The Diplomacies of Small States

International Political Economy Series

Series Editor: Timothy M. Shaw, Visiting Professor, University of Massachusetts Boston, USA and Emeritus Professor, University of London, UK

Titles include:

Timothy Cadman
QUALITY AND LEGITIMACY OF GLOBAL GOVERNANCE
Case Lessons from Forestry

Andrew F. Cooper and Timothy M. Shaw (*editors*)
THE DIPLOMACIES OF SMALL STATES
Between Vulnerability and Resilience

Andrew F. Cooper
INTERNET GAMBLING OFFSHORE
Caribbean Struggles over Casino Capitalism

Scarlett Cornelissen, Fantu Cheru and Timothy M. Shaw (*editors*)
AFRICA AND INTERNATIONAL RELATIONS IN THE 21st CENTURY

Anthony Leysens
THE CRITICAL THEORY OF ROBERT W. COX
Fugitive or Guru?

Valbona Muzaka
THE POLITICS OF INTELLECTUAL PROPERTY RIGHTS AND ACCESS
TO MEDICINES

Stefano Ponte, Peter Gibbon and Jakob Vestergaard (*editors*)
GOVERNING THROUGH STANDARDS
Origins, Drivers and Limitations

Mireya Solís, Barbara Stallings and Saori N. Katada (*editors*)
COMPETITIVE REGIONALISM
FTA Diffusion in the Pacific Rim

Peter Utting and José Carlos Marques (*editors*)
CORPORATE SOCIAL RESPONSIBILITY AND REGULATORY GOVERNANCE
Towards Inclusive Development?

International Political Economy Series
Series Standing Order ISBN 978–0–333–71708–0 hardcover
Series Standing Order ISBN 978–0–333–71110–1 paperback
(*outside North America only*)

You can receive future titles in this series as they are published by placing a standing order. Please contact your bookseller or, in case of difficulty, write to us at the address below with your name and address, the title of the series and one of the ISBNs quoted above.

Customer Services Department, Macmillan Distribution Ltd, Houndmills, Basingstoke, Hampshire RG21 6XS, England

The Diplomacies of Small States

Between Vulnerability and Resilience

Edited By

Andrew F. Cooper
Professor, Department of Political Science, University of Waterloo, Canada and Distinguished Fellow, Centre for International Governance Innovation, Canada

Timothy M. Shaw
Visiting Professor, University of Massachusetts Boston, USA, and Emeritus Professor, University of London, UK

The Centre for International Governance Innovation

Centre pour l'innovation dans la gouvernance internationale

First published 2009
Published in paperback 2013 by
PALGRAVE MACMILLAN

Palgrave Macmillan in the UK is an imprint of Macmillan Publishers Limited, registered in England, company number 785998, of Houndmills, Basingstoke, Hampshire RG21 6XS.

Palgrave Macmillan in the US is a division of St Martin's Press LLC, 175 Fifth Avenue, New York, NY 10010.

Palgrave Macmillan is the global academic imprint of the above companies and has companies and representatives throughout the world.

Palgrave® and Macmillan® are registered trademarks in the United States, the United Kingdom, Europe and other countries

ISBN: 978–0–230–57549–3   hardback
ISBN: 978–1–137–29767–9   paperback

This book is printed on paper suitable for recycling and made from fully managed and sustained forest sources. Logging, pulping and manufacturing processes are expected to conform to the environmental regulations of the country of origin.

A catalogue record for this book is available from the British Library.

A catalog record for this book is available from the Library of Congress.

10 9 8 7 6 5 4 3 2 1
22 21 20 19 18 17 16 15 14 13

Printed and bound in Great Britain by
CPI Antony Rowe, Chippenham and Eastbourne

Contents

Foreword: Studying Small States over the Twentieth into the Twenty-first Centuries

Vaughan A. Lewis

When the prime minister of newly independent Barbados spoke for the first time at the United Nations General Assembly, he alluded to a view about small states which he felt had become increasingly prevalent since the end of the First World War: that small states tended to be perceived as irritants in international relations, the causes or the occasions of disputation, including war, among larger powers.

Events of the post-Cold War period have no doubt given further currency to this view. The dissolution of the World Socialist System and the Soviet Union itself gave way to a myriad of states in Europe and Central Asia generally characterised as small. The new states seemed disposed to a variety of contentions, including: the legitimacy of the boundaries they inherited; the necessity for ethnic or cultural cohesion as the defining characteristic of the 'nation'-state; and fears of future domination by states larger than themselves, and in particular the now concentrated Russian Federation (for a contemporary review, see Ash 2000).

Of course, as is now well recognised, the various contentions in recent times have served as a reminder that certain kinds of issues relating to the behaviour of small states, and the behaviour of larger neighbouring entities towards small states have not changed much. Note the case of the small state inheritors of the Communist Yugoslav state for example. This suggests that the Cold War can be perceived as simply an interregnum between the First World War and the present period rather than, as used to be thought, a period of relatively peaceful stabilisation and economic expansion favouring integration of small- and medium-sized entities among themselves, or with larger and assumedly more 'viable' economic and political systems. Indeed, from today's perspective it is easy to understand the orientation of the first US president George Bush (and former Secretary of State Henry Kissinger) towards the maintenance of the Soviet Union after the fall of the socialist bloc, based on a belief that a large agglomeration such as the USSR would be more likely to ensure stability in the East-Europe–Central Asia arena, rather than if it were allowed to disintegrate into a number of small, likely unstable states.

We can refer to the latter orientation as a certain traditionalist view about the conditions likely to ensure global stability, reflective as it was of the attitude of the European colonial powers towards the movement to independence of their colonies in Asia, Africa and the Caribbean. There, in the post-Second World War period, both Britain and France sought to arrange various kinds of federations (and in the case of France even to seek a welding of autonomous African states and herself in a kind of 'EurAfrican' Community). This was in accordance with the view that the construction of large-scale sovereign political entities, even of multiple ethnicities and cultures, were more likely to permit long-term stability in the modern world. Stability, that is, in the multiple senses of security, economic viability and 'good government'.

In the terminology emanating from Britain during that period, good government meant 'representative and responsible government', which required reasonable amounts of material and human resources, to be satisfactorily maintained. In addition, these large-scale entities would permit easier articulation with the Great Powers in their task of maintaining international security, and provide, more likely, the sustenance of global peace.

In the immediate postwar period, this intellectual and policy position regarding the beneficial political and economic effects of large political entities seemed to be justified particularly by the British decolonisation of India where, in spite of the split of the subcontinent between India and Pakistan, the British insisted that the Indian principalities like Hyderabad should on no condition be allowed any form of state autonomy. Simultaneously there occurred the seemingly successful Dutch decolonisation of the Indonesian archipelago.

But as is well recognised now, the formula failed in cases such as: the relatively small federal agglomeration of the Anglophone Caribbean states (though of course the strategic nature of the Caribbean Basin gave them a significance beyond their size); the huge federations in East and Southern Africa, composed individually of territories with very large land areas, but undoubtedly perceived by the metropolitan states as small 'systems'; and the Federation of Malaysia, in part designed to provide a geopolitical bulwark comparable to newly independent Indonesia.

In turn, the late-1950s and 1960s independence, to use the words of a US State Department legal adviser, became a virtual 'industry of the metropoles'. The colonial preconditions for creating and sustaining political and economic viability having broken down, had been replaced by the notion of 'national liberation' where any substantial colonial power resistance was maintained, as for example in the case of the France in Algeria.

It was however the independence of Singapore in 1965 (after the failure of the Malaysian Federation) and its subsequent history of economic progress that, even more than the independence of the similarly small separate states of the Caribbean, began to establish – intellectually and methodologically – the variety of colonial notions about the relationships between size and viability.

These latter notions included the implicit belief that small size, particularly of island entities like those in the Caribbean, the South Pacific and off-shore states of the African continent, indicated a lack of capability for sustaining viability, and therefore necessitated some form of regional integration, or integration with other, most likely larger, entities. The relatively ready acceptance of the rapid integration of Zanzibar with the larger Tanzania exemplifies the prevailing attitudes of that time. The ejection of Singapore from the Malaysian Federation and the island state's subsequent history, however, permitted an alternative view of possible futures for small states. It is in that regard that discussion evolved on the so-called 'Singapore paradox'.

Vulnerability and viability

We can in general say that the functional parameters which allow us to assess the relationship between vulnerability and viability – the ability to survive as an identifiable unit in international relations – are as follows:

(i) Vulnerabilities deriving from the physical location of the state which we may refer to as *locational* or *territorial vulnerabilities*;

(ii) The extent of the administrative coherence (a function in part of the social coherence) of the state and the vulnerabilities arising in respect of the management of the state's policy operations and the stability of its decision-making – we can refer to this as the *extent of the state's Domestic Political Efficiency*. In this category we would locate also the belief system or systems of the population of the state, and of its political leadership;

(iii) The nature and extent of *economic vulnerability* of the state as an economic unit of particular geographical size in relation to both domestic resources and the networks of international transactions in which it is involved.

Vulnerability and the political context

Much of the discussion on small states in the developing world has tended to focus on the significance of economic viability, or the lack of it, and therefore to be situated largely within the discipline of economics. This in part was derived from a view that the 'material inequality' of states, to use David Vital's term, is the significant element in differentiating between states in terms of their capabilities.

But, as students of this subject are well aware, a long tradition exists that focuses on the ability of small states to sustain themselves in the play of international *politics*, from the perspective of the extent to which their specific geopolitical locations, taken in conjunction with their social and political constitutions or make-up, could fundamentally define the prospects for such sustenance. This focus leads to an emphasis not so much on smallness, but on 'weakness'; though it recognises at the same time that weakness cannot be perceived as a permanent defining characteristic simply of smallness. It can be a temporary characteristic of any kind of state regardless of size. And the conclusion of this kind of discussion really leads in the direction of *comparative analysis* of small states, in the same way that it can constitute a basis for comparative analysis of other kinds of states that share certain characteristics beyond mere physical size.

In terms of the wave of independence commencing in the late 1950s into the 1960s, an impetus to such comparative analysis regarding the new states' political capabilities for sustaining independence came to derive from events on the African continent, and in particular the crisis of attempted secession of Katanga that immediately followed the independence of the Congo, and the secession of Biafra from Nigeria in 1967. This gave rise to concern not so much with the assumed fragility of small entities – newly independent island entities in particular – but with the possibility of the persistent creation of small entities out of the large land masses of continental spaces. The political analysis and reporting of the term 'Balkanisation' began to return. Any comfortable assumption that the Indian precedent of the maintenance of large states of differing ethnicities and cultural/religious orientations might hold was now put severely in doubt (though it was apparent from the start that the French did not hold any such assumption, as they arranged to maintain large scale military forces in their former African territories).

With the early convulsions in Africa in the 1960s, a focus now came to be placed on the conditions under which relatively small land (as distinct from island) states could sustain themselves, such as from the threat of irredentism from neighbouring territories, given the spread of cultural or linguistic nationalities across borders. The conditions concerned related to (a) the ability to maintain political and administrative cohesion and (b) the ability to cope with external pressures within the context of the state's geopolitical location. A consideration that has assumed significance in more recent times, but did not have much prominence in the immediate independence period, is the ability of small states to maintain economic stability in the face of pressures emanating from the external (in particular external economic) environment, and therefore what instruments were necessary for adapting to such pressures. For one thing, the economic relations between the new states and their former metropoles were taken as possessing a reasonably long-term stability, an assumption more or less confirmed not only by the long-term stability of the postwar international economic system, but also by the solidifying of the pre-independence economic relations through the establishment of the Yaounde/Lomé Convention framework between the African, Caribbean and Pacific countries and the European Community.

As far as domestic political and administrative cohesion was concerned, the increasingly frequent *coup d'états* occurring in many countries on the African continent could not be taken as having analytical significance for students of comparative politics. S.E. Finer's early study, *The Man on Horseback* (1965), argued that this was not peculiar to the postwar/Cold War period. What was of more interest, and increasingly so to the international financial institutions, was the lack of administrative cohesion and social stability that would provide the conditions for long-term stable economic growth. But this, again, did not demonstrate itself to be a function of size, though the inability of states with small populations to attain a sufficient administrative division of labour to ensure an effective execution of policy was of some concern.

Location and the external environment

It is probably fair to say that the first significant work in the postwar period emphasising the issue of the relationship of the small state to its environment was David Vital's *The Inequality of States* (1967). Vital stressed that a state being able to survive as 'a small state alone', was an ideal type, designed to conceptually clarify the conditions, and the policies relating to these conditions, best appropriate for ensuring survival. Thus the ideal type assumes the condition of *isolation*, no doubt understood not only in the geopolitical, but also in the diplomatic sense.

Vital's model does not assume conditions of relative normality between states in the traditional sense of international theorising relating to traditional balance of power systems – systems in which small states may find themselves aware of the possibilities of liquidation. This 'rationalist theory' of the English School, deriving from the work of Martin Wight and Hedley Bull, emphasises this tradition of small state survival and the diplomacy that small states may seek to employ (Wight, 2002).

In modern parlance, from the perspective of small states, especially those existing in continental systems, this perspective could be referred to as a form of vulnerability theory in which the small state is analysed as perceiving itself in a continual situation of actual or potential turbulence, to which, as an open system itself, it is required to be continually adapting. Therefore, the small state is in a constant situation of fragility in respect of its external relations, to which policies of both domestic and international resilience need to be organised – as noted by Anthony Payne in the Afterword of this collection. In that context, the small state can be said to exist in a large or complex system in which in order to maintain its autonomy or identity, it must develop both domestic and international instruments, capabilities allowing it to 'match' the complex system. Within this category of instruments the diplomatic construction of various kinds of alliances falls (Bertalanffy, 1976).

This geopolitical perspective, analysed through the systems theory language of small and large (process and transactional) systems, can be translated from the arena of traditional geopolitics to that of geo-economics in the contemporary period. Here we can say that the international systems in which many small states found themselves located are now dissolving or disappearing. These systems were institutionalised (Commonwealth Preference/Lomé) in the form of asymmetrical economic alliances, which, for example, in the case of the Caribbean and Pacific island states provided long-term stability in both their domestic and international environments. The response to the disappearance of these systems would involve attempts to find alternative international systems, based on both domestic assets and internationally organised capabilities; however, owing to their small size and, likely, minimal assets and small presence in large systems, alternative systems are required to maintain the condition of asymmetry. In these circumstances, the distinction between small developing and large developing states becomes more emphasised, particularly as alternative opportunities for the export of commodities and sources of technological capability have become more available to the larger states.

Erling Bjol (1971) has put this in another way:

> By itself the concept of small state means nothing. A State is only small
> in relation to a greater one. Belgium may be a small state in relation
> to France, but Luxembourg is a small state in relation to Belgium, and
> France a small state in relation to the USA. To be of any analytical use
> 'small state' should therefore be considered shorthand for 'a state in
> its relationships with "greater states"'.

But we add to this that in considering 'relationships' we need to consider
not only institutional relationships, but process and structural relations
organised in systems that are reflected beyond institutional forms. Therefore, the examination of the behaviour of small states requires: (a)
differentiation between types of small states in terms of their location in
structural systems (systems of transactions) – comparative politics analysis; and (b) examination of how, and in what kinds of systems, particular
small states engage in *adaptation* (Rosenau, 1981) to the various elements
of the global system – comparative international relations analysis.

In fact, Bjol (1971) gives us an indication of an appropriate first
approach when he observes that:

> The problems, possibilities and behavior of small states vary consid-
> erably according to the types of international systems in which they
> operate – hegemonial systems, confrontation systems, integration sys-
> tems, security communities – according to the geographic parameters
> which condition their foreign policy, and according to their domestic
> structures.

We can take these as institutional systems. But if we understand the
types of systems of which he speaks here as being based on, or including, structural systems or transactions, his approach appears to be an
appropriate one for devising analytical frameworks regarding the study
of the comparative behaviour of small states – in terms of geographical or population size, and of small state regional systems; and also, of
states for whom military capability is not an instrument available for the
resolution of disputes or the pursuit of peaceful objectives.

Finally, contemporary international relations analysis takes into
account not only environmental transactions in the sense of *interactions*,
but aspects of the material environment, most importantly in ecological processes and factors that are relatively permanent aspects of some
country's existence. Harold and Margaret Sprout were instrumental in
bringing to academic attention the necessity to recognise this, and to give

it a significant place in international relations. At the level of government and policy, the president of the Maldives brought to the attention of Commonwealth Heads of Government in 1987, followed by the United Nations General Assembly, the significance for islands of sea-level rise, as well as the overwhelming potential for various kinds of environmental factors and the destruction of small island states. The report of the World Commission on Environment and Development (WCED), also known as the Bruntland Commission, subsequently reinforced the need for consideration of ecological factors as important elements in ensuring the sustainable development of small developing countries, as well as the importance of placing ecological factors within the purview of the international institutional framework (WCED, 1987). Finally, in 1994, the small states focus was brought to definitive institutional recognition at the United Nations Conference on Small Island Developing States (United Nations, 1994).

Small state analysis

From both an analytical and policy-making point of view then, the issues are those of:

(i) Understanding how small states can adapt in any specific environment or set of environments, and in particular those in which, at least in relation to entities acknowledged as larger than themselves, relations are asymmetrical;

(ii) Understanding the capabilities, and possibilities for action that states of relatively similar sizes in a particular geographical or geopolitical space have relative to each other in adapting to their relevant environments, and in adapting to each other's policy objectives and actions;

(iii) Understanding how space limitations affect policy objectives, including the ways in which the small state feels constrained by such limitations in seeking to adapt to its environment; and therefore understanding how enhancement of space through one or other modes of integration with other spaces can be undertaken;

(iv) Understanding how limitations of capabilities deriving from limited space can hinder or limit attempts to obtain some degree of control in pursuing effective adaptation to complex systems and their environments;

(v) Assessing the significance of late twentieth-century and early twenty-first-century innovation in the technology of communications, and the extent to which these affect the ability of small states to manoeuvre and to enhance or manipulate their control over complex systems. Put another way, how new technological capabilities can enhance the ability of small states' decision-makers to match complex systems in respect of particular objectives or challenges to their growth or to their maintenance of viability. This is an aspect of the resilience issue (explored by Briguglio and his colleagues in Briguglio and Kisanga, 2004; Briguglio et al., 2006); and

(vi) Assessing the limiting points between the gravitation of small states to a condition of (a) integration with another state or other states or (b) gravitation to a position approximating isolation, or the position of the 'small state alone'.

Timothy M. Shaw and Andrew F. Cooper have assembled an impressive slate of small states experts in this volume. Collectively, they have performed a great service to the study of small state behaviour in complex global systems through analysis of these many important issues.

VAUGHAN A. LEWIS
Former Prime Minister of Saint Lucia

References

Ash, Timothy Garton (2000) *History of the Present* (London: Penguin).

Bertalanffy, Ludwig Von (1976) *General Systems Theory: Foundations, Development, Applications* (New York: George Braziller).

Bjol, Erling (1971) 'The Small State In International Politics' in A. Schou and A.O. Brundland (eds), *Small States in International Relations* (New York: John Wiley & Sons).

Briguglio, Lino and Eliawony J. Kisanga (eds) (2004) *Economic Vulnerability and the Resilience of Small States* (London: Commonwealth Secretariat).

Briguglio, Lino, Bishnodat Persaud and Richard Stern (2006) *Toward an Outward-Oriented Development Strategy for Small States: Issues, Opportunities, and Resilience Building* (Singapore: World Bank Group/International Monetary Fund).

Finer, S.E. (1965) *The Man on Horseback: The Role of the Military in Politics* (London: Pall Mall).

Rosenau, James N. (1981) *The Study of Political Adaptation* (London: Frances Pinter).

United Nations (1994) *Report of the Global Conference on the Sustainable Development of Small Island Developing States*, Global Conference on the Sustainable Development of Small Island Developing States, 6 May, A/CONF.167/9.

Vital, David (1967) *The Inequality of States* (Oxford: Oxford University Press).

WCED (1987) *Our Common Future* (Oxford: Oxford University Press).

Wight, Martin (2002) *Power Politics*, Hedley Bull and Carsten Holbraad (eds) (New York: Continuum).

Preface to the Paperback Edition

Small states in a world of crisis and divergence: more/less vulnerability or resilience?

After a decade of the rise of new constellations of big states – notably in the form of BRICs/BRICS – and a half decade of crises, small state diplomacies are being more tested than ever. Whereas vulnerability may be exacerbated if exposed to the problems of the PIIGS of the eurozone; resilience is increasingly a function of relations with the emerging donors/economies/powers/states/societies not only from the old establishment of the G7/8 but key pivotal states from the global South. Furthermore, small states are intrinsically transnational with myriad cross-border relations of economies, ecologies, securities, societies, technologies. And on top of all these dynamics and dilemmas, we need to recognise the myriad non-independent countries which augment the number of small states: the more than 40 dependencies or 'overseas territories' of Australia, France, New Zealand, the Netherlands, UK and US. So there is almost one hundred such small countries with populations under one million if we juxtapose the nominally independent and dependent communities; with Paul Sutton (2011) we include states which perceive themselves to be small even if slightly over a million such as Lesotho, Mauritius, Swaziland, Timor-Leste and Trinidad and Tobago.

Analyses of International Relations (IR) generally and International Political Economy (IPE) increasingly recognise varieties of perspectives and policies. This revised overview suggests that the small state approach also merits such attention in addition to the African, Asian, BRICS, English, European and other genres. Small states continue to be a rich laboratory for innovation stretching the definition and practice of what the rules and accepted practices of IPE are. Yet, if animators of adjustment and resilience building, small states continue to be the receptors of disciplinary actions often imposed in an arbitrary and asymmetrical fashion.

The global financial crisis has showcased the value of studying Small States Diplomacies through the dualistic perspective of resilience and vulnerability. Small states had a good run in adapting to the new rules of the post-Cold War order. Harold James, although akin to Robert Keohane (1971) in an earlier phase of academic study, emphasising the role of the bigger small states, gives this category of countries pride of place as adapters: 'In the heyday of modern globalisation in the 1990s, it looked as if small open states would be the winners: New Zealand, Chile, Ireland, the Baltic Republics, Slovakia and Slovenia' (James, quoted by Rachman, 2009).

This cluster of countries were able to take advantage of the removal of barriers to international trade and investment, through a variety of means, some conventional (lowering taxes) and some very unconventional (making Iceland a banking centre) (Broome, 2011). Consistent with the flexibility built into the theme of resilience, some states have built up their economic niches using a well-thought strategy with a focus on education and technological infrastructure. Others adapted in a far more ad hoc – or even opportunistic manner. A good number of states saw themselves – and were seen by others – as being innovative risk takers.

Yet, as long suggested in the literature, small economies may be hit more swiftly than large economies and their downturns may become deeper (Handel, 1981). One of the hallmarks of the financial/economic crisis has been the return of the theme of vulnerability to the study of small states. As an article by Gideon Rachman in the *Financial Times* argued, a variety of small states have been among the hardest hit by the 'Great Recession'. Casualties have included most notably Iceland, Ireland, the Baltic states, in particular Latvia and Lithuania. Although the causes of this change in fortunes will continue to be debated, what stands out is the differentiation of effects: with the bailout terms imposed on a variety of small European countries – above all through IMF surveillance – being far more onerous at least in perception than those imposed on Spain.

Nor is this only a Euro-centric phenomenon. The city-state of Dubai risked falling into the same category when Dubai World asked a banking consortium for a six month moratorium on debt service to avoid possible default. Although this issue has brought out some impressive forms of crisis management, the episode conveyed an image of unanticipated vulnerability. As Rachman (2009) reminds us, Joseph Stiglitz, once conveyed the warning that: 'Small open economies are like rowing boats on an open sea.'

Under conditions of turbulence small states are placed in exaggerated forms of disadvantage in a world that privileges the bigs. The image of diplomatic vulnerability was magnified by the formation of the G20 as a new concert of powers. Far from being universalistic in form, the G20 has a highly restricted composition picked on a hierarchical basis. Looking at the G20 through a historical lens, it has some commonalities with past attempts to develop concerts of dominant powers in eras of transition. Stripped to its bare essentials the G20 can with some justification be categorized as the 'rule of big powers over the rest' (Aslund, 2009).

Reflective of the structurally imposed condition, small states continue to be disconnected from the most salient debates on the nature of transition in IR. Current shifts in the regional-global architecture continue to be almost universally perceived to be due not to any re-location among small actors but because of the emergence of the so-called BRICs – or alternative acronyms such as CHINDIA or the BASIC grouping– at the apex of the international hierarchy.

This emphasis on the changing hierarchy is reinforced by the obsession of Goldman Sachs and other segments from the financial and consulting world with finding a new upper middle group of countries as well with a focus on current and projected economic attributes. Goldman Sachs has conceptualized a 'Next 11' list of countries (including Bangladesh, Egypt, Indonesia, Iran, Korea, Mexico, Nigeria, Pakistan, Philippines, Turkey and Vietnam) that in its estimation have the economic trajectories necessary for entrance into this category (Goldman Sachs, 2007). Other analysts from the investment industry have also tweaked this concept of a new middle, either as CIVETs (Colombia, Indonesia, Vietnam, Egypt, Turkey and South Africa) or MIKT/MIST (Mexico, Indonesia, South Korea and Turkey).

Notwithstanding this evidence, however, we argue that the theme of resilience – especially diplomatic resilience – should not be discarded. If the potential for economic vulnerability has increased, the build up of various manifestations of diplomatic innovation in a number of selected small states is an impressive one. The image of the weakness of small isolated states is no longer good enough. Nor, conversely, is the notion of a large-scale ganging up of an assembly of Lilliputians – the so-called 'tyranny of the weak'.

The ongoing albeit nuanced privileging of resilience and resourcefulness reinforces the need to look closely at the diplomatic profile of small states both collectively and on an individual basis. In this narrative the image of small states is reconfigured in quite striking ways. Vulnerability is a naturally imposed and predictable condition in which the room for manoeuvre is severely constrained. Resilience by way of contrast is adaptive, whereas structural factors cannot only be resisted but re-shaped. Space for unorthodox diplomatic activity presents itself.

Qatar: exceptionally resilient

The case of Qatar – although not portrayed in a stand-alone chapter in the *Diplomacies of Small States* – exemplifies the subordination of vulnerability to resilience on a small country basis. Qatar, to be sure, has a number of strong economic attributes. Far from being a reactive small state, however, Qatar has moved to re-brand itself through some of the means advocates of the 'resilient' theme suggest. Using a blend of conventional and unconventional techniques, Qatar has become the poster illustration of how a small state can upgrade its diplomatic reputation to the point of being exceptionally resilient (Cooper and Momani, 2011).

Qatar is in many distinctive ways a hybrid diplomatic actor. Through one set of lenses its diplomatic profile plays to a familiar script: a small state as convener and helpful fixer. Through another set of lenses, though, Qatar has become a risk taker and unconventional player. The image of Qatar as the host of US Central Command regional headquarters is very different from its image as the pivotal hub for Al Jazeera.

As with other small states the theme of vulnerability has been accented with respect to Qatar by the global financial crisis. Nonetheless, what stands out is the degree to which this vulnerability on the part of Qatar is triggered by symbolic not instrumental factors. As with all other small states Qatar has been left out of the exclusive G20 club. But unlike many other small states Qatar has not come under attack by the G20 – through the assault on offshore financial centres (OFCs) or so-called tax havens.

An interesting sign of Qatar's sensitivity to the changing international 'club' context but also the extent of its comparative strength over other small states comes out in Qatar's decision to join with Singapore and Switzerland in the World Economic Forum's Global Re-design Initiative (GRI), a body seeking to channel the views of small and medium-sized UN states into the G20 process.

Qatar's willingness to take on this type of leadership role is significant. On the one hand, this initiative signals explicitly that Qatar's diplomacy has a global not a regional reach. On the other hand, it demonstrates that Qatar can work with the top tier small states and do so without the same sort of instrumental purpose that Singapore and Switzerland have on display. Unlike Singapore and Switzerland, Qatar has no ambition to be a G20 member. Nor unlike Switzerland (in the UBS case) has it needed to engage in intense bilateral negotiations as a form of damage limitation.

As a rule the financial crisis has increased the sense that these are years of living dangerously for small states. Big states – at least from the global

South – are in ascendancy. Familiar brands – as in the case of Switzerland – have become tarnished. Space for innovation – or at least unorthodox variations of innovation (whether in the case of OFCs or on Internet gambling by Antigua and other small states) – is diminished.

Still, Qatar reveals that there are important exceptions to this dynamic at odds with the image of exacerbated small state vulnerability. Qatar has become increasingly visible diplomatically. Regionally it has become a skilled mediator. It not only straddles the structure of political polarisation it leverages that condition to its own advantage – in terms of public and private diplomacy. Globally, it is on the cusp of becoming one of the key 'go to' states when architectural issues intensify. Although vulnerability has returned as the plight for many small states, the ability of Qatar to not only escape this predicament but to prosper in stressful times is a testament to the diversity in the constellation of small states, and why both International Relations generally and diplomatic studies specially needs to examine them through detailed analysis.

This is not to suggest that Qatar breaks the tradition of small state diplomacy that privileges solidarity. Collective voice opportunities are still the preferred option for many smaller states, as illustrated by the debate that has broken out about the differentiation in status among regions. Most notably, an attempt by the EU to upgrade its standing at the UN has raised concerns among a cluster of developing countries – led by CARICOM – which resent Europe being granted privileges other regions did not have (EurActiv, 2010).

Mapping the trajectories of Small States Diplomacies

Nor does the exceptional case of Qatar prove the rule that small states can achieve their goals by going up against big countries on an individual one on one basis. As Donna Lee highlights in this book, what is intriguing about diplomacies of small states is the creative use of partnerships. Through its 'Make Trade Fair' campaign, Oxfam worked with a number of small developing states to offset the 'rigged' world trade rules, such as in the case of the Cotton 4. These benign images are fractured in the Antigua case, also the subject of a chapter, for unlike a case such as the Cotton 4 (or for that matter, other cases beyond the WTO domain such as Vanuatu's appeal to NGOs to take over its delegation on environmental negotiations) (see Wapner, 2002), Antigua's partner was not an NGO but a segment of the international gambling industry it was seeking to protect. The companies at the core of the strategy were innovative leaders, but there was no disputing their material stake in the struggle.

These approaches embellish the link with the finding of loopholes or derogations in the international political economy, or what can be described as a phenomenon of 'slipping subtly through the nets of conformity' (Baldacchino and Milne, 2000: 238). What contradicts this image of unorthodoxy is the strong commitment that Antigua made to international rule making through the WTO.

Small states have also tapped into the entrepreneurial repertoire of middle states to play above their weight. A prime illustration is Singapore's leadership of the Global Governance Group or 3G group. An off-shoot of the World Economic Forum's Global Re-design Initiative (GRI) the 3G extended into a very diverse constellation of 28 small and medium-sized countries around the world: six from South East Asia and Asia Pacific (Singapore, Malaysia, Brunei, the Philippines, New Zealand and Vietnam); three from the Middle East (Bahrain, Qatar and the United Arab Emirates); three from Africa (Rwanda, Senegal and Botswana); eight from Europe (Sweden, Belgium, Ireland, Luxembourg, Switzerland, Liechtenstein, Monaco and San Marino); two from Latin America (Uruguay and Chile); and six from Central America and the Caribbean (Costa Rica, Guatemala, Panama, Jamaica, Barbados and Bahamas).

As with a number of small states diplomatic initiatives there was a strong element of self-help attached to this effort, especially on the issue of OFCs. This issue of fairness of representation came to the fore in some of the declaratory statements by the organisers of the 3G. As the Singaporean Foreign Minister George Yeo put it very bluntly in one interview: 'At the London meeting (of G20), financial centres became a major issue and countries like Singapore and Switzerland unexpectedly found themselves in the grey list and came under some pressure to alter the way we operate. This was without prior consultation with us, we were not involved in the discussions but we had to react to the decision taken by the G20 and we have reacted. That doesn't seem to me to be the right way to get things done. Hong Kong, which had a situation very similar to Singapore, had China to look after its interests so it is not on the grey list but Singapore was, and other countries too. So I think it is important that on issues that concern others, those who have major interest, should also be brought into the discussion. That is a matter of process; it would improve legitimacy and the sense of fairness' (quoted in Chowdhury, 2010).

Still, if a catalyst for action, the 3G could not have extended its scope of membership if it was only directed to a single issue. What the 3G did was to tap into the same sense of exclusion driving the regional critics but to re-configure this resentment into a larger campaign directed at engagement with the G20 under the banner of variable geometry. Using this device the 3G could make the argument that small countries should have access to the G20 on a functional basis – very much the same argument that middle powers made in the post-1945 period.

Small State Diplomacies in theory and practice after the 'global' crisis

Returning to the main theme of the book, vulnerability is a naturally imposed and predictable condition in which the room for manoeuvre is severely constrained. Resilience by way of contrast is adaptive, whereas structural factors cannot only be resisted but reshaped. Space for unorthodox diplomatic activity presents itself.

In some cases this turn towards unorthodoxy needs to be taken very seriously as path-breaking activity. If commonly cast in the role of the over-matched underdog – a proverbial 'David' in the IPE – Antigua's struggle with the US over Internet Gambling blows the stereotypes away. If ultimately unsuccessful due to structural limitations, Antigua demonstrated a huge amount of diplomatic capabilities not only in taking the case to the WTO but inside the beltway with a sophisticated form of lobbying (Cooper, 2011).

Such images should not cover up the high stakes attached to the dynamics of resilience/vulnerability of small states. When the Maldives held a cabinet meeting under water in October 2009, with the president and ministers donning scuba gear, it was not just a branding exercise but an act of frustration and even desperation about the lack of progress in dealing with the effects of global warming for low-lying nations. The newly independent country of South Sudan, although applauded for its resilience after its long liberation struggle with Sudan, faces enormous challenges in terms of reaching a peace deal that would settle frontier and citizenship disputes and the sharing of revenue from oil reserves that straddle the border. The government of Iceland has welcomed the attention of new economic and diplomatic partners in the aftermath of the financial crisis – China has built the largest embassy in Reykjavik and has made a number of investment overtures – but a backlash occurred when a Chinese business tycoon (and former state official) tried to buy a massive tract of land as a luxury eco-tourism resort.

At the same time, the image of small countries only acting alone needs to re-thought as well. Although not reverting back to the G77 and NAM, the collective pressure can be mobilised on an issue-specific basis, as revealed both in the regional and non-regional initiatives by groups of small countries to engage with the G20. The notion of the collective mobilisation through the 'tyranny of the weak' has to be reconsidered. As the 3G initiative demonstrates small countries can play big with lots of confidence, skill and resources.

This dynamic highlights the ad hoc, informal dynamic of small states activities. At the multilateral level, the G77 and NAM were not able to act as a protective shield for small states. At the regional level, traditional forms of trade preference were eroded (Heron, 2012). Nor, as the global financial crisis demonstrates all too acutely, could regional groupings – even one as creative and resourced as the European Union (EU) – cushion the blows in the aftermath of the 2008 shocks. The common assumption has been that membership in supranational organisations generally (Katzenstein, 1997) and the EU more specifically (Wallace, 1999) provides a sense of shelter allowing small states a greater ability to deal with unanticipated risks. However, as a recent study by Thorhallsson and Kirby conclude the situation is far more complex. To be sure, 'the case of Iceland indicates that a lack of economic and political shelter escalated the crisis'. Nonetheless, while 'The EU provided Ireland with assistance in absorbing the shock and helped in cleaning up after the crisis', its 'rescue package's onerous terms are seen by some to be prolonging the crisis'. A paradox exists also in that 'Iceland, the country without this shelter, is recovering more successfully than is Ireland' (Thorhallsson and Kirby, 2012: 16).

The study of small state diplomacy is an increasingly diverse and exciting project as reflected in analyses and debates in the current as well as previous decades (Ingebritsen et al., 2006, Bishop 2012, Lee and Smith 2010, Sutton 2011). In an altered setting where traditional assumptions about control at the apex of power have been eroded, 'non-hegemonic' IR/IPE projects (Higgott, 1991: 97) have considerably more space. Whether we have reached the point where it is 'No One's World' though is an exaggeration for most if not for all small states (Kupchan, 2012). If not as marginal to the study of IR/IPE conceptually or confining in practice as in the past, small states diplomacies still cannot accept assumptions about fairness or equal treatment as givens. As Bishop quite rightly notes in a review of the Small States Diplomacies volume, the structural constraints on action of this category of countries is still imposing (Bishop, 2012: 2). In times of crisis their stress will become more exaggerated. As such there remains the danger that small states in breaking the habit of neglect will be regarded largely as 'irritants' (Lewis, 2009: vii). Only by mustering the creative and steadfast repertoire, at the core of this book, will the power of agency be able to calm if not stabilise their precarious position. Such advances will translate in turn into a more sophisticated contextualised and contoured – if not privileged – appreciation in the literature.

References

Aslund, A. (2009) 'The Group of 20 must be stopped', *Financial Times*, 26 November.

Baldacchino, G. and D. Milne (eds) (2000) 'Conclusion' *Lessons from the Political Economy of Small Islands: The Resourcefulness of Jurisdiction* (Baskingstoke: Macmillan).

Baldacchino, G. and D. Milne (eds) (2006) 'Exploring Sub-National Island Jurisdictions', *Round Table* 95 (386) September: 487–627.

Bishop, M.L. (2012) 'The Political Economy of Small States: Enduring Vulnerability?' *Review of International Political Economy* 1–19.

Broome, Andre (2011) 'Negotiating Crisis: The IMF and Disaster Capitalism in Small States', *Round Table* 100, 413: 155–67.

Chowdhury, Iftekhar Ahmed (2010) 'The Global Governance Group ('3G') and Singaporean Leadership: Can Small be Significant?' ISAS Working Paper, no. 108, 19 May.

Cooper, A.F. (2011) *Internet Gambling Offshore: Caribbean Struggles over Casino Capitalism* (New York: Palgrave).

Cooper, A.F. and B. Momani (2011) 'Qatar and Expanded Contours of Small State Diplomacy', *International Spectator*, 46, 3: 113–28.

EurActiv (2010) 'Ashton speaking rights at UN face delay', 15 September.

Goldman Sachs (2007) 'The N-11: More Than an Acronym', Global Economics Paper no. 153.

Handel, M. (1981) *Weak States in the International System* (London: Frank Cass).

Heron, T. (2012) *The Global Political Economy of Trade Protectionism and Liberalization: Trade Reform and Economic Adjustment in the Textiles and Clothing Industry* (London: Routledge).

Higgott, R. (1991) 'Toward a Non-hegemonic IPE: An Antipodean Perspective', in C. Murphy and R. Tooze (eds), *The New International Political Economy* (Boulder, CO: Lynne Rienner).

Ingebritsen, C., I. Neumann, S. Gstöhl and J. Beyer (eds) (2006) *Small States in International Relations* (Seattle, WA: University of Washington Press).

Katzenstein, P. (ed.) (1997) 'The Smaller European States, Germany and Europe', in *Tamed Power: Germany in Europe* (Ithaca, NY: Cornell University Press).

Keohane, R.O. (1971). 'The Big Influence of Small Allies', *Foreign Policy* 2 (Spring): 161–82.

Kupchan, C.A. (2012) *No One's World: The West, the Rising Rest, and the Coming Global Turn* (Oxford University Press).

Lee, D. and N.J. Smith (eds) (2008) 'Special Issue: Small States in the International Political Economy', *Round Table* 97 (395): 201–303.

Lee, D. and N.J. Smith (2010) 'Small State Discourses in the International Political Economy', *Third World Quarterly* 31(7): 1091–105.

Lewis, V.A. (2009) 'Foreword: Studying Small States over the Twentieth into the Twenty-First Centuries', in A.F. Cooper and T.M. Shaw (eds) *The Diplomacies of Small States: Between Vulnerability and Resilience* (Basingstoke: Palgrave MacMillan), pp. vii–xv.

Rachman, G. (2009) 'How Small States Were Cut Adrift', *Financial Times*, 20 October 2009.

Sutton, P. (2011) 'The Concept of Small States in the International Political Economy', *Round Table* 100, 413: 141–53.

Thorhallsson, B. and P. Kirby (2012) 'Financial Crises in Iceland and Ireland: Does European Union and Euro Membership Matter?' *JCMS*: 1–18.

Wallace, W. (1999) 'Small European States and European Policy-Making: Strategies, Roles, Possibilities', in ARENA (ed.) *Between Autonomy and Influence: Small States and the European Union: Proceedings from ARENA Annual Conference 1998* (Oslo: ARENA Centre for European Studies).

Wapner, P. (2002) 'The Sovereignty of Nature? Environmental Protection in a Postmodern Age', *International Studies Quarterly*, 46, 2.

Acknowledgements

This collection is the first output of a burgeoning research project at The Centre for International Governance Innovation (CIGI) on the role of small states in the shifting global economic and diplomatic order. It is a direct result from a workshop convened at the Institute of International Relations (IIR) at the University of the West Indies (UWI) in St Augustine, Trinidad. The origins of this project, however, are rather diffuse. CIGI embarked on a major initiative on new forms of Caribbean economic governance which proved a catalyst for more focused work on the diplomacies of small states, with an emphasis on locating sites of innovation. This project also builds on the wider research agenda at CIGI devoted to illuminating the connections (and disconnects) between diplomacy and global governance.

In IIR, CIGI has found an ideal partner for this work. Given its four decades of experience and research expertise specifically on the Caribbean and on small states more generally, IIR has built an unparalleled brain-trust in these subject areas. Like the proverbial Olympic rings, our respective networks overlap and reinforce, as reflected in the impressive line-up of contributors to this collection with their set of prestigious affiliations. In particular, we welcome colleagues who span South and North, both sides of the Atlantic, and new and old generations. We appreciate their creativity and flexibility as well as generosity in analysing and debating alternative perspectives as the world of small states is impacted by emerging economies. Our thinking on the subject matter was also shaped by a number of experts. In particular, we want to thank Dr Vaughan Lewis who generously penned the Foreword to the collection and Tony Payne whose Afterword links this analysis with wider academic debates.

The production of the book benefited from the hard work of many individuals. In particular, Thomas Agar provided detailed research assistance while also taking on much of the textual work, smoothing out the style and syntax. As CIGI's research on diplomacy and linkages among big and small states has grown, Andrew Schrumm has skilfully coordinated these many activities with diligence and enthusiasm. Logistical support from Marilyn Ramon-Fortuné of IIR as well as Kristen Beaulieu and Briton Dowhaniuk of CIGI was invaluable to the successful February 2008 workshop in Trinidad. Joe Turcotte assisted in the preparation of the manuscript and Max Brem provided spirited guidance throughout the publication process.

As in all projects, CIGI's Executive Director John English created an environment amenable to productive research. In his role this year as Acting Executive Director, Daniel Schwanen has provided strong on-going support and intellectual leadership towards this and many related projects. CIGI's International Advisory Board of Governors has provided great encouragement and intellectual guidance for our vast research agenda.

CIGI was founded in 2002 by Jim Balsillie, co-CEO of RIM (Research In Motion), and collaborates with and gratefully acknowledges support from a number of strategic partners, in particular the government of Canada and the government of Ontario.

The final thanks are for Gemma d'Arcy Hughes, Renée Takken and their colleagues at Palgrave Macmillan. This volume and the entire International Political Economy series has benefited from their editorial guidance and professionalism. We are pleased that this publisher has chosen to support and enthusiastically advance the study of small states in a wider context.

This collection, and the networks on which it is based, will inform the preparations for and proceedings of two historic summits in Port of Spain in 2009 – Fifth Summit of the Americas (April) and the biennial Commonwealth Heads of Government Meetings (November) – as well as the deliberations of the 22nd annual meeting of the Academic Council of the United Nations System at UWI in June 2009 on Small, Middle and Emerging Powers in the UN System. So informed and challenged, we look forwards to continuing collaboration between CIGI and IIR and their 'Olympian' networks through the second decade of the new century.

ANDREW F. COOPER AND TIMOTHY M. SHAW
Waterloo and St Augustine

Notes on Contributors

Godfrey Baldacchino is Professor and Canada Research Chair in Island Studies at the University of Prince Edward Island, Canada; Visiting Professor of Sociology at the University of Malta, Malta; and Executive Editor of Island Studies Journal. His recent books include: *Extreme Tourism: Lessons from the World's Cold Water Islands*; *A World of Islands: An Island Studies Reader*; *Bridging Islands: The Impact of Fixed Links*; and *Pulling Strings*.

Jacqueline Anne Braveboy-Wagner is Professor of Political Science and International Relations in the Ph.D. Program at the Graduate School and University Center, and the City College of the City University of New York. She is the former director of the MA Program in International Relations at the City College and has held posts at Bowling Green State University and Tokyo Metropolitan University. In 2006–07 she chaired a government-appointed Committee to Review the Foreign Policy of Trinidad and Tobago. She has authored or edited nine books on the international relations of the Caribbean and on the global South, including *Institutions of the Global South* and *Small States in Global Affairs: The Foreign Policies of the Caribbean Community*.

Anthony T. Bryan is Senior Associate at the Center for Strategic and International Studies in Washington, D.C. and Professor Emeritus of the University of Miami. Previously he served as Professor and Director, Institute of International Relations at the University of the West Indies, Trinidad and Tobago, Senior Associate at the Carnegie Endowment for International Peace, and Senior Fellow at the Woodrow Wilson International Center for Scholars. He has held visiting professorships at Indiana University, the University of Texas, Georgetown University, and the Graduate Institute of International Studies in Geneva, Switzerland. Author and editor of numerous books and journal articles, his recent publications are on energy security and cooperation in the Americas.

Alan Chong is Assistant Professor at the S. Rajaratnam School of International Studies, Nanyang Technological University, Singapore. He has published widely on the notion of soft power and the role of ideas in constructing the international relations of Singapore and Asia. His publications have appeared in *The Pacific Review, International Relations* of the *Asia-Pacific*, *Asian Survey* and the *Review of International Studies*. His recent book is *Foreign Policy in Global Information Space: Actualizing Soft Power*. He is currently working on several projects exploring the notion of 'Asian international theory'. His interest in soft power has also led to inquiry into the sociological and philosophical foundations of international communication.

Andrew F. Cooper is Professor in the Department of Political Science at the University of Waterloo, where he teaches in the areas of International Political Economy, Global Governance and the Practice of Diplomacy and Distinguished Fellow, Centre for International Governance Innovation, Canada. He has been a visiting professor at the University of Southern California, Australian National University, Stellenbosch University and Harvard University. His recent books include *Global Governance and Diplomacy: Worlds Apart?*; *Celebrity Diplomacy*; *Regionalisation and Global Governance: The Taming of Globalisation?*; and *Tests of Global Governance: Canadian Diplomacy and United Nations World Conferences*.

Carlyle G. Corbin is an international adviser on democratic governance, and an adviser to the Fifth Constitutional Convention of the US Virgin Islands. He was formerly Virgin Islands Minister for External Affairs, a member of the territory's Political Status Commission and Secretary-General of the British Virgin Islands–US Virgin Islands Council. He is on the faculty of the University of the Virgin Islands' Institute for Future Global Leaders. He was UN expert on political missions to Bermuda and Turks and Caicos, as well as UN regional expert on decolonisation in the Caribbean and Pacific, and adviser to several Caribbean governments at the UN General Assembly. He has authored several books and articles on political evolution, and is Senior Editor for the *Overseas Territories Review*.

Daniel P. Erikson is Senior Associate for US policy and Director of Caribbean programs at the Inter-American Dialogue, the Washington-based policy forum on Western Hemisphere affairs. He is co-editor of *Transforming Socialist Economies: Lessons for Cuba and Beyond* and a contributor to several books including *Looking Forward: Comparative Perspectives on Cuba's Transition*; *Taking Sides: Clashing Views on Latin America*; and *Latin America's Struggle for Democracy*. He is the author of *The Cuba Wars: Fidel Castro, the United States, and the Next Revolution*. Past positions include research associate at Harvard Business School and Fulbright scholar in US–Mexican business relations.

Donna Lee is Professor of International Organisations and Diplomacy and University Senior Tutor, University of Birmingham, UK. She has held lecturing posts at several universities including the University of Nottingham, Leicester University, and Manchester Metropolitan University. Lee's research focuses on economic and commercial diplomacy, diplomatic theory, the GATT/WTO system and trade negotiations. Lee is currently a series editor (with Paul Sharp) for Palgrave Macmillan's *Diplomacy and International Relations* series. Recent books include *The WTO after Hong Kong*; and *The New Multilateralism in South African Diplomacy*.

Don D. Marshall is Senior Research Fellow at the University of the West Indies, Barbados. As a team member at the Sir Arthur Lewis Institute of Social and Economic Studies, he conducts research on international (financial) governance and the impact of ongoing globalisation on Caribbean states, economies and development practice. He has published extensively on these topics in journals such as *Third World Politics*, *Government and Opposition*, *Global Society*, and *Contemporary Politics*. He is author of *Caribbean Political Economy at the Crossroads*, co-editor of *Living at the Borderlines: Issues in Caribbean Sovereignty and Development* and is currently writing a manuscript on the genealogy of Caribbean offshore financial centres, resilience and challenges.

Debbie A. Mohammed teaches International Trade and Development at the Institute of International Relations, University of the West Indies, Trinidad, and is Coordinator of the Institute's Diploma and Internship Programs. Her research interests include CARICOM trade issues, the CSME, Competitiveness Strategies, Regional Food Security, Services and Small States and Development. She is a member of national and regional committees on the CSME. Recent publications include 'Size and Competitiveness: An Examination of the CARICOM Single Market and Economy (CSME)' *Round Table*, and 'Building Competitiveness in CARICOM States: The Role of Service Exports', in R. Ramsaran (ed.) *Size, Power and Development in the Emerging World Order*.

Keith Nurse is Director of the Shridath Ramphal Centre for International Trade Law, Policy and Services, University of the West Indies, Barbados. He has taught at the Institute of International Relations, UWI, Trinidad and Tobago, and at the Institute for International Development and Cooperation, University of Ottawa. Recent books include *Heritage Tourism in the Caribbean* and *The Cultural Industries in CARICOM*. He is also the co-editor of *Caribbean Economies and Global Restructuring* and *Globalization, Diaspora and Caribbean Popular Culture* and co-author of *Windward Islands Bananas: Challenges and Options under the Single European Market.*

Anthony Payne is Professor of Politics at the University of Sheffield in the UK. He has published extensively on the politics, political economy and international relations of the Caribbean. He also has a longstanding interest in the particular problems of small states, co-editing *Politics, Security and Development in Small States* and *Size and Survival: The Politics of Security in the Small Island and Enclave Developing States of the Caribbean and the Pacific.* His most recent related work is a CIGI paper, co-authored with Paul Sutton, entitled 'Repositioning the Caribbean within Globalisation'.

Naren Prasad is a Development Economist with the International Labour Organization's International Institute for Labour Studies and former Research Coordinator with the United Nations Research Institute for Social Development where he coordinated research projects in the area of Markets, Business and Regulation and Social Policy and Development. He is responsible for the 'privatisation of public services' project related to water, education, and health, as well as the 'Social Policy Index', which measures a country's priorities in terms of social policy. Prasad has worked with various United Nations agencies, including a position with UNESCO as a programme specialist. He has also worked with the International Labour Organization and is co-author of the *World Employment Report 2004–05: Productivity, Employment and Poverty.*

Timothy M. Shaw is Visiting Professor, University of Massachusetts Boston, USA, and Emeritus Professor, University of London, UK. He previously directed the Institute of Commonwealth Studies at the University of London and taught at Dalhousie University for three decades. Previous posts also include Carleton and Royal Roads universities. He has held visiting professorships in Europe, Asia and Africa, including current posts with Makerere University Business School and Mbarara University of Science and Technology in Uganda, and Stellenbosch University in South Africa. He is a Senior Fellow at CIGI and is a series editor for both Ashgate and Palgrave Macmillan.

Baldur Thorhallsson is Professor of Political Science and Chair of the Institute of International Affairs and the Centre for Small State Studies, University of Iceland. His research focuses particularly on small-state studies and European integration. He has published numerous articles on small states in Europe, European integration and Iceland's foreign policy. He authored two books on small states in Europe, including *Iceland and*

European Integration: On the Edge and *The Role of Small States in the European Union.* He teaches in the areas of small-state studies, European integration, international relations and Iceland's foreign affairs. He completed his Ph.D. in Political Science from the University of Essex in 1999.

William Vlcek is Lecturer at the School of International Studies, University of St. Andrews. He is the author of *Offshore Finance and Small States: Sovereignty, Size and Money* and has published research work on international measures to combat terrorist financing, as well as the Caribbean offshore financial centres in the *Round Table; British Journal of Politics and International Relations; International Journal of Politics, Culture and Society; European Security; European Foreign Affairs Review;* and *Global Change, Peace & Security.*

Abbreviations

ACP	African, Caribbean and Pacific states
ACS	Association of Caribbean States
ALBA	Bolivarian Alternative for the Americas (*Alternativa Bolivariana para las Américas*)
AOSIS	Alliance of Small and Island States
BASIC	Brazil, South Africa, India and China
BCCI	Bank of Credit and Commerce International
BMLAS	Barbados Mutual Life Assurance Society (later SAGICOR)
bpd	barrels per day
BRICs	Brazil, Russia, India, and China
BVI	British Virgin Islands
C4	The Cotton Four (Burkina Faso, Benin, Chad and Mali)
CARIBCAN	Caribbean Canada Trade Agreement
CARICOM	Caribbean Community
CARIFORUM	Caribbean Forum (CARICOM and the Dominican Republic)
CARIMET	Caribbean Metrology
CBTPA	Caribbean Basin Trade Promotion Agreement
ccTLD	Country Code Top Level Domain
CDF	Caribbean Development Fund
CET	Common External Tariff
CETDC	CARIFORUM–EC Trade and Development Committee
CHINDIA	China and India
CHOGM	Commonwealth Heads of Government Meeting
CICAD	Inter-American Drug Abuse Control Commission
COFA	Palau Compact of Free Association
COFOR	Caricom Council for Foreign and Community Relations
COTED	Council for Trade and Economic Development
CRNM	Caribbean Regional Negotiating Machinery
CSME	CARICOM Single Market Economy
DSM	Dispute Settlement Mechanism
EEA	European Economic Area
EEZ	Exclusive Economic Zones
EFTA	European Free Trade Agreement
EIC	East India Company
EITI	Extractive Industries Transparency Initiative
EPA	Economic Partnership Agreement

EPZ	Export Processing Zone
EU	European Union
FAO	Food and Agriculture Organization
FATF	Financial Action Task Force
FCO	Foreign and Commonwealth Office (UK)
FDI	Foreign Direct Investment
FTA	Free Trade Agreements
FTAA	Free Trade Agreement of the Americas
G-90	Group of 90
GATS	General Agreement on Trade in Services
GATT	General Agreement on Tariffs and Trade
GDP	Gross Domestic Product
GLISPA	Global Islands Partnership
GNI	Gross National Income
HOGC	Heads of Government Conference
ICRU	Icelandic Crisis Response Unit
ICT	Information and Communication Technology
IFI	International Financial Institution
IFPI	International Federation of the Phonographic Industry
ILO	International Labour Organization
IMF	International Monetary Fund
IOC	International Oil Company
IPE	International Political Economy
ITC	International Trade Commission
IR	International Relations
IWC	International Whaling Commission
LAC	Latin America and the Caribbean
MEUSAC	Malta–European Union Steering and Action Committee
MIITF	Marshall Islands Intergenerational Trust Fund
MFN	Most Favoured Nation
NAFTA	North American Free Trade Agreement
NAM	Non-Aligned Movement
NAMMCO	North Atlantic Marine Mammal Commission
NATO	North Atlantic Treaty Organisation
NCCT	Non-Cooperative Countries and Territories
NGO	Non-Governmental Organisation
NIEO	New International Economic Order
NOC	National Oil Company
NTUC	National Trade Unions Congress (Singapore)
OAS	Organization of American States
OECD	Organisation for Economic Co-operation and Development
OECS	Organisation of Eastern Caribbean States

OFC	Offshore Financial Centre
OPEC	Organisation of the Petroleum Exporting Countries
OSCE	Organisation for Security and Cooperation in Europe
PAP	People's Action Party (Singapore)
PdVSA	Petróleos de Venezuela, S.A.
PIIGS	Portugal, Italy, Ireland, Greece and Spain
PTA	Preferential Trade Agreement
RERF	Kiribati Revenue Equalisation Reserve Fund
S&DT	Special and Differential Treatment
SCP	Singapore Cooperation Programme
SICA	Central American Integration System (*El Sistema de la Integración Centroamericana*)
SIDS	Small Island Developing States
SIM	Inter-American Metrology System
SIRG	Summit Implementation Resource Group
SMD	Singapore Model of Development
T&T	Trinidad and Tobago
TCTP	Third Country Training Programme
TIEA	Tax Information Exchange Agreement
TNS	Transaction Network Services
TPB	Tuvalu Philatelic Bureau
TRIPs	Trade-related Aspects of Intellectual Property Rights
TTF	Tuvalu Trust Fund
UBS	Union Bank of Switzerland (originally)
UN	United Nations
UNAVI	United Nations Association of the Virgin Islands
UNCTAD	United Nations Conference on Trade and Development
UNDP	United Nations Development Programme
UNECA	United Nations Economic Commission for Africa
UNEP	United Nations Environment Programme
UNESCO	United Nations Educational, Scientific and Cultural Organisation
WCED	World Commission on Environment and Development
WIOC	West Indies Oil Company
WIPO	World Intellectual Property Organization
WOLA	Washington Office on Latin America
WTO	World Trade Organization

1

The Diplomacies of Small States at the Start of the Twenty-first Century: How Vulnerable? How Resilient?

Andrew F. Cooper and Timothy M. Shaw

Small states are mostly acted upon by much more powerful states and institutions ... Vulnerabilities rather than opportunities ... come through as the most striking manifestations of the consequences of smallness in global politics.

(Payne 2004: 634)

Resilience can be defined in many ways, but here it is defined as the ability to recover from or adjust to change. This definition is associated with the coping ability of an economically vulnerable country ... Resilience may be inherent or nurtured ... Nurtured resilience is that which is developed and managed, often as a result of some deliberate policy ... resilience building. On the other hand, a country can adopt policies which exacerbate its inherent vulnerability.

(Briguglio 2007: 105)

While there are now more small states than ever, the analytic and policy attention towards these states has not matched their proliferation. Hence the timeliness of this collection, which is designed as a catch-up exercise from both an academic and practical perspective and concentrates on the Caribbean. Reflective of a structurally imposed condition, small states continue to be disconnected from the most salient debates in International Relations (IR). Current theoretical shifts in IR to the regional-global architecture are almost universally perceived to be due

1

to the emergence of the so-called BRICs (Brazil, Russia, India, China) – or alternative acronyms such as the Next 11 (N11) – at the upper middle of the international hierarchy, and not to any relocation among small actors.

Yet this continuing bias towards re-ordering imposed by the big states – new or old – should not hide the impact that small states have in rethinking and reconfiguring practices of diplomacy. What small states lack in structural clout they can make up through creative agency. Indeed, in an increasingly multi-dimensional fashion, small states matter not only in the diplomatic domain, but also in the more general domain of global governance. Dominant images of weakness cannot be completely set aside, as witnessed by the number of failed or fragile states that fit the small states category (cases such as East Timor and Haiti are in the forefront), but this representation needs to be balanced by attention towards the innovative character of small states. Quite explicitly, it is this positive but under-played dimension that is the focus of this volume.

In geo-political terms, small states had some considerable leverage in the bipolar world because of their numbers. Leveraging the attributes of the Westphalian system in their favour, small states practiced much of their diplomatic activity within the United Nations, capitalising on the rule of one vote per sovereign state.

In the post-Cold War context, this form of collective activity via 'Third World' solidarity has eroded. Small states no longer attempt to work as part of a wider South-oriented trade union movement. Consistent with the trend towards fragmentation and a differentiated form of hierarchy, these states tend to compete with each other for niches in the global political/economic arena rather than cooperate. Globalisation has served to exacerbate differences and divergences. Inter-small state competition constitutes both upward mobility – such as Singapore, Iceland, Malta, Barbados, and Mauritius – and an alternative race to the bottom, most visible in the South Pacific as witnessed by Vanuatu, Nauru and the Solomon Islands.

In functional terms, the more successful small states adopt international practices that run on parallel lines to the classic middle power diplomacy associated with much bigger states, whether of a traditional (Canada/Australia/Nordics) or non-traditional (South Africa/Chile) variety (Cooper, 1997). Managing to break away on selective issue-areas, small states have revealed that they can adopt diplomatic practices that involve global networks advancing global governance on issues such as the land-mine ban or fisheries certification. It is worth noting here that before the agenda was taken up by a host of upper-level countries it was Trinidad and Tobago that took the initial lead on the International Criminal Court.

The proliferation of small states has also led to further forms of both inter- and non-state regionalisation. Smallness compels external cooperation for reasons of communication, development, environment, security, and technology. Such regional relations may constitute fuzzy boundaries as cultural, ecological, economic and strategic sectors do not necessarily nest neatly. The variety of post-imperial 'commonwealths' in the Caribbean (Clegg and Pantojas, 2008) is indicative of such complexities and is reflected in the diversity of the Overseas Countries and Territories of the EU Association (www.octassociation.org), half of which are in the Caribbean.

Symptomatic of the transformation in the analysis and practice of small states is the early work of David Vital (1967; 1971), undertaken at the height of the Cold War. His two monographs, both preoccupied with the state of Israel in the Middle East, were written in a period of intense bipolarity; they are contextually 'pre-globalisation' and are acutely realist with a concentration on conflict. Beyond Vital, the bulk of the literature in this period is premised on the assumption that small states could not simply assume their sovereignty/independence would be respected by greater powers. Greater powers often saw strategic relevance in interfering with the domestic policies of smaller states, and violated their territorial integrity when deemed necessary. This impression of vulnerability increased the closer a small state was in proximity to the greater power's sphere of influence (Mathisen, 1971: 49–66, 238–65; Schou and Brundtland, 1971: 31–7).

The context of the international economic system was just as problematic, as witnessed by the volatility of the oil shocks through the 1970s. Small states lacked diversification in their economy and were therefore more reliant on trade than larger states. Limited domestic market size and high transportation costs (a result of both remoteness from major markets and small cargo loads) further reduced their competitiveness and return. When the proximity to a larger state was close, economic dependence on a larger power merged into geo-political vulnerability (as found in the case of Swaziland, Lesotho and Botswana vis-à-vis South Africa) (Schou and Brundtland, 1971: 43–6; Commonwealth Secretariat/World Bank Joint Task Force on Small States, 2000: 6–7; Kisanga and Danchie, 2007: 55–97).

The post-Cold War era has in some ways brought with it greater vulnerabilities. For example, the early work of Lino Briguglio (1995) is concerned with post-independence island states, and is characterised not only by economic but ecological vulnerability, a notion that has become more acute with an appreciation of the dangers of climate change.

Yet, small states in the twenty-first century cannot be seen simply as structurally weak Lilliputians in a system controlled by the big and strong. Briguglio (2007: 105) for one has gone beyond vulnerability to advocate 'resilience', even 'nurturing', given the myriad opportunities and challenges of 'globalisation'. Briguglio affords considerable onus to the meshing of the operationalisation of resilience and the means by which diplomacies are used.

Keohane opened up some of these possibilities in his well-known 1971 article, 'The Big Influence of Small Allies'. But his privileging of diplomatic agency was still tempered by a number of analytical obstacles. Realist thinking still dictated that small states chose between a narrow set of choices, namely a bandwagon or a balancing approach. Moreover, the states that were given most of the attention in these studies were far more akin to middle powers than smaller states. Much of the older literature (pre-1990s) tends to focus on states that are under the population range of 10–15 million, categorising the world into Large States or 'Great Powers', Medium States or 'Medium Powers' and Small States or 'Small Powers'. When making specific reference to states below the 1–1.5 million people range, they were often referred to as Microstates (Vital, 1967; Dommen and Hein, 1985; Plischke, 1977).

The privileging of resilience and resourcefulness takes us in a very different, nuanced, and innovative direction. If many of the problems for small states need to be relocated, the need and the ability to find solutions require the same treatment. In this narrative the image of small states is reconfigured in quite striking ways. Vulnerability is a naturally imposed and predictable condition in which the room for manoeuvre is severely constrained. Resilience by way of contrast is adaptive, allowing structural factors to be resisted and reshaped.

As the construct of small states as simply system-takers is modified, the range of activity options is expanded. Instead of collective enterprises, so central to the Lilliputian-Gulliver image, a considerable emphasis is placed on individual actor-ness. Clearly there are commonalities of responses among small states as evidenced throughout this book. What jumps out from the collection's contributions, however, is the range of options open to small states. Consistent with the flexibility built into the theme of resilience, a few of the countries showcased within this volume have built up economic niches using well-planned strategies and a focus on education and technological infrastructure development. Other states have adapted in a far more ad hoc – or even opportunistic – manner.

All retain some aspects of conformity with respect to their diplomatic profile, traditionally associated with a club-orientation and state-centric diplomatic activity. In formal terms of sovereignty and jurisdictional issues, principles of non-interference continue to be the fundamental mantra of small state diplomatic culture. In practice, however, these principles are often contravened as most small states see themselves – and are often seen by others – as the mavericks and the rule-benders of the international system.

The increase in the supply of small states willing and able to be creative has coincided with the demand for such activity. In many cases, necessity has been the mother of innovation as both the severity of the crisis and its transnational nature have revealed themselves; this is especially so regarding environment-related issues. In other cases, adaptive capacity has gone hand in hand with an appreciation of both the risks and opportunities located in the dynamics of globalisation and liberalisation. The opening up of the global financial sector provided space for innovative small states to promote greater integration of their banking and investment services with larger economies, while exposing them to greater economic risks in times of crisis (see Sanders, 2008). Market conditions for commodities continue to have a bust/boom personality, with the added ingredient that import-driven inflation can offset rises in exports of raw materials. Manufacturing, for its part, is increasingly the preserve of selected members of the BRICs (most notably China) and the N11 and not the traditional twentieth century industrial states. Small states are therefore pushed to seek and maintain novel, and often precarious, areas of activity that are not conditioned by size or geographic location. This tendency is accentuated by the emergence on the front lines of international politics of the G20 – a forum that explicitly privileges big states/economies from the global South as well as the established G8.

From vulnerability to resilience and beyond?
Challenges/realities of practising small state diplomacy

The articulation of a 'vulnerability' agenda coincided with the dominance of the dependency lament around the new international economic order (NIEO) debate. During the debate, 'new' states in the South – the Third World – could together impact the two Norths: East and West. Vulnerability as both actuality and ideology was refined and advanced for the small island developmental states (SIDS), a process aided in particular by the still-new Commonwealth Secretariat with academic and method-ological support from Lino Briguglio and his colleagues at the University of Malta.

The need for different lenses to examine small states has animated many of the contributors to this book. Godfrey Baldacchino highlights the deficiencies in understandings of small states in his pivotal contri-bution. It is no longer good enough to simply present small isolated states as weak. The notion of a collective ganging up of an assem-bly of Lilliputians – the so-called 'tyranny of the weak' – also remains inadequate.

Naren Prasad builds on his own body of work (2004: 45), suggest-ing that 'most small islands distort international trade rules ... most of these successful strategies are based on rent-seeking activities which are generally considered unconventional.' Prasad goes on to identify some established and more recent strategies to exploit globalisation for small states: '[Export Processing Zone] EPZs, offshore financial centres, remit-tances, aid and rent-seeking and deriving other unconventional sources of income – go against mainstream thinking in economics.' Prasad proceeds to identify other current 'unconventional strategies': selling sovereignty, military bases, fishing rights, shipping registries, passport sales, philately, trust funds, telephone country codes, domain names, satellite businesses, and peacekeeping operations. He could also have added in the formal economy, Internet gaming (Cooper, 2008b), and cruise-ship visits, especially hubs (Chin, 2008), let alone myriad oppor-tunities in the informal sector such as drug and gun smuggling and money-laundering (Griffith, 2000).

Winston Griffith has recently argued that the Internet's ability to tran-scend distance means that resourcelessness should not be an obstacle to development, especially in education, services and skills. Rather, Griffith (2007: 941) argues that:

> Neither a country's economic smallness nor a lack of a diverse natural resource base is a constraint on its economic structure of production ... if a country has an abundance of knowledge skills at competitive prices, it can attract FDI which can help to diversify its economic structure of production.

Thus resilience as motif has replaced vulnerability in a few small states, especially 'developmental island states' such as Mauritius and Trinidad and Tobago. These states take their cues from other small developmental states such as Singapore, a newly industrialised country (NIC), as well as Iceland and Ireland in the North Atlantic. The lessons from Singapore, as traced by Alan Chong in extensive detail, are particularly intriguing as the state-based diplomacy of the late twentieth century is being eroded, if not completely transformed. The developmental state orientation, with its high promise and delivery of economic growth, is promoted not only by order and stability but through an increasingly sophisticated expression of soft power. Essential ingredients in this approach are both the projection of a normative doctrine (the championship of Asian Values) and instrumental deliverables (a generous foreign aid programme).

Yet the degree to which lessons can be transported between regions and across the equator remains in dispute. Singapore basks in its post-colonial success, initiated by a small nationalist elite pushing meritocracy. As detailed by Carlyle Corbin, some of the more successful economies are dependencies, such as Bermuda, the British Virgin Islands (BVI) and the Caymans in the wider Caribbean (www.ukota.org; Shaw, 2008: 77–80). Yet, amid these success stories, Corbin's analysis depicts the deeper contradictions located within these entities. Yes, they may be leaders in specific economic areas but they lag in the maturity of their political status. Whatever their developmental attributes these non-independent territories remain bastions of inequality on the periphery of both diplomacy and governance.

The case of Singapore is also quite different from the Caribbean Community (CARICOM) countries featured in Jacqueline Braveboy-Wagner's chapter. Akin to Singapore, these small-sized developing states have gone through an extensive decolonising process, but to a much greater and protracted manner than the latter. Moreover, they embraced collective efforts through the G77 caucus in the UN. Nevertheless, as Braveboy-Wagner's chapter fully articulates, the notion of vulnerability was reconstituted over a span of decades due in part to the politics of structural adjustment, the frustrations relating to changing traditional preferential trading arrangements, and the new security concerns post 9/11. Braveboy-Wagner demonstrates the growing resilience in selective issue-areas such as sustainable development and norm entrepreneurship. Although each has diplomatic particularities because of their geographic positions, concerns about global brands and communication strategies have become accentuated. In such an atmosphere of shape shifting it is anticipated that the foreign ministries of small states – embedded to the protocols of the past – will come under greater pressure to maintain their status.

Facing diverse and uncertain challenges: Case studies of small states' diplomacy vis-à-vis regional organisations

Notwithstanding these signs of adjustment on the ground, small states literature remains overly state-centric. It has remained so despite the intimate relations between economy/society and state-given smallness, histories of migrations, and proximity to the environment. If divergences in economic performance are to be interrogated, then, given globalisation, the roles of national and global civil societies, private companies and other diverse and competitive actors must be given the attention they deserve; each factor amplifying the opportunities and risks that influence the behaviour of small states.

Such a blend of challenges can be traced through a focus on regionalisation. Baldur Thorhallson's discussion on Iceland is indicative of some of these trends. At a state-centric level, the deepening engagement of Iceland with the European Union reflected core national interests. At a society level, though, this tendency reflected the rise of a prominent financial sector encouraged through greater liberalisation and privatisation. On both sides, a greater sense of confidence and inclination to take risks animated this type of re-orientation. The embedded sense of defensiveness turned into self-assertiveness with attendant over-confidence and over-stretch. There is no more pertinent recent example of how vulnerability and resilience have become closely intertwined. Iceland's culture of unconventional behaviour in its financial sector brought short-term advantages and exposed it to massive longer-term pitfalls.

Anthony T. Bryan brings attention to the controversial topic of Petro-Caribe and CARICOM. Dealing with the pressures emanating from the issue of energy security is a key test of resilience for the CARICOM countries. Still, as the small Caribbean energy-importing countries respond to these pressures through forging closer ties to Venezuela, resilience can turn into opportunism. Bryan convincingly depicts the dilemma, arguing: 'Dependence on oil and gas imports is higher in this region than anywhere else in the hemisphere, meaning that the potential for resource diplomacy is greater as well.'

As in other contributions, it is the ability of Bryan to nuance the PetroCaribe case that makes it so compelling. Details include a comparative discussion between the responses of the Caribbean states. Trinidad and Tobago, with its abundant energy resources, has remained resistant, but a range of other CARICOM countries have bought into the programme with sharply different implications. In Bryan's words the overall regional impact is one that 'emphasised the vulnerability of the regional institution'.

Each perspective highlights both the diversity and challenges before small states. One issue relates to the relevance of cross-regional/international associations. The Commonwealth has been an important forum for SIDS issues at the inter-state level, and now cooperates with the World Bank in an ongoing Joint Task Force (Shaw, 2008). As David McIntyre (2001: 117) notes:

> The Commonwealth has, indeed, become the premier small states forum. It has a higher proportion of small-state members than any other worldwide political organization ... From the mid-1980s, then, a small states dimension became a significant feature of Commonwealth activities.

Such sentiments are echoed by Paul Sutton (2001: 75): 'The Commonwealth has emerged as the intergovernmental champion for small states.' If the inter- as well as non-state Commonwealths can extend their reach to UK and other overseas territories (i.e. Australia and New Zealand), then their global coalition would have more clout as it would include Bermuda, BVI, and the Caymans.

The World Bank organises and hosts an annual Small States Forum in association with the Commonwealth as almost 30 of the 45 small states at the Forum are Commonwealth members. The orientation of the Forum suggests that given developments in global telecommunications, islands may no longer be at a disadvantage, at least in service sectors that rely on the Internet (www.worldbank.org/smallstates).

The other issue, of course, is the emerging sense of competition between bigger actors. According to Debbie Mohammed, relations between the EU and CARICOM can be just as controversial as those with Venezuela. Notwithstanding the passing of the hegemony of *dependencia*, the EU's aggressive selling of EPAs has dismayed the small states in the South as it has encouraged fissures between the African, Caribbean and Pacific regions. These negotiations contain high degrees of asymmetry, but despite these flaws the big picture continues to change. Eurasia or Eurafrica may become more salient than relations among the Southern regions (Gaens, 2008; Robles, 2004), while EU–small state connections become ever more apparent and imperative.

Some projections of state-based activity by small states still contain evidence of the club model's hold regarding the diplomacy of small states. In terms of causation, this orthodoxy goes back to the concept of legal equality as a fundamental characteristic of statehood and membership in the community of nations. Many international governmental organisations, as indicated above, operate on a 'one state, one vote' system that not only favours small states, but gives them a huge incentive to place weight on the symbolic attributes of sovereignty and club-membership. Status as an equal member in the society of states animates a good deal of the statecraft from this category of countries.

As Daniel P. Erickson illustrates this mode of diplomatic behaviour is accented by the convening function of major events for small states. The Commonwealth Heads of Government Meeting (CHOGM) allows small states, and their leaders, a particular high profile as hosts. For the last three years CHOGMs have been held in smaller countries – Malta, Uganda, or Trinidad and Tobago. Far more distinctive is the case of Trinidad and Tobago hosting the 2009 Summit of the Americas, which, unlike APEC, is without a set rotation worked out between its members. Nor is there a precedent of small states as hosts, as with the CHOGMs. As such the stakes for a state such as Trinidad and Tobago are much higher. As Erickson puts it, the 2009 Summit 'elevates the region from a historically marginal position to centre stage'.

Stretching out from these diplomatic 'club' activities are varied forms of networking. Certainly the 2009 Trinidad and Tobago Summit of the Americas promises once more to bring out the sensitivities that have built up over the years between the US and Venezuela and their respective allies. This is not the only potential confrontation, however. What should not be minimised is the overlapping struggle between a corporate-oriented agenda and societal groupings going back to the 2001 Quebec City Summit. Time will tell whether Trinidad and Tobago can get the Summit process back on track, with a rekindling of the original 'spirit of collegiality', or whether the 2009 Summit will be better remembered as an event featuring street demonstrations and barricades between the state leaders and societal forces!

Between conformity and the search for loopholes: Case studies of small states' diplomacy vis-à-vis international organisations

Tensions over club diplomacy go hand in hand with a tilt away from standard recipes for economic growth. The model followed by small states has deviated from one laid down in orthodox textbooks: from selling postage stamps, radio frequencies and flags of convenience to a range of formal/legal and informal/illegal services, such as cruise ships (Chin, 2008), ecotourism, Internet gambling (Cooper, 2008b), offshore banking and retirement communities to drug and gun-smuggling, respectively.

Some of these activities have become more pronounced because of constraints in other areas. Where international institutions allow small states to play an effective role, rules are abided by. This dynamic comes out in Donna Lee's chapter on small African state cotton diplomacy with respect to the WTO. In its coalitional form, and with its focus on a single commodity, this activity exhibits a backward looking style. Where it is completely different is in the new formal relationship developed between the Cotton 4 with Oxfam, shifting the nature of the 'club' towards a more networked format. Such innovation served as an indication that these small countries were not simply conventional patterns of the past.

Still, it is the obstacles as much as the opportunities that influence small state behaviour. The erosion of preferential trading systems through further globalisation has increased the difficulties small states face in maintaining a competitive international position economically, especially those already facing high transportation costs (Hurt, 2003: 161–76; Prasad, 2004: 45–8).

Shifting to an internal lens, small state 'governance' is different because of the intimacy of the ruled with their rulers. The elites across the club and network divides all know each other (Heine, 2006; Cooper and Legler, 2006). Thus integrity is even more crucial in such jurisdictions. Distinctions between state and non-state, or political and economic, tend to be blurred, and the external tends to be relatively more salient than in larger states, particularly the BRICs. To compensate somewhat for their often microscopic foreign ministries, public diplomacies that engage a wider set of non-state resources and networks would seem to be inevitable. Yet, up to recently, small states have not been known for the creative use of such partnerships.

One sign that this hold of orthodoxy is eroding comes out in Andrew F. Cooper's chapter on Antigua and its WTO Internet gambling dispute with the US. Having carved out a distinctive and lucrative niche in the global economy, Antigua (as a rentier state) and its allies within the gambling industry were determined to hold on to that advantage in spite of being branded as the proverbial 'Pirate of the Caribbean' by the US. Fighting this stigmatisation, without active help from its Caribbean neighbours, Antigua used new forms of private authority to defend its interests. It also used sustained and subtle forms of public diplomacy to re-configure its image as an innovator both with respect to regulation and as a technological service provider. As in the cotton case asymmetry could be reversed by the use of good arguments and persistence.

The gap between orthodox images and the unconventional behaviour of small states is stretched even further once other forms of specificity are brought into the mix. The identification and impact of assorted diasporas are central to small, especially island, state development: from social and financial relations to cultural and welfare, symbolised by call cards in distant metropolises. Given such historic migrations, the flow of remittances has become a major issue, not only through ubiquitous franchises like Western Union and MoneyGram – contemporary legacies of the 'barrel' culture – but informal channels.

Don Marshall reminds us how the stigmatisation of the unconventional behaviour of small Caribbean states is not at all a new phenomenon, with constant attempts to regulate spaces of money flows. The authoritative construction has been that small states are sites of 'considerable intrigue' with ties to the underworld. Consistent with the main theme of this collection, Marshall re-evaluates these contours of financialisation as a misunderstood ' "tool kit" of innovative instruments', built not on a basis of a conscious design but 'opportunist pragmatism'. Gambling was condoned both as a style of doing business in overall terms as well as a specific industry.

Even with this creative mentality there continues to be gaps in terms of the exploitation of niche economic opportunities. A fascinating case study examining obstacles of this sort comes out in Keith Nurse's chapter regarding the cultural industries. Caribbean small states have established high-profile brands in music and other forms of cultural expression. Nonetheless, cultural creativity has not been backed up by 'an entrepreneurial, managerial and marketing capability from within the Caribbean's business sector' or with respect to state support.

As Nurse acknowledges there are some recent signs of advance, via festival tourism for example. But most of the big ticket events remain connected with the diaspora. Gaps remain, however, as witnessed by the lack of massive global distribution networks. Symbolic appreciation of cultural industries as critical ingredients for identity formation and nation building is evident. What is lacking is an appreciation of cultural industries as a critical strategic resource.

In order to promote an adaptive culture, Briguglio (2007) has advocated that states nurture promising sectors in the twenty-first century. While some governments have encouraged growth in these areas, others have yet to accept Briguglio's advice. Such a development strategy implies that regimes must reach beyond the state, embracing a range of heterogeneous non-state actors. Can small states partner with non-state actors to minimise vulnerability and maximise resilience in the new century via public diplomacy (see www.publicdiplomacy.org)? Or even celebrity diplomacy (see Cooper, 2008a)? To give just one illustration of the nexus between entertainment and public/celebrity diplomacy, Rihanna (a major star in the music world, and a member of the Caribbean Diaspora) has been named an honorary youth and cultural ambassador of Barbados. Although more symbolic than instrumental, this innovative use of celebrity diplomacy reveals that small countries can be quick to make sure success stories at the individual level are linked to national rebranding.

If some organisations, notably the Commonwealth, are viewed often as champions of small states, other organisations are taken to be their adversaries. The OECD, in William Vlcek's contribution, falls very much in the latter camp, at least in terms of its attacks on tax havens or offshore financial centres. As Vlcek argues: 'The OECD has constructed a perception that the low-tax regimes offered by OFCs ... pose a threat to the tax base of OECD members.'

Although vulnerable to this sort of confrontation, Vlcek sees the Caribbean small state response as very much in accordance with the interpretation of resilience. As in the Internet gambling case, a good deal of this counter-attack was contingent on robust forms of public diplomacy with a focus on other issues such as capital flight from developing states. Unlike the Internet gambling case, however, no single small state was isolated in this fight. Vlcek concludes by stating that 'the small states demonstrated their resilience through claims for equal representation with the OECD states'.

Juxtaposition of relevant approaches and debates

Early small state/SIDS analyses emerged from political science and island studies in the initial post-independence era. Since then, as the number of small states and their issues have proliferated, so has the range of analytic assumptions and approaches as indicated in the third part of the Baldacchino (2007: 295–512) reader on development with chapters on security, political economy, governance, tourism, migration, gentrification and sustainability. The literatures increasingly span perspectives and debates through both uni- and multi-disciplinary analyses. Focusing on different periods, regions and issues means different rankings of factors and approaches, with ecology, illegal activity, new regionalisms, and new security arguably becoming more salient than before. As Baldacchino (2007: 1–30) suggests, island studies is more diverse and dynamic than ever.

Unlike the bipolar SIDS strategy of crying 'vulnerability', more public, contemporary diplomacy has involved using global rules against some of their authors: a rather robust form of resilience. Thus, to advance their OFCs out of the +/−40 world-wide, as William Vleck highlights, some of the SIDS have been able to turn the tables against the EU/G8/IMF/OECD advocates of the Harmful Tax Competition Initiative through the Financial Stability Forum, not wanting to get black-listed by the Financial Action Task Force (Marshall, 2007; Vleck, 2007 and 2008). Similarly, Antigua has been able to claim compensation from the US for trying to halt cross-border Internet gambling (Cooper, 2008b). In turn, small states might espouse the Extractive Industries Transparency Initiative (EITI) as it becomes established in the energy and mining sectors, as a further opportunity of verifying their financial integrity.

As may be expected, this exciting intellectual and practical agenda is overshadowed by a concentration on the new 'bigs' – BRICs, N11, etc. – and their thoughts and actions. It also is often subordinated to a Continental bias, including the renewed interest on Africa. Both of these trends, however, have enormous spill-over effects on small states. Whereas it has been the US/EU that traditionally dominated the theme of asymmetry in the small states literature, increasingly China, India, and Brazil have to be brought into the analysis. This necessitates deeper comparisons with Africa, in terms of BRICs diplomacy and hard and soft power. In either case we endorse Lemke's (2003: 116) plea for Africa, while fitting the sentiment within small state theory and policy: 'My goal is to offer specific steps to improve IR research designs so that Africa and the developing world more generally no longer go missing.'

More positively, sources on small states and islands have evolved from national and international agencies to local and global NGOs and think tanks as indicated in the list of websites below. Thus in 2007 alone, Chatham House (www.chathamhouse.org.uk) and CIGI (www.cigionline.org) generated innovative and distinctive analyses on the Caribbean given contemporary globalisation. Payne and Sutton (2007) were more comprehensive, critical and regional in their CIGI working paper than the Baker (2007) collection from London, which concentrated on more familiar formal economic and ecological factors rather than the range of informal relations including remittances. The question that remains is: what notions, sources, policies, and actors are going to advance the analysis and practice of the small states in the future?

Futures for small states: development for all/some/none?

Given the diversity of political economies/cultures among small states, no one projection about future trajectories is likely to emerge. Nevertheless, the divergence between vulnerability and resilience is stark (Briguglio, 2007; Briguglio et al., 2008) especially in terms of human development/security. Our edited volume will illuminate some of the choices and prospects between more 'fragile' communities and more ebullient 'developmental states'. Here we point to the unavoidable impacts of formal and informal globalisations along with responsive patterns of 'governance' at all levels. Information and Communications Technology (ICT) offers greater possibilities in these processes, allowing diverse participation in international relations at little cost and need for human resources.

The context to any such projections for the small state is cast between vulnerability and resilience given continuing, albeit uneven, globalisation, as indicated in the current debate and unease about the EU's imposition of regional EPAs. Such unease is compounded as dependencies become increasingly competitive with nominally independent regimes. While at the same time, economic vulnerabilities within leading industrialised states have become more pronounced. Constrained availability of credit and dwindling confidence in Western financial markets may play out over the long term to re-orientated multilateral trade and financial regulatory regimes, a process in which small states must insert resilient diplomacy.

At the end of the first decade of the new millennium, it is increasingly recognised that human and ecological resources are becoming more salient than traditional primary products in a relentless era of globalisation. This recognition is apparent in the handful of developmental island states, from Malta to Singapore and Mauritius to Bermuda and Caymans, thus far. Such a perspective reinforces the role of diasporas in terms of technology transfer and policy development as well as remittances/returns/retirements (Dawson, 2007). In the new century small states, as well as BRICs (Cooper et al., 2006; Shaw et al., 2007), the members of the G20, and N11s, contribute a lot to overlapping interdisciplinary fields such as development, environmental, and security studies in addition to established disciplines like political science and international relations. At odds with traditional perspectives, there is no single right way for small states to proceed; whether in Iceland or the Caribbean. They are free to push against orthodoxies in very different ways (both in terms of ideas and outcomes) from what was expected and possible in the past.

References

Baker, Gordon, (ed.) (2007) *No Island is an Island: The Impact of Globalization on the Commonwealth Caribbean* (London: Chatham House).

Baldacchino, Godfrey, (ed.) (2006) 'Special Issue: Sub-national island jurisdictions', *Round Table* 95(386): 487–626.

Baldacchino, Godfrey (2007) 'Introducing a World of Islands' in Godfrey Baldacchino, (ed.) *A World of Islands: An Island Studies Reader* (Charlottetown: UPEI): 1–29.

Briguglio, Lino (1995) 'Small Island States and their Economic Vulnerabilities', *World Development* 23(9): 1615–32.

Briguglio, Lino (2007) 'Economic Vulnerability and Resilience: Concepts and Measurements' in Eliawony Kisanga and Sarah Jane Danchie, (eds) *Commonwealth Small States: Issues and Prospects* (London: ComSec & CPA): 101–9.

Briguglio, Lino, Gordon Cordina, Constance Vigilance and Nadia Farrugia, (eds) (2008) *Small States and the Pillars of Economic Resilience* (London: Commonwealth Secretariat).

Chin, Christine (2008) *Cruising in the Global Economy: Profits, Pleasure and Work at Sea* (Aldershot: Ashgate).

Clegg, Peter and Emilio Pantojas, (eds) (2009) *Governance in the Caribbean: Challenges and Opportunities in the 21st Century* (Kingston: Ian Randle, forthcoming).

Commonwealth Secretariat (1985) 'Vulnerability: Small States in the Global Society' (London: Commonwealth Secretariat).

Commonwealth Secretariat (2007) *Small States: Economic Review and Basic Statistics, Volume 11* (London: Commonwealth Secretariat).

Commonwealth Secretariat/World Bank (2000) *Small States: Meeting Challenges in the Global Economy*, Final report of the Commonwealth Secretariat/World Bank Joint Task Force on Small States, March (London and Washington DC: Commonwealth Secretariat/World Bank).

Cooper, Andrew F. (1997) *Niche Diplomacy* (New York: Macmillan).

Cooper, Andrew (2008a) *Celebrity Diplomacy* (Boulder: Paradigm).

Cooper, Andrew (2008b) ' "Remote" in the Eastern Caribbean: the Antigua–US WTO Internet Gambling Case', Caribbean Paper No. 4, April (Waterloo: CIGI) (Available at www.cigionline.org).

Cooper, Andrew and Thomas Legler (2006) *Intervention without Intervening? The OAS Defense and Promotion of Democracy in the Americas* (Basingstoke: Palgrave Macmillan).

Cooper, Andrew, Agata Ankiewicz and Timothy M. Shaw (2006) 'Economic Size Trumps all Else? Lessons from BRICSAM', Working Paper No. 12, December (Waterloo: CIGI) (Available at www.cigionline.org).

Dawson, Laura Ritchie (2007) 'Brain Drain, Brain Circulation, Remittances and Development: Prospects for the Caribbean', Caribbean Paper No. 2, June (Waterloo: CIGI) (Available at www.cigionline.org).

Dommen, Edward and Philippe Hein, (eds) (1985) *States, Microstates and Islands* (London: Croom Helm).

Gaens, Bart, (ed.) (2008) *Europe–Asia Interregional Cooperation: A Decade of ASEM* (Aldershot: Ashgate).

Griffith, Ivelaw L. (2000) *The Political Economy of Drugs in the Caribbean* (London: Palgrave).

Griffith, Winston H. (2007) 'CARICOM Countries and the Irrelevance of Economic Smallness' *Third World Quarterly* 28(5): 939–58.

Heine, Jorge (2006) 'On the Manner of Practicing the New Diplomacy', Working Paper No. 11, October (Waterloo: CIGI) (Available at www.cigionline.org).

Hurt, Stephen R. (2003) 'Co-operation and coercion? The Cotonou Agreement between the European Union and ACP States and the end of the Lomé Convention', *Third World Quarterly* 24(1): 161–76.

Keohane, Robert O. (1971) 'The Big Influence of Small Allies', *Foreign Policy* 2, Spring.

Kisanga, Eliawony J. and Sarah Jane Danchie, (eds) (2007) *Commonwealth Small States: Issues and Prospects* (London: Commonwealth Secretariat).

Lemke, Douglas (2003) 'African Lessons for International Relations Research', *World Politics* 56(1): 114–38.

McIntyre, W. David (2001) *A Guide to the Contemporary Commonwealth* (London: Palgrave).

Marshall, Don D. (2007) 'The New International Financial Architecture and Caribbean OFCs: Confronting Financial Stability Discourse', *Third World Quarterly* 28(5): 917–38.

Mathisen, Trygve (1971) *The Functions of Small States in the Strategies of Great Powers* (Oslo: Universitetsfolaget).

Payne, Anthony (2004) 'Small States in the Global Politics of Development', *Round Table* 93 (376).

Payne, Anthony and Paul Sutton (2007) 'Repositioning the Caribbean within Globalization', Caribbean Paper No. 1, June (Waterloo: CIGI) (Available at www.cigionline.org).

Plischke, Elmer (1977) *Microstates in World Affairs: Policy Problems and Options* (Washington D.C.: American Enterprise Institute for Public Policy Research).

Prasad, Naren (2004) 'Escaping Regulation, Escaping Convention: Development Strategies in Small Economies', *World Economics* 5(1): 41–65.

Robles, Alfredo (2004) *The Political Economy of Interregional Relations* (Aldershot: Ashgate).

Sanders, Sir Ronald (2008) 'Storm Clouds Over Caribbean Financial Services', *HuntingtonNews.net*, 21 November.

Schou, August and Arne Olav Brundtland, (eds) (1971) *Nobel Symposium 17, Small States in International Relations* (New York: John Wiley & Sons).

Shaw, Timothy M. (2004) 'The Commonwealth(s) & Global Governance', *Global Governance* 10(4): 499–516.

Shaw, Timothy M. (2008) *Commonwealth: Contributions to Inter- & Non-state Global Governance*, Global Institutions Series (London: Routledge).

Shaw, Timothy M., Andrew F. Cooper and Agata Antkiewicz (2007) 'Global and/or Regional Development at the Start of the 21st Century? China, India and (South) Africa', *Third World Quarterly* 28(7): 1255–70.

Sutton, Paul (2001) 'Small States and the Commonwealth', *Commonwealth & Comparative Politics* 39(3): 75–94.

Vital, David (1967) *The Inequality of States: A Study of Small Powers in International Relations* (Oxford: Oxford University Press).

Vital, David (1971) *The Survival of Small States: Studies in Small Power–Great Power Conflict* (Oxford: Oxford University Press).

Vlcek, William (2007) 'Why Worry? The Impact of the OECD Harmful Tax Competition Initiative on Caribbean Offshore Financial Centres', *Round Table* 96(390): 331–46.

Vlcek, William (2008) *Offshore Finance and Small States: Sovereignty, Size and Money* (London: Palgrave Macmillan).

Part 1
Challenges/Realities of Practising Small State Diplomacy

2
Thucydides or Kissinger? A Critical Review of Smaller State Diplomacy

*Godfrey Baldacchino**

Setting the scene: Small states and the instrument of diplomacy

In *The Peloponnesian War*, Thucydides (1972: 402) highlights the effects of the general weakness of smaller states vis-à-vis larger, more powerful ones in a key passage where the Athenians remind the Melians that:

> you know as well as we do that, as the world goes, right is only in question between equals in power. Meanwhile, the strong do what they can and the weak suffer what they must.

Concerns about the vulnerability of small, weak, isolated states have echoed throughout history: from Thucydides, through the review by Machiavelli (1985) of the risks of inviting great powers to intervene in domestic affairs, through twentieth-century US-led contemporary political science (Vital, 1967; Handel, 1990) and Commonwealth-led scholarship (Commonwealth Secretariat, 1985). In the context of twentieth-century 'Balkanisation', the small state could also prove unstable, even hostile and uncooperative, a situation tempting enough to invite the intrusion of more powerful neighbours – a combination, according to Brzezinski (1997: 123–4) of a power vacuum and a corollary power suction.[1] In the outcome, if the small state is 'absorbed', it would be its fault, as well as its destiny, in the grand scheme of things. In his excellent review of small states in the context of the global politics of development, Anthony Payne (2004: 623, 634) concludes that 'vulnerabilities rather than opportunities are the most striking consequence of smallness'. It has been recently claimed that, since they cannot defend or represent themselves adequately, small states 'lack real independence, which makes them suboptimal participants in the international system' (Hagalin, 2005: 1).

There is, however, a less notable and acknowledged, but more extraordinary, strand of argumentation that considers 'the power of powerlessness', and the ability of small states to exploit their smaller size in a variety of ways to achieve their intended, even if unlikely, policy outcomes. The pursuance of smaller state goals becomes paradoxically acceptable and achievable precisely because such smaller states do not have the power to leverage disputants or pursue their own agenda. A case in point concerns the smallest state of all, the Vatican, whose powers are both unique and ambiguous, but certainly not insignificant (*Economist*, 2007). Smaller states have 'punched above their weight' (e.g. Edis, 1991); and, intermittently, political scientists confront their 'amazing intractability' (e.g. Suhrke, 1973: 508). Henry Kissinger (1982: 172) referred to this stance, with obvious contempt, as 'the tyranny of the weak'.[2]

This chapter seeks a safe passage through these two equally reductionist propositions. It deliberately focuses first on a comparative case analysis of two distinct 'small state–big state' contests drawn from the 1970s, seeking to infer and tease out the conditions that enable smaller 'Lilliputian' states (whether often or rarely) to beat their respective Gulliver. The discussion then proceeds to examine whether similar tactics can work in relation to contemporary concerns regarding environmental vulnerability, with a focus on two other small island states. Before that, however, the semiotics of 'the small state' need to be explored since they are suggestive of the perceptions and expectations that are harboured by decision makers at home and abroad and tend towards the self-fulfilling prophecy.

A declaration of bias

I cannot launch into this chapter without declaring my personal bias at the outset. I am a Maltese citizen and was one of six 'technical experts' on a nationally representative Malta–European Union Steering and Action Committee (MEUSAC) that participated in the detailed negotiations, led by the Minister of Foreign Affairs, surrounding the adoption of the *acquis communautaire* between the Maltese government and the European Commission. This led to Malta's eventual entry to the European Union in May 2004. Malta did not achieve all that it had hoped for – it did not manage to obtain an exemption from the use of plastic containers for beverages, for example – however, Malta *did* manage to secure the largest number of exemptions (72) from the *acquis* of the ten candidate countries at the time. This includes a much bigger, and very demanding, state – Poland, which came away with the second largest haul of exemptions (43). Malta even secured the only permanent derogation from the *acquis* among this group of accessing states: blocking non-permanent residents indefinitely from buying second homes in Malta. I agree with my colleague at the University of Malta, Roderick Pace, who has argued that 'Malta has used its small size to advantage in negotiating' (*Economist*, 2004).

So, where is the 'small state'?

In this chapter, I am deliberately using the word 'smaller' rather than 'small', resurrecting a usage preferred by Burton Benedict (1966; 1967) and Gerald Berreman (1978) that alerts readers to a tendency in the literature to equate 'large states' as 'normal'. This is hardly the case in practice. Out of 237 jurisdictions listed in the CIA *World Factbook* (2007), only 11 have populations exceeding 100 million; 23 have populations of over 50 million; while 158 have populations of less than 10 million (of which 41 have a resident population of under 100 000). Wikipedia has a list of 221 'countries by population', including sub-national jurisdictions, which ranges from the People's Republic of China to Pitcairn: the median (111th) position is occupied by Finland, with 5.3 million citizens.[3] Clearly, the so-called 'small state' is the typical state size (as it has also been for most of recorded history). In contrast, therefore, it is the *large* state which is the quirk and the anomaly – a condition that finds the state dealing with secessionist tendencies (Chechnya, Biafra, Aceh, Okinawa) and other conditions of 'giantism' (e.g. Lewis, 1991). There is also 'no widely accepted definition of a small state' (Crowards, 2002: 143). Moreover, and as had already been observed by Baehr (1975: 466), there is no sharp dichotomy between 'small' and 'large' states.

The earliest equation of 'large states as normal' probably emerged in the reference to the 'great powers' as the powers of consequence at the Treaty of Vienna in 1814, though Michael East (1973: 556) traces this new development to the Treaty of Chaumont of 1817. The model has, however, been driven primarily by US-based political scientists in the Cold War period. When the United Nations (UN) was set up in 1945, Luxembourg was the only smaller state member; by 1960, the UN only had two smaller states – Luxembourg and Iceland. Thereafter, smaller territories were becoming newly independent sovereign states with a fairly rapid frequency. However, certain 'large state' observers were seriously concerned with the implications of this trend for superpower balances. The involvement by these small (or worse, micro) states in sensitive global geopolitics was denounced as irresponsible interference, and was close to being deemed intolerable. These large state observers began taunting ways of packing up these potentially destabilising quirks of colonial retrenchment, whose claims for sovereignty they found absurd (Plischke, 1977: 9–10). At one point, the UN was also presented with a report by a 'Committee of Experts' that recommended associate membership for small states, without the right to vote (Harden, 1985: 17). With such rampant paranoia, smaller polities were pictured as dangerous, as 'problems' (Benedict, 1967; Diggines, 1985) and as anomalous – apart from being consistently regarded as inconsequential (Keohane, 1969). Barston (1973) questioned whether smaller states could have any meaningful foreign policy at all. Similarly, Watson (1982: 159) questioned whether smaller states had the 'resources, experience and sufficient institutional mechanisms to engage in effective dialogue with other states'.

Why call some states 'small'?

The nomenclature has stuck. First of all, international organisations have responded to the swelling number of smaller members. Among these, the Commonwealth Secretariat, in particular, has ushered in a range of studies focused on 'small states'. This was mainly in deference to its membership: no less than 32 of 54 Commonwealth members have populations of up to 1.5 million, but any neat definition has been skilfully avoided to embrace Jamaica, Papua New Guinea, Botswana, Lesotho and Namibia at its upper limits, 'even though their populations each exceeded 1.5 million' (Payne, 2004: 625–6). Moreover, in the wake of the 1983 US-led invasion of Grenada (one of the smallest members of the Commonwealth) and mercenary attacks on the Maldives (another Commonwealth member) in 1988, the Commonwealth Secretariat spawned a variety of educational and professional development programmes focused on small states (reviewed in Crossley and Holmes, 1999). The Commonwealth Secretariat has also supported the eventual development of a vulnerability index (e.g. Briguglio, 1995; Atkins et al., 2000) and continues to sponsor a modest literature peddling the concepts of *vulnerability* (reviewed in Bray, 1987) and, its more recent putative corollary, *resilience* (e.g. Briguglio et al., 2006; Kisanga and Danchie, 2007). Other notable contributions have been made by such institutions as UNESCO, through its International Institute for Educational

Planning in Paris and its regional offices in Jamaica and Samoa (Bray, 1992; Lillis, 1993). Parallel studies evoked an analogy with Jonathan Swift's Lilliput (Swift, 1965), to suggest not just a chronic weakness in the face of a world driven by Gullivers, but also as indicative of an inability to adopt proactive policies in international relations (e.g. Sutton and Payne, 1993).

Secondly, critical commentary about smaller states is typically driven by academics based in first-world universities. All other things being equal, the smaller the jurisdiction, the less likely that it will have the internal capacity necessary to generate research about itself. So the 'small state' finds itself in an environment where it may be largely defined by others, without the capacity to counter such representations.

But would the will to counter such skewed representations be there at all? It appears not: the 'small states' appear willing to tag along in this naming exercise. The third explanation for such a trend becomes the growing number of 'small island developing states' (SIDS) which have been active in regional and international fora. This has led the United Nations to sponsor their own 'mini-Rio' summit: the 'Island Matters, Islands Matter' Global Conference, held in Barbados in 1994, which adopted a Programme of Action for the Sustainable Development of SIDS. This was followed by an International Review Meeting, held in Mauritius in 2005, resulting in the 'Mauritius Strategy' for the Further Implementation of the Programme of Action for the Sustainable Development of SIDS. Today, practically all the UN agencies – including UNEP, UNDP, UNCTAD, as well as the World Bank – recognise the category of small island developing states. (The category tends to exclude 'developed small states' – including non-island Luxembourg and Liechtenstein but also insular Iceland – raising concerns as to whether smaller size is actually synonymous with the ills with which it is nonchalantly attributed.) Moreover, the Alliance of Small and Island States (AOSIS) was set up to present these countries with a coordinated and unified international voice: 37 of the world's 51 island states are members (Depraetere and Dahl, 2007: 101, Table 5). AOSIS's interests were recognised in the UN Framework Convention on Climate Change (Ashe et al., 1999).

Finally, the appellative 'small', alongside 'vulnerable', has become a useful rallying cry for those that are strategically defining themselves as 'small states'. This composite condition, quantified into an index, has been used to lobby international support for special economic privileges to be granted to small economies. The international community has been politely supportive, acknowledging and taking note of the heightened vulnerability concerns of small developing states, including major references in both the Barbados 1994 and the Mauritius 2005 declarations; yet the concept remains elusive and subject to some scepticism (e.g. Hein, 2004). The World Bank would only go as far as agreeing that small states have 'special characteristics which should be noted by global institutions' (Commonwealth Secretariat/World Bank, 2000; see also Payne, 2004: 626). Moreover, openness – one of the alleged components of economic vulnerability – is itself a key basis for the competitive export-orientation of small economies and which have prevented their lapse into protectionism and autarchy (Baldacchino, 2000). More recently, but reminiscent of Katzenstein (1985), a fresh flurry of research into the international relations of small states has emerged in the context of European integration (e.g. Thorhallsson, 2000). As if to add further confirmation of the absence of any rigorous definition of a small state, all the members of the European Union except the 'big six' (France, Germany, Italy, Poland, Spain and the United Kingdom) and all EU applicant and candidate countries except Turkey, are considered small (reviewed in Neumann and Gstöhl, 2004).

Thus, the 'small state' is defined in contradistinction to the 'big state': small states are assumed to be price takers in a largely inhospitable global market, while big states are deemed more likely to be price makers. Small states are deemed to be more vulnerable to such external shocks as invasions, externally directed coups and mercenary attacks, unlike larger states. Small states are deemed to be unable to provide or afford international overseas representation, unlike larger states. And this goes on. Smallness becomes an important quality to peddle if it is deemed to represent a condition of dependency, fragility or vulnerability. It becomes the hook to attract the interest of donors, fan the 'soft imperialist' aspirations of benign larger states, or facilitate aid and grants in cash and in kind by regional powers concerned with a small state's allegedly inherent instability, initiatives from which small states would then arguably benefit. Indeed, certainly in Commonwealth circles, 'vulnerability has often been deployed as a surrogate for smallness' (Payne, 2004: 626). This theme will be revisited below in dealing with environmental diplomacy.

Imagine the consternation, surprise and high drama when small (often island) states *do not* play this game and indeed seek to influence international relations according to their own interests, and succeed.

Comparative case study A: Two damned dots

'If you think you are too small to make a difference, try sleeping in a closed room with a mosquito' – African proverb.

Imagine the governments of two smaller island states, with no standing armies, with populations of less than a third of a million each, heading into a confrontation with the United Kingdom. The respective smaller state governments have either flimsy majorities or shaky coalitions. And yet, in both cases, the wishes of the smaller state prevailed over those of the ex-imperial power, with the support and additional pressure of the USA. In the context of the Cold War and the Soviet Threat of the early 1970s, both Iceland (in the North Atlantic) and Malta (in the Central Mediterranean) played their cards, and won. In an obvious reference to the fictitious 'teeny-tiny' European Duchy of Grand Fenwick, they were mice, and yet they roared (Sellers, 1959). However, the community of 'great powers', including the United Kingdom, was not amused. *The Economist* magazine (1971), reviewing – and reviling – both Malta and Iceland in the same article, thought fit to title this feature 'Damned Dots'.

Much has been written about the standoff between Malta Prime Minister Dom Mintoff and British Prime Minister James Callaghan in 1971–72 (e.g. Smith, 1975; Wriggins, 1975). The episode has also featured among the cases studied at the Program on Negotiation at the Harvard Law School. In spite of a parliamentary majority of just one, Mintoff threatened to evict British military forces from Malta (then with a population of 325,000) and turn over air and naval facilities – deemed to have 'negative strategic value' to NATO and Britain – to the Soviet Union. By deploying 'maverick diplomacy' and playing the role of a 'power broker', which has been described as 'wholly unsuited for an economically weak, tiny island nation' (Micallef, 1979: 250), Mintoff succeeded against all odds in obtaining a 300 per cent increase in British development assistance to Malta (Baldacchino, 2002: 202).

At around the same time in the North Atlantic, an Icelandic government composed of an unwieldy three-party coalition unilaterally expanded sovereignty over 'its' fishing grounds by extending its territorial waters from 12 to 50 miles, even in the face of an international agreement that had been previously secured with the United Kingdom, and refused to recognise the jurisdiction of the International Court of Justice over the matter. Britain (population approximately 60 million) rushed to defend its economic interests by sending military vessels to the contested zone, while Iceland (population approximately 290 000) sent its coastguard vessels, which were armed with trawl wire cutters. Iceland, comments Kurlansky (1997: 166), acted 'shockingly tough'. '[U]sing the Royal Navy to bully an unarmed small state' (Ingimundarson, 2003: 96), and couching the episode in heavy colonial discourse, the confrontation generated much international sympathy for Iceland, both from developing countries and from public opinion in the West. Meanwhile, a nationalist discourse secured support at home. All along, Iceland resorted to an underdog argument: 'a small state was fighting for its economic survival against big powers, whose sole aim was to get their greedy hands on Iceland's economic resources' (Ingimundarson, 2003: 105). Moreover, this was not just *any* economic resource: Iceland was (and still remains) heavily dependent on its fishing industry.

When the tension subsided, and the two smaller states emerged better off from their respective confrontations, it is easy to conclude that were it not for their strategic values, the US would not have applied pressure on Britain urging it to accommodate the pesky microstates. And yet, these two European economies were already squarely within the commercial and ideological circuit of the West: any isolationist policies would have spelled economic ruin, as US President Nixon hinted to Icelandic Prime Minister Jóhannesson in June 1971 (Ingimundarson, 2003: 115). With the benefit of hindsight one may add that these strategies even led to political ruin, as both Malta's and Iceland's foreign policies eventually backfired. Indeed, it could be suggested that the smaller states won their battle, but did not win their war.

It would be more appropriate to conclude that larger states do not want to be seen to be bullying smaller states, unless that smaller state can be convincingly depicted as harbouring communists, terrorists or other reprehensible categories. Public opinion, at home and abroad, can be swayed and galvanised into protest action by such notions as imperialism or neo-colonialism. Moreover, the manner in which smaller states undertake international diplomacy is also typically much more focused and more driven by 'heroic' individuals (such as prime ministers) than would happen in larger, democratic countries that are used to pluralism, internal consultation and protracted deliberation by committee (e.g. Singham, 1968). This can disarm larger states who find that a showdown with an intractable negotiator is not necessarily a foregone conclusion (e.g. Pirotta, 1985). The stakes are also laid out differentially: a concession by a larger player to a smaller one may not be so onerous, and can always be dismissed as an act of generosity or gratuity; in contrast, the failure by a smaller state to secure its interests via international diplomacy with a larger state may be simply catastrophic, with possible negative implications for the larger state itself.

Of course, these episodes may very well be the exceptions that justify the rule. Indeed, if we fast forward to the present, there are hardly any victories yet to be declared by smaller states when it comes to a different, perhaps more serious, topic of international statecraft: environmental vulnerability. In spite of a unity of purpose, as seen through the development of AOSIS and a widespread recognition of the dual phenomena of global warming and sea-level rise, there is as yet no tangible evidence that smaller states are winning the argument. Why? Or, better, why not? Why is it that the lessons of the past have not yet informed the present? Where are the contemporary Maltas and Icelands in the diplomatic war against environmental catastrophe?

Comparative case study B: Threatened paradises

There have been considerable attempts by smaller island state governments to generate regional and international interest in the condition of their islands, especially low-lying island states at the risk of sea-level rise. There is now irrefutable scientific evidence of the human impact on climate, especially the global rise of mean surface temperature by around 2°Celsius by the year 2100. One consequence of this temperature change will be sea-level rise, due mainly to the thermal expansion of the oceans, as well as to the thawing of glacial ice. A mean rise of some 50 cm is projected by 2100 (Charles et al., 1997: 67–9).

Of course, being a smaller island is not the critical factor in terms of vulnerability to sea-level rise: various larger countries, including the US and China, have extensive low-lying coastlines that are just as vulnerable, and particularly where there are heavily populated areas near the coast, such as Bangladesh. However, the problem is especially acute for small island states with fragments of finite, small and low-lying land areas because even a modest rise in sea-level could mean total or near total submersion. These island populations have no hinterland to turn to, unlike larger countries. Their whole land area, especially in the case of atolls, consists in vulnerable coastline. The four smaller island states most seriously affected by this predicament are the Maldives, the Marshall Islands, Tuvalu and Kiribati.

Is the past instructive in any way? There have been some high profile evacuations of islanders in the twentieth century: notably from Tristan da Cunha in 1961 and from Montserrat in 1995, both with the connivance of the United Kingdom, and both due to volcanic eruptions. Yet, these two island jurisdictions are both overseas territories of the UK, and so the UK had a measure of responsibility to ensure their well-being. Both evacuations were temporary. Moreover, a volcanic eruption is a much more sudden and visually dramatic event than creeping sea-level rise: perhaps the former more easily captures the imagination of sympathetic onlookers than the latter. The ravages of the 2004 'Boxing Day' tsunami, whose horrors were captured on amateur video and circulated world-wide via the Internet, similarly galvanised considerable international attention, and from which affected islands were significant beneficiaries.

Unlike overseas territories like Tristan or Montserrat, smaller island states enjoy a sovereignty which seems to have excised the responsibility of other (larger, non-island) states from the consequences of sea-level rise on the former islands' inhabitants. These smaller island states appear to have resorted to a combination of technology, as well as bilateral and multilateral diplomacy, to seek a full and satisfactory resolution to their problem.

The Republic of the Maldives, a sprawling archipelago with a population of 311 000, is very much at the frontline on two of these three measures. Flooding in 1987 threatened the country. More flooding, this time associated with the 2004 tsunami, submerged the whole archipelago, albeit for a few minutes. The Maldives government had raised the issue before the 1989 *Small States Conference on Sea Level Rise*, which it hosted and at which the Association of Small and Island States was initiated, with this concern foremost on its agenda. The country was also the first to sign the Kyoto Protocol. President Gayoon has been campaigning vigorously on the international stage for the acknowledgement of the predicament of his country and that of similar SIDS, as well as for calls for remedial action. His impassionate address to the United Nations at the June 1992 Earth Summit was poignant:

> I stand before you as a representative of an endangered people. We are told that as a result of global warming and sea-level rise, my country, the Maldives, may sometime during the next century, disappear from the face of the Earth. ...
>
> Let this not be a time in the history of mankind when those who can really help decline to do so, while the very survival of the peoples of low-lying, small island nations is at stake. As I speak here today, there are 225 000 people in my country, and many tens of thousands more in other small island states, expecting strong and immediate international action to save our countries. (Gayoon, 1992)

The latest, smaller island state to attempt a major diplomatic exercise is the Seychelles. Seychelles President James Michel took the lead in setting up the Sea-level Rise Foundation in 2005 – a 'global initiative to establish a platform of excellence on sea level rise' – and the Global Islands Partnership (GLISPA) which is trying to mount a common 'global strategy' against the causes of sea-level rise (http://www.sealevel-rise.org/).

But such 'political solutions' do not seem to have gotten anywhere, except perhaps expanding awareness '[t]hat hasn't done much yet to slow down sea-level rise' (Hamilton, 2008). And so the Maldives has turned to technological remedies: a massive sea wall, made up of concrete tertapods, that surrounds the entire capital of Male (2km long and 800m wide); and now Hulhumale, a brand new, flood-resistant island (CDNN News, 2004; DEME, 2008). Japan paid for the Male sea wall; international donors, it is hoped, will pay for further human-made construction.

Such engineering strategies represent measures that could mitigate or postpone the effects of sea-level rise; but they do not attack its causes. Nor is the solution necessarily a long-term one. They represent similar technology-driven measures that are being contemplated by developed countries threatened by sea-level rise, such as the Netherlands. Of course, the Dutch have had to struggle against the infiltration of water for most of their history; they do not need convincing regarding the seriousness of the issue (Woodward, 2001; Palca, 2008).

The danger is that as more states, small and not so small, consider adopting piecemeal engineering solutions to their own national problems, the urgency and thrust of a common collective position will be dampened. The resort to a global, largely diplomatic solution may no longer be seen as essential. And, thus, the pressure to reduce the causes behind sea-level rise may fall. The belief in 'science as miracle cure' may thwart steps that would attack the root causes of environmental vulnerability. So much for Gayoon's expected 'strong and immediate international action to save our countries'. Indeed, the Maldivian story may be an example of the frustration in seeking a global concerted solution to a global problem, and the resort to the more familiar 'chequebook diplomacy' game with which smaller states are familiar (and which is perhaps one key reason why they assiduously call themselves '*small states*'). Larger, typically donor, countries are also comfortable with this stance since it allows them to display and offer munificence and development assistance.[4] Could it be that the attempt to seek international visibility via the sea-level rise platform is nothing more than a ploy to arm-twist donors into a new line of credit? Environmental vulnerability may be replacing economic vulnerability as the new justifying mechanism for maintaining 'MIRAB' economies (dependent on migration and remittances that finance private households and on aid that finances their government bureaucracies) (Bertram, 2006). Or else, is it also possible that the official leadership of SIDS may have fully internalised patterns of thought that represent them as weak victims of global trends?

Tuvalu has been trying a diplomatic route similar to the Maldivian one, though with a few other twists. The island archipelago's total population is just 11 000 people, who live on nine coral atolls totalling ten square miles. The country, securing independence in 1979, became a member of the United Nations in 2000 and maintains a mission at the UN in New York. Tuvalu's only other diplomatic office is its High Commission in Suva, Fiji. The promotion of concern about global warming and sea-level rise is Tuvalu's 'major international priority' (US State Department, 2007). Tuvaluan government representatives have been vocal advocates of the Kyoto Protocol, as well as champions of a global mitigation of climate change through reduced emissions. They have also expressed public disappointment with those governments that fail to manifest similar support (Sopoanga, 2003). As Acting Prime Minister Toafa observed:

> We in Tuvalu live in constant fear of the adverse impacts of climate change and sea-level rise. With a height of a mere 3 m above sea level, our livelihoods and food security are already affected badly, with increasing salinity in ground water, land erosion, coral bleaching and total anxiety. The threat is real and serious, and is of no difference to a slow and insidious form of terrorism against Tuvalu. (Toafa, 2004: 4)

The attempt to portray Tuvaluans as victims of terrorism does not seem to have triggered the expected response, however. Back in 2002, Tuvaluan Prime Minister Koloa Talake even raised the prospects of pursuing legal redress for climate change damage in international tribunals and the domestic courts of the US (the main terrorist threat?); so far, no litigation proceedings have been commenced (Farbotko, 2005a).

More ingeniously, Tuvalu has appealed to Australia, the hegemon in the South Pacific, to arrange for the acceptance of its citizens as 'climate refugees'. But Australia – during a period when there was much public debate about the country's policy towards asylum seekers – refused to even discuss the matter, claiming that there is, as yet, no international recognition of such a refugee category. When Tuvalu turned to New Zealand for help, that country agreed to accept the whole of Tuvalu's population but only when that country becomes uninhabitable. Meanwhile, current applicants for entry to New Zealand remain subject to the conditions of the Pacific Access Category that covers Tuvalu, Fiji, Kiribati and Tonga. The PAC allows only 75 people to emigrate from Tuvalu to New Zealand per year and imposes a series of stringent requirements (Kenny, 2007).

The diplomatic efforts continue. Enele Sopoanga, Tuvalu's ambassador to the UN (and one of Tuvalu's two ambassadors), addressed a climate change conference in Nairobi:

> The delegate from the tiny Pacific nation of Tuvalu proposed a thought experiment as he addressed the United Nations summit on climate change on its final day in Nairobi.
>
> Imagine the world knew global warming was about to destroy 43 nations – *'but not which 43'*, Enele Sopoaga, Tuvalu's UN ambassador, told the summit on Friday. If that were the case, 'we suggest that all parties would be striving for big reductions in greenhouse gases'.
>
> Instead, the 43 that could be wiped out by rising sea levels are the small island states – among the most powerless in the world. 'What will history say of us if we let whole countries disappear?' asked Mr Sopoaga in a plea that moved delegates to applause'. (Button, 2006)

Discussion

The reportage of the above episode in the *Sydney Morning Herald* deserves some critical commentary. The reference is to a 'thought experiment' by the delegate of a 'tiny nation', 'among the most powerless in the world'. The article is titled 'Tiny Tuvalu Packs a Powerful Punch'. The delegate's 'plea' is moving; and is met by 'applause'.

Paradoxically, those who were moved by Sopoanga's words continue to not stand up to be counted when called upon to take actions that could mitigate global warming. Indeed, Farbotko (2005b) has shown, in her gripping analysis of the representation of Tuvaluans in the *Sydney Morning Herald* (as above), that these islanders are often portrayed in the metropolitan press as victims of tragic circumstances beyond their control. They fit easily into quaint stereotypes of dehistoricised vulnerability and 'paradise in peril', which the rest of the world can watch – absolved of any responsibility – as they unfold, almost like a slow-motion movie, and presumably from a safe and distant vantage point (DeLoughrey, 2007: 214). Island life is treated as 'an eccentric curiosity … caricatured as naïve and idealistic' (Tallack, 2008). For those who want a closer experience, certain island jurisdictions – like Greenland, and the Maldives – have actually started marketing their tourist industry with a dark twist: appealing to those who wish to visit paradise 'before it is too late' (Farbotko, 2005b: 285).

It is quite disheartening and unsettling to discover that the interests of the First World in the lives of small state islanders can continue to be held, even if tentatively, when islands and islanders are depicted much like threatened exotic *curiosa* in a grand walk-through museum of civilization. Bikini, the Pacific atoll that gave its name to a sexy swim-suit, is far better known internationally as a byword for erotic seduction than as a site of radioactive fallout and agonising death (Gillis and Lowenthal, 2007: iv). Some islanders may be silently thankful that even a perverse interest by the international community is better than no interest at all (Baldacchino, 2008). Like 'paradise', the attributes of 'small size' may ensure some visibility, but the representation of that visibility is stymied and trivialises the subject matter to grotesque lows, possibly below the surface of the waves.

The way in which the world thinks and speaks about small states, including the smaller states themselves, and how the latter conceives of themselves as foreign policy recipients rather than actors, remains thoroughly contaminated by the exclusive uni-dimensional portrayal of smaller states as (albeit cute) victims of global trends (climate change, trade liberalisation, financial regulation, drug cartels, etc.). This tendency to emphasise weakness and fragility continues to be reflected in documents produced by the very same organisations that speak on their behalf. Smaller states are now firm believers in their own chronic vulnerability, and are looking for 'resilience' and 'capacity building' to mitigate their handicap. Many of the ruling elites of smaller states play along in this social construction of negative identity since this ensures them greater access to (dwindling?) official development resources. It is bitterly ironic, therefore, that the very reason why smaller states and their condition have gained the attention of global organisations seems to prevent the world as much *as the smaller states themselves* from appreciating capacities for proactive action and foreign policy initiatives.[5] Perhaps Mintoff and Jóhannesson considered themselves to be lions, rather than mice. It appears that the 'tyranny of the weak' is an unfortunate consequence of amnesia.

Conclusion: That sinking feeling

So who provides the correct analysis for smaller state diplomatic behaviour: Thucydides or Kissinger? The US debacle in Vietnam certainly suggests that might can be proved wrong; and Thucydides goes on to describe how, although the Melians lost the 'battle' and were decimated, they still managed to portray the Athenians as morally degenerate, and Athenian democracy collapsed not long afterwards.

The pattern which appears to emerge is that smaller states are especially good in diplomatic adventures where (a) they are essentially bilateral (one-on-one); (b) the smaller state commands the moral high ground such that it whips up domestic support and distorts the international media campaign in its favour, drumming up sympathy even from non-state actors; and (c) the issue at stake is essentially financial or economic. A broadly similar set of explanations may pertain equally well to the recent *Antigua versus USA* rulings by the World Trade Organisation (PokerPages.com, 2007).[6] Locating the issue within the geo-strategic considerations of superpower conflict raises the stakes. The best theatres for this to unfold in contemporary times are: (a) the China–Taiwan struggle for international recognition; and (b) in the voting patterns of the International Whaling Commission, where the commercial whaling interests of Japan could be seen to match the funding requirements of various smaller states (BBC News, 2006; Bertram and Poirine, 2007: 365). In spite of the considerable number of smaller states on the world stage, and their ability to make their presence – and their plight – felt in international fora, especially at the UN through AOSIS, and more recently through GLISPA, their lobbying has not generated much tangible benefit beyond rhetoric, sympathy and applause. Concern about such foreign policy failure was already evident in the Mauritius International Review Meeting of 2005; and while a study concluded that it would be unfair to say that AOSIS has failed, 'the underlying goals of the coalition ... were not achieved' (Chasek, 2005: 135). Cooperative, multilateral, smaller state diplomacy has proved largely futile, *not* so much because smaller states have limited policy capacity, but mainly because no larger country has been embarrassed to act through its failure to respond to smaller state concerns, and no larger country has deemed its own economic or strategic interests unduly threatened by the slow sinking of the 'languid sensual world' of tiny Tuvalu (Pollock, 2005), or even of a slightly less tiny Maldives. The Tuvaluans are meanwhile voting with their feet; already, there are more Tuvaluans living overseas than on their doomed archipelagic homeland. In spite of the islanders' attempts, the dangers posed to their smaller low-lying jurisdictions by climate change may not have turned them (yet?) into 'the ecological conscience' of climate politics (Oberthür and Ott, 1999: 26; Payne, 2004: 633).

One remains hopeful that the Netherlands should not prove averse to granting some technical and other development assistance on favourable terms to the Maldivian government, enabling the Dutch to showcase some of their coastal barrier know-how on Hulhumale.

Notes

* My gratitude to the discussants of the workshop on small state diplomacies convened by the Centre for International Governance Innovation (CIGI) at the Institute of International Relations, St Augustine Campus of the University of the West Indies, Trinidad and Tobago, 20–23 February 2008. Special thanks to Andrew F. Cooper, Donna Lee, Vaughan A. Lewis, Debbie Mohammed, Keith Nurse, Naren Prasad, Baldur Thorallsson and William Vlcek. Additional useful comments were received from Philip Nel, Kathleen Stuart and Jordan Blake Walker. The usual disclaimers apply.
1. I acknowledge these terms to UPEI graduate student Jordan Blake Walker.
2. I have heard Olafur Ragnar Grimson, president of Iceland, use the same term, but with some obvious glee rather than any associated contempt.
3. For current list, see http://en.wikipedia.org/wiki/List_of_countries_by_population. The list should include a 222nd member, Kosovo, as from 17 February 2008.
4. The typical 'small state–large state' display of largesse these days arises in the context of the diplomatic recognition of either the People's Republic of China or the Republic of China/Taiwan. See Harris (2006) in the Caribbean. This has replaced the Cold War polarity for smaller states and affords them a continuing opportunity to seek critical foreign aid 'from the highest bidder'. In fact, 'governments have fallen and elections have been fought on the issue of whom to support' (Nadkami, 2007).
5. I am grateful to Philip Nel for these ideas.
6. For a more in-depth look at this case, see Cooper's chapter.

References

Ashe, J.W., R. Van Lierop and A. Cherian (1999) 'The Role of the Alliance of Small and Island States in the Negotiation of the United Nations Framework Convention on Climate Change', *Natural Resources Forum* 23(3): 209–20.

Atkins, J.P., S. Mazzi and C.D. Easter (2000) *A Commonwealth Vulnerability Index for Developing Countries: The Position of Small States* (London: Commonwealth Secretariat).

Baehr, P.R. (1975) 'Small States: A Tool for Analysis', Review Article, *World Politics* 27(3): 456–66.

Baldacchino, G. (2000) 'The Challenge of Hypothermia: A Six-Proposition Manifesto for Small Island Territories', *Round Table: Commonwealth Journal of International Affairs* 89(353): 65–79.

Baldacchino, G. (2002) 'The Nationless State? Malta, National Identity and the European Union', *West European Politics* 25(4): 191–206.

Baldacchino, G. (2008) 'Studying Islands: On Whose Terms?', *Island Studies Journal* 3(1), May: 37–56.

Barston, R.P. (1973) 'Introduction' in R.P. Barston (ed.), *The Other Powers: Studies in the Foreign Policies of Small States* (London: George Allen & Unwin): 13–28.

BBC News (2006) 'Japan gains key Whaling Victory', *BBC News*, 19 June, http://news.bbc.co.uk/1/hi/5093350.stm, accessed on 26 August 2008.

Benedict, B. (1966) 'Sociological Characteristics of Smaller Territories and their Implications for Economic Development' in M. Banton (ed.), *The Social Anthropology of Complex Societies* (London: Tavistock): 23–34.

Benedict, B. (ed.) (1967) *Problems of Smaller Territories* (London: Athlone Press for the Institute of Commonwealth Studies).

Berreman, G. (1978) 'Scale and Social Relations', *Current Anthropology* 19(2): 225–45.

Bertram, G. (ed.) (2006) 'Beyond MIRAB: The Political Economy of Small Islands in the 21st Century', *Asia Pacific Viewpoint*, special issue, 47(1).

Bertram, G. and B. Poirine (2007) 'Island Political Economy' in G. Baldacchino (ed.), *A World of Islands: An Island Studies Reader* (Malta and Canada: Agenda Academic and Institute of Island Studies): 323–78.

Bray, M. (1987) 'Small Countries in International Development', Review Article, *Journal of Development Studies* 23(2): 295–300.

Bray, M. (1992) *Educational Planning in Small Countries* (Paris: UNESCO, International Institute for Educational Planning).

Brzezinski, Z. (1997) *The Grand Chessboard: American Primacy and its Geostrategic Imperatives* (New York: Basic Books).

Briguglio, L. (1995) 'Small Island States and their Economic Vulnerabilities', *World Development* 23(9): 1615–32.

Briguglio, L., G. Cordina and E.J. Kisanga (eds) (2006) *Building the Economic Resilience of Small States* (Malta and London: University of Malta and Commonwealth Secretariat).

Button, J. (2006) 'Tiny Tuvalu Packs a Powerful Punch', *Sydney Morning Herald*, 20 November, http://www.smh.com.au/news/world/tiny-tuvalu-packs-a-powerful-punch/2006/11/19/1163871272168.html, accessed on 26 August 2008.

CDNN News (2004) 'Need More Space? Build an Island', *CDNN News*, 11 December, http://www.cdnn.info/industry/i041211/i041211.html, accessed on 26 August 2008.

Charles, E., et al. (1997) *A Future for Small States: Overcoming Vulnerability* (London: Commonwealth Secretariat).

Chasek, P.S. (2005) 'Margins of Power: Coalition Building and Coalition Maintenance of the South Pacific Island States and the Alliance of Small and Island States', *Review of European Community and International Environmental Law* 14(2): 125–37.

CIA (2007) *World Factbook* (Washington, DC: Central Intelligence Agency).

Commonwealth Secretariat (1985) *Vulnerability: Small States in the Global Society* (London: Commonwealth Secretariat).

Commonwealth Secretariat/World Bank (2000) *Small States: Meeting Challenges in the Global Economy*, final report of the Commonwealth Secretariat/World Bank Joint Task Force on Small States, March (London and Washington DC: Commonwealth Secretariat/World Bank).

Crossley, M. and K. Holmes (1999) *Educational Development in the Small States of the Commonwealth: Retrospect and Prospect* (London: Commonwealth Secretariat).

Crowards, T. (2002) 'Defining the Category of 'Small' States', *Journal of International Development* 14(2): 143–79.

DEME (2008) *Creating Land for the Future* (Belgium: Dredging Environmental and Marine Engineering), http://www.deme.be/projects/maldive_hulhumale.html, accessed on 26 August 2008.

DeLoughrey, E.M. (2007) *Routes and Roots: Navigating Caribbean and Pacific Island Literatures* (Honolulu: University of Hawaii Press).

Depraetere, C. and A.L. Dahl (2007) 'Island Locations and Classifications' in G. Baldacchino (ed.) *A World of Islands: An Island Studies Reader* (Malta and Canada: Agenda Academic and Institute of Island Studies): 57–106.

Diggines, C.E. (1985) 'The Problems of Small States', *Round Table: Commonwealth Journal of International Affairs* 74(295): 191–205.

East, M. (1973) 'Size and Foreign Policy Behaviour: A Test of Two Models', *World Politics* 25(4): 556–77.

The Economist (1971) 'Damned Dots', London, The Economist Newspapers, July 31: 16.

The Economist (2004) 'Smallness Pays', London, The Economist Newspapers, February 26, http://www.economist.com/displayStory.cfm?story_id=2461814, accessed on 26 August 2008.

The Economist (2007) 'God's Ambassadors', London, The Economist Newspapers, July 21: 58–60.

Edis, R. (1991) 'Punching above their weight: How small developing states operate in the contemporary diplomatic world', *Cambridge Review of International Affairs* 5(2): 45–53.

Farbotko, C. (2005a) 'Tuvalu, Climate Change, and the Possibilities for Legal Redress', paper presented to Clean Air Society of Australia and New Zealand Conference, Hobart, Tasmania.

Farbotko, C. (2005b) 'Tuvalu and Climate Change: Constructions of Environmental Displacement in the Sydney Morning Herald', *Geografiska Annaler* 87B(4): 279–94.

Gillis, J.R. and D. Lowenthal (2007) 'Editorial Introduction', *Geographical Review* 97(2): iii–vi.

Gayoon, M.A. (1992) Address by His Excellency Maumoon Abdul Gayoom, President of the Republic of Maldives, at the United Nations Conference on Environment and Development, Rio De Janeiro, Brazil, 12 June, http://www.un.int/maldives/unc(ed.)htm, accessed on 26 August 2008.

Hagalin, T. (2005) 'Real Independence of Microstates in International Organizations and State Relations', paper presented at 14th Convention of the Nordic Political Science Association, Reykjavik, Iceland, August, http://registration.yourhost.is/nopsa2005/papers/Thorhildur%20Hagalin.doc, accessed on 26 August 2008.

Hamilton, J. (2008) 'Maldives Build Barriers to Global Warning', *National Public Radio*, 28 January, http://www.npr.org/templates/story/story.php?storyId=18425626, accessed on 26 August 2008.

Handel, M. (1990) *Weak States in the International System* (London: Frank Cass).

Harden, S. (1985) *Small is Dangerous: Micro-States in a Macro World* (New York: St Martin's Press).

Harris, T. (2006) 'The Dynamics of International Diplomacy: The Case of China and Taiwan in the Caribbean, 1971–2005', *Journal of Caribbean International Relations* (2): 122–37.

Hein, P.L. (2004) 'Small Island Developing States: Origin of the Category and Definitional Issues' in *Is Special Treatment of Small Island Developing States Possible?* (Geneva and New York: UNCTAD): 10–22.

Ingimundarson, V. (2003) 'A Western Cold War: The Crisis in Iceland's Relations with Britain, the United States, and NATO, 1971–74', *Diplomacy and Statecraft* 14(4): 94–136.

Katzenstein, P. (1985) *Small States in World Markets: Industrial Policy in Europe* (Ithaca, NY: Cornell University Press).

Kenny, Z. (2007) 'Global Warming Refugees: Left to Drown?', *Green Left*, 17 March, http://www.greenleft.org.au/2007/703/36535, accessed on 26 August 2008.

Keohane, R.O. (1969) 'Lilliputians' Dilemmas: Small States in International Politics', *International Organization* 23(2): 291–310.

Kisanga, E.J. and S.J. Danchie (eds) (2007) *Commonwealth Small States: Issues and Prospects* (London: Commonwealth Secretariat and Commonwealth Parliamentary Association).

Kissinger, H. (1982) *Years of Upheaval* (Boston: Little, Brown and Co).

Kurlansky, M. (1997) *Cod* (New York: Vintage Books).

Lewis, J.P. (1991) 'Some Consequences of Giantism: The Case of India', *World Politics* 43(3): 367–89.

Lillis, K.M. (ed.) (1993) *Policy, Planning and Management of Education in Small States* (Paris: UNESCO, International Institute for Educational Planning).

Machiavelli, N. (1515/1985) *The Prince*, translated by H.C. Mansfield, 2nd edition (Chicago: University of Chicago Press).

Micallef, J.V. (1979) 'Mediterranean Maverick: Malta's Uncertain Future', *Round Table* 68(275): 238–51.

Nadkami, D. (2007) 'Views from Auckland: Chequebook Diplomacy Gets Some Serious Notice', *Islands Business*, http://www.islandsbusiness.com/ islands_business/index_dynamic/containerNameToReplace=MiddleMiddle/ focusModuleID=17653/overideSkinName=issueArticle-full.tpl, accessed on 26 August 2008.

Neumann, I.B. and S. Gstöhl (2004) *Lilliputians in Gulliver's World? Small States in International Relations*, Working Paper 1-2004, Reykjavik, Centre for Small State Studies, University of Iceland, http://www.hi.is/solofile/1008303, accessed on 26 August 2008.

Oberthür, S. and H.E. Ott (1999) *The Kyoto Protocol: International Climate Change Policy for the 21st Century* (Berlin: Springer).

Palca, J. (2008) 'Dutch Architects Plan for a Floating Future', *National Public Radio*, 10 February, http://www.npr.org/templates/story/story.php?storyId=18480769, accessed on 26 August 2008.

Payne, A. (2004) 'Small States in the Global Politics of Development', *Round Table* 93(376): 623–35.

Pirotta, J.M. (1985) 'Unruffled Persistence: Borg Olivier's 1952 Negotiations with the British Government', *Melita Historica* 9(2): 171–84.

Plischke, E. (1977) *Microstates in World Affairs: Policy Problems and Options* (Washington, DC: American Enterprise Institute for Policy Research).

PokerPages.com (2007) 'USA loses WTO Appeal in Online Poker & Online Gambling Case', 2 April, http://www.pokerpages.com/poker-news/current-affairs/usa-loses-wto-appeal-in-online-poker–online-gambling-case-29626.htm, accessed on 26 August.

Pollock, E. (2005) Rough Cut: Tuvalu –That Sinking Feeling. Global Warming, Rising Seas, *Frontline World*, 6 December, http://www.pbs.org/frontlineworld/rough/2005/12/tuvalu_that_sin_1.html#, accessed on 26 August 2008.

Sellers, Peter (director) (1959) *The Mouse that Roared*, Columbia Pictures/ Open Road Productions, http://www.allmovie.com/cg/avg.dll?p=avg&sql=1:33517, accessed on 26 August 2008.

Singham, A.W. (1968) *The Hero and the Crowd in a Colonial Polity* (New Haven, CT: Yale University Press).

Smith, S.C. (1975) *British Documents on the End of Empire Project: Malta*, Series B, Volume 11 (London: University of London, Institute of Commonwealth Studies).

Sopoanga, S. (2003) Statement by The Hon. Saufatu Sopoanga OBE, Prime Minister and Minister of Foreign Affairs of Tuvalu, 58th UN General Assembly, September 24, http://www.un.org/webcast/ga/58/statements/tuvaeng030924.htm, accessed on 26 August 2008.

Suhrke, A. (1973) 'Gratuity or Tyranny? The Korean Alliances', *World Politics* 25(4): 508–32.

Sutton, P.K. and A. Payne (1993) 'Lilliput under Threat: The Security Problems of Small Island and Enclave Developing States', *Political Studies* 41(4): 579–93.

Swift, J. (1726/1965) *Gulliver's Travels: Lemuel Gulliver's Travels to Several and Remote Regions of the World* (London: Methuen).

Tallack, M. (2008) 'Farewell from Fair Isle', *New Statesman*, 28 January, http://www.newstatesman.com/200801280003, accessed on 26 August 2008.

Thorhallsson, B. (2000) *The Role of Small State in the European Union* (Aldershot: Ashgate).

Toafa, M. (2004) Statement by The Hon. Maatia Toafa, Acting Prime Minister and Minister of Foreign Affairs of Tuvalu, 59th UN General Assembly, September 24, http://www.un.org/webcast/ga/59/statements/tuveng040923.pdf, accessed on 26 August 2008.

Thucydides (431BC/1972) *History of the Peloponnesian War*, translated by Rex Warner (London: Penguin Classics).

US State Department (2007) *Background Note: Tuvalu*, Bureau of East Asian and Pacific Affairs, October, http://www.state.gov/r/pa/ei/bgn/16479.htm, accessed on 26 August 2008.

Vital, D, (1967) *The Inequality of States: A Study of the Small Power in International Relations* (Oxford: Oxford University Press).

Watson, A. (1982) *Diplomacy: The Dialogue between States* (London: Eyre Methuen).

Woodward, C. (2001) 'Netherlands battens its Ramparts against Warming Climate', *National Geographic News*, 4 September, http://news.nationalgeographic.com/news/2001/08/0829_wiredutch.html, accessed on 26 August 2008.

Wriggins, W. Howard (1975) 'To the Highest Bidder: Malta, Britain and NATO', *Round Table: Commonwealth Journal of International Affairs* 64(1): 167–85.

3
Small but Smart: Small States in the Global System

*Naren Prasad**

> Laws are generally found to be nets of such a texture as the little creep through, the great break through and middle-sized alone are entangled in.
>
> William Shenstone (1714–63),
> *Essays on Men, Manners, and Things*

Small states, often island or enclaves, frequently make news headlines because of their economic or political instabilities: the 'failed state' of the Solomon Islands, the imminent collapse of Nauru, the crisis of East Timor, and ethnic tensions and coups in Fiji are but recent examples. Small jurisdictions are also sometimes accused of being 'modern day pirates', bent on distorting international financial rules or operating on the margins of the financial system by creating offshore financial centres (OFCs) and attracting 'unscrupulous' sources of funds (*Economist*, 2007). Aside from these examples, however, there are many other small developing states that have made a successful transition to modernity, with quite envious standards of living and decent quality of life.

There has been some scattered research on the general issues of small states, mainly as a result of conferences and the sustained scholarship of the Commonwealth Secretariat. However, no systematic global attempt has yet been made to understand how some small states (like Iceland, Malta, Barbados and Mauritius) have (so far) managed to avoid the inevitable catastrophe that their small size forecasts in principle.[1]

Small states have always fascinated people as they were associated with adventure, isolation, darkness, dream, splendour and paradise, especially in the case of island states. Small states have been studied from different angles. Some researchers, like Charles Darwin (evolution on the island of Galapagos), Margaret Mead (*Coming of Age in Samoa*), and

Bronislaw Malinowski (ethnography in Papua New Guinea), were interested in studying small states because of their microcosmic environment and their inhabitants. Historians and political scientists have studied small states as a group of countries in the international relations context including aspects related to foreign affairs, security, power relations, diplomacy, peace and war.[2]

During the 1960s and 1970s, there was an increased interest in small states and their development process as a result of several factors. First, at this time it was argued that the size of countries and their natural resource base were important determinants of economic growth. In addition, the question of viability of small states was also studied both during and in the aftermath of decolonisation. Most of the publications that emanated at this time were the result of international conferences on small economies. During the 1980s and 1990s, publications on small states continued to grow, especially those pertaining to the problems and challenges related to administration, economies of scale and security issues within these countries. The Commonwealth Secretariat, with over a third of its members classified as small economies, has been genuinely interested in studying small states. It sponsored many international conferences on small states and their vulnerabilities. In addition, it published many reports such as *Vulnerability: Small States in the Global Society* (Commonwealth Secretariat, 1985) and *A Future for Small States: Overcoming Vulnerability* (Commonwealth Secretariat, 1997). The Commonwealth Secretariat also published an influential report jointly with the World Bank entitled *Small States: Meeting Challenges in the Global Economy* (Commonwealth Secretariat and World Bank, 2000). One of the recommendations of this publication was the creation of a Forum on Small States where international donors report on their activities within small states. As a result, small states have managed to garner additional support and attention from international donors.

Reviewing the earlier literature on small states, the titles of these publications reveal a sense of inherent weakness, vulnerability and pessimism. However, more recently there has been a surge of optimism, including some research regarding resourcefulness and resilience in small states. Baldacchino, for example, argued that small states use their power of jurisdiction to advance their development cause (Baldacchino, 2000; 2005; 2006; Baldacchino and Greenwood, 1998; Baldacchino and Milne, 2000). If we look at the statistics, we tend to find that small states have been characterised by relatively good socio-economic performance. In other words, we observe that despite being highly vulnerable, small states are able to design ingenious strategies to cope with their inherent vulnerability. As a result these countries have developed 'economic resilience', defined as a state's 'ability to economically cope with or withstand its inherent vulnerability as a result of some deliberate policy' (Briguglio and Kisanga, 2004: 20). A resilience index was created comprising of four indicators: macroeconomic stability, microeconomic market stability, good governance, and social development. However, due to data constraints, many small states are not included in the index (Briguglio, et al., 2006).

Prasad (2003; 2004) argues that small states have developed a unique set of strategies to cope with their vulnerabilities. These successful strategies involve a mixture of economic and political approaches. Some small countries and territories have benefited from niche products in services, such as hosting offshore financial centres and tourism. Prasad shows that economic activities in the service sector (tourism and offshore financial centres) and in light manufacturing (export processing zones) have lead to better economic growth in small islands compared with strategies relying on agriculture and remittance. Some small states have excelled in small-scale, high-value products and have put their island identity to good use (Prasad and Raj, 2006).

Small states are able to use their sovereignty and political status, rather than their economic influence, to advance their cause. Here, they often resort to using non-market solutions or non-orthodox approaches, such as relying on their power to negotiate aid and derogations in international systems, as well as emigration, which provides an outlet for its population. Baldacchino puts it neatly that 'the history of economics in the real world is, after all, none other than a continual attempt to distort and usurp the free market to one's perceived advantage' (Baldacchino, 1993: 37–8). Economic text books preach that as a result of having a small proportion of total trade at the global level, small states can avoid retaliation, even if they break trading rules. Chang (2002) and Reinert (2007) also show that the industrial countries have always manipulated or imposed global trade rules to others to suit their interest.

Small countries seldom conform to the orthodox prescriptions of economic development. Instead they are, or can become, experts in 'slipping subtly through the nets of conformity' (Baldacchino and Milne, 2000: 238). Mainstream thinking considers the economic success of island countries to be an exception. We will demonstrate that most of the development strategies pursued by small islands are at odds with this view since we regard the economic success of small states as the status quo, with some exceptional 'failed states'.

This chapter demonstrates that small states are able to manipulate the global system in their favour, first by distorting international trade rules and secondly through rent-seeking activities. The author also argues that although small countries, often island territories, are considered vulnerable, they have nonetheless succeeded in adopting unconventional, yet effective development strategies to overcome such vulnerabilities. They have effectively designed strategies to earn foreign currencies to finance their growing imports. This chapter will demonstrate that small states are experts in searching for loopholes in the international system, asking for leniency and seeking special arrangements or derogations with developed or metropolitan countries. Indeed, small countries use their 'smallness' very effectively, especially by playing the game of 'importance of being unimportant' or the 'power of being powerless'.

After defining the category of small states and its characteristics, this chapter demonstrates that small states have used preferential systems and describes the challenges that exist in the aftermath of eroding preferences. The final section analyses how the major development strategies pursued by small islands, such as OFCs and remittances, aid and rent-seeking, and other unconventional sources of income, go against mainstream economic thinking.

Definitions

There is no unanimously accepted definition of small states. The notions of small and large states are relative concepts. Small states can be defined by the size of their population, GDP, land area, level of trade or by a combination of all four of these indicators. Population is the most widely used criterion for small states. Recently the Commonwealth Secretariat and the World Bank have proposed to use a maximum of 1.5 million residents to classify countries as small. However, there is no theoretical justification for taking a particular size as a cut-off point. By using the COMSEC/World Bank view as a definition of small states, a total of 45 states can be classified as small. If we use composite indicators as proposed by Crowards (2002) or take the level of global trade as proposed by Davenport (2002) we still have the same number of countries.

Statehood is interpreted in terms of political sovereignty, in the sense that most states today are members of the United Nations. Of the 192 member states in the United Nations, 46 have a population of less than 1.5 million; 30 of these are islands or archipelagos, of which 25 are identified as Small Island Developing States.

Table 3.1 Socio-economic statistics of small states

Country	Land (Sq km)	Population	GNI (current US$ millions)	GDP per capita	Growth (2000–03 average)	Poverty	Gini index
Antigua and Barbuda	440	75 779	716.0	9 134.65	2.47	12.0	0.53
Bahamas	10 070	311 560	4 840.0	15 591.00	1.23	9.3	0.46
Bahrain	620	690 865	610.0	11 851.67	3.47	6.0	
Barbados	430	268 788	2 520.0	9 372.93	-0.12	13.9	0.39
Belize	22 800	261 500	899.0	3 446.65	7.70	33.0	0.40
Bhutan	47 000	839 443	584.0	642.30	6.85	25.3	0.34
Brunei	349	347 270			2.95		
Cape Verde	4 030	452 230	784.0	1 251.78	5.00	44.0	
Comoros	2 170	578 993	323.0	364.98	1.46	60.0	
Cook Islands	240	18 250		5 349.28	7.57	12.0	
Cyprus	9 240	763 143	9 100.0	12 153.75	3.78	25.5	0.34
Djibouti	21 980	686 270	641.0	834.73	2.17	45.1	
Dominica	750	71 175	239.0	3 597.53	-2.24	30.0	0.35
Equatorial Guinea	28 050	475 930	454.0	3 215.10	8.81		
Estonia	43 211	1 361 125	8 510.0	4 418.70	6.65	8.9	0.37
Federated States of Micronesia	702	121 318	261.0	1 832.83	2.18	27.9	0.41
Fiji	18 270	821 800	1 960.0	2 222.50	2.25	25.5	0.49
Gabon	257 670	1 301 100	5 210.0	3 889.38	1.83	62.0	0.48
Gambia	10 000	1 368 400	370.0	321.07	3.70	40.0	0.40
Grenada	340	103 025	388.0	3 830.63	1.64	32.0	0.45
Guinea-Bissau	245 860	1 427 325	3 600.0	146.25	0.28	20.8	0.47
Guyana	196 850	763 935	698.0	950.16	0.08	43.0	0.43
Iceland	100 250	285 750	10 300.0	30 276.75	2.94		

(*Continued*)

Table 3.1 Continued

Country	Land (Sq km)	Population	GNI (current US$ millions)	GDP per capita	Growth (2000–03 average)	Poverty	Gini index
Kiribati	717	93 647	84.6	569.09	1.73	51.0	0.31
Luxembourg	2 586	442 250	23 600.0	45 398.75	3.56	5.5	0.40
Macao, China	21	437 000		14 956.00	5.65	19.0	
Maldives	300	283 520	680.0	2 377.90	5.73	43.0	
Malta	320	395 250	3 660.0	9 706.65	1.42	15.0	0.30
Marshall Islands	181	52 325	139.0	1 903.30	1.40	20.0	0.54
Mauritius	1 850	1 204 800	5 220.0	3 973.55	4.58	12.1	0.37
Palau	458	19 792	130.0		1.85		
Qatar	11 437	604 158				20.3	0.38
Samoa	2 850	175 050	265.0	1 474.78	4.55	53.8	0.44
Sao Tome & Principe	1 000	152 675	50.2	323.64	3.90		
Solomon Islands	27 540	437 425	247.0	621.60	−4.95		
St Kitts and Nevis	269	45 955	299.0	7 413.25	2.38	32.0	0.37
St Lucia	610	158 435	644.0	4 195.98	−0.44	25.1	0.43
St Vincent and the Grenadines	340	109 833	356.0	3 125.48	1.83	37.0	0.56
Suriname	161 470	431 408	1 150.0	2 155.85	3.49	70.0	0.46
Swaziland	17 200	1 076 650	1 890.0	1 343.68	2.36	40.0	0.61
Seychelles	455	82 102	678.0	7 324.43	−0.54	19.0	0.47
Timor-Leste	14 609	819 500	341.0	438.44	5.01	41.0	0.35
Tonga	718	100 900	161.0	1 606.20	2.75	22.7	0.42
Trinidad and Tobago	5 130	1 300 525	10 100.0	6 708.85	6.57	21.0	0.40
Vanuatu	14 760	203 480	279.0	1 124.73	0.58	40.0	0.58

Source: Author's calculations based on Development Indicators, World Bank, 2007; for Gini coefficient various IMF country reports.

Characteristics

Compared with larger and continental countries, small (island) states tend to have distinctive geographic, social, demographic and economic characteristics, which may affect their development strategies and prospects in significant ways. These characteristics include geographic features such as remoteness and isolation (measured by transport costs); vulnerability to natural disasters (measured by the number of natural disasters); and a limited resource base (measured by the preponderance of primary production). The social, political, and administrative features of small islands include the intensity of social cohesion; issues relating to the public and private sectors; and the demographic issue of significant emigration. This latter issue is a major concern to many small states because of the fear and reality of 'brain-drain' and because it is not known whether remittance can compensate such losses. Finally, the majority of small states are democracies (Anckar, 2002; Anckar, 2004; Srebrnik, 2004). The socio-economic characteristics of the aforementioned 45 small states are shown in Table 3.1.

The existence of economies of scale (mainly linked to domestic population) is a major factor in business strategies. Owing to their small size, small states require external markets for their exports to achieve economies of scale, and therefore it is not surprising to see that small islands rely on trade (exports and imports) to a greater extent than larger countries. Consequently these countries have an exceptionally high degree of openness to external economic developments with respect to trade, capital flows, and technology. Exports tend to be concentrated in a narrow range of commodities and markets and a dependence on foreign resource flows. However, certain public services cannot be imported, and therefore higher costs must be borne.

In an empirical study Winters and Martins (2004) show that small islands are in a disadvantaged position when doing business in the global market because of inherent costs associated with smallness. Their study takes into consideration the following related business costs faced by island countries: air freight, sea freight, wages, telephone, electricity, water, fuel, land, bank, corporate tax, import duties, and personal air travel. Taking these factors into consideration, their study concludes that small islands face excessive business costs attributed to the above cost variables mainly because of their size.

Even lucrative tourism developments cannot survive unless selected premium markets are targeted. Winters and Martins (2004) find that the cost disadvantage for (micro) islands in the manufacturing sector (clothing and electronic assembly) would be 36 per cent compared with the median-sized country, and 58 per cent for tourism. As the size of the country increases, this cost disadvantage decreases. For example, in very small islands (bigger than micro islands), such as Vanuatu, the cost disadvantage for the manufacturing sector would be 14 per cent and 29 per cent for tourism. Incentives to some extent play a significant role in offsetting these costs in order to lure investors to consider smaller economies as their hosts. In addition, there are negative returns on capital in small islands. Even if labour costs were zero, small islands' exports in manufactured goods would still be higher than the world price. The study's conclusion is rather pessimistic.

Preference

Despite their huge cost disadvantage, several island economies have managed to survive through relying on trade. This has been achieved by capitalising on preferential trading agreements, using their sovereignty, and developing small transient market niches which create quasi-rents, remittance, and aid (Prasad, 2004).

All the small island countries except Maldives are ACP (Africa, Caribbean, and Pacific) member states and enjoy privileged market access to the European Union. ACP preferences constitute a one-way trade preference for 71 countries in Africa, the Caribbean and the Pacific (47 countries from south of the Sahara in Africa, 16 island nations from the Caribbean, 8 island nations from the Pacific, of which 39 of the ACP countries are classified as least developed countries). These preferences are not available to all developing countries, nor are they restricted to least developed countries, therefore violating WTO rules. As a result, these preferences are being eliminated progressively in order to comply with WTO rules of free trade. Consequently, many small countries dependent on these preferences are facing considerable challenges owing to this loss of revenue, as shown in Table 3.2. According to Grynberg and Silva (2007), small islands will lose approximately 300 million dollars each year, mainly representing income loss through sugar and banana exports. As a result, these islands could 'search for less social sources' to compensate for revenue losses. Small remote islands are difficult to police if their governments are not sympathetic to global objectives.

Offshore financial centres

Some islands have ventured into developing OFCs as one of their development strategies (see Vlcek's chapter). Many small economies

Table 3.2 Income loss through preference elimination, US dollars

	Total	Sugar	Banana	Welfare loss
Fiji	72 423 863	72 423 862	144	62 962 159
Mauritius	97 656 428	97 656 580	156	87 952 867
St. Lucia	5 857 891		5 857 891	5 729 651
Guyana	33 810 466	33 828 128	943	29 802 679
Barbados	12 548 562	12 548 501		11 606 598
Jamaica	43 041 144	38 928 567	4 112 577	40 677 038
Belize	18 582 235	15 261 334	3 314 849	16 033 295
Dominica	2 146 916		2 146 916	2 052 398
St. Vincent	2 980 128		2 980 128	2 916 459
Suriname	2 220 770		2 220 770	2 476 196

Source: Grynberg and Silva, 2007: 139.

have opted for the strategy of providing offshore financial services as part of their development strategy since as early as the 1960s. The strategy of OFCs has produced positive results, but recent international efforts to curb money-laundering has led many centres to review their strategy.

Figure 3.1 shows the importance of financial services to a country's economy. For many small states such as Luxembourg, Switzerland, Barbados, Grenada, Vanuatu and Trinidad and Tobago, financial services exports account for 10 per cent or more of total services exports.

OFCs are considered by bigger countries to represent 'illegitimate or questionable' activities with 'capital-distorting effects'. Their activities are seen as 'economic piracy' since they manipulate tax competition (Baldacchino and Milne, 2000: 6). Small countries therefore have a more capital intensive production and higher per capita output than larger countries. Others argue that small jurisdictions have the right to compete in the global financial services sector precisely because they have a comparative advantage (Sanders, 2002: 345).[3]

Smaller countries use their sovereignty to set up these centres – what Palan refers to as the 'commercialization of state sovereignty' (Palan, 2003: 151). OFCs work by unbundling sovereignty, allowing local regulatory authorities to establish the local regulatory environment, while encouraging multinational banks to make use of their jurisdiction (Hudson, 1998). In other words, the authorities sell some powers over their space. The main characteristic of an OFC is its ability to offer a

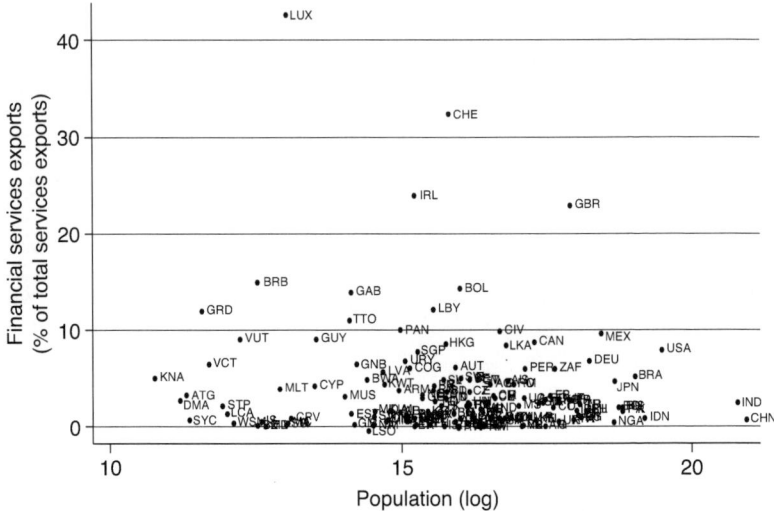

Figure 3.1   Financial services exports as a percentage of total service exports
Source: Author's calculations based on Development Indicators, World Bank, 2007.

regulatory environment that is different and legally separate from that available onshore in other countries (hence 'offshore'). The authorities provide a different set of rules for the financial sector with total security, secrecy and no or low tax.

The existence of a strong tourism sector appears to be a pre-condition (*causa sine qua non*) for an OFC (McCarthy, 1979; Hampton and Christensen, 2002).[4] Tourism and offshore finance require the same services such as rapid air transport links, hotels, restaurants, shops and attractive climates. Typically, the country first becomes a destination for wealthy individuals and some then invest and establish residence. Bankers and accounting firms bring their knowledge and experience, adding to the virtuous circle.

Despite growing international initiatives against OFCs (for example by the OECD, IMF, the Financial Stability Forum, and the United Nations) OFCs are still considered a 'workable option' for many small economies (Woodward, 2006: 686). *The Economist* (2007) argued that the international initiatives to clamp down on OFCs are overblown and OFCs that improve the working of the global financial system should be allowed to exist. It is argued that OFCs serve some bigger countries like the USA into financing their government budget deficits. In addition, large multinational corporations find OFCs very useful as they are able to pay less or no tax on their earnings. However, some smaller OFCs, Vanuatu for example, do not have a sufficient regulatory capacity to enact international standards regulations, having succumbed to international pressure. Other OFCs, more established and capable of 'manufacturing niches out of the untidy compromises of the global financial governance', have flourished (Woodward, 2006: 696). In other words, being small helps these countries to change the existing rules and laws quickly to react to new opportunities. In a recent article, Dharmapala and Hines (2007) demonstrated that better-governed jurisdictions have a far greater chance of success in creating viable OFCs.

Remittance, aid and rent seeking

Rent-seeking activities are an alternative way for small islands to use their economic and non-economic resources and advantages such as political ties, strategic geographic location, international security, and goodwill, thus using their jurisdiction as an economic resource (Baldacchino, 2000; Baldacchino and Milne, 2000). Likewise, Kakazu (1994) suggests that rent-seeking activities need not be considered as merely generating unproductive resource transfers, but as economically logical strategies for small island economies to shift their limited resources from producing uncompetitive products as long as there are opportunities for income gain.

It is often argued that remittances have a developmental role and help generate economic growth. Remittance seems to be more stable than official development assistance, and recently it has surpassed foreign aid flows to developing countries. Remittance flows world-wide were over 270 billion dollars in 2006, and more than half of this went to developing countries. Remittances from foreign workers are the second largest source of external funding for developing countries, after foreign direct investment.

The importance of remittances is much more meaningful if we examine per capita remittances or remittances relative to gross domestic product (GDP). During the period 2000–04, Lebanon received closer to $1300 in remittances per capita, followed by Tonga which received $585, and Jamaica a close third (as shown in Figure 3.2). The countries that receive high per capita remittance flows are small states. Similarly, data reveals that small countries also receive high amounts of remittances in proportion to their GDP, the highest being that of Tonga (around 40 per cent of GDP), Lesotho and Jamaica.

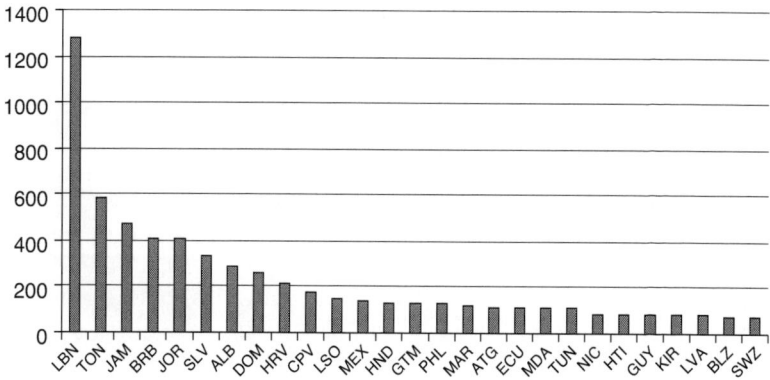

Figure 3.2   Per capita remittance (US$)
Source: Author's calculations based on Development Indicators, World Bank, 2007.

Aid is also particularly important to small states. Figure 3.3 shows the per capita aid receipt according to population size. It shows that aid is significantly high in small countries. For example, Marshall Islands, Federated States of Micronesia, and Tonga receive over $600 of aid per capita.

In certain respects, the strategy of relying on remittances and aid is considered rent-seeking. Rent-seeking includes profitable activities that do not directly result in real output but have the potential for ultimately yielding benefits (Kakazu, 1994: 55). Most small economies that rely on remittances or aid have a commercial deficit, implying its domestic demand cannot be met by its own productive resources.[5] Therefore, its consumption level is sustained by continuous inflows of rent generated abroad. As Kakazu (1994: 57) puts it: 'rent is an integral part of the international transfer of resources from a "surplus" country to a "deficit" country'.

This chapter has shown that preferential agreements are instruments that divert trade and include a grant element (like aid), giving rise to a 'clientelist donor–recipient' relationship of rent-seeking. We also show that small island countries have a different economic logic and subscribe to 'unorthodox, yet effective' strategies and policies (Rodrik, 2001: 21).

Unorthodox development strategies

Apart from the classic strategies mentioned above, there are other sources of income for small island states. Many states may be too small and

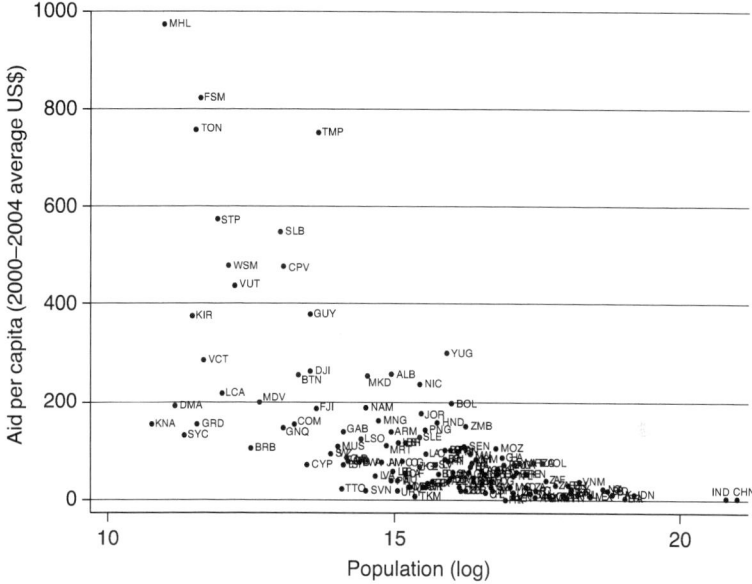

Figure 3.3 Per capita aid by population (US$)
Source: Author's calculations based on Development Indicators, World Bank, 2007.

remote for commercial investment and may, therefore, have to look beyond orthodox strategies and the usual service economies such as tourism. The difficulties posed by smallness in achieving economic development in many small islands have resulted in the islands choosing somewhat unusual development strategies.

Selling sovereignty

In this era of increased globalisation many small islands states sell their sovereignty to other countries in order to finance their budget or to get foreign aid. According to Greenpeace (2002), Japan, has given more than US$323 million of 'aid' in exchange for votes in the International Whaling Commission in order to reverse the global whaling ban through its fisheries grant aid.[6] During the Cold War era the East and the West competed to gain geo-strategic access in remote islands (such as Pacific, Indian Ocean, Caribbean). Similarly, the China–Taiwan relationship benefits some small islands as Taiwan provides ample foreign-aid benefits to small nations that choose to officially recognise it.[7] Small island nations have used their not insubstantial leverage of diplomatic recognition, along with an implied favourable UN vote on issues of concern to both Chinas, to win economic favours from each of the two claimants to Chinese rule. Therefore, sovereignty has been an important asset in allowing small islands to structure their international linkages. In addition, in exchange for their votes, small states possess considerable opportunities for rent-seeking in the international institutions such as the United Nations.

Military bases

Other small island countries provide strategic military bases for developed countries (or sites for weapons testing including nuclear tests). For example, Palau and the United States negotiated a Compact of Free Association in the 1980s. This agreement gives the US military rights in Palau for 50 years, in exchange for some $627 million paid over the agreement's first 15 years. The compact took effect in 1994, the same year Palau gained independence and joined the United Nations. The following year, the new nation received nearly $250 million in front-loaded compact payments, though the allocation fell to about $120 million in 1996 and to some $15 million in 1997, with similar annual incomes set for the following 12 years (Nero et al. 2000). Marshall Islands has a similar agreement with the United States as well.

Fishing rights

The Exclusive Economic Zone (EEZ) for each country reserves exclusive rights to exploit, develop, manage and conserve natural resources in and under the sea within 200 miles (320 kilometres) of their shore (including fishing, oil, gas and minerals). Many small islands have given these rights to other countries with domestic processing industries (Japan, USA, Taiwan (China), China, and South Korea) to fish their waters in return for access fees. The impact of this on the economy of the small state can be substantial; for example, 50 per cent of Tuvalu's government revenue comes from fishing license access fees. In 2000, there were 949 tuna fishing vessels in the EEZ of the Pacific. Currently the access fee for each country ranges from 2.2–10 per cent of gross revenue. Small islands in the Pacific received around US$60 million in access fees from foreign fishing activity in 1999, compared with US$15 million in 1982 (Gillett, 2001: 13).

The tuna fishery in the Western Pacific is the largest and possibly most productive in the world, with annual catches now of around 2 million tonnes per year of the main market species of tuna. This represents close to 50 per cent of global production of these species (Asian Development Bank, 2005). Revenue from these access agreements is important to Pacific island countries and, in some cases, can represent more than 50 per cent of direct government revenue, with the contribution of access fees to GDP estimated to range from 0.01 per cent to 43 per cent in 1999 (Gillett and Lightfoot, 2001). The direct value of access to Pacific island countries was estimated at US$60.3 million, representing around 5–6 per cent of the value of the catch in the Pacific island countries region (approx. 1 million tonnes in 1999).

Shipping registries

The flag of convenience started after the First World War when some non-traditional maritime countries (Panama, Liberia, and Honduras) started registering foreign owned vessels under their flags. This was mainly for economic reasons, in exchange for exercising minimal control over the operations and activities of the vessel (Osieke, 1979). There are around 14 countries, mainly small states such as Panama, Honduras, Liberia, Belize, Cyprus, Marshall Islands, Mauritius, St. Vincent and the Grenadines, and Vanuatu that operate flags of convenience. The revenue coming from registrations fees for some countries can be significant. Its worthwhile noting that 'Flags of convenience' represent around 50 per cent of the world fleet (Klikauer and Morris, 2001). Another example is Vanuatu, which has about 500 merchant and fishing vessels currently flying the Vanuatu flag of convenience, representing significant revenue for the government at around $2500 per ship (18 February, 1999 – Radio Australia). Other countries such as Sao Tome and Principe have also ventured into such practices to earn hard currency.

Selling passports

Other islands, like Kiribati, Federated States of Micronesia, Samoa, Tonga, Grenada, St Lucia, Sao Tome and Principe and Tuvalu, have ventured into selling their national passports to rich businessmen as a source of revenue. The Kiribati government, for example, has received more than US$5.5 million through its Kiribati Foreign Investor Passport Program for Asian businesspeople. The programme encourages rich businesspeople from Asian countries to set up investments that are different from those already in existence in Kiribati (Pacific Islands News Association, 2001).

Marshall Islands also started similar schemes from the mid-1990s, selling hundreds of passports to Asians (primarily in China), earning the country tens of millions of dollars. Natural-born Marshall Islanders, however, can live, study and work in the United States without needing a visa under the Compact of Free Association signed by the two states. Tuvalu also has an Investment Passport Scheme, although this contributes very little to the government's revenue.

Philately

Less controversial is the sale of philately, which contributes to the revenues of smaller islands, such as Tuvalu and Sao Tome and Principe. In Tuvalu, annual philatelic revenues at one point grew to well over US$500 000 (government reserve funds totalled less than this amount). Currently, the philatelic profits amount to around US$50 000 annually. The Tuvalu Philatelic Bureau (TPB) was established after the state's independence in 1978 and for its first few years, was the country's major foreign exchange earner. For a few years, TPB was the country's third largest employer (Knapman et al., 2002).

Trust funds

Trust funds can be an effective way to accumulate, preserve, grow, and mobilise capital for development (Graham, 2005). The Kiribati Revenue Equalisation Reserve Fund (RERF) was established in 1956 during the United Kingdom's colonial administration of the Gilbert (now Kiribati) and Ellice Islands (now Tuvalu). The RERF was capitalised using tax revenue from phosphate mining, and it was established to help balance the government's future recurrent budget in anticipation of phosphate exhaustion. The value of the fund has grown from $556 000 (1956) to nearly $600 million today. From 1991 to 2002 the fund's annual average contribution as a percentage of total government revenues was about seven per cent.

The Tuvalu Trust Fund was established in 1987 through a multilateral international agreement among Tuvalu, New Zealand, the UK and Australia. The fund was initially capitalised with A$27.1 million in contributions from the UK (A$8.5 million), New Zealand (A$8.282 million), Australia (A$8 million), Tuvalu (A$1.6 million), Japan (A$0.695 million) and the Republic of Korea (A$0.031 million). It was set up to contribute to the financial stability of Tuvalu by providing an additional source of revenue for recurrent expenses and to set the country on a path towards greater financial autonomy. The value of the fund had grown from its original $27.1 million to $81.3 million as of spring 2004. Between 1997 and 2001 the fund's annual average contribution to government revenues was 20 per cent.

The Palau Compact of Free Association (COFA) Trust Fund was established in 1995 under section 211 of the Compact of Free Association with the United States. This was a front-loaded fund capitalised with a US$66 million contribution from the US in 1995 and a $4 million follow-up contribution in 1997. The primary objective of the fund is to augment the government's recurrent budget. The fund had grown from its original $66 million to nearly $150 million as of March 2004 including the $4 million subsequent contribution in 1997.

Republic of the Marshall Islands (RMI) established its Marshall Islands Intergenerational Trust Fund (MIITF) in 1999 to help the government achieve budgetary self-reliance. A number of sources capitalised on the fund: US$750 thousand from RMI, ADB injections of $1.8 million (under the Public Sector Reform Program loan) and $2 million (under the Fiscal and Financial Management Program loan), and supplementary Compact funds in fiscal years 2002 and 2003 worth $15.5 and $14 million respectively (these were the so-called 'bump-up' funds). As of late 2003 the fund had reached just over $33 million but had yet to be formally invested.

In addition to the Kiribati Revenue Equalisation Reserve Fund (RERF) and the Tuvalu Trust Fund (TTF), the Compact of Free Association (COFA) Trust Funds between the United States and Palau, FSM, and RMI; the Nauru Phosphate Royalties Trust; the Tonga Trust Fund; the Tuvalu Falekaupule Trust Fund; and the Marshall Islands Nuclear Claims Fund are analysed.

Country code

Some small countries also use some controversial measures to raise revenues such as the sale of their international telephone routing code. As small countries have simple three-digit area codes, residents of the United States or Europe can dial these numbers without realizing they are making expensive international calls. In the case of Tuvalu, its country code 688 was used by international telephone sex firms, which enables callers paying by credit card to maintain their anonymity. This generated up to a US$1 million in revenues per annum, and after eight years it contributed approximately 10 per cent of the national budget. After strong moral objections from the local churches, the government decided to end this operation in the late 1990s (Field, 1997). Other countries in the

Caribbean (such as Guyana) and in the Pacific (like Vanuatu) are also involved in such practices.

Domain names

Another new source of revenue is sales of Internet domain names. All countries are assigned a two-letter country code top-level domain ccTLD, such as .fr for France or .au for Australia (there are altogether 243 ccTLDs). Many small states have sold the rights to their ccTLDs to private firms in exchange for money and access to information technology. These corporations then market the domain name to anyone wishing to register with them. Tuvalu is a good example. It was given the country domain name extension .tv when Internet addresses were handed out. In 1999 the government of Tuvalu signed a contract with USA-based DotTV Corporation International to market and manage its ccTLD '.tv' indefinitely. Having learned from past misjudgments, government officials sought legal and technical assistance to negotiate a marketing agreement. In return for the exclusive rights to sell second-level domain addresses, the government would receive US$1 million per quarter for 12.5 years and 20 per cent equity in the company. In mid-2001 the DotTV Corporation ran into financial difficulties and in December 2001 the company was purchased by VeriSign, Inc., the domain administrator for '.com'. Tuvalu's share of the sale amounted to about US$10 million, which was received as a lump sum. The new contract with VeriSign provides Tuvalu with US$2.2 million per annum plus 5 per cent of all revenue exceeding US$20 million sales per year. VeriSign holds the rights to market '.tv' for 15 years (Knapman, 2002: 10). This money was transferred into the Tuvalu Trust Fund and used to finance its development budget, including the installation of its first streetlights and the inaugural tarring of Funafuti's roadways (Finn, 2002), electricity to the outer islands, extension of its only airstrip (Gaither, 2001), and it was able to pay its UN membership fee and provide better services to its people (Sheehan, 2002: 12).

Other countries such as Moldova also reaped similar benefits after marketing its ccTLD, which happens to be .md. Niue's two-letter ccTLD, .nu, means 'now' in several Scandinavian languages (Drezner, 2001). By marketing its domain name to those countries, Niue has generated enough revenue to be the only nation providing free Internet service to all its residents. Other domain names which are frequently sought include Tonga's (.to) used to make memorable URLs such as www.go.to, Turkmenistan (.tm) used for trade-marking, and the Democratic Republic of the Congo (.cd) used for promoting music.

Satellite business

Some small islands have also launched into the satellite business. A first example involves the Kingdom of Tonga, which was a bold pioneer in establishing political control over orbital slots and turning that control to economic advantage. Tonga has tried to earn income by claiming orbital satellite slots under international law, then selling them to telecommunications carriers. After initially claiming 27 satellite slots, Tonga received seven after larger countries and telecommunications companies objected to the small nation snapping up chunks of space (Price, 1999). The skies over Tonga represent the last unoccupied stretch of the geo-stationary orbital arc. This is the area, 22 300 miles above the equator, where an orbiting satellite's forward speed equals the earth's rotational velocity, meaning from the earth's surface, the satellite appears stationary (*Omni*, 1994). These geo-stationary satellites carry international television hook-ups, telephone communications and data transmissions. Until recently few nations aside from the United States, the former Soviet Union and some of the European countries had either the capability or the need to launch sophisticated communications satellites.

Peacekeeping operations

Fiji supplies troops to the United Nations peacekeeping operations. There are many benefits for such operations for the country, especially in creating employment opportunities for its youth, boosting government revenue (at one stage it was Fiji's third largest earner), upgrading of military skills and boosting Fiji's international image in the global system (Ishizuka, 1999).

Many small island countries have virtually no goods to export. Their external balance, as well as their external service balance, suffers from a substantial deficit. However, this trade deficit is more than balanced by income receipts from abroad through some of the original initiatives led by the governments of these countries.

Internet gambling

Although at the margins of legality, Internet gambling also provides considerable revenue to some small islands such as Antigua and Barbuda. It was argued by Antigua that the offshore gaming industry employed over 2000 people and generated over US$7 million in licence fees per year (UNDP, 2006). As a result of severe legislative pressure from the United States, employment within the sector declined to less than 200 people in 2003. In response Antigua and Barbuda presented arguments to the WTO panel showing that the US government's legislation against transactions between US financial institutions and Antigua and Barbuda-based Internet gaming companies was in breach of the US government's obligations under the General Agreement on Trade in Services (GATS). The Disputes Panel at the WTO has ruled that a revenue loss of US$21 million per year has occurred. Accordingly the WTO recommends that Antigua may request authorisation to suspend the obligations under the TRIPS Agreement at a level not exceeding US$21 million (see Cooper's chapter).

Conclusions

Despite being vulnerable and at the mercy of external donors, small economies have invented ingenious systems to overcome the difficulties posed by their smallness. The recognition of this vulnerability has been a political exercise, which has brought the smaller economies, particularly small islands, into the limelight in international discussions. This chapter has shown that small economies pursue development strategies based on preferential treatment that goes against the international trade theory of free trade. Rather than investing in productive activities to finance imports, small islands prefer to create offshore financial centres, considered illegitimate by larger countries, and engage in rent-seeking. In addition small countries use their political ties and strategic location to create ingenious sources of additional income and to negotiate aid. Lastly their sovereignty (and its instruments) is considered an important economic asset, enabling many small economies to pursue their 'development' in relatively successful, albeit peculiar, ways. In summary, small island economies are at odds with the prescription of economists since they are champions in breaking and distorting rules. These are perfectly logical choices for small economies or, in some cases, they are not choices at all.

This chapter has also demonstrated that the importance of being unimportant allowed many small economies to pursue distinctive national policies to seek favourable deals that concede special advantages. Many small economies behave like 'modern day pirates', in search of exceptions, loopholes, special arrangements and derogations in the world systems. As seen from the small economies' perspectives, globalisation is not homogeneous, uniform or equal, but rather 'pluralistic, messy and often richly asymmetrical', consisting in 'derogations, exceptions, and special arrangements' (Baldacchino and Milne, 2000: 239). Wise and intrepid, the leaders of small islands try to make the most of global opportunities while engaging the forces of globalisation on its own terms.

Notes

* I would like to thank Nicola Hypher for useful comments on earlier drafts of this paper.
1. For example, in 1960, James Meade, the Noble Prize winner in Economics (1977), had forecast that Mauritius was doomed to failure because of heavy economic dependence on a single crop (sugar), high levels of vulnerability to terms of trade shocks, rapid population growth, and potential for ethnic tensions.
2. For a literature review see (Ingebritsen et al., 2006)
3. Well-educated, computer-literate populations, lower levels of business cost, good telecommunications infrastructure, low levels of tax, etc.
4. Although in some countries that provide offshore financial services, such as Nauru and Vanuatu, the tourism sector is not effectively developed.
5. Most islands, especially in the Pacific, have balance of payments deficits of 50 per cent to over 100 per cent of imports, meaning that more than half the imports are financed through current transfers (remittance, aid) or by capital inflow (borrowing, FDI). Apart from remittance and aid as current-account transfers, it should be noted that certain island states (Kiribati, Nauru and Tuvalu) earn interest and dividends on financial assets held overseas (Bertram, 1999a). These are sources of disposable income that do not arise directly from the sale of commodities.
6. Some of the countries supporting Japan's position in exchange to aid are: St Lucia, Antigua and Barbuda, Dominica, Grenada, St Kitts and Nevis, St Vincent and Grenadines, Solomon Islands, and other countries including Panama, Morocco, Guinea, Namibia and Gabon. Japan is using overseas aid to persuade poorer nations, without any direct interest in whaling, to support Japan's pro-whaling stance at the International Whaling Commission.
7. Taiwan has full diplomatic ties with 28 countries, which are mainly small. Solomon Islands; Marshall Islands; Tuvalu; Nauru; Vatican City; Belize; Costa Rica; Dominica; the Dominican Republic; El Salvador; Grenada; Guatemala; Haiti; Honduras; Nicaragua; Palau; Panama; Paraguay; St Kitts and Nevis; St Vincent and the Grenadines; Burkina Faso; Chad; the Gambia; Liberia; Malawi; Sao Tome and Principe; Senegal; and Swaziland.

References

Anckar, D. (2004) 'Direct Democracy in Microstates and Small Island States', *World Development* 32 (2): 379–90.

Anckar, D.A.G. (2002) 'Why are Small Island States Democracies?', *Round Table* 365(1): 375–90.

Baldacchino, G. (1993) 'Bursting the Bubble: The Pseudo-Development Strategies of Micro-State', *Development and Change* 24 (1): 29–51.

Baldacchino, G. (2000) *Lessons from the Political Economy of Small Islands: The Resourcefulness of Jurisdiction* (Houndmills, UK: Macmillan Press).

Baldacchino, G. (2005) 'The Contribution of Social Capital to Economic Growth: Lessons from Island Jurisdictions', *Round Table* 94 (378): 31–46.

Baldacchino, G. (2006) 'Innovative development strategies from non-sovereign island jurisdictions? A global review of economic policy and governance practices', *World Development* 34 (5): 852–67.

Baldacchino, G. and R. Greenwood (1998) *Competing Strategies of Socio-economic Development for Small Islands* (Charlottetown, PEI: Island Studies Press).

Baldacchino, G. and D. Milne (2000) *Lessons from the Political Economy of Small Islands* (Houndmills, UK: Macmillan Press).

Bertram, G. (1999) 'The MIRAB Model Twelve Years On', *The Contemporary Pacific* 11(1): 105–38.

Briguglio, L. and E.J. Kisanga (eds) (2004) *Economic Vulnerability and Resilience of Small States* (Malta and London: Islands and Small States Institute of University of Malta/Commonwealth Secretariat).

Briguglio, L., G. Cordina and E.J. Kisanga (eds) (2006) *Building the Economic Resilience of Small States* (Malta and London: Islands and Small States Institute of University of Malta/Commonwealth Secretariat).

Chang, H.J. (2002) *Kicking Away the Ladder: Development Policy in Historical Perspective* (London: Anthem Press).

Commonwealth Secretariat (1985) *Vulnerability: Small States in the Global Society: Report of a Commonwealth Consultative Group* (London: Commonwealth Secretariat).

Commonwealth Secretariat (1997) *A Future for Small States: Overcoming Vulnerability: Report by a Commonwealth Advisory Group* (London: Commonwealth Secretariat).

Commonwealth Secretariat and World Bank (2000) *Small States: Meeting Challenges in the Global Economy: Report prepared for the Commonwealth Secretariat/World Bank Joint Task Force on Small States* (Washington, DC: Commonwealth Secretariat/World Bank).

Crowards, T. (2002) 'Defining the category of small states', *Journal of International Development* 14 (2): 143–79.

Davenport, M. (2002) *Alternative Special and Differential Arrangements for Small Economies* (London: Commonwealth Secretariat).

Dharmapala, D. and J.R. Hines (2007) *Which Countries Become Tax Havens?*, *American Law and Economics*, Association Annual Meetings, Paper 48.

Drezner, D.W. (2001) 'Sovereignty for Sale', *Foreign Policy* (126): 76–7.

Economist (2007) 'Offshore and beyond the pale: Financial centres', 24 February.

Field, Michael J. (1997) 'Tuvalu Joining Passport Sale Business', Agence France Presse, 31 October.

Finn, Gerard A. (2002) 'Small is Viable', *Pacific Magazine*, July, http://www.pacificmagazine.net/issue/2002/07/01/small-is-viable, accessed 25 November 2008.

Gaither, Chris (2001) 'For a Tiny Pacific Nation, Its Domain Is Its Treasure', *New York Times*, 16 July.

Gillett, R.D. (2001) *Tuna, a Key Economic Resource in the Pacific Islands: A Report Prepared for the Asian Development Bank and the Forum Fisheries Agency* (Manila: Asian Development Bank).

Gillett, R. and C. Lightfoot (2001) *The Contribution of Fisheries to the Economies of Pacific Island Countries*, Report prepared for the Asian Development Bank, the Forum Fisheries Agency and the World Bank (Manila: Asian Development Bank).

Graham, B. (2005) 'Trust Funds in the Pacific: Their Role and Future', *Pacific Studies Series* (Manila: Asian Development Bank).

Greenpeace (2002) 'Aid for Votes Greenpeace Briefing', http://whales.greenpeace. org/, accessed on 26 August 2008.

Grynberg, R. and S. Silva (2007) 'Preference-dependent economies in the Doha round: impacts and options' in S. Bilal and R. Grynberg, (eds), *Navigating New Waters: A reader on ACP-EU trade relations* (London: The Commonwealth Secretariat).

Hampton, M.P. and J. Christensen (2002) 'Offshore Pariahs? Small Island Economies, Tax Havens, and the Re-configuration of Global Finance', *World Development* 30 (9): 1657–73.

Hudson, A.C. (1998) 'Placing trust, trusting place: on the social construction of offshore financial centres' *Political Geography* 17 (8): 915–37.

Ingebritsen, C., I. Neumann, S. Gstöhl and J. Beyer (eds) (2006) *Small States in International Relations* (Seattle and Reykjavik: University of Iceland Press/University of Washington Press).

Ishizuka, K. (1999) 'Fiji: A micro-state and its peacekeeping contribution', *Peacekeeping and International Relations* 28 (3): 18–21.

Kakazu, H. (1994) *Sustainable Development of Small Island Economies* (Oxford: Westview Press).

Klikauer, T. and R. Morris (2001) 'Crews of Convenience from the South West Pacific: The "German" Sailors of Kiribati', *New Zealand Journal of Industrial Relations* 26 (2): 185–98.

Knapman, B., M. Ponton and C. Hunt (2002) *Tuvalu: 2002 Economic and Public Sector Review* (Manila: Asian Development Bank).

McCarthy, I. (1979) 'Offshore Banking Centers: Benefits and Costs', *Finance and Development* 16 (4): 45–8.

Nero, K.L., F. Brel Murray and M.L. Burton (2000) 'The Meanings of Work in Contemporary Palau: Policy Implications of Globalization in the Pacific', *Contemporary Pacific* 12 (2): 319–48.

Omni (1994) 'Chutzpah in orbit: Meet the new power in the telecommunication', 16(11): 20.

Osieke, E. (1979) 'Flags of Convenience Vessels: Recent Developments', *American Journal of International Law* 73 (4): 604–27.

Pacific Islands News Association (2001) 'Millions through Passport Sales, says Kiribati', 5 February.

Palan, R. (2003) 'Tax Havens and the Commercialization of State Sovereignty', *International Organization* 56 (1): 151–76.

Prasad, N. (2003) 'Small islands' quest for economic development', *Asia-Pacific Development Journal* 10 (1): 47–67.

Prasad, N. (2004) 'Escaping Regulation, Escaping Convention: Development strategies in small economies', *World Economics* 5 (1): 41–65.

Prasad, N. and S. Raj (2006) 'The Perils of Unmanaged Export Growth: The Case of Kava in Fiji', *Journal of Small Business and Entrepreneurship* 19 (4): 381–94.

Price, M. (1999) 'Satellite broadcasting as trade routes in the sky', *Public Culture* 11 (2): 387–403.

Reinert, E. (2007) *How Rich Countries Got Rich ... and Why Poor Countries Stay Poor* (London: Constable).

Rodrik, D. (2001) *The Global Governance of Trade: As if Development Really Mattered* (New York: United Nations Development Programme).

Sanders, R. (2002) 'The fight against fiscal colonialism: the OECD and small jurisdictions', *Round Table* 365 (1): 325–48.

Sheehan, Genevieve (2002) 'Tuvalu Little, Tuvalu Late: A country goes under', *Harvard International Review* 24(1): 11–12.

Srebrnik, H. (2004) 'Small Island Nations and Democratic Values', *World Development* 32 (2): 329–41.

UNDP (2006) UNDP Barbados, Country Profiles: Antigua and Barbuda, 'Introduction', http://www.bb.undp.org/index.php?page=antigua-barbuda, accessed on 27 May 2008.

Winters, L.A. and P. Martins (2004) *Beautiful but Costly: Business Costs in Small Economies* (London: Commonwealth Secretariat).

Woodward, R. (2006) 'Offshore Strategies in Global Political Economy: Small Islands and the Case of the EU and OECD Harmful Tax Competition Initiatives', *Cambridge Review of International Affairs* 19 (4): 685–99.

World Bank (2007) *World Development Indicators* (Washington, DC: World Bank).

4
Singapore and the Soft Power Experience

*Alan Chong**

Soft power is a product of nurture. It is the ability to get others to want what you want through cooptation or appeal, as opposed to hard, coercive power (Nye Jr., 2004). This is practically applicable to both small and large states alike, but for the former, it requires the transformation of political size and an intense trial of communitarian will. Given the ambit of the discussion covered in the Commonwealth Secretariat Report *A Future for Small States – Overcoming Vulnerability* published in 1997, soft power is a logical panacea for vulnerability. This report noted that 'vulnerability is ... the consequence of the interaction of two sets of factors: (1) the incidence and intensity of risk and threat, and (2) the ability to withstand risks and threats (resistance) and to "bounce back" from their consequences (resilience)' (Commonwealth Secretariat, 1997: 13). Furthermore, it observed that small states' security starts at home. Social cohesion in most small states is a major resource which adds to resilience and lessens internal insecurity. Small states exhibit an enviable record of political stability. While this is to be welcomed there is no room for complacency, since if order does break down in small states conflict can quickly 'escalate beyond the survival of a particular regime to the survival of the core values of the society itself' (Commonwealth Secretariat, 1997: xi). If this report can be regarded as a sample of small state leaders' perceptions of their territories' foreign policy parameters, soft power is integral to attaining small state goals in the international system for a number of reasons that are also characteristic of itself.

First, soft power derives from an 'intermestic' condition in national governance. The policies of a domestic government are either a re-action to or anticipation of international trends. Owing to the relatively minuscule size of small states, the adaptability of their governments tends to involve the persuasion and mobilisation of civil societies and business sectors in a consensual direction. In large measure the effective-ness of soft power depends on how far government and society can act in unison. I have labelled this the communitarian basis of soft power since it involves 'packaging' a way of life while minimising its short-comings (Chong, 2007: 55). Joseph Nye's original formulation of soft power has merely hinted at this aspect in his repeated references to American non-traditional power indices, such as diplomatic respectabil-ity, the popularity of ideological exports, as well as music and film. The communitarian aspect literally entices the goodwill and admiration of others if it can demonstrate efficacy. Secondly, soft power is premised on its ability to circulate omnidirectionally, that is to say, it cannot be targeted at only a select audience. Soft power, unlike the peacetime pro-paganda of the interwar years, or the wartime propaganda practised by belligerents against one another, is the long-term propaganda of com-munity discourse. It is similar to an open shop window allowing all manner of passers-by to view its displays and to inquire within. Thirdly, soft power demands consistency and credibility from its practitioners. If government and society cannot project a measure of unity for the purposes of foreign policy projection, then the latter could hardly be expected to be taken seriously abroad. Therefore, ideological projec-tion of peaceful developmental intentions should not be vitiated by frequent recourse to the use of force across borders by the soft power wielder. Likewise, as the example of Cold War-era superpower compe-tition showed, boasts of the economic and civilisational superiority of one's model should not be undermined by dissidents articulating con-vincing counter-claims of food shortages and human rights persecution. In Nye's comparison, in the end the Soviet Union's extensive propaganda was weaker than its American rival simply because defectors' disclosures of life behind the 'Iron Curtain' could be corroborated more effectively than official explanations in communist-controlled newspapers and radio.

In this short chapter, I intend to offer a concise explanation of Singapore's soft power strategy with a view towards highlighting its strengths and weaknesses. This will be achieved through a brief ana-lysis of the origins of its soft power in its route to independent statehood and developmental experience. Thereafter, Singaporean soft power effec-tiveness will be examined through a few demonstration cases such as the Asian Values Debate, the export of the Singapore Model of Development, and humanitarian aid diplomacy. It is hoped that the Singaporean case will offer some constructive lessons in small state resilience triumphing over vulnerability.

The origins of Singaporean soft power

It can be argued that soft power posed a philosophical attraction for the leaders of the Republic of Singapore because of geographical circumstances and the unfolding of the nationalist trajectory that sought to end British colonialism within Southeast Asia. It must be stressed at the outset that generating soft power was a choice, not an inheritance. The British colonial legacy was a strategic nightmare that was at once demographic, geopolitical, economic and administrative. When Singapore was founded in 1819 as an 'Emporium', it formed part of a design to extend Britain's nascent commercial empire under the auspices of the East India Company (EIC). As a forerunner of the late twentieth-century multinational corporation, it was never tasked with moulding a future nation-state. The brief for the EIC's man on the spot was to manoeuvre within the geopolitical interstices between the archipelagic Dutch East Indies and the local Malay potentates, in order to secure a foothold in the intensifying rush for profitable colonies in Southeast Asia (Raffles, 1973: 88–90). The British acquired Singapore Island for a literally princely sum, by recognising one Malay royal family over another while promising the former protection in Singapore. The British secured a strategic prize just in time. Since the 1500s, Spain had already staked out the Philippine islands across the South China Sea, while the French were showing interest in nearby Indochina. Economic considerations further encouraged the EIC to undercut their regional rivals by virtually eliminating all taxes on traders and entrenching Singapore's reputation as the freest port in the region. In tandem with being a cost-cutting destination, the British liberally encouraged immigration from China and India to provide a ready pool of labour for menial tasks involved in building the infrastructure of roads, public buildings, harbour services, raw material processing and warehousing. Singapore was intended to be the export outlet of the hinterland of the Malay Peninsula to the north and, where possible, all of maritime Southeast Asia. Singapore's deep harbour – situated along the major east–west shipping channel between the Indian Ocean, the Straits of Melaka, and the South China Sea – encouraged flows of goods, ideas and people of all religions and cultures through its port. This state of affairs continued for nearly a century and a half, with Singapore serving as both the premier export outlet for British extractive industries in Malaya and as the 'Gibraltar of the East' from which British gunboat diplomacy exerted its presence in the region. Furthermore, administrative consolidation since the late 1800s ensured that the island was ultimately invested with a separate governorship by 1946.

The Japanese Occupation of the island hardly disturbed its strategic status between 1942 and 1945. In fact, the Japanese military command sought to enhance Singapore as the headquarters of their Southeast Asian empire. It was symbolic that the humiliating surrender of the British and Commonwealth troops took place in Singapore, following a 70-day campaign that saw the island coordinating the ill-fated defence of the entire British Malaya.

The Japanese Occupation also stoked the nascent centrifugal streams of anti-colonial nationalism on the island. Given the British policy of liberal immigration, the native Malay population was rapidly reduced to minority status by the burgeoning population of Indian and Chinese immigrants who, nevertheless, exhibited divided loyalties in relation to Singapore. By the 1930s nationalist stirrings in both China and India were beginning to exert their gravitational pulls on their racial diaspora in Singapore. Anti-colonial sentiments in Singapore surfaced in many local migrants' associations in tune with developments in their ancestral homelands. Likewise, Malay nationalism in Singapore imbibed currents from mainland Malaya and Islam in the Middle East. The Japanese invaders played on these sentiments through their propaganda of a Greater East Asia Co-Prosperity Sphere. The British did not help matters with an indecisive attitude towards preparing the local education and welfare systems for self-government. The British military surrender to an Asian power reinforced the increasingly widespread local perception that His Majesty's Government was never seriously interested in protecting Asian indigenous interests. Instead, the hiatus in British authority from 1942–45 demonstrated the instrumental dispensability of Singapore's society in relation to the wider strategy of defending an overstretched British empire. Nevertheless, the experience of growing up in a hierarchically organised colonial order inspired some of the local born Chinese, Indian and Malay elites to aim towards accessing the colonial English-speaking 'high culture' through education, either within the island's educational institutions or abroad, in metropolitan Britain itself. This group formed the nucleus of the People's Action Party (PAP), the most successful of the ten nationalist political parties that contested British supremacy during the limited local elections held between 1955 and 1959. The first generation leaders of the PAP, Lee Kuan Yew, Toh Chin Chye, Sinnathamby Rajaratnam, Kenneth Byrnes and Goh Keng Swee, had all developed a sense that the vision of a postcolonial, independent Singaporean nationhood and statehood required a multi-racial umbrella party that pushed an agenda that eroded racial inequalities through enlarging the economic pie and making government appointments on the basis of meritocracy. This group felt that a distinctive Singaporean foreign policy identity was synonymous with the domestic struggle for democratic legitimacy and anti-colonialism and deployed their talents for eloquent political communication accordingly. In the polarising *milieu* of Third World nonalignment politics during the 1960s, the PAP elite felt it judicious to align itself with the dominant currents represented by India, Yugoslavia, China, Egypt and Algeria. Furthermore, this served as a foil for difficult negotiations with the British for self-government on one hand, and on the other, talks with the Alliance government in control of an independent Malayan state from 1961 onwards. In this way, even though the PAP government was not constitutionally a fully sovereign entity before 9 August 1965, it was pursuing a foreign 'policy without authority' (Boyce, 1965) in an attempt to brand its identity at home and abroad as socialist, democratic, multi-racial and pragmatic. These aspirations were not always reconcilable but it could be said that the complicity of geography with colonial legacies rendered the independent state of Singapore a vacuum of identity that lent itself to the transformative leadership of the PAP government.

The developmental strategy of the PAP government was a version of authoritarian corporatism engineered towards building an export-oriented industrialised economy. Given the island's dearth of natural resources to exploit and a land area of barely 700 square kilometres, this could not be achieved with hard power. The fledgling state's only credible resources were its workforce and its reputation; both having to be built from scratch. In this way soft power was derived from a narrative of efficient hospitality to foreign investment coupled to a reality that matched it. Domestically this justified a disciplined structure of employer–worker relations where both had to be persuaded through strong arguments to re-imagine themselves as stakeholders in a communitarian effort to lift Singaporean prosperity. Negotiations for national wage increases and bonuses were channelled into a closed-door setting where the government sat alongside representatives of the employers' federations and trade unions to decide on increases that kept pace with projected economic indices. Likewise, legislation made it difficult to initiate sudden labour stoppages without consequences. In return for acquiescence, the PAP state, through its affiliated National Trades Union Congress (NTUC), offered workers a wide range of subsidised health care and homes, budget retail outlets, incentives for skill upgrading, insurance coverage, and loans at favourable rates. Furthermore, the Central Provident Fund was established as a state-administered compulsory pension system that ensured each citizen would keep part of his salary in reserve for housing provision, education, and geriatric needs. On a pragmatic, welfarist basis there was thus no reason not to buy into a PAP state that was serious about growing the economic pie for all, including the working class. Politically, corporatism meant that the PAP was dedicated towards retaining its pre-eminence through regularly large electoral mandates where Singaporeans indicated their overall satisfaction with the economic deliverables at the expense of possessing untrammelled personal freedoms. Such pragmatic logic appears to have ensured that opposition votes at election time would not pose a serious threat against a hegemonic party that seems to have entrenched itself through indefatigable instrumental legitimacy. Increasingly, however, civil society groups monitoring the environment, the plight of the elderly and artistic preservation have found favour within this corporatist set-up. Democratisation at a glacial pace appears to have been the preference of more than 60 per cent of the electorate who had regularly voted for the PAP's continuity as a reliable economic provider.

In short, the PAP state's articulation of soft power was a narrative of corporatist developmentalism aimed at attracting foreign capital as an engine of externally-driven growth while distributing material gains to the population through qualified welfarism. In tune with the lucid clinical language employed by the PAP elite, I have conceptualised the 'Singapore Model of Development' (SMD) as comprising three 'Cs'. First, 'Credibility' applied to political promises, programmes and politicians, including talent promotion and uncompromising anti-corruption vigilance. Secondly, the 'Cohesion' of the nation-state, was to be manifested in the qualities of teamwork, diligence and harmony of purpose in the face of common adversity. And thirdly, 'Confidence' was to be actualised through paternalistic leadership, its virtues in implementing strict law and order, and its planning for a long-term communitarian good (Chong, 2007: 104–5). On the surface, these three 'Cs' appear unremarkable but these are a statement of the PAP's *modus operandi* that ought to be read in tandem with other popular Singaporean political parlance such as 'teamwork', 'pragmatism', 'flexibility while retaining the fundamentals of good government', and 'welcoming the world as a united nation'. In this way soft power as discourse could variously defend the SMD as a workable model of non-western exceptionalism; project it as a poster child for benign neoliberal globalisation; demonstrate the importance of cohesive organisation in foreign policy projection; and gain friends as a beacon of successful development in line with nation-building. Moreover, the articulators of soft power had to possess a good turn of phrase, intellectual charisma, and a willingness to debate within academic and current affairs forums with global exposure. In this respect the interviews and writings of ministers and diplomats of the likes of Lee Kuan Yew, S. Rajaratnam, Wong Kan Seng, Goh Chok Tong, Kishore Mahbubani, and Tommy Koh served as veritable delivery vehicles for soft power (Chong, 2006; Mahbubani, 2008).

Singapore and the Asian Values Debate

The SMD had come under fire from western liberal commentators virtually since independence in 1965. The lightning rods were many: the PAP's legislation concerning the domestic and foreign media; the closure of newspapers linked to communist subversion from abroad; the restructuring of labour-management relations for a corporatist political economy; the employment of the Internal Security Act for detaining subversives without trial; and the so-called 'climate of fear' pervading Singaporean civil society as a cumulative result of the preceding measures. Ironically, Singapore even withdrew from the Socialist International in 1976, citing its double standards and lack of empathy towards the PAP's developmental priorities. Throughout the 1980s, the Republic was embroiled in a series of libel disputes with leading western news magazines such as *Time, Newsweek, Asiaweek, Far Eastern Economic Review* and the *Asian Wall Street Journal* over correcting what the PAP leaders perceived to be misrepresentations of local politics. But it was interesting to note that the PAP government did not ban these publications outright. It resorted to open legal proceedings under existing Singaporean law, and restricted their circulation to institutional subscribers in the country. In a few cases the PAP government challenged these media owners to demonstrate their journalistic aspiration for delivering pure news by deleting advertisements from their published copies. This came to represent a pattern of careful calibrated response from a weak state perceived as 'soft authoritarian' by outsiders. The basic premise of attracting foreign capital could not be undermined, while asserting the sovereignty of the elected government of Singapore over its domestic political *modus operandi*. The PAP government further deflected severe sanctions through its firmly anti-communist alignment with Western postures towards the communist world, especially following the reversals in America's war in Vietnam from 1968 onwards.

The Asian Values Debate erupted as a significant diplomatic row between Singapore and the West, chiefly due to a conjunction of factors at the end of the Cold War. The apparent victory of liberal democratic capitalism over the communist model gave the fillip to western

ideologues seeking to realise a comprehensive democratic peace divi-
dend during this historical moment. The two successive administrations
of President Bill Clinton in the US upped the ante by declaring the pursuit of human rights and democratisation as their primary foreign policy
priorities. This predictably stoked a series of long-running diplomatic
confrontations with the US's Asian and Middle Eastern allies, placing
them ironically within the same ideological camp as Saddam Hussein's
Iraq, fundamentalist Islamic Iran and Castro's Cuba. In Asia, China,
North Korea, Indonesia, Malaysia, Singapore, Myanmar, Vietnam, and
Cambodia came under the spotlight for their authoritarian practices.
This coincided with the widespread perception that the causes of economic decline in the West were a result of illiberal economic practices in
non-western newly industrialising countries that were destined to realise
the 'Pacific Century' at the expense of the traditional hegemony of the
transatlantic powers. Post-Cold War attention towards the revival of
inter-civilisational and inter-religious dissension in international relations was ignited by the genocidal events in former-Yugoslavia and
sub-Saharan Africa. Samuel Huntington's 1993 thesis of the 'clash of
civilisations', along with Francis Fukuyama's 'end of history' argument
(articulated in 1989), helped crystallise a world-wide perception that the
West was gearing up for a new cold war to eviscerate non-western civilisations that were illiberal and, by extension, inimical to transatlantic
interests. Singapore's articulation of the SMD came under threat, and
given Singapore's sizable socio-economic stakes in a modernising post-
Mao China, the PAP elite turned their elocutionary powers to bear on
the issue.

Singaporean foreign policy spokesmen modulated their SMD discourse
with the aim of: (a) putting up a credible wall against perceived western
sermonising on political liberalism in development prognoses; (b) gal-
vanizing an Asian or non-western political front in support of China's
self-determined political and economic transition; and (c) to assert
normatively Asian countries' political equality with the West after the
divisions of the Cold War. The strategy was designed to counter strad-
dled intellect and coercion with a response designed to be both subtle
and forceful. The clearest statement comes from Lee Kuan Yew's widely
cited *Foreign Affairs* interview: 'It is not my business to tell people what's
wrong with their system. It is my business to tell people not to foist
their system indiscriminately on societies in which it will not work'
(quoted in Zakaria, 1994: 110). The Singaporean position in the debate
was to undergo three serious tests. The first was the 1993 United Nations
World Conference on Human Rights at Vienna, where the UN sought
to obtain a landmark declaration of universal humanitarian principles

by the international community entailing some morally binding reference for posterity. As expected, the unravelling of international order polarised the participants into two broad camps, pitting the West, Latin America and most of Africa, against an Asian and 'Arab-Islamic' coalition articulating exceptions on human rights. Singapore was invited by the conference chair to mediate both positions during the final stages of the drafting of a joint declaration on the basis that it was perceived as intellectually partisan but diplomatically realistic. As Singapore's foreign minister Wong Kan Seng explained it, while murder is always murder and 'no one claims torture as part of their cultural heritage', the Singaporean experience 'is that economic growth is the necessary foundation of any system that claims to advance human dignity, and that order and stability are essential for development'; hence 'a pragmatic approach to human rights is one that tries to consolidate what common ground we can agree on, while agreeing to disagree if we must' (Chong, 2007: 110).

The next discursive confrontation was less gentlemanly, in part because the stakes directly involved Singapore's legal sovereignty. Michael Fay was an 18-year-old American student at an expatriate school in Singapore indicted by a Singaporean court for vandalising public and private property. His crime was spray-painting more than a dozen cars without permission and retaining the public street signs he and his group of friends from the Singapore American School had pilfered. Fay was sentenced to six strokes of caning and a fine of S$3500. The Clinton administration criticised the decision on three grounds. First, caning was a barbaric and outmoded form of torture and inhumane punishment. Secondly, since the SMD believed in privileging communitarian order through strict observance of law, the 'Singaporean-Asian Confucian state' was a reprehensible authoritarian example contrary to everything western, American, liberal, and democratic. Thirdly, Fay was a young, inexperienced individual deserving of leniency. These reasons were cited in President Clinton's intercessionary letter to the President of Singapore and in his public statements before and after the implementation of the sentence. The Singaporean authorities relented slightly but with a qualification that did nothing to abate liberal anger. While the six strokes of caning were reduced to four, the official explanation for the concession noted that 'to reject his [Clinton's] appeal totally would show an unhelpful disregard for the President and the domestic pressures on him on this issue. Therefore even though the Cabinet found no merit in Fay's petition, it sought a way to accommodate President Clinton's appeal without compromising the principle that persons convicted of vandalism must be caned' (Chong, 2007: 113). Washington threatened to deny its vote for Singapore's hosting of the first WTO ministerial conference scheduled for 1996. However, given the fallout from the 'clash of civilisations' stemming from the Clinton Administration's ancillary rows with other Asian states over assorted human rights and economic pressures, Singapore's position attracted unstinting diplomatic support from Asia, including Japan. The Japanese position declared 'we are sympathetic *as an Asian nation* to the proposal to hold the first [WTO] ministerial conference *somewhere in Asia*' (Chong, 2007: 114, emphasis added). Just a few weeks before Fay's caning, President Clinton himself admitted indirectly on television that the SMD resonated as a form of developmental soft power, which evoked conflicting sentiments in him:

> [O]n the one hand, I don't approve of this punishment, particularly in this case. Now having said that, a lot of the Asian societies that are doing very well now have low crime rates and high economic growth rates, partly because they have very coherent societies with strong units where the unit is more important than the individual, whether it's the family unit or the work unit or the community unit ... What's happened in America today is, too many people live in areas where there's no family structure, no community structure and no work structure. And so there's a lot of irresponsibility. And so a lot of people say there's too much personal freedom. When personal freedom's being abused, you have to move to limit it. (Clinton, 1994)

This long quote from President Clinton captures the effect of Singaporean/Asian soft power as an authoritarian developmental discourse in international politics. If the SMD is to be convincingly regarded as a superior model, it should not only be demonstrated by the words and deeds of the originator, it ought to be echoed by the adopters and neutrals, and where possible, conceded by the opposition. Apparently this debate resonated in Singapore's ongoing attempts to foster the Asia–Middle East Dialogue as a decidedly non-western initiative at interregional economic, political and cultural exchanges where both regions' political authorities have amicably decided at the outset that the matter of regime acceptability should not be a bar to mutually beneficial constructive engagement.

Promoting the SMD: The Singapore Cooperation Programme

The promotion of the SMD as a formal version of a foreign aid programme is a relatively recent policy. The Republic claims to have trained

53 000 officials from 168 countries since 1992 under the Singapore Cooperation Programme (SCP) (SCP, 2008). Like most aid efforts it aims to cultivate goodwill towards Singapore from every quarter of the international community. It achieves this through some unusual characteristics. First, the spirit of aid is in idea transfer as opposed to 'hard' technology and monetary grants. As it says on its website, 'give a man a fish and he will eat for a day. Teach a man to fish and he will eat for the rest of his life' (SCP, 2008). Secondly, the foreign ministry does not take a rigid ideological view when inviting interested parties into its programmes. Officials interviewed by the author (Chong, 2007: 130–1) have repeatedly emphasised modesty in applying the SMD holistically to any one context. Instead, the interested foreign party is offered choices of 'curricula' from a long menu: transportation planning and management, public administration and law, banking policy, health care, to even professional English proficiency. The onus lies upon the aid recipient to adopt the SMD selectively or as a whole. Most of the 168 countries have opted for selective expertise transfer, whereas Vietnam, China and certain municipal authorities in Indonesia and India have opted for a wholesale reproduction of 'mini-Singapores' in townships and special economic zones. Furthermore, Singapore offers technical training for workers in the Indochinese states through the Initiative for ASEAN, as well as the Singapore Scholarship, tenable for undergraduate study in any of Singapore's full-fledged universities. Thirdly, there is the feature of international partnership and synthesis in putting together some of these developmental curricula under the label of Third Country Training Programmes (TCTP). These third parties include not only developed states such as Britain, Canada, Denmark, Germany, and Japan, but also prominent neoliberal institutions such as the World Bank and International Monetary Fund (IMF), as well as emerging powers such as India and South Korea. Afghanistan, Cambodia, Vietnam, Laos, and Timor-Leste are some examples where the TCTP have proved beneficial while also being faithful to the spirit of soft power as socialisation into the norms of a developmental epistemic community. Fourthly, the Singapore Cooperation Programme appears to be run on a budget with manpower and expertise shared out among 88 ministries, educational institutions, state corporations and their subsidiaries. This manifests the practical meaning of developmental corporatism and the notion of 'Singapore Incorporated'. The amount spent on 'aid' is not delineated separately in the published national budget for the foreign affairs ministry. Nonetheless, given that the latter's budget has stayed within 0.2 per cent of national GDP between 1999 and 2008, and the fact that the overall expenditure

for the ministry has doubled from S$153 million to S$346 million, the S$105.9 million set aside for participation in international organisations and the Cooperation Programme in 2008 alone speaks of a very efficient shoestring aid policy (Ministry of Foreign Affairs, 2008a; 2008b). The ministry does not appear to have attempted to quantify the results of aid as soft power either.

Consequently, it is extremely difficult to assess the success of the Cooperation Programme except where external parties provide feedback. One indication came during the final phase of the Asian Values Debate on the diplomatic front. This coincided with the Asian Financial Crisis (1997–99) when Singapore bucked the trend of unmitigated economic disaster with only a temporary spike in unemployment, low growth, and no rioting in the streets. Many critics ignored it as the inconvenient statistic, while painting it as the indirect target of 'Asian misgovernance' charges. The SMD's espousal of communitarian ethics ignored all the cronyism, corruption and other financial misdemeanours in Malaysia, Indonesia, Thailand, the Philippines and South Korea, charged the critics. Yet, ironically, both the IMF and World Bank signed up with the TCTP amid the crisis to utilise Singapore's services as a 'good governance' consultant. Additionally, where China and Vietnam were concerned, full-scale copying of the SMD through top-down fiat proved problematic by the late 1990s owing to bureaucratic resistance from middle-level and regional party officials who were resentful of a loss of power under the guise of reform. It required repeated high-level ministerial visits from Singapore to re-ignite the momentum whenever bottle-necks were encountered on the ground in promoting industrial parks and reforming investment laws. Perhaps the better endorsements of the SMD come from two very diverse sources: Britain and Nigeria. Erstwhile London Mayor Ken Livingstone had implemented Singapore-style road pricing over the objections of motorist rights advocates and other libertarians in 2003, and consequently confounded these critics when the scheme rapidly ended congestion in Central London. Livingstone remarked in an interview that while 'Britain gave the world William Shakespeare, ... it is really Singapore which has led the world in the best way of easing traffic jams in city areas' (Chong, 2007: 138). From Nigeria, Demola Bakare, a Singapore Cooperation Programme participant, wrote in Nigeria's anti-corruption journal that it is 'easier to have a good clean government, and a good clean system, than for an anti-corruption agency to clean up a corrupt government and a crooked system ... In this [way], like Singapore, Nigerian leaders should strategically focus on three related areas of legislation, enforcement and adjudication as a package' (Bakare, 2007).

Humanitarian aid diplomacy

As an extension of the SMD, the humanitarian aid dimension of Singapore's soft power was never intended as a prominent feature. Humanitarian operations were an appendage of the notion of good governance at home – the incorporation of civil defence units into the internal security structure; the token disaster relief operation in friendly states; and more evidently in foreign policy, a visible but modest stake in fleshing out the country's commitment to the spirit of virtuous membership in the UN. Nonetheless, for the ministries of defence, home affairs and foreign affairs, the operational distance between physically supporting a UN mandate and the standard operational readiness for military ventures by air, sea and land would be very short (Boey, 2005). This is by virtue of the SMD's constant emphasis on credibility and cohesion. Teamwork and a united response to crisis are learned traits of the Singaporean political economy.

The official responses to the Indian Ocean tsunami disaster in 2004–05, along with the aftermath of Cyclone Nargis in Myanmar and the Sichuan earthquake in China in 2008, have shifted Singapore's humanitarian relief policy into high gear. Three points of analysis can be drawn from these relief efforts. First, Singaporean participation in relief operations manifests community in a tangible way to both foreign governments and their publics. Both Singaporean leaders and relief-receiving governments have acknowledged that during the tsunami disaster the Singaporean effort was a major gesture of identifying positively with a 'community of fate' on the basis that a neighbour's calamity within an interdependent region should morally transcend principles of sovereign non-interference. Similarly the spontaneous response to the Myanmar people's plight was an act of charity in spite of the Yangon military regime's xenophobic intransigence. One might also say that comparable government-sanctioned fundraising gestures pertaining to the Sichuan earthquake attested to the special quality of Singapore–China ties. Secondly, the 'community of fate' logic implicitly required an omnidirectional exercise of soft power: bystander parties, be they nongovernmental organisations (NGOs) or nation-states, ought to be included in a joint effort while accommodating their respective degrees of political sensitivities. During the three relief operations Singaporean officials exercised great care communicating with their counterparts in the affected countries, deferring to the latter's problem identification and articulation of needs on the basis that the 'locals know best' how and where the outsider's sincere help should be deployed (Lim, 2005).

This degree of diplomatic legitimacy varied from Indonesia to Myanmar and China for reasons of national pride. Reflecting these disparities in sensitivity, Singapore dispatched three helicopter landing ships, six heavy lift Chinook helicopters and over 900 military and civilian staff to Indonesia's worst-hit Meulaboh district; while the Myanmar and China efforts witnessed the participation of only single teams of civil defence personnel in bit parts (Sim, 2008). Furthermore, the operational logic of NGOs had also to be accommodated by an SMD that had thus far operated on corporatist authoritarian principles. It is therefore significant that the Singapore Red Cross, Mercy Relief, the Parkway Health Group and Habitat for Humanity played important, and often unsung, medical and reconstruction roles in Indonesia's Aceh province long after the Singapore Armed Forces' emergency infrastructure-patching efforts wound up. Likewise, in the Myanmar case the sizable Myanmar expatriate community in Singapore and their wider Buddhist fraternity among Chinese Singaporeans carried out a spontaneous donation and delivery campaign that contrasted with the official caution of the Singaporean authorities towards the military regime. Nevertheless, in both the tsunami and Nargis efforts the Singaporean prime minister either initiated or persuaded key aid givers and recipients to convene a relief coordination conference to draw up plans for synchronisation of aid flows and a division of labour to ensure that no areas were neglected. Thirdly, it is this passion for sorting out the finer details of implementation that reinforced a widespread sense that the Singaporeans were good administrative Samaritans, since they operated the SMD that took pride in consistency and credibility in delivering on its promises. Jan Egeland, then Head of the UN's Office for the Co-ordination of Humanitarian Affairs, expressed the hope that following the tsunami relief effort Singapore would work more closely with other UN relief efforts 'because it is a rich and efficient society' (Low, 2005).

Ramifications of a Singaporean soft power experiment

Singaporean soft power is evidently a risky gamble for a small state fashioned by British imperial design as a junction of exchange for a regional Southeast Asian hinterland and little else. The nationalist PAP elite nurtured this historical feature as a foundation for survival through the *enlargement* of the island's utility to the rest of the world and beyond. Most of this enlargement was not physical; it was achieved through ideas. More specifically, it was through the political communication abroad of a Singapore Model of Development that lent itself to various diplomatic uses. The relative economic success of the SMD, as measured by its regularity in top ten rankings in indices of economic competitiveness, incorruptibility, and trading volume by international neoliberal institutions since the 1990s, suggests that ideational power has little correlation to physical size. Yet ironically, any idea must be translatable into some manifestation of achievement. Therefore, in the long run the SMD must be able to sustain relevance to global discourses on development and governance. Though the Asian Values Debate is no longer bandied about in global discourse by its proper name, it does not mean that exceptionalism has been buried in the current *milieu* of international diplomacy. It simply means that exceptionalism must always anchor its relevance through comparison and learning. This is why soft power is a luxury a small state can afford if it is prepared to risk scrutiny and the uncertainties of positive feedback within the context of generating its appeal to a wider community of states and peoples. Soft power is thus indistinct from strategies of resilience.

Note

* I wish to thank Jean Tan for invaluable research assistance in the preparation of the final section of this chapter.

References

Bakare, D. (2007) 'Corruption Control: The Singapore Model', *ICPC [Independent Corrupt Practices and Other Related Offences Commission] Monitor* 1 (3), https://app.scp.gov.sg/index.asp, accessed on 1 June 2008.

Boey, D. (2005) *Reaching Out – Operation Flying Eagle. SAF Humanitarian Assistance after the Tsunami* (Singapore: SNP).

Boyce, P. (1965) 'Policy without Authority: Singapore's External Affairs Power', *Journal of Southeast Asian History* 6 (2): 87–103.

Chong, A. (2006) 'Singapore's Foreign Policy Beliefs as "Abridged Realism": Pragmatic and Liberal Prefixes in the Foreign Policy Thought of Rajaratnam, Lee, Koh and Mahbubani', *International Relations of the Asia-Pacific* 6 (2): 269–306.

Chong, A. (2007) *Foreign Policy in Global Information Space: Actualizing Soft Power* (New York: Palgrave Macmillan).

Clinton, W.J. (1994) Transcript of Remarks by President Clinton on MTV's 'Enough is Enough' Forum on Crime, *US Newswire*, 19 April.

Commonwealth Secretariat (1997) *A Future for Small States: Overcoming Vulnerability. Report by a Commonwealth Advisory Group* (London: Commonwealth Secretariat).

Lim, L. (2005) 'HELP – Why Singapore Reached Out', *Straits Times (Singapore)*, 15 January.

Low, E. (2005) 'Top UN Relief Official Praises Singapore Efforts', *Straits Times (Singapore)*, 7 January.

Mahbubani, K. (2008) *The New Asian Hemisphere: The Irresistible Shift of Global Power to the East* (New York: Public Affairs).

Ministry of Foreign Affairs (2008a) 'Singapore Budget 2008 – Expenditure Overview: Ministry of Foreign Affairs', http://www.mof.gov.sg/budget_2008/expenditure_overview/mfa.html, accessed on 31 May 2008.

Ministry of Foreign Affairs (2008b) 'Budget Highlights: Financial Year 2008', http://www.mof.gov.sg/budget_2008/speech_toc/downloads/FY2008_Budget_Highlights.pdf, accessed on 31 May 2008.

Nye Jr., J.S. (2004) *Soft Power: The Means to Success in World Politics* (New York: Public Affairs).

Raffles, T.S. (1973) 'The Founding of Singapore. (Letter to Colonel Addenbrooke from Singapore, dated 10 June 1819)', in M. Sheppard (ed.) *150th Anniversary of the Founding of Singapore* (Singapore: Times Printers).

SCP (2008) 'About Us – Introduction to SCP', http://app.scp.gov.sg/, accessed on 31 May 2008.

Sim, C.Y. (2008) ' "Respect Autonomy of Disaster-Hit States" George Yeo says Outsiders must Accept that Affected Governments Know their Local Situations Better', *Sunday Times (Singapore)*, 18 May.

Zakaria, F. (1994) 'Culture is Destiny: A Conversation with Lee Kuan Yew', *Foreign Affairs* 73 (2): 109–26.

5

Dependency Governance and Future Political Development in the Non-Independent Caribbean

Carlyle G. Corbin

Since the formation of the United Nations in 1945, a doctrine of self-determination and absolute political equality has prevailed as the guideline for the decolonisation of the global South. However, after decades of progress and the actualisation of political autonomy for numerous small states, the process has stalled for the remaining small, non-independent territories. Cosmopolises such as the US and UK are now exercising a top-down authority over their dependent territories through policies that while ensuring sustained economic progress, have created a democratic deficit and political vulnerability based on unequal status.

An historical context

At the beginning of the twentieth century, the international process was dominated by Europe with vast territorial holdings in Africa, Asia and the Pacific, and Latin America and the Caribbean. The United States as a newer colonial power acquired the territories of Guam, the Philippines, Cuba and Puerto Rico after the defeat of Spain in the Spanish-American War in 1899. The Danish West Indies was also acquired by the United States from Denmark (1917) for military strategic considerations surrounding the First World War.

In the Americas territorial holdings have been considerable with the Dutch in the Netherlands Antilles and Dutch Guiana; the French in Martinique, Guadeloupe and French Guiana; the Portuguese in Brazil; the Spanish in other parts of pre-independent Latin America; the British in large parts of the English-speaking Caribbean.

By the end of the Second World War, the political status of most of the territories under colonial rule still remained unresolved, and a motivating factor in the creation of the United Nations in 1945 was devising means of determining the disposition of these territories. This was the genesis of the era of decolonisation, with Articles 1 and 55 of the United Nations Charter (1945) maintaining the fundamental purpose and principle 'to develop friendly relations among nations based on respect for the principle of equal rights and self-determination of peoples'. Three additional chapters of the Charter were devoted to the dependent territories (United Nations, 1990a: 4), as 72 dependencies were placed voluntarily on the United Nations non self-governing list by the respective administering powers (United Nations, 1946).

Between 1946 and 1959 eight of these territories became independent while 21 others were removed from the United Nations list on account mostly of what were deemed significant constitutional changes in their political relationship with the cosmopolitan country. Resolutions were adopted by the United Nations General Assembly validating these changes, resulting in the de-listing of Puerto Rico (1953), as well as the Netherlands Antilles (1955), neither of which had explicit rights to modify their political status through a process of self-determination in accordance with their constitution/charter (Igarashi, 2002: 42–62). The French territories in the Caribbean and Pacific were removed from the United Nations list unilaterally without benefit of United Nations concurrence (United Nations, 1990a: 5).

The United Nations' adoption in 1960 of the Decolonisation Declaration, and a companion resolution defining the three legitimate models of political equality, gave important clarity to the prerequisites for a full measure of self-government sufficient to remove a territory from non self-governing designation (Corbin, 2006a: 3). The addition of 16 newly independent African states to the United Nations in 1960 gave further impetus to decolonisation, resulting in the acceleration of the process of self-determination for many of the Caribbean territories. This was most noted in the independence of a first wave of small island Caribbean countries including Jamaica and Trinidad and Tobago in 1962, Barbados and Guyana in 1966, the Bahamas in 1973 and Grenada in 1974, following the break-up of the Federation of the West Indies in 1962.

The formulation of the West Indies Associated States model in 1967 was put forth by the United Kingdom as a compromise between the political expectations of the remaining smaller Caribbean territories under British administration and prevailing perceptions which questioned the viability of microstates (Geiser et al., 1976: 22). The new arrangement included the territories of Antigua, Dominica, Grenada, St Kitts–Nevis–Anguilla, St Lucia and St Vincent, and was the latest attempt by the British at multi-island dependency governance to date (Igarashi, 2002: 116–17).

An important rationale for this approach was to devise an internationally acceptable governance model in response to intensified United Nations focus on the prevailing colonial arrangements. A United Nations assessment of the West Indies Associated States model undertaken in 1967 determined, however, that it did not meet the standard of free association as adopted by the General Assembly in Resolution 1541 (XV) of 1960, and that the decolonisation mandate still applied to those territories. This association later dissolved with the attainment of independence by its individual countries beginning with Grenada (1974), followed by Dominica (1978), St Lucia (1979), St Vincent (1979), Antigua and Barbuda (1981) and St Kitts and Nevis (1983).

By the middle of the 1980s, Bermuda, Turks and Caicos Islands, Cayman Islands, Montserrat, Anguilla and the British Virgin Islands, under United Kingdom administration, and the US Virgin Islands, under United States jurisdiction, all remained as non self-governing territories. With the independence of Namibia at the beginning of the 1990s, most of the remaining 17 non-self-governing territories were small island developing countries in the Caribbean and Pacific.

Contemporary dependency and self-governing models

From 1990 through 2008 only Timor-Leste achieved a full measure of self-government, and among the 16 non self-governing territories left behind are those which remain the subject of sovereignty disputes (Gibraltar, Western Sahara, Falklands Islands/Malvinas). These began to dominate United Nations deliberations, limiting the attention paid to the small territories. Accordingly, the decolonisation process has largely stalled, according to a 2007 report of the United Nations Office of Internal Oversight Services (United Nations, 2007b: 1). It has been concluded that the lack of success in the contemporary decolonisation process is directly proportionate to the lack of implementation of United Nations decolonisation resolutions (Trask, 2008: 4).

In addition to the non self-governing arrangements in the Caribbean and Pacific, there are also a number of self-governing models which have been legitimised by the international community. The Netherlands Antilles and Aruba emerged as self-governing countries in association with the Kingdom of the Netherlands through autonomous measures contained in the Kingdom Charter, while the erstwhile dependent territories of Guadeloupe, Martinique and French Guiana became politically integrated/assimilated into the French Republic. The former New Zealand-administered territories of the Cook Islands and Niue developed acceptable autonomous association arrangements, and the Federated States of Micronesia, the Marshall Islands and Palau negotiated an equally valid but different form of association with the United States influenced by Cold War military considerations.

The dependency periphery

There are also territories which could be considered in a dependency periphery. These include Puerto Rico, which was removed from the United Nations non self-governing list before the criteria for full self-government was fully defined (Corbin, 2003: 3) and French Polynesia, which was removed from non self-governing status unilaterally without United Nations concurrence. Since there is no United Nations mechanism to review de-listed territories, no formal assessment of the level of self-governance of these models has been undertaken.

Concerns over premature de-listing from formal United Nations reviews have been consistently expressed. The former president of French Polynesia noted in 2007 that 'it is vital that [French Polynesia] be re-inscribed on the list of non self-governing territories at the United Nations Decolonization Committee' (Temaru, 1997: 6).

Political actors in Puerto Rico in recent years have taken a different approach, having failed to gain the re-listing of Puerto Rico in the 1990s. By 2005 the focus was shifted to achieving a United Nations decision to add the case of Puerto Rico as a separate United Nations agenda item. This strategy was endorsed by the three active political parties in the territory in statements to the United Nations Special Committee on Decolonisation in 2006 and 2007. The Committee, in turn, adopted a 2007 resolution which 'requests the General Assembly to consider the question of Puerto Rico comprehensively in all its aspects' (United Nations, 2007a: 8). If this request was granted, the procedure would be similar to the General Assembly's actions towards the French-administered (but non-listed) Indian Ocean territory of Mayotte.

The individual islands of the Netherlands Antilles may also be emerging into the dependency periphery category in the wake of the ongoing process of political dismantling under way in 2008 as a result of earlier referenda on each of its five islands. The two major islands, Curacao and Sint Maarten, are slated to become separate countries in the Kingdom of the Netherlands, but would not be as autonomous as the present Netherlands Antilles model of association, particularly in the areas of financial management and security. This developing model does not sit well with much of the political leadership in Curacao, the capital of the more autonomous Netherlands Antilles until the restructuring of the five-island grouping is completed. These concerns appear not as immediate in Sint Maarten where, under the present arrangement, the main preoccupation is the ability to deal directly with Amsterdam, rather than through the central government in Curacao. Whether this weaker autonomous model of association conforms to the minimum standards of self-government in association is the subject of significant concern, especially in Curacao (Corbin, 2006b: 2).

The other three smaller Dutch islands of Bonaire, St Eustatius and Saba have opted for political integration as overseas provinces of the Dutch Kingdom. The consequence of this new reduction of local governance is only surpassed by the potential repercussions to the wider Caribbean of three new parts of the European Union appearing in the region, with implications for the exclusive economic zone, and other resource and security considerations.

Governance and political equality

While the self-governing countries and the integrated departments in the Caribbean have met international standards of self government through the attainment of integration, free association or independence, the non self-governing territories have yet to be provided an opportunity to decide on a legitimate political status through a popular consultation in the form of an acceptable act of self-determination. Over time this has resulted in the development of complex dependency arrangements, which do not meet the minimum requirements of full self-government as defined by international norms of democratic governance. The view that some territories are content with the status quo political standing, despite their inherent democratic deficiencies, is indicative of the existent information deficit on the relevance of the international decolonisation process to the political development of non self-governing territories (Lewis, 2004: 1). The lack of such information available to the territories has been a persistent theme articulated by representatives of elected territorial governments and non-governmental organisations alike.

Accordingly, awareness of the principles of complete and absolute political equality is critical if the people of the territories are to develop a full measure of self-government. This perspective has been consistently articulated by Caribbean member states at the United Nations in the international debate on decolonisation since the beginning of the First International Decade for the Eradication of Colonialism in

1992. This regional position has contributed significantly to countering the argument that the territories have passively evolved into an acceptable form of self-government as a result of certain internal colonial reforms, albeit without the necessary rebalancing of the power relationship between the territories and their respective administering powers. Reference to the existing dependency models is illustrative of this conclusion.

In the British dependent territories, modifications to the internal constitutional arrangements announced in a new 1999 United Kingdom policy were clear examples of changes in form, but not in substance (OTR, 1999: 1–4). Hence, the difference in nomenclature from *dependent* to *overseas* territories was coupled with the overriding retention of the United Kingdom's powers of unilateral authority to legislate for the territories through the mechanism of order-in-council, and to administer the islands through reserved constitutional powers of the British-appointed governor. It is to be emphasised that the modernisation of the dependency arrangements, as envisaged in the 1999 policy, was not intended to fundamentally change the political status of the territories *vis à vis* the United Kingdom. This was duly confirmed in an updated United Kingdom policy document published in 2007, which indicated that 'overseas territories governments should not expect that in the constitutional reviews currently under way the UK will agree to changes in the UK Government's reserved powers' (OTR, 2007b: 5).

Yet, even as the policy confirmed the continuation of the status quo, a strategy of 'colonial accommodation' was devised with the aim of gaining international legitimacy for the prevailing dependency arrangements as forms of self-governance (OTR, 2007a: 6–9). This is evident in the position of the United Kingdom representative who, in a statement to the United Nations Fourth Committee in October, 1998 argued that 'in no cases have territories remained British through coercion or repression (or) have been denied the opportunity to make their views known'. It is unclear, however, by what method the people of these territories had chosen to remain in their present dependency status since the available options have been limited to either independence, or continued and enhanced dependency status.

The United Kingdom policy did provide for the replacement of the dependent territory citizenship with that of British citizenship, permitting the right of abode in Britain, but provided no accompanying political powers such as voting rights and representation in the legislative body of the cosmopolis enjoyed by other British citizens. It is to be emphasised that such political powers are essential elements of full civil and political rights, as recognised by the International Covenant on Civil and Political Rights, as well as other human rights instruments.

The modernised dependency arrangements provide for further applicability of other British and European Union laws and regulations, including the application of European Union, Organisation of Economic Cooperation and Development (OECD), and Financial Action Task Force (FATF) regulations affecting the financial sector, and the further application of European Union laws on human rights through orders-in-council on issues in relation to corporal and capital punishment. Pressures continue to mount on the territories such as Anguilla and the Cayman Islands to include language in the bill of rights sections of new constitutional provisions under review, which are considered adverse to the social and religious norms of those respective societies.

At the same time, the elected governments of the British-administered territories continue to emphasise the importance of devolution of power – as opposed to its reversible delegation – as critical to the evolution towards democratic governance, while the United Kingdom continues to state that such devolution of power would only be granted if accompanied by a timetable for independence. Within this political landscape, the elected leadership of the Turks and Caicos Islands, and the British Virgin Islands were able to achieve through negotiation significant delegation of authority in their new constitutions of 2006 and 2007, respectively, even as these powers are subject to constitutional override by the British government.

While the prevailing contemporary colonial conditions continue to pertain, the United Kingdom continues to articulate in the United Nations debates that 'the colonial era is over, and that colonialism as a practice is dead'. This contrasts deeply with the objective reality that unilateral authority, rather than democratic self-government, still characterises the governance model. Because of the absence of the views of the elected governments of most territories in international decolonisation deliberations, the colonial contentment argument continues to be made without sufficient challenges.

International principles of governance also have resonance in the US dependencies in the Caribbean. The case of the US Virgin Islands is especially relevant in the wake of the inconclusive political status referendum held in 1993 resulting in a state of political dormancy. Unlike Bermuda where only the political option of independence was before the voters in its 1995 referendum, the US Virgin Islands referendum in 1993 had seven options, many of which were as indistinguishable to the voters as they were to the political status commission responsible for public education. This led to predictably significant confusion, with the inconclusive result more a function of the lack of awareness of the political options within the community than an acceptance of the status quo dependency arrangement. However, this did not prevent the result from being projected in the international community as a vote in favour of colonialism by consent. The territory reverted in 2007 to the election of the Fifth Constitutional Convention with the mandate to draft an internal constitution in compliance with the present dependency status. This limits the exercise to one of colonial reform, but is touted by United States authorities as a significant step in the political development process.

This perspective was articulated by the United States representative before the United Nations Fourth Committee as early as October 1998 when questions were raised as to the efficacy of applying the term non self-governing to the United States administered territories. The representative argued that the phrase was 'not wholly applicable to residents ... who are able to establish their own constitution, who elect their territory's public officers and who have a voice in the US Congress'. This incomplete description of the political status of US territories failed to acknowledge the fundamental limitations on the political rights of the people that caused the territory to be listed as non self-governing in the first instance. These limitations were addressed in a 1998 statement of the United Nations Association of the Virgin Islands (UNAVI) to the Fourth Committee of the United Nations which outlined the political inequality inherent in the present political relationship in the US territories. The statement identified such areas as lack of voting rights in the US political process, the requirement that territorial constitutions be written in compliance with the unilateral application of United States laws and the lack of voting representation in the United States Congress. The report emphasised that these conditions were indicative of a political relationship in which the vested authority of the territory is not with the people, but rather in the US Congress in which the territory has no vote. It questioned how such an unequal political arrangement could be projected as a legitimate form of democratic governance.

Notwithstanding these clarifications, the 1998 United States statement to the Fourth Committee continued to call for the territories under its administration to be 'dis-inscribed' from non self-governing territories status, although nothing in the argument could be supported by any reasonable criteria of self-determination. The real intent appeared to be the redefinition of the present arrangements as self-governing for the sole purpose of removing the nuisance of international oversight on decolonisation. The 1998 United States policy statement with respect to the US Virgin Islands went on to argue that the people 'prefer the current arrangement and [have] freely select[ed] that status'. In the wake of the documented inconclusive results of the 1993 referendum, which was declared null and void, it is clear that the people have not expressed support or rejection of the present status, but reverted to it by default. Further, any concurrence of such an arrangement, given the prevailing democratic deficiencies, could only be due to a genuine lack of awareness among the people of the genuine political status options available to them. This lack of awareness is common among people of many of the small island territories in the Caribbean and Pacific despite decades of un-implemented United Nations resolutions calling for public education programmes to explain the legitimate political options.

A further United States policy shift rejecting the three internationally recognized political status alternatives is also significant given that the US had until then historically supported the relevance of political integration and free association, respectively, as a counterweight to previous United Nations emphasis on independence.

Since no constitutional changes have taken place in any of the remaining non self-governing territories to meet objective criteria of self-determination, the new United Kingdom and United States policies, if endorsed by UN member states, could leave the territories in a perpetual state of political and constitutional dependency. So far the international community has maintained its stance in support of international principles of self-determination. It is unclear, however, how long this support can be sustained as diplomatic pressures are brought to bear on many United Nations member states whose voting records and policies are subject to heightened scrutiny, and often linked to developed country economic support.

There is also the factor of decolonisation fatigue, which appears to be growing even among a number of countries of the Non Aligned Movement, which themselves had earlier emerged from colonialism. Even though these countries have consistently supported the principles of self-determination and decolonisation, some are growing increasingly frustrated at the lack of progress on implementing the decolonisation mandate as the Second International Decade for the Eradication of Colonialism hastens to an end.

Colonial accommodation

In the context of the present political climate, it is to be recalled that the attempted legitimisation of the prevailing dependency arrangements has been a strategy attempted for decades. In a 1990 United Nations seminar held in Barbados on constitutional advancement in the non-independent Caribbean, the model of protectorate status was proposed for the British territories in the Caribbean as an alternative to what was termed the economic infeasibility of independence and the inflexibility of free association. The seminar ultimately dismissed the legitimacy of the arrangement as not sufficiently self-governing and reaffirmed the importance of maintaining the minimum standards of autonomy required in the free association definition (United Nations, 1990b).

The model of sustained autonomy was introduced three years later in 1993 for the French- and New Zealand-administered territories in the Pacific at the United Nations Decolonisation Seminar in Papua New Guinea. The model introduced the concept of a retained 'residual power' for the cosmopolitan country to make laws for the territory, with cosmopolitan country jurisdiction over criminal and civil proceedings of the judiciary, among other areas. As in the case of the Barbados Seminar in 1990, this model was rejected on similar grounds of insufficient autonomy (United Nations General Assembly, 1993).

Also proposed in 1993 was a model of partial incorporation of the United States territories with the grant of participation in US presidential elections via one collective Electoral College vote shared by the five territories. It did not advocate for direct participation in the United States legislative process, a fundamental tenant of full political rights. The spectre of one-fifth of one Electoral College vote in exchange for the privilege of probable revenue diversion from the territorial to the United States treasuries was not particularly appealing to territorial representatives (Corbin, 2003: 11).

Similar ideas were offered for the British territories, particularly the 1998 legislative Representation of Dependencies at Westminster Bill which would have permitted a non-voting petitioner from the individual British territory to address the House of Commons from the bar on relevant issues that the Speaker of the House determined to be related exclusively to that territory. This concept, based on the non-voting delegate model of partial representation of the US territories in the US House of Representatives (lower house) of the Congress, was not included in the 1999 British dependent territory policy (Corbin, 2003: 11).

International support for continued vigilance

After a period of post-Cold War adjustment from an East–West to a North–South paradigm of international relations, the global community, for the most part, has continued to state its support for political equality as the continual standard for the remaining territories. Caribbean countries have been especially clear in this respect. In a 2000 statement to the UN General Assembly on behalf of the Caribbean Community (CARICOM), Antigua and Barbuda ambassador Dr Patrick A. Lewis reaffirmed the longstanding CARICOM recognition that 'none of the non self-governing territories in the Caribbean have met the essential criteria of full and absolute political equality as defined by the UN General Assembly in its landmark resolutions'.

Ambassador Lewis went on to confirm that: 'these principles of political equality must remain the operative standard to be applied to the self-determination process of the remaining territories [and] is essential in order to avoid the inadvertent legitimisation by the international community of un-equal, politically dependent, arrangements that still characterise the present political status of those territories.'

The linkage of human rights conventions and the contemporary decolonisation process was also reaffirmed by Caribbean governments. Ambassador Julian R. Hunte of St Lucia in a 2000 statement to the Third Committee of the General Assembly supported UN Secretary-General Kofi Annan's expression in his 2000 annual report that defined 'self-determination as a fundamental human right in the Charter of the United Nations, the two principal human rights covenants, the Declaration on the Right to Development, and other international instruments and declarations'. Ambassador Hunte pointed out that 'increased attention is being paid to the issue of self-determination by the Commission on Human Rights, which adopts resolutions on the issue, and by the Human Rights Committee, which considers periodic reports on compliance with the International Covenant on Civil and Political Rights'. He also referred to support in the 2000 Millennium Declaration which upheld 'the right to self-determination of peoples under colonial rule'.

Subsequent expressions in this light were made by CARICOM countries before the Third and Fourth Committees throughout the present decade. In 2007 the statement of the 14 independent CARICOM states was delivered by Ambassador Crispen Gregoire of Dominica to the United Nations Fourth Committee, who noted that 'the people of these territories continue to express their concerns ... regarding the democratic deficiencies inherent in the arrangements governing them, and regarding the inconsistency of United Nations action in accelerating the decolonisation process'. He emphasised 'the importance of undertaking the necessary measures to bring the era of new millennium colonialism to a conclusion, and fully endorse[d] the [decolonisation] measures contained in United Nations resolutions, and in the United Nations budget'.

These statements of support for the principles of self-determination and resultant decolonisation reaffirm the international consensus on the importance of the contemporary self-determination process. The differences in perspective on these issues between the administering powers and most of the rest of the international community lie in the specific aspects of the political status of the dependency, and whether those elements conform to the principles of political equality. In this sense, the objective reality clearly favours the realisation that the basic principles of political equality, as defined in international instruments, are essential to the development of true democratic governance, and the adherence to such principles by those states which administer territories would effectively accelerate the process of self-determination.

From dependency to self-governance

For the remaining small island territories, the devolution of power and the provision of more autonomy to the elected governments are vital to fostering their political and economic future as they proceed towards full and absolute political equality, either by full integration with an independent state, free association with an independent state, or independence. Increasing autonomy can take many forms as governments of these territories mature and systematically develop the capacity to take on more powers. Thus, there exists an organic link between the attainment of more autonomy and the capacity to minimise economic vulnerability to the international market. In this regard it has been established that, in addition to the vulnerabilities of small size, economies of scale, distance from external markets, limited economic diversification and other factors shared with fellow small island developing countries, the non-independent territories are also faced with the added vulnerability of the democracy deficit that characterises the system of dependency governance. Accordingly, the inability of these territories to manoeuvre autonomously within the international economic system limits their resiliency to external shocks.

In a number of territories, where the economic progress has been steady and sustained, the insufficiency of autonomous authority in order to react quickly to fast-paced developments in a globalised world remains a formidable challenge to their adaptive capacity. Lobbying for the delegation of authority or an entrustment on a particular competence is a far too cumbersome procedure. European policy unilaterally imposed on the international financial sector of these territories by such bodies as the Organisation of Economic Cooperation and Development (OECD), among others, renders the important financial sector particularly vulnerable to subjective assessment, especially when the offshore sector in the territories becomes an attractive and competitive alternative for international investment. The provision in the British dependent territory policy limiting the borrowing authority of the territories is another illustration which weakens the resilience of these territories to effectively engage the international economic system.

These challenges are especially glaring since most of the British-administered territories no longer receive financial grant-in-aid from the United Kingdom, and feel that their internal economic decisions should be their own. Montserrat as the one territory still receiving grant-in-aid, largely due to the aftermath of the volcanic crisis, has itself been thwarted by the United Kingdom's lack of concurrence with the territory's request to foster its own economic sustainability through regional economic integration with the emerging Caribbean Community Single Market and Economy (CSME).

At the same time the United States territories, whether in the Caribbean or Pacific, are in varying stages of economic difficulty with high debt ratios in relation to their gross national product, and are more dependent than ever on grant programmes from Washington. This serves to limit their perspective on future political options, and a psychological dependence on US support has emerged in earnest. Their interest in building resiliency through regional economic and technical cooperation or integration has also been severely limited, whether in the denial of the US Virgin Islands to seek associate membership in CARICOM and the Organisation of Eastern Caribbean States (OECS), or similar restrictions against American Samoa and Guam in regards to the Pacific Islands Forum.

Within this framework it is remarkable that most of the non-independent territories in the Caribbean have been able to maintain encouraging levels of economic performance. Some have argued that the retention of the constitutional link with the larger countries is a major contributing factor to their economic sustainability, while others attribute their resilience to the internal economic stewardship despite the stated constraints.

In the specific case of the British territories in the Caribbean, the continued unilateral authority exercised by the administering power could result in an unintended/intended effect of nudging these territories into independence, especially since the British have removed the options of free association and integration from the negotiating table. Further, the longstanding United Kingdom position that any real devolution of power would be granted only within the context of a timetable for independence has framed the debate. It may be the case that some of the territories in 2008 may be ready to seriously consider such a timetable if they determine that continued constitutional dependency might impede their future sustainable development.

Conclusion

As has been displayed throughout this chapter, the process of ensuring absolute political equality, as mandated by the UN Charter, has increasingly slowed, if not almost come to a complete halt. This lack of progress has been the source of great frustration for the allies of decolonisation. The volatility of current global markets reveals a requirement for states to have the freedom and mobility to quickly and effectively adapt to change. The lack of self-determination currently existent in the governance structures of the majority of non self-governing territories, has left them vulnerable to the shocks of the new global system and in a perpetual state of inequality.

References

Convention between the United States and Denmark Providing for the Cession of West Indies, 17 January 1917, New York, US Treaty Series, No. 629.

Corbin, Carlyle (2003) 'Governance, Dependency and Future Political Development in the Non-Independent Caribbean', Paper presented to the *Society for Caribbean Studies Conference*, Bristol University, United Kingdom.

Corbin, Carlyle (2006a) 'Criteria for the Cessation of Transmission of Information Under Article 73(e)', *Overseas Territories Report*, 5 (5).

Corbin, Carlyle (2006b) 'Decolonization and Self-Government in the Netherlands Antilles', *Overseas Territories Report*, 5 (3).

Geiser, Hans J., Pamela Alleyne and Carrol Gajraj (1976) *Legal Problems of Caribbean Integration* (St Augustine: Institute of International Relations).

Igarashi, Masahiro (2002) *Associated Statehood in International Law* (The Hague, London and New York: Kluwer Law International).

Lewis, Patrick (2004) Statement on Behalf of Antigua and Barbuda to the Organisational Session of the Special Committee on Decolonisation, 11 February.

Overseas Territories Review (1999) 'British Territories Review Options in Wake of UK Policy Announcement', 2 (5).

Overseas Territories Review (2007a) 'UN Struggles to Implement International Decolonization Agenda', Special Edition (May).

Overseas Territories Review (2007b) 'UK to Extend Control Over its Colonies', 2 (5).

Temaru, Oscar (1997) *Independence and Sovereignty for Te Ao Maohi* (Faa'a Tahiti: Te Ao Maohi/French Polynesia).

Trask, Mililani (2008) *Statement on the United Nations Decolonization Process: Collective Global Intervention of the Pacific, the Caribbean and Puerto Rico*, Seventh Session of the United Nations Permanent Forum on Indigenous Issues, New York.

United Nations (1946) *Transmission of Information under Article 73(e) of the United Nations Charter*, Resolution 66/1, 14 December (New York: United Nations General Assembly).

United Nations (1990a) 'Thirty Years of the Decolonisation Declaration', Department of Special Political Questions, Regional Cooperation, Decolonisation and Trusteeship, Publication No. 39 (New York: United Nations).

United Nations (1990b) *Report of the Regional Seminar in Observance of the Thirtieth Anniversary of the (Decolonization) Declaration*, Barbados, A/AC.109/1043.

United Nations (2007a) *Report of the Special Committee on the Situation with regard to the implementation of the Declaration on the Granting of Independence to Colonial Countries and Peoples*, Special Committee Decision of 12 June 2006 concerning Puerto Rico, New York, A/62/23.

United Nations (2007b) *Report of the Office of Internal Oversight Services on the in-depth evaluation of political affairs: decolonization and question of Palestine*, Report to the Committee on Programme and Coordination, New York, E/AC.51/2007/2/Add. 3.

United Nations General Assembly (UNGA) (1993) *International Decade for the Eradication of Colonialism*, Report on the Regional Seminar to Review the Political, Economic and Social Conditions in the Small Island Non-self-governing Territories, 8–10 June, Papua New Guinea, A/AC.109/1159.

6
The Diplomacy of Caribbean Community States: Searching for Resilience

Jacqueline Anne Braveboy-Wagner

Since the end of the Cold War, a majority of nations have reassessed their foreign policy directions and strategies, and have restructured their foreign services to meet today's challenges. This chapter summarises these challenges and their effects on the content and conduct of diplomacy in the small Caribbean Community (CARICOM) states, focusing primarily on the larger Caribbean countries.[1]

International perceptions of small state and Caribbean diplomacy

The international community's perspectives with respect to the problems of small developing states have changed contextually over the years, matched by changes in the foreign policies of the small states themselves. In specifically referring here to small-sized 'developing' states, I differentiate from past literature's focus on the small states of Europe which, though sharing a sense of security and resource vulnerability with all the late-emerging small-sized states, have been able to advance economically – some to a very high level – by adopting smart financial, agricultural, or manufacturing strategies at a time when the world was relatively accommodating to their needs. On the other hand, the developing countries as a group (small and large) have had their socio-economic progress hampered by a range of circumstances, including: political and economic legacies of the colonial enterprise; the decolonisation process; the difficulties of reducing their economic dependence on the northern countries once they became independent; the lasting effect of the Cold War polarities; the internal ethno-political conflict artificially muted during the Cold War; their own wanting efforts at governance; severe social problems stemming from rapid modernisation and industrialisation; and the inexorable deepening of global integration.

In the 1960s, when a number of small developing states in Africa and the Caribbean became independent, the international community – which had accepted the wealthier Luxembourg and Iceland into the United Nations in 1945 and 1946 respectively – began debating the viability of small states based largely on prevailing perceptions of sovereignty (for more, see Braveboy-Wagner, 2003: 152–4). Some considered these states to be quasi-sovereign and not likely to be able to properly meet the responsibilities of global citizenship. As late as 1977 the suggestion was made that small states should not be granted 'full status and rights in the councils of the collective global community' and they should not participate in the 'broader international conferences, organizations and affairs', dealing with matters 'distant to their national interest' (Plischke, 1977: 24).

Unequal status was, however, clearly not acceptable to the emerging developing states, no matter how small. In the atmosphere of heightened expectations engendered by the wave of decolonisation, the new Non-Aligned developing nations were eager to have their voice heard and respected in the United Nations and other global fora. Fortunately for them, despite some 'big power' reluctance, the UN placed the principle of sovereign equality over other instrumental calculations. Armed with their equal votes, the new states were able to expand the membership of the Security Council and the Economic and Social Council, still today the most significant changes that the UN has undergone since its inception.

The first small Caribbean states that emerged to independence at this time – Jamaica and shortly thereafter Trinidad and Tobago (1962), followed by Barbados and Guyana (1966) – shared the view that their activities should extend beyond the local/regional arena, even though they moved early to create a regional free trade area. The UN was particularly important to them as a forum allowing each of them to have a global voice. Thus by the mid-1970s they had claimed such elective offices at the UN as the vice presidency of the General Assembly (Trinidad and Tobago in 1966, followed by the other three states), the chairmanship (Jamaica and Trinidad and Tobago) and vice chairmanship (Guyana in particular) of various General Assembly committees, as well as less visible positions (Braveboy-Wagner, 2007: 130–4). Moreover, Jamaica and Trinidad and Tobago opened additional missions to the UN offices in Geneva early on, as well as Washington DC, as the English-speaking Caribbean states chose to become members of the hemispheric Organization of American States (OAS), beginning with Trinidad and Tobago in 1967. (Guyana, however, was excluded from joining the OAS because of its border dispute with Venezuela.) These multilateral linkages promoted by the newly independent CARICOM states supplemented the non-regional bilateral links with the United States, Canada, and Europe that they established primarily for economic purposes. Still, an early sign of their desire for diversification of external ties could be seen in the establishment of Guyana's embassies in Brazil and Venezuela, Jamaica's embassy in Mexico, and Trinidad and Tobago's embassies in Brazil, Venezuela and India.

By the late 1970s, the global community had largely left behind the unresolved debate over sovereignty and viability, and policy attention was diverted instead to the large-scale development concerns of *all* the emerging nations. The Non-Aligned Movement and the Group of 77 caucus had already embarked on their quest for a New International Economic Order intended to foster greater equity between the developed North and the postcolonial South. Developing countries had turned their attention to the issue of neocolonialism and the problems of excessive and continuing dependence on the metropolitan powers. Countries were eager to reduce the economic (and cultural) domination of the North and to claim autonomous space in *political* decision making as well. The UN was fully engaged in this debate, offering various solutions for improving the terms of trade and for more aid to, and investment in, developing countries. In particular, with respect to small states, the UN sought to adopt special policies for small-island developing states as well as least-developed nations and land-locked nations. A wide range of social subjects were also on the UN's agenda, spurring the first set of global conferences on food, population, the environment, the habitat, child welfare, and gender, among others. In all of these activities the small nations of the Caribbean (the 'Big Four' now having been joined by the other islands and Belize), were strong participants. Moreover, after having adopted generic pro-West policies after independence, the English-speaking Caribbean states were caught up in the third world's alternative experiments, opting for more nationalistic stances both at home and abroad, and in some cases, for outright socialist strategies (specifically, Guyana, Jamaica, and Grenada). The more nationalistic they were at home, the more expansive their diplomatic linkages across the third world and the socialist bloc. They also tried to deepen their self-reliance (as recommended by the UN) by strengthening their regional integration movement, that is, forming the Caribbean Community in 1973, and by trying to diversify their trade and technical cooperation with such advanced developing countries as India and Brazil.

In the 1980s the growth of environmentalism and concerns about resource depletion were added to the global agenda at a time when successive oil price increases brought on global recession. Policies of structural adjustment were adopted by or imposed upon most developing countries by the international financial institutions, as economic liberalisation began to be heavily promoted by the United States, which was later to be taken up by other developed countries, as well. Meanwhile, the notion of 'vulnerability' took centre stage in policy discussions involving small states, who were seen as particularly vulnerable to economic and environmental threats, domestic, political and ideological conflict, uncivil transnational elements (such as drug traffickers) and to the traditional threats emanating from great powers and larger neighbours. Therefore, while still looking for multilateral help to resolve these problems, CARICOM states, like other developing nations, began to focus more on domestic development issues and to favour the use of bilateral foreign policy strategies rather than multilateral 'posturing' (as some saw it).

The late 1980s (bringing with them the end of the Cold War) and the 1990s were characterised by the deepening of the global trend toward liberalisation and increasing attention to the process of globalisation. As small states worried about their ability to compete in a liberal economic world, they sought 'special and differential treatment' in their trade negotiations. Such treatment was theoretically acceptable to the newly-formed World Trade Organization (WTO), although it proved to be a less effective bargaining strategy in hemispheric and bilateral negotiations. In any event, caught off guard by global developments, CARICOM nations spent most of the 1990s attempting to preserve vital preferential trading arrangements with the North and to postpone complete trade liberalisation as long as possible. Slowly recognising the inevitability of global liberalisation, CARICOM states moved to accelerate their efforts at diversification of both domestic economic production and external trade partnerships, both of which have been carried forward into the 2000s.

Meanwhile, small developing states were also swept up by new security concerns. The events of 11 September 2001 intensified world-wide fear about radical Islamic terrorism, and imposed new burdens on small states, including CARICOM states, with respect to aviation, marine operations, trade, finance and almost all aspects of international business. Meanwhile, the march of globalisation intensified the effects of financial crime, drug trafficking, trafficking in arms and persons and other transnational problems on small countries; these effects required urgent cooperation between all countries, regardless of size.

Relevant new policies of the region

The 1990s saw a turn toward enhanced outward-looking regionalism throughout most of the world, and as a result CARICOM refocused its energies on strengthening its integration arrangements. The result was the launching of the CARICOM Single Market and Economy (CSME) in 2006, which aims to remove remaining restrictions on trade and the movement of capital, goods and labour across the region, while enhancing functional cooperation among its members. A revised institutional structure was put in place to facilitate this process.

The strengthening of regionalism has also represented an important step in the attempt to move away from a reliance on preferential trading arrangements with the United States, Canada and Europe. These arrangements have been of considerable benefit to the primary producing countries of the region allowing CARICOM countries to focus on working out gradual timetables for the inevitable liberalisation. As of 2008, regarding North America, this has taken the form of requests to extend the existing preferential arrangements with Canada (CARIBCAN) and the United States (CBTPA) while preparing for new free trade arrangements. In the case of Europe, an Economic Partnership Agreement, discussed elsewhere in this book, has already been signed anticipating liberalisation of most products traded between the two regions (including Cuba and the Dominican Republic) within 15 to 25 years.

At the hemispheric level, CARICOM's trading interests were threatened by the creation of the North American Free Trade Agreement (NAFTA) – but eased temporarily by 'NAFTA parity' – and there were divided voices as to the benefit of a Free Trade Area of the Americas (FTAA), which has since stalled and been replaced by a push for bilateral, bi-regional, and region-to-region accords. (Some CARICOM countries have also demonstrated interest in the Venezuelan-initiated alternative to the FTAA, the Bolivarian Alternative for the Americas (ALBA).) It is important to note that with the launch of the CSME the region is bound to rules prioritising negotiations as a unit with third parties. For this purpose the region established a Regional Negotiating Machinery in 1997. Even though the trade liberalisation process encompassed by the FTAA has stalled, the attendant Summit of the Americas process continues focusing on functional integration, with the full participation of CARICOM states.

In the larger world (or as some say, the 'glocal') arena, the CARICOM region has also been at the forefront of promoting sustainable development issues. Small-island developing states share unique environmental and economic vulnerabilities stemming from open economies, difficulties of achieving economies of scale, transportation difficulties, vulnerability to natural disasters, threats to biodiversity, threats to the marine ecology, threats emanating from climate change, and so on. The CARICOM states have been 'norm entrepreneurs' (Keck and Sikkink, 1998), helping to bring global attention to these special problems at UN environmental conferences, while consistently supporting measures to ensure environmental sustainability. However, significant differences remain between governments and local non-governmental groups in this regard.

The transnational security problems mentioned earlier have affected the region quite profoundly. The problems of drug trafficking and money laundering have not only created tensions with North America and Europe (particularly the dominant neighbour, the United States) but have also brought major threats to the social and institutional fabric of regional countries – that is, increased crime, health problems and criminal justice challenges, to list only a few. Likewise, the dependence of some countries on substantial offshore operations has brought them into conflict with developed countries. As already mentioned, regional states dependent on travel and trade with the United States have had to institute often financially onerous counter-terrorism measures (aviation and port controls, the introduction of machine-readable passports, vigilance in visa issuance and so on). Spurred by this need, the region has developed an architecture of security cooperation that belatedly represents some spill-over (to use the functionalist term) beyond the slow process of economic integration.

State (foreign) policies

While the preceding section discussed briefly what the region as a whole has done to accommodate global changes, the fact is that foreign policy is still very much a state-based activity; that is to say, it is conducted in the national or self-interest of states – not to be confused with the realist notion of pure power-seeking – and devised in the context of the uniqueness of domestic environments. It is, in other words, an 'inside–outside' activity, resting on the foundation of the legally constituted and internationally recognised state (Hill, 2003: 30–7).

Nevertheless, foreign policy (that is to say, the official purposive activities of states targeted towards the abroad) has clearly changed in both content and conduct as the world has modernised and become more integrated. In this respect, every author points to the breakdown of the international-domestic distinction and the emergence of non-state actors as significant players in world politics. Although the central state apparatus remains important to the devising and official conduct of foreign policy, today there is the increasing and independent involvement not only of many bureaucratic actors, but also of sub-state entities (like provinces, cities and counties in foreign policy) sometimes in a way that contradicts official policy. It is also clear that regional and international organisations have continued to expand their roles *vis-à-vis* states in international affairs. Similarly, the role of transnational entities, groups as well as corporations, has continued to grow along with the trend towards globalisation and liberalisation. Another change comes in the form of the rise of transnational civil society, that is to say, non-state international groups that advocate globally with state and international organisations. Transnational/global civil society goes beyond traditional labour and business organisations to include activists in a host of nongovernmental organisations, and epistemic communities concerned with social and environmental issues (Haas, 1992: 3; Keck and Sikkink, 1998).[2] Their mission is aided by linkages at the local, national and transnational level; their vigorous advocacy has earned them a place as information providers and purveyors of alternative public policy ideas at the decision-making tables of international organisations.

The foreign policy of CARICOM states today, as of all states, is impacted by these considerations. The strategies devised by officials, in the context of the particular and expanding configuration of interests, constitutes a formal foreign policy, but since other state agents also make 'foreign policy', the official policy is more representative of the extent that governments are able to coordinate the disparate voices and interests.

While scholars find it useful for various reasons to put small states into one analytical category (for example, Hey, 2003) – and while small states all tend to share an openness to external or systemic influences and to suffer from human resource and (in the case of developing states) financial limitations – from this foreign policy (inside-out) point of view, there is no blanket prescription for small countries when it comes to something as specific as devising foreign policy and designing foreign services. This applies to the category of 'small-island developing states' used earlier as well. There are some general similarities in the conduct of, and influences on, small-state foreign policy, but in the final analysis foreign policies are devised to suit *national* priorities and domestic social configurations. Thus, there can be no small-state foreign policy per se, only commonalities in foreign poli*cies*; that is, one can only speak of certain *issues* and strategies that such states might hold in common.

As noted earlier, there is wide recognition today that a new level of foreign policy initiation/coordination is developing at the regional level. However, except for the European Union (EU), no regional movement, certainly not CARICOM, has progressed to the stage where the region's bureaucrats dictate more than narrow administrative policies and economic regulations approved by, and dependent for their sustenance on, governments. CARICOM has no supranational structure and even in the purely economic arena, differences in national priorities and national circumstances continue to generate serious arguments and divisions.

It is generally accepted that developing countries hold as their first priority the achievement of economic development; thus the primary role of state foreign policy is to support and promote domestic economic policies. Because of the different types of economies within CARICOM, this means that beyond a general agreement by all states on basic economic integration matters, member countries will conduct dissimilar foreign economic policies. Thus, for example, Jamaica, with an economy focused on the export of bauxite, coffee and bananas as well as a heavy dependence on tourism, has logically been among the countries most involved in supporting international and bilateral initiatives to stabilise commodity prices and diversify the markets for commodities. Its foreign policy has been oriented towards searching for tourism niches and projecting abroad an image of stability and attractiveness to tourists. Jamaica earns significant revenue from its cultural tourism; hence its efforts in free trade negotiations are geared towards ensuring that European as well as other markets are as open as possible to its artistes as well as its products.

On the other hand, the Eastern Caribbean primary producers have exerted most of their efforts on preserving preferential arrangements with the developed countries. This is very different from the focus of Trinidad and Tobago. This energy-producing country must gear its policies towards preserving, expanding and diversifying the sources of foreign investment and the markets for its oil and gas, and must have in place the necessary diplomatic intelligence to monitor energy developments globally and regionally. (Developments in nearby Venezuela are particularly important.) Trinidad and Tobago is also the most industrialised country of CARICOM and a major exporter of manufactured goods to the region. Hence strategies have to be devised to support the role of manufacturers in the region and develop niches abroad.

These different interests are also clearly translated into different, and not necessarily compatible, geographical foci in foreign policy. While all Caribbean countries depend very heavily on the US market, Trinidad and Tobago's current interest is in serving as a bridge to Latin America. On

the other hand, the Bahamas, with a strong economy based on financial services and tourism, has long oriented its policies largely towards
the United States, eschewing membership in the Caribbean common
market. Eastern Caribbean countries have tended to remain focused on
traditional Northern partners. Belize's location in Central America has
dictated strengthening bilateral relations with its neighbours and membership in the Central American Integration System (SICA). Jamaica has
been in the forefront of diversifying towards Asia, opting in the 1980s
to send trade missions to Southeast Asia, opening the only CARICOM
embassy in Japan at a time when Japan was the world's economic superpower, and today turning its attention in a very deliberate way to trade
and investment with China. In the case of Suriname, the traditional
economic focus on the Netherlands is being supplemented by growing
relations with CARICOM as well as diversified linkages with the United
States and South America. Also, in keeping with new trends most CARI-
COM countries have begun to engage in vigorous foreign policy outreach
to a most important group of non-state actors: their huge diasporas resid-
ing in the North. Here, again, Trinidad and Tobago finds itself somewhat
at odds with its neighbours in that it is not highly dependent on diaspora remittances and therefore engages the diaspora relatively weakly.
For Trinidad and Tobago remittances amounted to 3.3 per cent of Gross
Domestic Product in 2006, whereas remittances for Jamaica were 18.3
per cent, and for Grenada and St Vincent 31.2 per cent and 26.4 per cent
respectively (International Fund for Agricultural Development, 2007:
14).

While the discussion has focused so far on economic strategies, CARI-
COM states also act differently in security and in multilateral diplomacy.
Guyana and Belize continue to face territorial threats from Venezuela
and Guatemala (however muted those may be today) and have therefore devised foreign policies – primarily multilateral alliances – intended
to ensure the continued preservation of their basic security. Suriname
has deepened security linkages with neighbouring Brazil. Jamaica and
Guyana have ambitions to acquire international status and have therefore emphasised strong performance in international organisations. On
the other hand, Trinidad and Tobago has used its economic resources
largely to cement its regional rather than global leadership, and is now
initiating technical assistance and outreach to African countries. Despite
their lack of resources, some of the smaller Eastern Caribbean countries
have also been very active in the UN, St Lucia having the distinction
of being the smallest country to assume the presidency of the General
Assembly (in 2003).

In sum, foreign policy is a unique enterprise wedded to each country's domestic configuration and needs. CARICOM countries, no matter how small, have differing priorities. Thus while the various national foreign policies often coincide, it is also true that national foreign policies and priorities clash, most often on economic issues – which is common in most integration movements – but most *notably* on political issues. Examples in the 2000s include severe disputes over the marine border and fishing rights between Trinidad and Tobago and Barbados, necessitating resolution of the first issue by the International Tribunal on the Law of the Sea, and conflict between Trinidad and Tobago and the rest of the region (except Barbados) with respect to Venezuela's offer of energy assistance under its PetroCaribe initiative – which is discussed elsewhere in this volume.

Resilience in diplomacy?

In view of what has been said about the regional and national policies that have been put in place, it can be said that today the CARICOM small states prioritise three facets of diplomacy: economic diplomacy first, that is, strategies that will allow both the states and the region to achieve their goals of economic development based on their particular economic structures; security diplomacy to deal particularly with the new transnational threats; and some combination of consular/diasporic diplomacy to help achieve both security as well as economic goals. In addition, it should be noted that *human* security (including poverty alleviation) is a concept that has been supported strongly by CARICOM states, as is the concept of environmental sustainability. One would expect that the adherence to these goals would be reflected primarily in vigorous multilateral diplomacy. This is not to suggest that CARICOM states have specifically defined their diplomacy in these terms. Rather, these conclusions are drawn inductively. In particular, most governments have issued directions since the 1990s to their diplomats to prioritise economic diplomacy and, since the 2000s, security and consular affairs have gained in significance.

Since research on small states has turned from an emphasis on vulnerability to a focus on 'resilience' (as noted in the Introduction to this book), a pertinent question that can be asked here is: to what extent has CARICOM demonstrated a capacity for diplomatic resilience? Unfortunately, as noted earlier, CARICOM states were slow to respond to global economic changes. In other areas they have engaged in piecemeal *ad hoc* approaches in dealing with new dilemmas, treating issues only as they arise and usually under pressure from external forces, rather than pursuing well-planned diplomatic strategies.

Part of the problem stems from the decline of the foreign services, especially in the areas of forward planning and intelligence gathering. As other bureaucratic units have risen in prominence, the role of these services has been overlooked. In the rest of this chapter I consider some reasons for this decline and what needs to be done to improve the capacity of the services to ensure that they are able to engage in proactive diplomacy. As background, however, it is worthwhile to consider what other foreign services are doing and what the expanding responsibilities of diplomats today are.

How have others adapted?

Since the 1990s foreign ministries around the world have been retooling in order to meet new objectives formulated by their governments in order to reflect the new global realities. For example, a White Paper prepared by the UK Foreign and Commonwealth Office (FCO) in 2003 and updated in 2006 noted that, 'The FCO needs to adapt to the challenges of the twenty-first century. Delivering services, influencing others and shaping change needs a flexible and targeted diplomatic network.' Ten strategic priorities were defined (primarily in security and consular matters) to provide the framework for deploying the FCO's efforts 'as resources remain tight and demand for our services grows' (United Kingdom Foreign and Commonwealth Office, 2006). The UK's approach has been subsumed under the title 'Active Diplomacy for a Changing World'.

The United States has also made changes in its foreign service to suit its new priorities, in this case building sustainable democracies around the globe. Secretary of State Condoleeza Rice introduced the idea of 'transformational diplomacy', which entails, among other things, greater diplomatic outreach and tighter coordination between diplomatic and donor assistance initiatives (United States State Department, 2007). In the pursuit of this transformational diplomacy the emphasis has been on the 'right numbers of people in the right places' (Wolfson, 2006). The changes include greater attention to public diplomacy, and to bring US diplomats – now often barricaded in fortified embassies – closer to the streets.

In 2005 Canada identified new goals, including initiatives to better meet the need to respond quickly to international crises, strengthen human rights and human security assistance, and promote multilateralism and public diplomacy. The North American presence was to be strengthened, a regional approach was to be encouraged and more diplomats would be sent out of headquarters to key areas, such as Asia and the Middle East (Foreign Affairs and International Trade Canada, 2005).

Among countries of the global South, Thailand has adopted a new foreign ministry structure that reflects the interrelatedness of issues rather than specialisation. Without citing private details, it can be said that a 'CEO model' was adopted throughout the government to increase efficiency. In the foreign ministry, the ambassador is the CEO performing as an assistant to the prime minister in carrying out government policies overseas in cooperation with representatives of other agencies (Srivihok, 2006). Malaysia was said to favour outsourcing some of the peripheral functions of the foreign ministry (DiploFoundation, 2006). Colombia undertook four sets of reforms between 1992 and 2004, matching changes intended to promote greater efficiency in the public service as a whole. New themes and geographical targets were defined for the twenty-first century and the Foreign Service was reorganised to try to cover both areas as leanly as possible (Tickner et al., 2005: 8–30).

Along with changes in foreign policy foci as well as in the services, the very role of the diplomat has changed in the twenty-first century. Diplomacy is no longer just 'the application of intelligence and tact to the conduct of official relations between the governments of independent States' (as elaborated by the venerable Sir Ernest Satow) but also the acquisition of a range of technical skills. To borrow from one characterisation of the twenty-first century diplomat:

- Twenty-first century diplomats must not only be proficient in languages, but in intercultural communication.
- They must be good managers; know how to get the most from their employees, while developing each one of them to their fullest potential.
- They must understand the global issues.
- They must understand the important role that public diplomacy plays.
- They must have the negotiating skills to deal effectively with governments, the media, NGOs and the private sector.
- And they must be comfortable with the latest technologies, which will be changing in ways we cannot even imagine today (Grossman, 2001).

Given the fact that foreign ministries and foreign services are challenged today by the rise in prominence of other bureaucratic agencies, foreign ministries also risk further decline in their status by not paying close attention to 'improv[ing] their relations with politicians and, perhaps most importantly of all, relat[ing] effectively to the Head of Government's agenda' (Wilton Park, 2005). There is a history of leaders' irritation with diplomatic services and some of this is unavoidable: Margaret Thatcher referred to the UK department as the Department for Foreigners because she thought it was too soft in defending British interests. Jesse Helms felt similarly disposed about the State Department (Hill, 2003: 80). More recently, French President Sarkozy expressed the view that the Quai d'Orsay should be eliminated (Sciolino, 2007). Of course no government seriously wants to eliminate its ministry of Foreign Affairs altogether. These political comments are often made in the context of natural frustration over bureaucratic inertia as well the desire to exert control over resistant bureaucrats. Often politicians find themselves having to seek help from same ministry personnel whom they earlier decried. On the other hand, it is certainly true that more than ever before foreign policy is directly linked to domestic demands. Today, so many foreign policy issues are *intermestic* that it has become more difficult for foreign ministries to claim special space away from the complexities of politics and society. It is also true that resources for the ministries of Foreign Affairs in most countries have been decreased as other ministries become more active in international affairs. Foreign ministries have had to adjust to these realities and retool to ensure that they can work on many issues on smaller budgets.

How have the CARICOM services fared?

There are many issues that affect the functioning of foreign services, as a whole, and small states, in particular, but only three are selected for discussion here: the organisation of CARICOM foreign services, management and coordination issues, and two problems affecting the personnel.

Organisational issues

Are CARICOM foreign services organised in such a way as to reflect the priorities of the twenty-first century? Here I focus on the ministries of the four more developed nations as the smaller countries have fewer structural divisions within their ministries. There is continuing debate as to the proper mix of functional and thematic units within foreign ministries, but the (world-wide) trend today is towards thematic lines and CARICOM countries are following these trends as well. In view of the discussion so far in this chapter, one would expect that the foreign ministries of the CARICOM countries would be organised to deal strongly with trade and other economic affairs, security issues, and disaporic issues, among other priorities. And indeed, in terms of economic issues, Jamaica and Barbados fit the expectation; they currently deal with trade issues within the foreign ministry. In the case of the former, foreign trade is a unit combined in terms of management with maritime and aviation affairs, whereas in Barbados trade is clearly a top priority, designed as a separate but equal part of the ministry itself.[3]

Why are there no trade divisions in the ministries of Guyana and Trinidad and Tobago? The trade portfolio is handled by separate powerful ministries. There has in fact been a general uncertainty in the region as to whether trade divisions are usefully located within foreign ministries or whether trade is so important that it should fall within the purview of separate more technically-proficient ministries of trade. The uncertainty has resulted in a continual linking and delinking of the two ministries since the 1980s – a factor that has, incidentally, led to the decline in both morale and personnel in some foreign ministries. Where there are separate ministries of trade, there appears to be a parallel decline in the political and financial resources allocated to the foreign ministry.

Trade divisions are not to be confused with what is generally termed 'international economic' divisions, which refer specifically to departments handling multilateral economic affairs, including the agendas of the WTO and other UN agencies. These are still seen as within the purview of foreign ministries. The divided arrangement does, in fact, lead to an odd and inefficient compartmentalisation of responsibilities; on the positive side, it does provide the foreign ministries a platform from which at least partly to influence the trade agenda.

A good deal of the work of the foreign ministries today focuses on CARICOM integration, and in this respect Trinidad and Tobago is unique in having established a separate unit in the foreign ministry devoted specifically to this area long ago. Other foreign ministries deal with CARICOM within their Americas divisions, which are also growing in importance as countries deal with NAFTA and FTAA issues and deepen their bilateral relations with Latin American countries, particularly in the case of Trinidad and Tobago, Guyana and Suriname.

My conclusion is that with respect to economic affairs there seems to be adequate organizational capacity within CARICOM foreign ministries, but that major handicaps exist in terms of resource allocations, as well as a persistent lack of coordination between Foreign Affairs and Trade (where separated). It may be added that in the case of the smaller Eastern Caribbean countries complaints abound that the political authorities tend to elevate trade and finance ministries over foreign affairs ministries.

Unlike economics the importance of security issues today is not readily reflected in the structure of the CARICOM foreign ministries. Not unexpectedly, traditional security threats continue to be reflected in Guyana's Frontiers Unit Department. However, *transnational* security issues do not seem to occupy any special space within any of the ministries. On the other hand, it is true that there has been an intensification of the work of the longstanding consular units that now deal with more and more security-linked decisions. Also reflective of increased security concerns is the growth of Legal Divisions that were originally established to deal specifically with the law of the sea negotiations of the 1970s and 1980s. According to the Jamaican foreign ministry's web site, the work of the Jamaican legal unit, which expanded to the extent that it required a separate unit established in 1996, now includes issues dealing with asylum, civil aviation (open skies), drugs, maritime issues, the International Criminal Court, and mutual legal assistance treaties, as well as CARICOM and bilateral treaties, and the work of the Caribbean Court of Justice, among other areas (Jamaica Ministry of Foreign Affairs and Foreign Trade, 2008).

The multilateral divisions of the foreign ministries have also seen their work expand to include global trade negotiations (already mentioned), as well as the traditional international organisational issues. Also, notably, consular units – which are usually combined with Protocol Divisions – have been upgraded in many countries to include diasporic units, variously termed the Overseas Department (Jamaica), Facilitation Unit for Returning Nationals (Barbados), or the Remigration Office (Guyana). Obviously this is in accord with the intensified thrust today to attract diasporic reinvestment.

Structural reform cannot be effective without accompanying reform in information and registry services, and in most CARICOM countries modernisation of all government ministries in this area has been prioritised. While this is a stated priority of most foreign ministries, ministries appear to be struggling to find the financial and human resources needed to upgrade these services. In particular IT upgrades are sometimes hampered by older infrastructure, as well as by country-wide technological limitations. The negative impact on the ability to communicate quickly and securely, to access timely information, conduct research, and other such activities, has hampered the ability of foreign services to engage in a more robust diplomacy.

In a related vein, the foreign ministries of CARICOM are particularly weak in terms of their public outreach. Despite the presence of public affairs units in most foreign ministries, neither relations with the media and general public (public affairs) nor communication abroad (public diplomacy) have been prioritised. This is an important omission, especially since today non-governmental organisations both at home and abroad are increasingly clamouring to be allowed a role in policy making. As a result the work of the foreign ministries has remained relatively mysterious to the public, which contributes to a growing disrespect towards diplomacy's possible role in the country's development.

Efficient management

Are CARICOM foreign services well-managed? Indeed, there are a number of problems that have fostered inefficient management, particularly at a time when best practices are being promoted in the public services as a whole. There is only space here to highlight two general issues: the first concerns the dysfunctional patterns of communication between the foreign ministry and the other line ministries that are becoming more and more involved in foreign affairs, to the extent that these ministries have established their own mini-foreign affairs units. This is not peculiar to the Caribbean: so many bureaucratic units are involved in foreign affairs today that no foreign ministry is able to act as an efficient gatekeeper to the abroad. However, CARICOM foreign ministries seem to be particularly estranged. Stories abound of foreign ministries not being informed or asked to coordinate the visits of key officials abroad or not being given adequate time to prepare the protocol for upcoming visits by important officials to the home country. Major international activities are undertaken by other ministries without any input from the foreign ministry, leaving foreign ministry personnel marginalised and too often demoralised.

Some of the problem, however, is attributable to inefficiencies of the foreign ministry itself. There are numerous complaints about the lack of a timely response to requests made to the foreign ministry by line ministries, the public or even the embassies and consulates. Heads of mission are compelled to act more independently than is desirable. The concept of an 'instructed mission', which works so well in the US context, is hard to apply within CARICOM given this penchant for delayed responses.

Overarching all of this is the issue of planning and competency: foreign ministry personnel often find it difficult to articulate what they are expected to do and what the bureaucratic expectations for their ministry, in general, and for the service, as a whole, are. Planning tends to be *ad hoc* and sectoral so that overarching goals are unclear. Moreover, in a rationalist age, many of the operations of the foreign service lack transparency, and evaluative criteria are not in place. Yet, as Christopher Hill sees it, foreign ministries can no longer argue for their necessity 'on the spurious justifications that only diplomats understand foreigners or the processes of negotiation' (Hill, 2003: 81). CARICOM foreign services still tend to fall on this dated line of argument.

Finally, problems also exist at the mission level. Beyond the issue of whether such small missions and so few missions can be effective in dealing with the multitude of issues they now confront, many missions are overburdened, lack clear guidance, lack good managers and do not have in place any criteria by which to evaluate and reward good performance.[4]

Personnel issues

More than anything else, the fate of the foreign services and the ability to extract what the country needs from the international environment, rests in the hands of the employees of the Foreign Service, and diplomats in particular. There are many reasons why the diplomats of CARICOM are not well prepared for the twenty-first century, but only two can be discussed here. First, because the foreign ministries of the Caribbean (like those in most areas of the globe) have been downsized considerably in the past few decades, there is a shortage of staff at a time when the work agenda has expanded considerably. A circular argument pertains whereby the political authorities are reluctant to invest more resources in the Foreign Service without proof of performance even as the service renders poor performance because of the shortage of staff. Moreover, the greatest need is for very specialised staff at a time when skilled and educated personnel are attracted to better-paying opportunities in the private sector and elsewhere. While some ministries have increased their hiring of temporary, contract staff at home and abroad, the use of too many contract employees may bring its own problems with respect to loyalty, 'turf' and morale.[5]

Second, the rapid changes in the global environment call for the availability of continuous and relevant training opportunities for all Foreign Service staff. In view of the staff shortages, this training also has to be accomplished on-site where feasible. Unfortunately, training institutes that were established earlier in the region in Trinidad and Tobago and in Guyana – the latter as part of the Foreign Ministry – have for various reasons ceased to fulfil their original functions. (Another institute established by the Jamaican Foreign Ministry has yet to begin functioning in 2008.) There is, therefore, an urgent need to institutionalise training programmes, to put in place transparent processes for selection of employees for training, and to ensure that whatever training is offered is matched to career niches that are appropriate for future diplomatic operations. Here it is worth recalling what was said earlier about the skills needed by the twenty-first century diplomat: as Grossman notes, they include proficiency in languages (non-traditional as well as traditional), proficiency in intercultural communication, managerial skills, knowledge of diverse global issues, and the skill to negotiate not only with governments but also with the media and various stakeholders that are now fully monitoring and expecting to participate in foreign policy process (Grossman, 2001). Without adequate training of new employees, the aging CARICOM foreign services will not be able to adapt to the new realities.

Conclusion

Major changes in the region and across the globe have necessitated changes in the role of diplomats and in the priorities and structure of foreign services the world over. However, the CARICOM countries have been slow to adapt, having focused initially on fighting a rearguard and *ad hoc* action against the encroachment of liberalisation and the forces of globalisation. This chapter has addressed some of these issues, as well as the bureaucratic problems that continue to hinder the development of a more robust diplomacy for CARICOM states. Despite the region's fears, the CARICOM region is proving to be relatively resilient now that it has accepted the inevitability of global change. However, a parallel effort to streamline the foreign services is only just beginning. Only by ensuring that these small services are able to operate as efficiently as possible can the region hope to implement a robust and resilient diplomacy, which is necessary to harness the abroad and achieve development aspirations.

Notes

1. Haiti is also a member of CARICOM but is not referenced in this chapter. Although the Haitian diplomatic establishment, which has been very pro-active, shares a number of limitations with the foreign services of the rest of the region, there are diplomatic implications for the country's unique political and economic history that have to be addressed separately.
2. Epistemic communities are 'network[s] of professionals with recognized expertise and competence in a particular domain and an authoritative claim to policy-relevant knowledge within that domain', in other words, knowledge-based communities. See Haas (1992: 3).

3. Information on Trinidad and Tobago is from private sources. The Ministry's web site (www.foreign.gov.tt) does not contain organisational information at the time of writing.
4. CARICOM countries maintain relatively few diplomatic missions abroad and these are staffed at a low level. In 2006–07 Jamaica had 14 missions abroad, Trinidad and Tobago 12, Guyana and Belize 10, Suriname 9, Barbados 7, and other states 5 or 6. For financial reasons the trend has been towards contracting rather than expanding missions, except for Trinidad which opened one more in 2007 and was expected to open three more later, and Belize which opened four missions in the 1990s. Even more importantly, the missions abroad tend to be staffed by two or three diplomats at most, along with locally-recruited support staff.
5. These issues are analysed in greater detail in Braveboy-Wagner (2007), chapter 7.

References

Braveboy-Wagner, Jacqueline (2003) 'Making Room for the Smallest States', in J. Braveboy-Wagner (ed.) *The Foreign Policies of the Global South: Rethinking Conceptual Frameworks* (Boulder, CO: Lynne Rienner): 147–61.

Braveboy-Wagner, Jacqueline (2007) *Small States in Global Affairs: The Foreign Policies of the Caribbean Community* (CARICOM) (New York: Palgrave Macmillan).

DiploFoundation (2006) Conference on 'Challenges for Foreign Ministries: Managing Diplomatic Networks and Optimising Value', Geneva, 31 May–1 June.

Foreign Affairs and International Trade Canada (2005) 'Our Priorities', http://www.geo.international.gc.ca/cip-pic/IPS/IPS-Diplomacy4-en.asp, accessed on 25 July 2007.

Grossman, Marc (2001) 'Technology and Diplomacy in the 21st Century,' Speech to 'NetDiplomacy 2001: The Internet and Foreign Policy Conference', Washington, DC, 5 September, http://www.state.gov/p/us/rm/6580.htm, accessed on 25 July 2007.

Guyana Ministry of Foreign Affairs (2008) Home page, http://www.minfor.gov.gy/, accessed on 10 April 2008.

Haas, Peter M. (1992) 'Introduction: Epistemic Communities and International Policy Coordination', *International Organization* 46 (1): 1–35

Hey, Jeanne A.K. (ed.) (2003) *Small States in World Politics: Explaining Foreign Policy Behavior* (Boulder, CO: Lynne Rienner).

Hill, Christopher R. (2003) *The Changing Politics of Foreign Policy* (New York: Palgrave Macmillan).

International Fund for Agricultural Development (2007) *Sending Money Home: Worldwide Remittance Flows to Developing Countries* (Rome: IFAD).

Jamaica Ministry of Foreign Affairs and Foreign Trade (2008) Home page, http://www.mfaft.gov.jm/, accessed on 10 April 2008.

Keck, Margaret E., and Kathryn Sikkink (1998) *Activists Beyond Borders* (Ithaca, NY: Cornell University Press).

Plischke, Elmer (1977) *Microstates in World Affairs: Policy Problems and Options* (Washington: American Enterprise Institute Press).

Sciolino, Elaine (2007) 'Portrait of President, Craving Power, Enthralls France', *New York Times*, 24 August.

Srivihok, Vitavas (2006) 'CEO Ambassador: Challenges of the International Management of External Relations', Paper presented at DiploFoundation conference, Geneva, 31 May–1 June, http://www.diplomacy.edu/conferences/MFA/papers/srivihok.pdf, accessed on 25 July 2007.

Tickner, Arlene, Oascar Pardo and Diego Beltrán (2005) *El Estado del Servicio Exterior y La Carrera Diplomatica de Colombia* (Bogotá, Colombia: Universidad de los Andes, 5 August).

Trinidad and Tobago Ministry of Foreign Affairs (2008) Home page, http://www.foreign.gov.tt, accessed on 10 April 2008.

United Kingdom Foreign and Commonwealth Office (2006) *Active Diplomacy for a Changing World* (International Priorities), White Paper, 29 March, http://www.fco.gov.uk, accessed on 25 July 2007.

United States State Department (2007) *Strategic Plan 2007–2012*, http://www.state.gov/s/d/rm/rls/dosstrat/2007, accessed on 25 July 2007.

Wolfson, Charles (2006) 'Rice Seeks to Transform Diplomacy; Wolfson: Secretary of State Touts Transformational Diplomacy', *CBS News*, 20 January.

Wilton Park (2005) 'Diplomacy Today: Delivering Results in a World of Changing Priorities', Conference Report WPS05/4, 3–6 March.

Part 2
Case Studies: Small States' Diplomacy vis-à-vis Regional Organisation

7
Can Small States Choose Their Own Size? The Case of a Nordic State – Iceland

Baldur Thorhallsson

Introduction

The aim of this case study is to explain why Iceland has changed its international approach and become a more active player in the international arena since the mid- and late 1990s. Iceland's increased activity in the international system is explained by five interrelated features: a redefinition of interests; greater economic resources; greater administrative resources; a change of perception and preference by a large part of the Icelandic political elite; and an external pressure reflecting the view of international actors. All these features have led to a policy change at the domestic level. There has been a move away from an international approach built on historical bilateral relations, with a narrow focus on the concrete economic advantages to be gained from all overseas activity, to an approach based on more broadly defined interests and increased international activity within multilateral organisations. Accordingly, Iceland is moving out of Keohane's 'system-ineffectual' category, that is, being a state which simply adjusts to the international system and cannot change it. Recently, Iceland can be regarded as belonging to Keohane's 'system-affecting' category, that is, being a state that cannot influence the international system on its own but can do so together with other states (Keohane, 1969: 295–6).

The decision by the Icelandic government in 1998 to apply for a seat in the Security Council of the United Nations (UN) demonstrates the shift from a reactive international approach to greater activity in the international arena. Iceland joined most of the international organisations created after the Second World War, but unlike other Nordic states, it did not seek an active role within them. The Icelandic governments attached importance to bilateral relations with neighbouring states in terms of trade and defence: the Nordic states, the United States and Britain (Thorhallsson, 2005). Emphasis was placed on obtaining concrete economic advantages from all overseas activity, whether these concerned the extension of Iceland's fishing zone, trade agreements or protection by the US military. The work of the UN (with the exception of the establishment and application of the Law of the Sea), the North Atlantic Treaty Organization (NATO) and the Council of Europe, were not placed high on the agenda. Governments prioritised beneficial trade deals with European states and joined the European Free Trade Association (EFTA) in 1970 and the European Economic Area (EEA) in 1994. However, as soon as market access for Icelandic fish and marine products was achieved, little importance was attached to the work of those institutions except when issues concerned Icelandic core interests and the unavoidable routine day-to-day business within them. Politicians did not engage in building a decisive civil service, including a foreign service, in order for Iceland to become actively engaged in these institutions (see detailed discussions in Thorhallsson, 2002 and 2005). Moreover, Icelandic policy-makers, have been reluctant to apply for membership within the European Union (EU) since it might jeopardise the resilience of the economy (Oddsson, 2004). This prevented Iceland from belonging to Keohane's 'system-affecting' category of states which can influence the international system with other states, as stated above. This is in contrast to the other Nordic states, primarily Sweden, Norway and Denmark, which can be said to have belonged to this category in the postwar period because of their international activity. Keohane distinguished between large and small powers by examining whether their leaders have a decisive impact on the international community. His third category is 'system-determining, or system-influencing', consisting of states that can influence the international system through unilateral or multilateral action (Keohane, 1969: 295–6).

However, since the late 1990s, the Icelandic government has become increasingly engaged in the international community, emphasising a traditional small state multilateral approach. Iceland has become more active within international organisations such as NATO, the European Council, the Organisation for Security and Co-operation in Europe (OSCE), the World Trade Organisation (WTO), the World Bank and organisations of the UN, such as the Food and Agricultural Organization (FAO), the UN Education, Scientific and Cultural Organisation (UNESCO), and a number of UN commissions. Iceland has also taken on leadership duties in the Arctic Council and the Council of the Baltic Sea

States. Aid for development has increased substantially along with work within international organisations dealing with aid and development. In 2000 Iceland created an Icelandic Crisis Response Unit (ICRU) explicitly earmarked for possible use by NATO, the EU, the UN and the OSCE. The ICRU is a non-military 'peacekeeping force' of individuals (police, doctors, nurses, lawyers, air traffic controllers, administrators, etc.) available for rapid deployment abroad. In 2001 and 2002 it contributed to a mission in the Balkans in which all four international bodies named above were involved. Its main missions have been the management of the international airports in Pristina in Kosovo and Kabul in Afghanistan. Furthermore, since the mid-1990s, the Foreign Service has extended its activity to a number of countries and opened embassies in China, India, Japan, Canada, South Africa, Finland and Austria.

Moreover, Iceland's central administrative capabilities have increased considerably in the last two decades. In terms of number of personnel, the Icelandic Foreign Service has nearly doubled in size over the last decade. Its ability to produce detailed reports on Iceland's status and policy choices in Europe and elsewhere has changed fundamentally (see detailed discussions in Thorhallsson, 2006a). The administration is now much more capable of taking an active part in the international arena.

Yet recently Iceland's burgeoning international presence has suffered its share of setbacks. In 2008, the vulnerability of Iceland, as a small economy and a small international actor, became evident in the financial crisis as well as its campaign to become a member of the UN Security Council. The small Icelandic currency (the króna) fell rapidly while the three main Icelandic banks collapsed, forcing the Icelandic government to take over their operations. Moreover, the country came to an economic standstill as foreign trade crumbled due to the breakdown of the foreign currency market in the country. The Icelandic government, despite considerable effort, failed to get immediate loans and other economic assistance from both its neighbours and international institutions.

Internationally, Iceland had failed to guarantee the country a permanent shelter within the EU framework, including the European Central Bank, even though it took an active role in the Four Freedoms through its membership in the EEA. Iceland got into a major dispute with Britain and the Netherlands because of their demands that Iceland should honour its legal obligations within the EEA to depositors in overseas branches of the Icelandic banks. The British government used its antiterrorist law to take over the assets and operations of the two Icelandic banks in Britain, causing one of the banks to fall instantly, and substantially worsening the economic crisis in Iceland. Britain also managed to delay much needed economic assistance promised by the International Moneatry Fund (IMF) until the dispute had been settled.

Moreover, Iceland failed to get elected to the UN Security Council in mid-October 2008. This was because of a limited record of activities within the UN, a small foreign service compared to the competitive states, Austria and Turkey, and a campaign by Britain against Iceland in the week before the vote in the UN General Assembly. Accordingly, the case of Iceland in 2008 once again indicates how the fate of a small economy is tied to external conditions and the actions of larger neighbours despite rapid economic growth and a considerable increase in international activity.

Explanations

Acknowledging the setbacks that have occurred, it is still worth analysing what has led to this policy shift in Iceland. Why has Iceland moved away from its reactive international approach with its focus on bilateralism and adopted an active international approach based on multilateralism? As introduced above, Iceland's increased activity in the international system is explained by five interrelated features: a redefinition of interests; greater economic resources; greater administrative resources; a change of perception and preference by a large part of the Icelandic political elite; and external pressures reflecting the view of international actors.

A redefinition of interests

The Icelandic political elite was highly ambitious concerning domestic affairs throughout the twentieth century. Icelandic society was transformed from being a very poor undeveloped agrarian society to a rich industrial and commercial society. The prioritisation of the elite was clear: self-determination over the country's landmass and surrounding waters. Accordingly, the elite managed to gain independence from Denmark (domestic rule in 1904, sovereignty under the Danish Crown in 1918 and a republic in 1944) and full control over the 200-mile fishing zone surrounding the island in 1976 (after steady successful extensions of the zone). This was combined with an aim for a more successful economy and higher living standard – though Iceland's priorities in this respect were perhaps not always correctly focused.

Throughout the twentieth century fish and marine products were far the most important exports of goods accounting for 95 per cent in 1940 (National Economic Institute, 2001). Accordingly, Iceland's trade policy had a clear objective: to guarantee its fish and marine products access to important markets mainly in Britain, the EU and US. On the other hand, fish and marine products have declined significantly in importance in the last four decades. In 2006 fish and other marine products accounted for just over 50 per cent of merchandise exports and roughly one-third of total exports, down from 82 per cent and 60 per cent respectively in 1991 (Central Bank of Iceland, 2007). The economy has diversified bringing into the picture exports of aluminium and medical and pharmaceutical products, a tourist industry and recently a financial sector. The export of manufactured goods has grown rapidly and accounted for 38 per cent of merchandise exports in 2008 while service accounted for almost 35 per cent of total export revenues (Central Bank of Iceland, 2007). The government has had to respond to and focus on a much wider range of interests internationally. For instance, it has extended its work within the WTO and expanded its Foreign Service to distant markets. The international work of the government now bears the hallmark of protecting the new financial sector, and its operational consequences abroad, as well as export-oriented companies such as pharmaceuticals.

There has been a shift of priorities from a narrow focus on direct benefits from overseas relations to more broadly-defined interests in terms of the importance of contributing to the work of the international community. For instance, Iceland's increased activity within the WTO is seen as contributing to better market access for Icelandic products around the globe. Also, the opening of the embassies in China, Japan and India is a response to the growing and potential importance of these markets for Icelandic companies (Ásgrímsson, 2004). The pivotal role of these states internationally is also recognised by decisions to open embassies in their capitals. Moreover, Icelandic governments did not take an active part in the work of the World Bank in the twentieth century, but attached importance to membership in the IMF due to the several economic benefits Iceland received from IMF membership[1] and not from the World Bank (International Monetary Fund, 2005; Institute of Economic Studies, 2005). In 1997 a report issued by the Icelandic Ministry for Foreign Affairs stated that Iceland had done little to increase its expertise and its level of development assistance. The consequences have been that Iceland has had difficulty in taking on duties within the group of the Nordic and Baltic states in the World Bank Group (Haralz, 1997). In a report that followed in 2003 the government was encouraged to take a more active part in the governing and the work of the Group (Ingólfsson and Haralz, 2003).[2] In the last decade, Iceland has increased its development aid substantially and there were plans for considerable annual increases in overseas assistance before the financial crisis. Accordingly,

Iceland has increased its international activity in order to facilitate aid in international organisations, such as the World Bank, opened an embassy in Africa, and works more closely with developing states within the UN. Increased international activity is seen as being of benefit to Iceland in the long run. For instance, Iceland's increased aid expenditure and international cooperation with small developing states was obliviously linked to its bid for an elected, rotational seat on the Security Council. Membership within the Security Council was seen to benefit Iceland in that cooperation with distant countries could help to build coalitions concerning Icelandic trade interests in other international organisations.

Furthermore, the Icelandic government was forced to re-examine its defence policy after the US government decided to close down its military base in the country in 2006, leaving Iceland without a military presence. However, the defence treaty signed between the two states in 1951 – originally based on a defence and trade agreement from 1941 – is still in place. But since the withdrawal of the US military, Iceland has sought formal defence cooperation with European states, such as Norway and Denmark, as well as other NATO members based on the Atlantic Treaty. In the process that led to the military withdrawal Iceland recognised its obligations to contribute to its own defence after considerable pressure for the US – previously paid for and operated entirely by the US. In the late 1990s, Iceland became more active within NATO and started to contribute to its operations. This was a part of the government's policy to share some of the NATO burden in the hope of helping to maintain the US military presence in the country (Bailes and Thorhallsson, 2006). Since this strategy's failure, Iceland's defence policy no longer focused entirely on cooperation with the US. Iceland now works more closely with European states, emphasises its work within NATO, and has since had its first defence budget in 2008. Hence, Iceland's economic and political interests are becoming much wider in all respects.

Greater economic resources

Iceland was one of the poorest states in Europe at the beginning of the twentieth century and received development aid until 1976 (Gísladóttir, 2008); yet, its economic development over the century was remarkable, and has been so particularly since the mid-1990s. The resilience of the Icelandic economy coincides with neoliberal policies and membership in the EEA since the early 1990s. The Icelandic economy was transformed through various measures such as tax reductions, the privatisation of state-run businesses – particularly banks – and improvements in the corporate environment. Access to common markets, aided by the compulsory implementation of EU regulations in competition and finance though EEA membership, led to greater prosperity. Accordingly, Icelandic governments managed to enhance the flexibility of the economy, labour, and product markets within the policy framework of the country and the EEA.

The liberalisation and privatisation process led towards a rapid growth of the financial sector. This growth was originally led by favourable fish prices, a global economic recovery, a rise in exports, and foreign investment in the aluminium sector. It was sustained by private consumption and investment in the non-traded goods sector mainly financed by foreign credit. Historically, Iceland's prosperity was largely built on its comparative advantages in abundant marine and energy resources. However, growth in the twenty-first century has been boosted by services located mainly in the financial services sector. From 1945 to 2006, the average annual growth rate of GDP was about 4 per cent and from the mid-1990s Iceland has experienced one of the highest growth rates of GDP among the Organisation for Economic Co-operation and Development (OECD) countries. Despite the small size of the economy, the smallest within the OECD, reflecting the 310 000 inhabitants of the country, Iceland's Gross National Income (GNI) per capita was the sixth highest among OECD countries and the eighth highest in the world, amounting to US$36 000 in 2006 (Central Bank of Iceland, 2007). In addition, Iceland was ranked first out of 177 countries on the 2007/2008 Human Development Index published by the UN (UN Development Programme, 2007/2008).[3]

The economic boom beginning in the mid-1990s, and the increased revenue that has followed, has allowed governments to move from a relatively large public sector deficit in the 1980s and early 1990s to a series of budget surpluses. The fiscal balance has been well above the OECD average (Central Bank of Iceland, 2007). This has enabled the government to allocate more resources to the central administration. For instance, a decisive Foreign Service has been built and all ministries and their institutions have afforded to spend more time and resources on external relations. Besides, the government has been more affluent and politicians more willing than before to contribute to international aid and take part in international burden sharing. Accordingly, there has been less necessity to focus entirely on getting direct economic benefits from overseas activities.

That said, the vulnerability of a small economy has become evident in the case of Iceland during the credit crisis in 2008. The rapid foreign expansion of Icelandic banks and companies, mainly based on foreign borrowing, led to major constraints on the economy and the króna. The Central Bank of Iceland has had difficulties in defending the króna due to its lack of liquidity. In mid-2008 the IMF concluded that the Icelandic economy was at a difficult and uncertain turning point: 'the long home-grown, foreign-funded boom was coming to the end. Its legacies are overstretched private sector balance sheets, large macroeconomic imbalances, and high dependence on foreign financing' (IMF, 2008). The Icelandic banks were hit hard by the credit crisis, as the cost of borrowing rose. The banks responded by slowing lending growth and rationalising balance sheets.

The króna, fell rapidly in the first half of 2008, making life somewhat more comfortable for the export-oriented industries. At the same time, export costs increased considerably due to foreign borrowing and the higher cost of imported material. In response to the fall of the króna, The Central Bank of Iceland concluded bilateral swap facility arrangements with the Central Banks of Sweden, Norway and Denmark to bolster its international liquidity. The facilities are a precautionary measure made to provide the Central Bank of Iceland with access to euros if needed. Each agreement provides up to EUR 500 million, where the Central Bank of Iceland can acquire euros against the Icelandic króna. The swap agreements are facilities that may be drawn upon by the Central Bank of Iceland when and if necessary (Central Bank of Iceland, 2008). However, the Icelandic Central Bank failed to bolster its external liquidity any further. Requests from the Central Bank and the Icelandic government to the neighbouring central banks and governments in the Nordic states, the UK and the US, to come to Iceland's rescue were declined. These states doubted the government's ability to stand by its overgrown financial sector.

Accordingly, the swap facility arrangement did not prevent a further fall of the króna, reduced to an all-time low against the euro a few weeks after the agreements were made public (Oakley, 2008). In autumn 2008 the three main Icelandic banks were nationalised by the government as they faced bankruptcy caused by 'lending stops' abroad. The foreign currency market collapsed leading the country to an economic standstill. The Icelandic government sought emergency loans and assistance from the IMF as well as from the EU emergency fund and several states around the globe, including Russia and China. The IMF came to the rescue and provided the Icelandic government with a $2.1 billon loan. The IMF economic assistance package included a promise by several states to loan Iceland about $3 billion in order. However, Britain and the Netherlands turned against Iceland in order to guarantee the savings of their citizens in overseas branches of the Icelandic banks. They argued that the Icelandic government was obligated to guarantee all deposits of up to about EUR 20000. Iceland claimed that these obligations were covered by the Icelandic Depositors' and Investors' Guarantee Fund set up by the EEA rules and if the fund is unable to fully meet its obligations, as was the case, the Icelandic government did not have to step in. The British government used its anti-terrorist law to take over the assets and operations of the two Icelandic banks in Britain, putting the banks and the Icelandic Ministry of Finance and the Central Bank on the British government's list of terrorist organisations (a list that includes al Qaeda). Britain and the Netherlands used their influence to delay the much needed emergency loan from the IMF, a loan from the EU emergency fund and loans from the Iceland's closes allies, the Nordic states. In fact, they managed to block all attempts by the Icelandic government to foreign currency loans as well as other forms of economic assistance. Iceland finally gave in to this pressure in order to prevent total economic collapse – since the stock of foreign currency in the Icelandic Central Bank was rapidly coming to nothing – with the Bank providing foreign currency to only Icelandic companies importing food, medication and fuel.

The Icelandic government was 'left without friends', as the Icelandic prime minister put it, and failed to secure new friends despite several attempts at getting loans from Russia and China. Iceland's closest neighbours, the Nordic states, were all on the side of Britain and the Netherlands, fearing that if Iceland would not be obligated to stand by guaranteeing all deposits up to about EUR 20000, the credibility of the whole financial sector within the EEA might be in danger. Iceland was faced with bilateral negotiations with the Britain and the Netherlands without access to the decision-making processes within the EU institutions. The IMF did not provide Iceland with an immediate shelter, failing to stand by its agreement with the Icelandic government and succumbing to pressure from Britain not to formally approve the agreement and put it into action until the dispute between Britain and Iceland had been settled.

The Central Bank of Iceland was simply 'too small' to defend the extensive foreign expansion of Icelandic banks and companies. Moreover, the króna did not stand a chance in the credit crisis due to the large Icelandic financial sector operating abroad. Consequently the viability of the króna has gone. Owing to the fluctuation of the króna and its collapse, the Icelandic business community is united in urging the government to explore the possibility of adopting the euro. Furthermore, a broad consensus has developed among economic sectors in Iceland – with the exception of the agrarian and fisheries sectors – and Iceland's most influential labour union for negotiation with the EU on accession: one of the main reasons given for membership is the importance of receiving backup from the European Central Bank. Furthermore, in June/July 2008 an opinion poll indicated that about 60 per cent of voters wanted the government to start negotiations with the EU on accession and the adoption of the euro; of the remainder of respondents, equal numbers were opposed to such moves or undecided (Capacent Gallup, 2008).

The grand coalition government, consisting of the centre-right Independence Party (IP) and the Social Democratic Alliance (SDA), has been divided on the EU and the euro questions. However, the leading IP, which has traditionally fiercely opposed EU membership and the adoption of the euro, is now reviewing its European policy. The party has given in to severe pressure from the business community and decided, in the midst of the current economic turbulence, to examine in detail the pros and cons of EU membership. After one of his ministers called for adoption of the euro within the framework of the EEA (Bjarnason, 2008), the leader of the IP and prime minister, Geir H. Haarde announced that the government's committee on Europe would look into this possibility as well as tying the króna to the euro. However, Haarde has expressed doubts about these possibilities without full EU membership (Icelandic Public Radio, 2008), an option he has previously opposed. The leader of the SDA and the foreign minister, Ingibjörg Sólrún Gísladóttir agrees with Haarde that adopting the euro without joining the EU is an unlikely possibility.

Hence, the vulnerability of the small Icelandic economy has become evident in the financial crisis. Iceland benefits enormously from EEA membership (i.e. access to the common market), participation in the Four Freedoms of the EU, with the exceptions of the Common Agrarian Policy and the Common Fisheries Policy, and credibility due to the fact that Iceland has to implement exactly the same financial legislation and regulatory framework as EU member states. However, Iceland lacks the shelter of the European Central Bank and faces a massive economic downturn 'dominated by external considerations' (IMF, 2008). The IMF predictions in the summer of 2008 had all become evident by the autumn: the króna could depreciate more if the outflow of capital continues; external liquidity risk remains a key concern, caused by the foreign debt of the private sector – chiefly banks – and domestic risks such as inflation, house and equity prices, and household and corporate indebtedness (IMF, 2008). The 'economic miracle' of the last decade is over. The volatility of a small economy is once again evident.

Icelandic governments have reluctantly sought shelter within the framework of European integration in order both to guarantee access to the European market and respond to economic downturns. This was the case with EFTA membership in 1970 and EEA membership in the early 1990s. Yet again, the government, led by the IP, is considering the EU alternative and adopting the euro. A question mark has been added to Iceland's capacity to nurture the resilient nature of its economy without the protection of EU membership.

Greater administrative resources

The increased capacity of the Icelandic central administration over the past two decades has gone hand in hand with greater economic resources, a wider range of interests, and the growing importance of international organisations and change in the priorities of politicians. The ability of the civil service to engage in information gathering and policy-making has increased enormously. It is able to form its own polices, that is, it is less dependent on interest groups and policy-making in other Nordic states, and has the ability to skilfully pursue its policy objectives. Over the last decade, the Icelandic Foreign Service has nearly doubled in size in terms of number of personnel (see Figure 7.1), and its expertise on a wide range of international affairs has also increased (Thorhallsson, 2002; Thorhallsson, 2004).

Iceland's membership within the EEA required all ministries and many of their institutions to hire experts in the field of European integration in order to engage effectively in EEA policy-making and to implement EEA regulations. Moreover, the administration's engagement in European integration has given officials greater room for manoeuvre in their day-to-day work since politicians are largely absent from the formal EEA decision-making system (Lægreid et al., 2004). This may have given officials greater confidence concerning policy-making and representing Iceland abroad since, historically, Icelandic politicians have interfered to a greater extent in the work of the bureaucracy than in the other Nordic states (Kristinsson, 1993). Membership within the EEA also forced ministers to increase expertise within their ministry by professionally hiring specialists instead of using appointments to return political favours. A wider range of economic and political interests, a more complex international system, and a greater importance of international institutions, such as the WTO, the EEA and the Arctic Council, have required

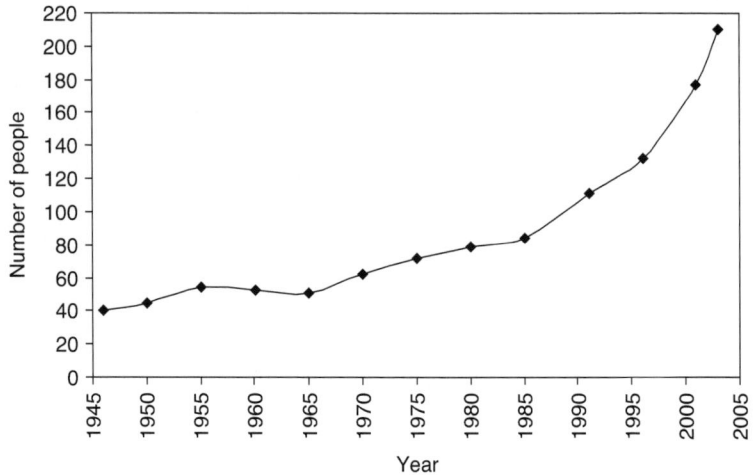

Figure 7.1   The number of people working in the Icelandic Foreign Service from 1945 to 2003, all personnel included.
Source: Based on data from Ministry for Foreign Affairs, Government of Iceland, 2003.

profound knowledge within the administration. Accordingly, the administration has been engaged in a steady and successful capacity build.

The consequences are clear; Iceland has been able to take on considerable leadership duties abroad. For instance, Iceland assumed the chairmanship of the Council of Europe for the first time in 1999 – earlier having always argued that it did not have the administrative capacity to tackle the chairmanship duties that rotate among member states. Iceland also chaired the Arctic Council from 2002 to 2004 and held the presidency of the Council of the Baltic Sea States from mid-2005 to mid-2006. It has also taken on leadership roles within the WTO, the World Bank and the FAO, UNESCO and other organisations and commissions of the UN. Moreover, the extensive operations of the ICRU at the international airports in Pristina and Kabul, mentioned above, have been acknowledged.

Furthermore, since the mid-1990s, the Foreign Service has extended its activity to a number of countries. Figure 7.2 shows the rapid rise in the number of Icelandic separate embassies/missions abroad in the last decade. Iceland opened a number of embassies/missions in the 1940s but, in the 40-year period that followed, only four new separate embassies/missions were established abroad (Ministry for Foreign Affairs, Government of Iceland, 2006). Iceland did not regard it as important to establish embassies to serve individual states abroad (Ásgrímsson, 2004).

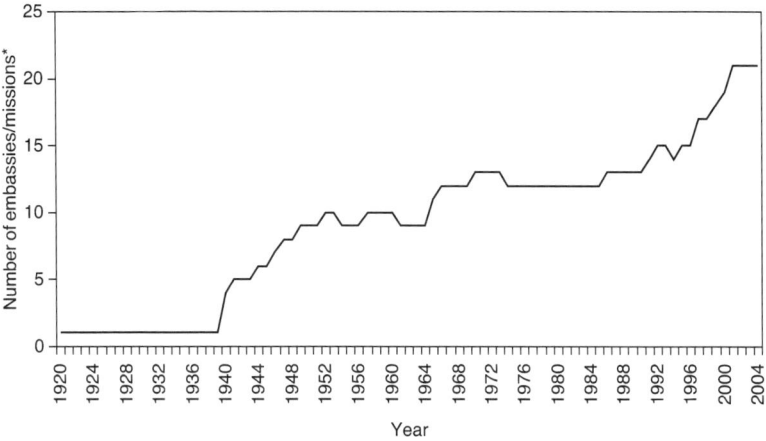

Figure 7.2   The number of Icelandic embassies/missions abroad

Note: *The number of Icelandic embassies/missions is defined as the number of separate foreign-service offices abroad, i.e. embassies, permanent missions and consulates-general with special ambassadors, permanent representatives or consuls-general.

Source: Based on data from Ministry for Foreign Affairs, Government of Iceland, 2006.

A change of perception and preference by the political elite

The opinions of relevant domestic actors, particularly political leaders, regarding the state's ability to engage in international affairs cannot be ignored. The willingness of leaders to participate in the international community is also of key importance in understanding a state's external policies. Political leaders' preferences and perceptions of their state and the international environment is a base upon which they build their state's international engagement. 'Preference size' includes three features of the domestic political elite: ambitions, prioritisation and ideas regarding the international system. 'Perceptual size' is the size of a state as viewed by domestic actors in comparison with other states (Thorhallsson, 2006b). This reflects how political discourse may determine how actors view states' sizes and capabilities (see for instance Hansen, 2002; Hálfdanarson, 2004). There are three issues here: first, the changed view of the Icelandic political elite regarding Iceland's size and external capabilities; secondly, the 'new' belief or ideology of decision-makers that Iceland has obligations in the international arena and should contribute to the well-being of individuals and international organisations; and finally, the belief that a small state like Iceland can have a say internationally.

In the last century, domestic actors in Iceland regarded the state as having considerable internal capacity in terms of the ability to build up the infrastructure and provide a decent living standard. However, until the mid- to late-1990s, the Icelandic political elite did not regard Iceland as having the external capacity needed to engage in wide-ranging international activity. Icelandic politicians lacked the ambition to play an active part in the international arena and seemed not to have believed that Iceland could have a say within international institutions (see detailed discussion in Thorhallsson, 2005).

The political discourse in Iceland was based on self-determination regarding the extension of the fishing zone, diminishing or increased dependency on the US military presence in the country and the lack of political will to transfer power from Reykjavik to the institutions of the EU (Thorhallsson, 2005). Also, it centred on the necessity of deriving concrete benefits from overseas activity (Haarde, 2006a). Policy-makers opted for a reactive international approach based on bilateral contacts with neighbouring states. Why should a state try to influence decisions taken in international organisations if its policy-makers steadily regard it as impossible for them to do so?

This view of the Icelandic political elite was in sharp contrast to the views of the elite in other Nordic states, who regarded themselves and their states as being fully capable of participating actively in the international community. Moreover, the postwar political discourse in other Nordic states was characterised by the obligation to participate in the international system (Archer, 2003). For instance, other Nordic states provided 25 per cent of all military personnel deployed in UN peacekeeping operations during the Cold War (Embassy of Norway in Copenhagen, 2005; Ministry of Foreign Affairs, Government of Denmark, 2005).

On the other hand, as has been stated above, there has been a complete turnaround in Iceland's international approach in the last ten years. Iceland has become more active in all of the international institutions, mentioned above. This policy change would not have occurred were it not for the changed views of a large portion of the Icelandic political elite concerning Iceland's priorities, role and duties, internationally. The Icelandic government also regards Iceland as having a duty to contribute to the international community (I.S. Gísladóttir, 2007; I.H. Gísladóttir, 2007; Haarde, 2006a; *Morgunblaðið*, 2003). This has led to Iceland's contribution to a number of international institutes and commissions. Iceland has not only become highly ambitious in its international activity by taking a more active part in the work of these organisations, but its prioritisation has radically changed in the last ten years. This is manifested in the Policy Statement of the present government which states that: 'Human rights, increased development cooperation and a focus on peaceful resolution of disputes will be the new cornerstones of Icelandic foreign policy. ... Iceland should aim for leadership in the campaign against marine pollution and in global work to counter climate change' (Policy Statement, 2007).

A considerable number of politicians now seem to consider it possible for the country to influence decisions taken within international institutions. Moreover, Iceland is seen as having a role to play and the ability to contribute to the international community (Haarde, 2007). Also, the Icelandic political elite, at least the present governing elite, has changed its view regarding the international system itself. Its perception regarding the international system has changed since Iceland, despite its smallness, is seen as having a say within it.

The intensive debate in 2004 and 2005, about whether or not Iceland should continue with its application to become a member of the UN Security Council, showed two opposing camps disagreeing on Iceland's international approach. On the one hand there was the traditional camp arguing for an international approach based on economic gains, with little or no belief that Iceland could exercise influence in international institutions and in the international system generally (see Oddsson, 2002; *Morgunblaðið*, 2005a; *Morgunblaðið*, 2005h). This is founded on the notion of Iceland's smallness compared to other states, its limited administrative capacity and the conviction that membership within the Security Council would not bring Iceland any direct benefits (see *Morgunblaðið*, 2005b). The financial burden that would result from increased international cooperation also plays a part in the debate. In 2004 and 2005 the Icelandic foreign minister, Oddsson, a former prime minister for more than 13 years (1991–2004) and leader of the right of centre Independence Party, raised doubts about the continuation of the campaign for a seat in the Security Council because of the estimated high cost involved. He was supported by a number of MPs in his party (*Morgunblaðið*, 2005c; *Morgunblaðið*, 2005d; *Morgunblaðið*, 2005e). On several occasions during his premiership Oddsson questioned whether a small state like Iceland could have any say in an international organisation like the European Union.

On the other hand there was the camp that continues to regard Iceland as being capable of taking an active part in the international community and having duties towards the outside world (Haarde, 2006a; Haarde, 2007). The foreign minister, Geir H. Haarde, also from the Independence Party and who took over from Oddsson in September 2005, restated the government's policy to campaign for a seat in the Security Council for 2009–2010. He argued that the reason for the campaign was to place Iceland in a position to be able to influence decisions which concern the international community. He stated that the administration is not too small to take on the duties associated with membership on the Council and would manage this by relocating personnel within the Foreign Ministry and having staff from other ministries work temporarily in the Foreign Ministry. He claimed that Iceland's main goals in the Council would be to promote the core values of the country's foreign policy, that is, human rights, freedom, respect for peace, and security (Haarde, 2006b). Moreover, Iceland's main aim would be disarmament and to prevent the further spread of nuclear weapons (Haarde, 2006a). This latter view prevails now under another foreign minister from May 2007, leader of the Social Democrats, Ingibjörg Sólrún Gísladóttir. She is enthusiastic about Iceland's new and more active international role and regards Iceland as having duties towards the outside world. Under her leadership Iceland intensified its campaign to get a seat in the Security Council emphasising Iceland's ability to contribute to human rights, particularly women's rights, and assist developing states, particularly small developing states (Gísladóttir, 2008). Gísladóttir has had the full backing of Haarde (now prime minister).

The prime reason for Iceland's historical absence from the Security Council is the lack of enthusiasm on the part of previous governments in Iceland to play an active part in the international community. They did not see any reason for Iceland to join the Council, since this would not provide any direct economic benefits for Iceland. In 1998 Iceland was the only Nordic state not to have applied for a seat on the Council. Moreover, Iceland has not taken on the presidency of the UN General Assembly – a post which all the other Nordic states have held, as well as Luxembourg (1975) and other countries of 'similar size' such as the Former Yugoslav Republic of Macedonia (2007), Saint Lucia (2003), Malta (1990), Lebanon (1958) and Ireland (1960–61), all of which were less economically advanced than Iceland (UN General Assembly, 2008). In autumn 2008 Iceland lost its bid for a seat on the Security Council after a humiliating defeat by Austria and Turkey. Iceland received only 87 of 192 votes for one of two rotating European seats on the Security Council. Austria got 133 votes and Turkey 152 votes, achieving the two-thirds margin needed for election in the secret balloting. The result can partly be explained by the lack of interest the Icelandic government has shown regarding UN work over the years. Also, the Icelandic Foreign Service found itself marginalised in the election campaign against the much larger and more widespread Foreign Services of Austria and Turkey. Furthermore, Britain's campaign against Iceland's membership in the last few days before the vote, due to the financial dispute, lost Iceland many votes in the Commonwealth and the small Caribbean island states. The election defeat is a serious blow to those within the Icelandic government who have campaigned for a more assertive and active international role for the country. The defeat also indicates the fractal position of Iceland as a small state in the international community despite its effort to increase its international activities.

External pressure

The perception of international actors, such as pressure groups, firms, states and international institutions, regarding a particular state's ability to influence the international arena cannot be ignored in the new globalised system. This is because the attitudes of these actors may shape the notion of the size of the state and influence its international approach and how other actors respond to its actions (Thorhallsson, 2006b).

International organisations, governments and a number of intergovernmental organisations have put increased pressure on Iceland to contribute more to the international community in the last decade. For instance, this has been the case with NATO, the World Bank, the EEA and the UN and its member states. There has also been growing pressure from organisations working on human rights and development assistance. The US government also put considerable pressure on Iceland from the early to mid-1990s to contribute to its own defence and to shared duties with NATO member states.

Moreover, in 2005, as the debate on whether or not to continue the campaign to seek membership on the Security Council intensified in Iceland, both the prime minister and the foreign minister stated that they were under considerable pressure from their Nordic counterparts to continue the campaign (*Morgunblaðið*, 2005f; 2005g). The prime ministers of the other four Nordic states raised their concerns about Iceland's potential withdrawal of its Security Council application. They emphasised the need for a Nordic state to be represented at the Council's negotiation table and stated that they would be very disappointed if Iceland withdrew its application. Furthermore, they argued that one of them would have campaigned for the seat in the 2009–2010 period in the Council if Iceland had not decided to run in 1998 – and that it was now too late for them to start a campaign (*Morgunblaðið*, 2005b).[4]

One could argue that the views of these actors regarding Iceland's international capabilities has changed in recent years since Iceland has become more affluent and gradually more self-assertive internationally. This external pressure has had several implications for Iceland's international activity. For instance, it has led to the establishment of the ICRU (Bailes and Thorhallsson, 2006) and a considerable increase in Iceland's development aid, which has been much less, as a proportion of GDP, than that given by the other Nordic states (Haralz, 1997; Ingólfsson and Haralz, 2003).

The case of whaling provides an example of the pressure on Iceland to participate in the international scene and to follow its norms and rules. In 2002 Iceland found itself obliged to rejoin the International Whaling Commission (IWC) having left it ten years earlier in protest at not being allowed to continue whaling for commercial purposes. The decision to withdraw from the IWC was in sharp contrast to the position adopted by other whaling nations, such as Norway and Japan, which continued to work with, and promote their policies in, the IWC. This attempt to challenge the authority of the IWC can be seen in the light of the traditional view of Icelandic governments to have the right to make their 'own decisions' regardless of international rules – such as the matter of the Icelandic fishing zone – and deal with issues outside international organisations. In the 1990s Iceland made an attempt to start whaling again, having stopped whaling for scientific purposes in 1989 (after international pressure), by creating an international organisation, the North Atlantic Marine Mammal Commission, together with other whaling nations. This approach failed completely (Halldórsson and Stefánsson, 2001) and Iceland sought to rejoin the Commission in order to be able to start whaling for scientific purposes. Thus, Iceland decided to accept international rules concerning whaling, that is, to work within the IWC, which it has done since 2003. This brought Iceland into line with other whaling nations that accept the IWC's authority and co-operate with countries world-wide within its framework.

To summarise, the pressure from the international community to contribute more on the world stage is clearly felt by the Icelandic government. Iceland has felt obligated to take part in the burden sharing of the more affluent members of several international organisations. Reluctance to follow international norms and rules is neither an attractive option nor even a realistic option for a small state wishing to be taken seriously and needing to protect its wide-ranging interests internationally.

Conclusion

Iceland has become a more active international actor in the last decade, a policy change occurring at the domestic level. There has been a fundamental shift in foreign policy primarily aimed at securing direct Icelandic interests towards a much broader international approach. Iceland's increased activity in the international system has been explained by five interrelated features. First, a more diversified domestic economy and a more complex international arena have led to a redefinition of interests. The Foreign Service has had to widen its appeal in order to respond to this new environment. Second, increased economic resources based on the economic boom from the mid-1990s have given successive governments an opportunity to allocate resources to international affairs. Iceland's government was seen to be more affluent and capable of engaging in activities previously regarded as a luxury. On the other hand, the small Icelandic economy has been hard hit by the financial crisis. The massive overgrown financial sector, which was built on expansion abroad by foreign borrowing, has collapsed with severe consequences for the economy and the fall of the króna. The volatility of the small economy is evident, and the Icelandic government is once again considering seeking economic shelter within the framework of European integration, that is, by considering adopting the euro. Also, the Independence Party is reviewing its policy towards EU membership which might lead to a policy change within the government. Third, the central administration has been strengthened and the Europeanisation of the civil service has increased its expertise and independence. The human capital of the country has also increased in terms of a better educated workforce capable of engaging in international activities. Consequently, the Foreign Service and other ministries and institutions dealing with international affairs are much more capable of decisive policy-making, of carrying out their duties and taking on leadership domestically and internationally. That said, the smallness of the Icelandic Foreign Service was clearly a disadvantage in its campaign for a seat on the UN Security Council as it faced the bigger and more widespread foreign services of competing states Austria and Turkey. Also, the budget deficit which Iceland faces in the coming years due to the economic downturn will lead to a downscaling of the Foreign Service. Fourth, Iceland has chosen to become a more active player in the international arena, a conscious choice. Most Icelandic politicians now regard Iceland capable of contributing to the international community and being able to have a say within international organisations. Governments still prioritise Icelandic core economic and political interests internationally but their list of international engagements has become much longer. Iceland is not only seen to have a duty to protect its core interests, but also its obligations to the outside world. In other words, Iceland is becoming much more ambitious internationally, taking on duties previously unconsidered. On the other hand, Iceland's failure to get a seat in the Security Council could lead to a backlash in the country's attempt to become a more active player on the world stage. Moreover, Icelandic governments have failed to secure the county a permanent economic and political shelter. Iceland's closest allies failed it when the country faced its most serious economic crisis in decades, as did the international institutions such as the EEA, the IMF and the Nordic Council. The Icelandic government has not had access to EU decision-making despite the fact it has to implement most of the EU rules, such as concerning the financial sector, though membership within the EEA. Accordingly, Iceland implemented rules related to the free movement of capital without having any say about the rules and the shelter of EU institutions, including the European Central Bank. Thus, Iceland was left defenceless in the credit crisis. Finally, there has been considerable pressure from international actors for Iceland to take on greater international responsibility. The view of these actors on Iceland's capacity has shifted in recent years along with the increased confidence of Icelandic actors abroad. Iceland has yielded to the pressure in order to take part in the burden sharing of the international community and in the hope of securing long-term benefits for Icelandic society.

As a result, and in the light of the country's reactive approach until the mid- to late1990s, one could say that Iceland has chosen a new role internationally based on its revaluation of its size. Accordingly, Iceland has chosen a new size based on the features discussed above. Political leaders in Iceland have transformed the country from belonging to Keohane's 'system-ineffectual' category into a country capable of influencing the international system together with other states within Keohane's 'system-affecting' category. Iceland's increased activity within the UN, NATO and other multi-lateral organisations is noticeable in this sense. That said, the reluctance of Icelandic governments to take full part in European integration by joining the EU has left the country without an economic and political shelter. This has left Iceland stranded by the EEA Agreement – only implementing its rules without having any say within the EU.

States can choose the extent to which they take part in the international community, given that they have the necessary resources and political will to carry out given tasks. Political elite in a state such as Iceland, which has built up its internal capacity, can transform its domestic capabilities into an active international approach. This is precisely what Icelandic governments have done during the last decade. Iceland is now preparing for the next step towards greater participation in the international community by re-examining its stand towards EU membership.

Notes

1. Such as financial assistance in the form of beneficial loans; economic advice (which was very much needed owing to a lack of domestic expertise, the fluctuating economy and, more specifically, Iceland's currency, the króna), and technical assistance to its financial institutions.
2. On the other hand, Iceland has occasionally taken on duties within the World Bank Group and the IMF through its participation in the Nordic and (since the early 1990s) Baltic states' group in the past few decades (Central Bank of Iceland, 2005).
3. Iceland was in second place on this index from 2003 trailing only Norway (UN Development Programme, 2005), but moved to first place in 2007. The index compares the standard of living in 177 countries. These are assigned a Human Development Index (HDI) rating, which combines four variables: life expectancy at birth; adult literacy rate; combined gross enrolment ratio for primary, secondary and tertiary schools and GDP per capita (PPP US$).
4. Elections to the Council, for terms of two years, are held within the UN every second year, and one of the other four Nordic states (Norway, Denmark, Sweden and Finland) has always campaigned for membership every other term, i.e. the policy of the Nordic states is to have one of their number represented in the Council every other term.

References

Archer, C. (2003) 'The Nordic States Contribution to the International System' in T. Seppä, K. Touminen, U. Vesa, and T. Väyrynen (eds), *Studying the World and Changing It* (Tampere: Tampere Peace Research Institute): 217–29.

Ásgrímsson, H. (2004) *Skýrsla Halldórs Ásgrímssonar utanríkisráðherra um utanríkis- og alþjóðamál* (Reykjavík: Ministry for Foreign Affairs).

Bailes, A. and B. Thorhallsson (2006) 'Iceland and the European Security and Defence Policy' in Alyson Bailes, Gunilla Herolf and Bengt Sundelius (eds) *The Nordic Countries and the European Security and Defence Policy* (Oxford, Oxford University Press): 328–48.

Bjarnason, B. (2008) *Evruaðild-Guðnaráð-nýfrjálshyggja*, 12 July, http://www.bjorn. is/pistlar/nr/4538, accessed on 26 August 2008.

Capacent Gallup (2008) '*Samtök iðnaðarins. Viðhorf almennings til ESB*', June/July, http://www.si. is/media/althjodlegt-samstarf/2008–06- ESB-almenningur.pdf, accessed on 26 August 2008.

Central Bank of Iceland (2005) *Ísland og Alþjóðagjaldeyrissjóðurinn*, http://www.sedl abanki.is/?PageID=320, accessed on 26 August 2008.

Central Bank of Iceland (2007) *The Economy of Iceland 2007*, http://sedlabanki.is/ lisalib/getfile.aspx?itemid=5387, accessed on 26 August 2008.

Central Bank of Iceland (2008) *The Central Bank of Iceland concludes swap facility arrangements*, http://www.sedlabanki.is/?PageID=287&NewsID=1766, accessed on 26 August 2008.

Embassy of Norway in Copenhagen (2005) *Information* (Copenhagen: Embassy of Norway in Copenhagen).

Gísladóttir, I.H. (2007) Speech, 'Mannréttindi í íslenskri utanríkisstefnu: Hvers vegna?', University of Akureyri, Akureyri, 10 December, http://www.utanrikisra duneyti.is/haskolafundarod/nr/4012, accessed on 26 August 2008.

Gísladóttir, I.S. (2007) *Speech* at the conference: Alþjóðasamstarf á 21. öld og öryggisráð Sameinuðu þjóðanna, 7 September, University of Iceland, Reykjavik, http://www.utanrikisraduneyti.is/frettaefni/raedurISG/nr/3831, accessed on 26 August 2008.

Gísladóttir, I.S. (2008) Speech at the Fifty-Second Session of the Commission on the Status of Women, 25 February, United Nations, New York, http://www.utanrikisraduneyti.is/frettaefni/raedurISG/nr/4116, accessed on 26 August 2008.

Haarde, G.H. (2006a) 'Rétt að fara í átak til að upplýsa almenning', interview in *Morgunblaðið*, 9 March.

Haarde, G.H. (2006b) Interview on Icelandic National Radio(RUV) Channel 1, 9 March.

Haarde, G.H. (2007) Speech at the conference: *Alþjóðasamstarf á 21. öld og öryggisráð Sameinuðu þjóðanna*, 7 September, University of Iceland, Reykjavik.

Hálfdánarson, G. (2004) 'Discussing Europe: Icelandic nationalism and European Integration' in B. Thorhallsson (ed.) *Iceland and European Integration: On the Edge* (London and New York: Routledge).

Halldórsson, G.E. and H.J. Stefánsson (2001) *Hvalveiðar: Áhrif, afleiðingar og almenningsálit*, B.A. dissertation (Reykjavík: Faculty of Social Sciences, University of Iceland).

Hansen, L. (2002) 'Introduction' in L. Hansen and O. Wæver (eds) *European Integration and National Identity: The Challenge of the Nordic States* (London and New York: Routledge).

Haralz, J.H. (1997) *Um þróunarsamvinnu Íslands*, 16 April (Reykjavík: Ministry for Foreign Affairs).

Icelandic Public Radio (Ríkisútvarpið) (2008) 'News' (Fréttir), Icelandic Public TV News, 14 July.

Ingólfsson, H.Ö. and J.H. Haralz (2003) *Ísland og þróunarlöndin: Álitsgerð um þróunarsamvinnu Íslands og þátttöku í starfi alþjóðastofnana*, 1 September (Reykjavík: Ministry for Foreign Affairs).

Institute of Economic Studies (2005) Information, 25 August (Reykjavík: Institute of Economic Studies).

International Monetary Fund (2005) Interview with an official, 25 August.

International Monetary Fund (2008) *Iceland-2008 – Article IV Consultation Concluding Statement*, 4 July.

Keohane, R.O. (1969) ' "Lilleputians" Dilemmas: Small States in International Politics', *International Organization* 23(2): 291–310.

Kristinsson, G.H. (1993) 'Valdakerfið fram til Viðreisnar 1900–1959', in G. Hálfda- narson, and S. Kristjánsson (eds) *Íslensk þjóðfélagsþróun 1880–1990* (Reykjavík: Félagsvísindastofnun Háskóla Íslands and Sagnfræðistofnun Háskóla Íslands).

Lærgreid, P., R.S. Steinþórsson and B. Thorhallsson (2004) 'Europeanization of Central Government Administration in the Nordic States', *Journal of Common Market Studies* (2): 347–69.

Ministry of Foreign Affairs, Government of Denmark (2005) *Information* (Copenhagen: Ministry of Foreign Affairs).

Ministry for Foreign Affairs, Government of Iceland (2003) *Information*, May (Reykjavík: Ministry for Foreign Affairs).

Ministry for Foreign Affairs, Government of Iceland (2006) 'Sendiráð, fastanefndir og ræðisskrifstofur 1918–2002', http://www.utanrikisraduneyti.is/utanrikisth jonustan/soguleg- yfirlit/#VII, accessed on 26 August 2008.

Morgunblaðið (2003) 'Halldór Ásgrímsson utanríkisráðherra fjallaði umframboð til öryggisráðs SÞ á Alþingi. Ákvörðun um framboð til öryggisráðs SÞ markar tímamót', 14 November.

Morgunblaðið (2005a) 'Vaxandi efasemdir eru um möguleika Íslands', 25 January.

Morgunblaðið (2005b) 'Öryggisráðið og aðrar leiðir', 27 January.

Morgunblaðið (2005c) 'Verra en í Eurovision', 2 March.

Morgunblaðið (2005d) 'Óöruggt sæti í öryggisráði', 30 April.

Morgunblaðið (2005e) 'Áleitnar spurningar hafa vaknað um kostnað', 30 April.

Morgunblaðið (2005f) 'Fullur stuðningur við framboð Íslands til Öryggisráðsins', 29 June.

Morgunblaðið (2005g) 'Mörg fordæmi fyrir því að ríki hætti við', 14 July.

Morgunblaðið (2005h) 'Stórþjóð eða örþjóð – Staksteinar', 18 September.

National Economic Institute (2001) *Historical Statistics 1901–2000*, 14 December, http://www.ths.is/rit/sogulegt/english.htm.

Oakley, D. (2008) 'Sharp rise in CDS spreads increase pressure on Iceland', *Financial Times*, http://www.ft.com/cms/s/0/972bf7fc-4317-11dd-81d0- 0000779fd2ac.html, accessed on 26 August 2008.

Oddsson, D. (2002) 'Ávarp forsætisráðherra á aðalfundi Samtaka atvinnulífsins', Speech, 25 January, http://forsaetisraduneyti.is/radherra/raedur-og-greinar/nr/ 365, 26 August 2008.

Oddsson, D. (2004) 'Iceland's Economic Performance', Address before the American Enterprise Institute, Washington, DC, 14 June, http://eng. forsaetisraduneyti.is/minister/speeches-and-articles/nr/1391, accessed on 26 August 2008.

Policy Statement (2007) *The Policy Statement of the Government of the Indepen- dence Party and the Social Democratic Alliance*, 23 May, Iceland: Thingvellir, http://eng.forsaetisraduneyti.is/news-and-articles/nr/2646, accessed on 26 August 2008.

Sverrisdóttir, E. B. (2006) Ekkert knýr á um aðild Íslendinga að ESB. Morgunblaðið, 1 April, http://www.mbl.is/mm/gagnasafn/grein.html?grein_id=1074899, accessed on 8 August 2008.

Thorhallsson, B. (2002) 'Consequences of Small Administration: The Case of Iceland', *Current Politics and Economics of the European Union* 11 (1): 61–76.

Thorhallsson, B. (2004) 'Shackled by smallness: a weak administration as a deter- minant of policy choice' in B. Thorhallsson (ed.) *Iceland and European Integration: On the edge* (London and New York: Routledge): 161–84.

142   *The Diplomacies of Small States*

Thorhallsson, B. (2005) 'What features determine international activities of small states? The international approach of Iceland until the mid 1990s', *Stjórnmál og stjórnsýsla – veftímarit* 1(1): 105–54.

Thorhallsson, B. (2006a) 'Iceland's Involvement in Global Affairs since the mid-1990s', *Stjórnmál og stjórnsýsla – veftímarit*, Stofnun stjórnmála og stjórnsýslu, Háskóli Íslands, 2(2): 197–223.

Thorhallsson, B. (2006b) 'The Size of States in the European Union: Theoretical and Conceptual Perspectives', *Journal of European Integration*, 28(1): 7–31.

UN Development Programme (2005) *The 2005 Human Development Index (HDI)* (New York: United Nations).

UN Development Programme (2007/2008) *Human Development Report – Iceland – The Human Development Index – going beyond income*, http://hdrstats.undp.org/countries/country_fact_sheets/cty_fs_ISL.html, accessed on 26 August 2008.

UN General Assembly (2008) *President of the 62nd Session United Nations General Assembly*, http://www.un.org/ga/president/62/presskit/listpast.shtml, accessed on 26 August 2008.

8
PetroCaribe and CARICOM: Venezuela's Resource Diplomacy and its Impact on Small State Regional Cooperation

Anthony T. Bryan

The world energy map is changing and global competition for oil and natural gas is increasingly more aggressive. As demand grows, oil and natural gas become obvious strategic commodities susceptible to being used for geopolitical leverage. Potential confrontations over oil and gas supplies and transportation networks once again have developed into geopolitical flashpoints. At the same time, energy security has emerged as an important factor, but its traditional focus on procurement and market stability has been bolstered by politics and strategic calculations.

Global dynamics of resource diplomacy

The structural shifts in global energy markets and political alliances are manifested in displays of 'petro-politics' and the increased use of resource diplomacy. For example, a newly assertive Russia is making Russian nationalism in global politics a more important factor by flexing its military muscle in some former states of the now defunct USSR, bolstered by the political leverage it exercises over Europe on account of huge Russian oil and natural gas reserves. China, a global power, is conducting a foreign policy highly motivated by the urgency to satisfy its enormous energy needs. The search for energy has resulted in China's political outreach to the Middle East, Africa and Latin America. Iran, one of the world's great oil producers, is challenging the United Nations, the United States, and the West for the right to develop its nuclear power capabilities.

In the Americas a similar dynamic is being played out *inter alia*: between Bolivia and its main export markets, Brazil and Argentina, over natural gas prices; the Bolivian government's nationalisation of foreign oil company operations such as Petrobrás (the Brazilian state oil company) within its borders; and, Bolivian refusal to ship natural gas to Chile because of a deep-seated and emotive historic national rivalry. But it is Venezuela, led by the ubiquitous President Hugo Chávez that is playing the resource diplomacy game with notable success.

Venezuela

Venezuela has massive oil and gas resources. It has proven oil reserves of 80 billion barrels and 151 billion cubic feet of natural gas. Latin America holds the largest petroleum reserves in the world after the Middle East, and Venezuela possesses nearly 70 per cent of the total proven Latin American hydrocarbon reserves (Energy Information Agency, 2008). If extra heavy crude oil is included, the country's oil reserves rival those of Saudi Arabia. Venezuela is taking advantage of its oil largesse to leverage development, promote regional integration, and reduce dependence on the United States. President Chávez, who was given congressional authority to rule by decree until July 2008, has since used new decrees to augment the state's control over the economy and financial system. He also admits to using 'oil as a geopolitical weapon' (Kozloff, 2005) to reconfigure strategic alliances in Latin America and the Caribbean, to re-fashion global alliances, and to leverage political influence in the US. Venezuela's particular brand of 'resource nationalism', involving the recentralisation of control over the domestic energy industry, taking ownership and profit potential away from international oil companies (IOCs) and giving national oil companies (NOCs) majority interests in most concessions, has also encouraged the administrations of President Evo Morales in Bolivia and Rafael Correa in Ecuador to try similar approaches.

Venezuela's petro-politics is intended to take advantage of its revenue from oil resources and move the country towards greater control over its domestic energy sector. Before the end of July 2008 President Chávez issued a number of new decrees that appear to form part of a renewed effort to augment the state's control over the financial system. (EIU, 2008) During his tenure he has deepened what he calls 'twenty-first century socialism' by nationalising some banks, an international cement company, and private energy companies operating in Venezuela in the telecommunications, electricity, and natural gas sectors, as well as heavy crude oil upgrading projects in the Orinoco River Basin. The IOCs have been invited to stay on as minority partners, and most (with the notable exception of major player Exxon) have indicated a willingness to continue investing despite Chávez's tightening terms, including tax and royalty increases. The possibility that the Orinoco belt could contain the largest pool of crude oil reserves in the world is a major magnet for them. The technology for producing and refining the 'extra heavy' crude oil in the Orinoco belt has been developed for some time now by foreign oil majors.

Under the administration of President Chávez the national oil company, Petróleos de Venezuela, S.A. (PdVSA) has become a driver of Venezuela's foreign policy and an instrument in Venezuela's regional political power plays. Despite his regular harsh and sometimes vitriolic anti-US pronouncements, Chávez's actual energy and foreign policies are more nuanced, even as they become more nationalistic. The reality is that most of the oil that Venezuela exports is still shipped to the United States, where the refining capacity now exists for the country's heavy crude. US companies still provide the bulk of Venezuela's imports of goods and services, despite Venezuela's diversification of its oil markets globally and its joint investment in a myriad of new refinery projects in Asia, the Middle East and Latin America. Although Venezuela has been threatening to sell its US-based oil refineries, its gasoline outlets (CITGO stations), and rethinking its long-standing gasoline supply contracts, the current US position as Venezuela's major market and trading partner in energy commodities will not be replaced anytime soon.

One of the most successful ventures in Venezuela's resource diplomacy is its current relationship with Cuba. What began as an innocuous set of agreements has become a major alliance in which strategic assets are exchanged. These assets include energy resources, large financial transactions, joint business ventures, information technology, development aid, intelligence services, highly-trained personnel, and military assistance. The alliance has appeal to both Cuba and Venezuela because each country is exchanging assets that are inexpensive for the sending country but of enormous strategic value to the receiving country. In this relationship people really matter, as evidenced by Cuba's regional 'medical diplomacy', which provides medical personnel not only to Venezuela but also many countries in the Latin American/Caribbean region. The scholarship programme for medical training in Cuba is also the type of active diplomacy that has won friends in the region. There are other gains for Cuba as the primary beneficiary of Venezuela's initiatives. It has gained critical breathing space in the management of its foreign and economic policy, particularly now in shaping the post-Fidel Castro transition. Venezuela's close relationship with Cuba also provides

President Chávez with enormous international political stature, despite serious political and financial costs arising from the severe polarisation of domestic politics in Venezuela.

In spite of the varied images conveyed internationally about President Chávez, it is difficult to deny that his regional PdVSA-backed investments and ventures in oil exploration, infrastructure, and the financing of social projects in Venezuela and other parts of the Americas, have created a somewhat unsteady and reluctant commonality of interests in the region. Several recent regional polls have suggested that many Latin Americans do not like Chávez personally or his politics. Many in neighbouring countries also resent his very public and outrageous name calling of their leaders, and what they perceive as interference in their sovereign affairs (WOLA, 2007).

Obviously it is one thing to oppose President Chávez politically in Venezuela, it is quite another for energy deficient Caribbean neighbours, or leaders with similar ideological views in South America, to refuse his money. Demands of poverty alleviation and decreased income disparity placed upon regional governments and provided the Venezuelan government with fortuitous opportunities for regional influence. In the past four years Venezuela's oil money has rescued Ecuador's deficit budget more than once, helped Argentina place successful bond issues, and is financing, what President Chávez conceives as, the energy integration of Latin America and the wider Caribbean. The mechanism for such energy integration is PetroAmérica (a holding company for all state-owned energy projects in Latin America and the Caribbean), and its subsidiaries: PetroCaribe, PetroSur and PetroAndina. In fact, Petro-América is being acclaimed by Venezuela as the cornerstone of an energy ring that will enable the region to be self-sufficient and have leverage to set prices, not as a Latin American OPEC (Organization of the Petroleum Exporting Countries, of which Venezuela is a founding member) but as an ally of OPEC. In essence, the current Venezuelan approach to resource diplomacy lies in the development of a strong NOC bolstered by high oil prices, and legitimised by a Chávez-inspired 'twenty-first-century socialism' that, in the view of this writer, occupies a nebulous philosophical comfort zone somewhere between Simón Bolivar and Santa Claus!

Generally, the possibilities of using petroleum for political influence in Latin America are somewhat limited owing to the energy-richness of the area. Venezuela, Mexico, Colombia, Ecuador and Trinidad and Tobago are exporters while Argentina and Bolivia produce enough to satisfy their internal demand. The net petroleum importers are Peru, Brazil, Chile, Paraguay, Uruguay, and all the Central American and Caribbean countries except Trinidad and Tobago. The Andean region also appears to be one where oil diplomacy would have minimal impact because of its vast reserves of petroleum, natural gas, coal and hydroelectric power. But political, social and ethnic crises in the region (particularly in Bolivia) allow neighbouring governments and global powers to try to influence vulnerable governments (Arriagada, 2006).

PetroCaribe

Central America and the Caribbean are the regions where Venezuelan resource diplomacy can have its greatest impact. In the case of the Caribbean, heavily indebted small nations, struggling to develop social and economic transition programmes, adjusting to declining revenues, and facing the erosion of traditional preferential markets for commodities such as sugar and bananas, are searching for ways to respond to their energy-related financial problems. The countries of the Caribbean island chain, along with mainland Guyana, are among the most indebted states in the world on a debt-to-GDP basis. Expected high energy prices over the next decade will have a further negative impact on their foreign currency reserves and balance of payments. With the exception of Trinidad and Tobago, crude oil and refined petroleum make up the bulk of Caribbean import needs. Dependence on oil and gas imports is higher in this region than anywhere else in the hemisphere, meaning the potential for resource diplomacy (as well as resource dependency) is greater as well (Bryan, 2007).

The PetroCaribe initiative, launched by Venezuela in July 2005, has provided budgetary and development options for some of the countries in the region currently suffering from the loss of traditional preferential export markets. At first glance the basic PetroCaribe agreement is straightforward. It is a framework agreement within which each signatory agrees on how much oil or petroleum products it requires from Venezuela. Depending on the world price of oil, a fixed percentage is assigned to the recipient nation in the form of a soft loan. If oil is at $50 per barrel, the loan to the nation concerned will be set at 40 per cent of the value of the overall purchase; if, for example, oil goes to $100 per barrel or beyond, 50 per cent of the cost of the imports is deferred for a period of 25 years at a concessionary rate of 1 per cent.

During the PetroCaribe Summit in Maracaibo, Venezuela in mid-July 2008, the government of Venezuela agreed to increase the deferred financing portion to 60 per cent once the price exceeds US$100 per barrel, a reaction to the unprecedented increases in oil prices during 2007 and

2008. Further, should the price exceed US$200 per barrel, the deferred portion will be increased to 70 per cent. Under the latest agreement, up to 50 per cent of PetroCaribe members' energy bills could potentially be paid for with agricultural products, and services (including tourism). At the Summit it was also announced that an oil block in the Orinoco belt would be assigned to PetroCaribe's member countries. Also significant was the Summit participants' decision to establish a Fund to support PetroCaribe member countries in expanding agricultural production and improving food security, while making 100 000 tons of urea per annum available to PetroCaribe members at a discount of 40 per cent of the prevailing market price. President Chávez also decided to contribute 50 cents towards the Fund for every barrel of oil exported, estimated to amount to US$760 million per year.

The original agreement was signed by 12 of the 15 members of CARI-COM plus Cuba and the Dominican Republic on 7 September 2005. The nations signing the agreement were Antigua and Barbuda, the Bahamas, Belize, Cuba, Dominica, the Dominican Republic, Grenada, Guyana, Jamaica, Nicaragua, Suriname, St Lucia, St Kitts and Nevis, and St Vincent and the Grenadines. The only countries that chose not to sign on were Barbados and Trinidad and Tobago. The programme was extended to Haiti in January 2006 after the election of the new president, René Preval. Honduras joined the alliance in December 2007, and Guatemala became the eighteenth member in July 2008.

So far the results of the programme for PetroCaribe members have been mixed. As of mid-2008, only Cuba and Jamaica have been receiving regular fuel shipments while other members are receiving shipments only sporadically. Within CARICOM Jamaica has benefited most from shipments and PdVSA has helped to finance Jamaican development projects, such as a $500 million refinery upgrade and expansion under an agreement that will give the Venezuelan state oil company a 49 per cent stake in the facility. Venezuela has taken over the role of principal supplier, providing almost 24 000 barrels per day (bpd) out of the 28 000 bpd consumed in the country in 2007. There have also been loans to aid the completion of major highway projects in Jamaica, support for Air Jamaica, the Clarendon Alumina plant, and the Sugar Company of Jamaica. The Port Authority of Jamaica is also looking to the PetroCaribe fund for financial assistance to facilitate the expansion of the country's ports and operations (*Jamaica Observer*, 13 August, 2008).

Progress on implementing PetroCaribe is slow because PdVSA has encountered serious problems dealing with the management of such small quantities, particularly where the infrastructure for delivery has to be created. Among recipient nations only the Bahamas, Jamaica and Suriname have appropriate refineries. Caracas has upgraded Cuba's Cienfuegos refinery as well as a refinery in the Dominican Republic. There are also separate agreements with Cuba, the Dominican Republic and Jamaica for the improvement and expansion of their refining capacity, designating them as refining centres to supply fuel and fuel products to CARICOM states. Under a deal struck in December 2006 between PdVSA and the West Indies Oil Company (WIOC) pertaining to the rental of fuel storage facilities, Antigua and Barbuda (which owns 25 per cent of WIOC) will become a collection centre and trans-shipment point in the distribution of diesel, jet fuel, and gasoline to Eastern Caribbean countries. Yet delivery member countries have fallen short of expectations. As of December 2007 PetroCaribe members were receiving 145 000 barrels daily (rather than the 200 000 barrels per day originally planned) of which 95 000 barrels go to Cuba.

While the PetroCaribe arrangement between Caribbean countries and Venezuela might be working as a buffer against high oil prices, import countries are sinking deeper into long-term debt. Inevitably, PetroCaribe has proved to be a great accelerator of debt for the Caribbean members. In the case of Jamaica the debt had reached J$33 billion (US$476 million) by April 2008 (*Jamaica Gleaner*, 2008). In December 2007 PetroCaribe members' collective debt for Venezuelan crude stood at US$1.2 billion and was expected to grow to US$4.5 billion by 2010 (CNN, 2007). Given the large increases in oil prices in 2008, the debt figure is certain to have increased substantially since the December figure.

CARICOM and the reaction to Venezuela's resource diplomacy

The issues surrounding PetroCaribe have posed diplomatic challenges for the CARICOM region as an entity. Both Trinidad and Tobago and Barbados declined to sign the PetroCaribe agreement. Trinidad and Tobago was concerned that its state-owned Petrotrin refinery stood to lose about 30 per cent of its sales of petroleum products, fuel oil, diesel, and gasoline to the Caribbean. Approximately 56 per cent of Petrotrin's product sales are in the Caribbean market. Phoenix Park Gas Processors Ltd, which traditionally supplies natural gas liquids to the CARICOM region, also expected to suffer a decline in sales (ENERGY Caribbean, 2007a).

The government of Trinidad and Tobago was particularly angered by the almost total acceptance of the Venezuelan initiative without reservations. From the outset, Prime Minister Patrick Manning criticised the way in which Caribbean states rushed to sign the agreement in spite of its apparent weaknesses. He indicated that the initiative would force out private oil firms, leaving the region dependent on a single state-run supplier – Venezuela's PdVSA. He also suggested that Petrotrin, the traditional supplier to CARICOM, would be hurt financially and that Trinidad and Tobago could stop selling its oil and petroleum products to its neighbours and seek extra-regional markets. In such a case, guarantees could not be offered to countries attempting to resume buying oil and petroleum products from Trinidad and Tobago if the PetroCaribe agreement eventually faltered (BBC Caribbean, 2006). In the case of Barbados, the minister of energy explained that his country saw no need to sign on to PetroCaribe because: its crude oil is already refined in Trinidad; PetroCaribe would not deliver discounted prices for petroleum products; petroleum products originating in Venezuela would attract the 20 per cent Common External Tariff (CET); and the agreement would result in debt accumulation at a tremendous rate (Wood, 2005).

The PetroCaribe arrangement also undercut Trinidad and Tobago's two regional initiatives: an oil facility to CARICOM countries including a loan initiative to finance the purchases of petroleum products above the price of $30 a barrel of oil; and a CARICOM Petroleum Fund (established in 2004) that makes an annual grant to member states to help them in developing their economies.

As of July 2008 neither Trinidad and Tobago nor Barbados had joined PetroCaribe, but their positions had become more accommodative indicating an awareness of the serious economic circumstance of their CARICOM neighbours. Indeed, shortly after PetroCaribe was established, Prime Minister Manning of Trinidad and Tobago agreed to act on behalf of his CARICOM colleagues in negotiations with the Venezuelan government on the operational aspects of PetroCaribe. Trinidad and Tobago also removed the CET protection on its petroleum refinery to 'facilitate' the PetroCaribe arrangement between Venezuela and other CARICOM members, knowing, even then, that Petrotrin was facing a disadvantage in losing some of its markets in the Caribbean. (By giving up the CET, Venezuela does not incur additional costs or tariffs when it supplies oil to CARICOM members under the PetroCaribe arrangement.) In fact, Petrotrin's usual Caribbean market sales of around 60 000 bpd have fallen by half since the 2005 creation of PetroCaribe. But Petrotrin is meeting the challenge by improved product lines, new markets and an intensive refinery upgrade (Hutchinson-Jafar, 2008). At the end of its 2007 fiscal year, Petrotrin declared its highest revenues ever, thanks largely to soaring oil prices on the international market and the ability to sustain export levels. Company revenues for the year ending September 2007 reached US$4.2 billion, an increase of 2.5 per cent over 2006.

In addition, Trinidad and Tobago, despite the PetroCaribe initiatives, continues to be generous in support of its neighbours by raising the level of its contributions to its CARICOM Petroleum Fund. As of March 2008, US$190 million had been disbursed to the fund and another $US500 million committed through the creation of a special window that would allow OECS countries to access an infrastructural development fund as well as monies for poverty alleviation, natural disaster relief and national security. Trinidad and Tobago has also agreed to provide $US38 million to the Caribbean Development Fund (CDF) and transfer $US20 million from its CARICOM Petroleum Fund to the CDF. The motives are obvious. Trinidad and Tobago controls 80 per cent of CARICOM's intra-regional trade and it is in the country's interest to ensure that the integrity of its regional trade partners is not compromised (*Newsday*, 2008).

Increasingly, Venezuela is being viewed as a regional partner by energy dependent CARICOM countries and PetroCaribe looks like a real attempt to find a regional solution to the supply problems that they face. But as each country reports its progress under the PetroCaribe framework agreement, it is clear that there are variations between the individual country terms that are negotiated with Venezuela. It is also obvious that some countries, such as Jamaica and Antigua and Barbuda, have been able to negotiate better side agreements than others. Venezuela's financing arrangement as presently structured may also cause problems for the emerging Caribbean Single Market and Economy (CSME).

In regional political, business, and diplomatic circles, there has been concern that the PetroCaribe arrangement might have an impact on Caribbean diplomacy, in particular, voting patterns in multilateral institutions and regional bodies such as the United Nations and the Organization of American States (OAS). In July 2006 such diplomatic concerns were put to the test when Venezuela lobbied and received bloc support from CARICOM leaders in its (failed) quest for a non-permanent seat on the United Nations Security Council. Despite pressure from the United States to support Guatemala, the CARICOM countries were quite disinclined to do so because of Guatemala's continuing antagonism towards Belize in its border dispute with that country. In fact, neither the Venezuela–Guyana border dispute nor Venezuela's claim to Bird Island (Isla de Aves) off Dominica was deemed by the CARICOM governments as sufficient reasons to deny support for Venezuela's campaign for the Security Council seat. Apparently, a long-term economic relationship that could compromise future independent action relating to border issues does not as yet seem to be a concern for the current crop of CARICOM leaders. While there are still valid questions about the potential use of PetroCaribe as a political instrument, so far Venezuela has not yet gained any clear political advantage in the international arena through the arrangement. But such anxiety will continue to surface. Current diplomatic concerns include: Venezuela's military arms build-up during 2007 and 2008 (supposedly to counter the US Fourth Fleet); its territorial dispute with Guyana; and its territorial challenge to Barbados regarding two of the latter's 24 offshore oil blocks offered to foreign companies being in Venezuela's maritime zone (a potentially difficult process to arbitrate since Venezuela is not a signatory to the UN Convention of the Law of the Sea).

ALBA

While some Caribbean leaders may be concerned about the ability of PdVSA to support such economic largesse in the future, there is also suspicion that PetroCaribe may create new strategic alignments that respond to Venezuelan President Hugo Chávez's long-term political objectives. This includes the formation of the Bolivarian Alternative for America (ALBA), which he considers an alternative to the proposed (and stalled) Free Trade Area of the Americas (FTAA) and a weapon in his ideological war with Washington. ALBA is seen by its proponents as an attempt at regional economic integration that is not based primarily on trade liberalisation, but on a vision of social welfare and mutual economic aid (Altmann, 2008; Arreaza, 2004). The ALBA was formed on 14 December 2004 with Venezuela and Cuba as its first members. Since then Bolivia and Nicaragua have joined and Dominica became the first CARICOM country to sign the agreement on 15 January 2008. Antigua and Barbuda and St Vincent and the Grenadines, though not members, have attended ALBA meetings.

Since his election to office in 2004, Prime Minister Roosevelt Skerritt of Dominica has forged a relationship with Cuba's Castro and Venezuela's Chávez, which has resulted in Dominica (population 72 000) receiving substantial aid from both countries. About 1000 Cuban and Venezuelan experts in energy, education, health care, agriculture, tourism, housing and other forms of construction are working in Dominica. Under the PetroCaribe agreement, crude oil from Venezuela will be stored in huge amounts in Dominica for distribution to other Caribbean countries. Construction of a US$80 million dollar oil refinery with Venezuelan cooperation is also proposed. Dominica pays for 40 per cent of its

PetroCaribe oil imports – that is, about 900 barrels a day – with its main export, bananas. The Venezuelan government said it has given Dominica a US$10.1 million grant to expand the Melville Hall Airport, forgiven the island nation's US$1.5 million debt, and assisted in restoring the sight of some 500 blind Dominicans in either Cuba or Venezuela. In education, about 2000 Dominican students enjoy Cuban and Venezuelan scholarships in computer science, medicine, engineering, sports, physics, math, and agriculture.

Although other CARICOM governments are sympathetic to Dominica's economic plight and its efforts to improve it, Dominica's ALBA membership has generated considerable debate in the region among both policy-makers and commentators over CARICOM's inability to reach foreign policy consensus on Venezuela's initiatives in the region. In fact both PetroCaribe and ALBA have become divisive foreign policy issues (as has the question of the continuing recognition of Taiwan by some CARICOM states) within the region. Some prominent regional scholars and technocrats believe that Dominica and others who support ALBA regard it as just another avenue for obtaining economic aid that is not available within the CARICOM regional integration grouping and have dismissed the arguments of others that ALBA could undermine CARICOM. Other actions undertaken by CARICOM member states cited as being at variance with regional commitments and responsibilities are: the efforts of Jamaica and Trinidad and Tobago to act unilaterally in the early 1990s to qualify for 'NAFTA parity' treatment by the United States; the separate negotiations by CARICOM countries with the US on the drug interdiction 'Shiprider' agreements; and Trinidad and Tobago's agreement on a Free Trade Agreement (FTA) with Costa Rica, disallowed by the Council on Trade and Economic Development of CARICOM, and eventually negotiated as a CARICOM–Costa Rica FTA (Girvan, 2008; Richards, 2008). The issue for the longer term, therefore, is the extent of the cohesiveness of CARICOM foreign policy as new global configurations alter old allegiances and traditional diplomatic positions unravel.

Regional energy policy

No one would deny that PetroCaribe provides a lifeline at the precise moment at which many Caribbean nations feel there is no longer any interest among traditional partners in supporting them. But whether it is good for regional integration, or individual poor and small energy-dependent states, are open questions. Since February 2003 a six-member committee, appointed by CARICOM's Heads of Government, has been trying to deliver a clear Regional Energy Plan utilising the expertise of Trinidad and Tobago. Many analysts now regard the plan as somewhat of an anti-climax since, even under the CSME, an energy policy document will be an umbrella that recognises the right of individual states to pursue their own policies (ENERGY Caribbean, 2007b).

As it now stands PetroCaribe, even with its warts, poses a barrier to the implementation of a CARICOM regional energy policy. Indeed, Trinidad's role as a regional energy supplier is becoming more marginal. PetroCaribe has shifted the regional dominant energy supplier from Trinidad and Tobago to Venezuela. In the process, even Trinidad's role as a potential partner for Venezuela in the processing of natural gas from the Plataforma Deltana field may be less certain.

The PetroCaribe agreement is not in itself the model of regional energy cooperation that can serve CARICOM properly. The agreement is based primarily on the primacy of Venezuelan oil with its current high revenue stream due to global markets, and the export of commodities and minerals for the continuation of profligate budgetary policies and social programmes. If Chávez leaves the scene, either by nature or by force, and PdVSA and Venezuela have new presidents, what will happen with Cuba's oil debt and PdVSA's investments in the region and abroad?

Hemispheric energy policy and security is a big league game in which the long-term strategic interests of the US, Brazil and Venezuela cannot be set aside. A common approach by CARICOM, as envisioned in the formulation of a Caribbean energy policy, can help to transform Petro-Caribe, as well as the region's relations with Venezuela, into approaches that have less potential for politics to trump economics. Similarly, while Venezuela now has regional integration mandated in its constitution, and uses energy resources for economic development, the personification of Venezuelan foreign policy in President Chávez has given rise to serious concerns that certain bilateral and multilateral relations in the region could eventually be aborted (Bryan, 2007).

The challenge for CARICOM

The question that emerges for CARICOM is whether as a regional group it is able systematically to respond to external changes and potentially divisive issues and do so with consensus, instead of on an ad hoc and individual country basis. At the 11th Meeting of the CARICOM Council for Foreign and Community Relations (COFOR) in Antigua and Barbuda, on 9 May 2008, Secretary-General Edwin Carrington pointed out that CARICOM's adoption of Community positions on major hemispheric and international issues has been one of the greatest strengths of the Community. He warned that a departure from the pursuit of that obligation will significantly weaken the Community and its individual member states. He sees the current task as one to promote and protect the Community's strategic interest. Carrington charged the various ministers of foreign affairs to determine how the region should respond to the challenges; what new initiatives could be mounted by the region; and what mechanisms the region needs to put in place to attain the Community's objectives (Carrington, 2008).

In the case of CARICOM, when one tries to match integration theory with practice, it appears that the current regional integration movement is weak because of generic political and institutional factors. The integration process is constantly undermined as national and sectional interests are advanced over regional ones. Conflicts arise over priorities and objectives because of differing approaches to the notion of regionalism. Consequently, the formulation and implementation of policies by member countries, at both the national and regional levels, are not based on a solid system of ideas or ideology that recognises how inextricable the deepening and consolidation of the integration process is to the development of each individual territory. In fact, given the adversarial nature of Caribbean politics, regional decisions often become hostage to domestic power politics. There is no supranational authority with the power to enforce or implement decisions, thus many CARICOM decisions are simply impotent, left unimplemented, or are soon forgotten. In addition, measures that find agreement at the regional political or technical levels are subject to domestic non-compliance because of a lack of local government enthusiasm or adequate funding for sufficient technical capacity to carry out the mandate. Given the existing circumstances, member countries tend to pursue their different development and political strategies pragmatically, without consultation or coordination with other member states. This is particularly troublesome in the realm of foreign policy where the coordination is one of the tenets of the regional grouping (Bryan and Bryan, 1999).

The impact of PetroCaribe on CARICOM has further emphasised the vulnerability of the regional institution. While vulnerability is a constant condition of small states, Caribbean academics have often pointed to weaknesses in the theory, practice and structure of the regional movement (Lewis, 2008a; 2008b). One scholar has posited that over the years of its existence, CARICOM has been able to promote the co-existence of regional integration at one level and regional fragmentation at another. In fact, he concludes that, strictly speaking, if the term 'integration' is considered to mean the emergence of a new and separate community of identity into which previous national identities are progressively submerged, then CARICOM is not an integration movement at all. The end result is not the replacement of national and political action, but rather its 'reinforcement' (Payne, 2007). In the seminal Report of the West Indian Commission in 1992, *Time for Action*, and in subsequent expert recommendations to CARICOM Heads of Government, there are repeated assertions that CARICOM continues to remain a community of sovereign states (West Indian Commission, 1992). The Commission's recommendation to endow CARICOM with executive responsibility for implementing decisions was rejected along with the opportunity to prepare collectively for changes in the perspectives of the region's global partners with respect to trade and liberalisation.

Today, several factors shape CARICOM's regional space. While demands in the global political economy create an incentive for deeper integration, the history of a failed attempt at federation, and the political culture within each member state mitigate against political union. What seems to be emerging is a 'half-way house' reflected in a shift from the solely inter-governmental framework to an emerging model necessary in facilitating the establishment of the Caribbean Single Market and Economy. Some revisions to the CARICOM institutional structure have been made during the past 15 years but the institutional difficulties persist (Grenade, 2005). Although CARICOM has a complex organisational structure in place, its institutions may not have the capacity to lead member states through the fundamental reforms needed to confront the new external challenges. The decision-making process, including the establishment of effective and better integrated enforcement mechanisms, must be strengthened if regional and external images and effectiveness are to be improved. CARICOM countries are being compelled by globalisation to respond to a more dynamic trade, business, and foreign policy environment.

Conclusion

Since the inception of PetroCaribe, Venezuela has started to emerge as the most important single development partner for its members. The economic relationship with Venezuela now appears to be central to the region's short- and medium-term stability. It is estimated that the PetroCaribe oil agreement is responsible for 43 per cent of the $US4.7 billion cost of the 59 million barrels of oil sent to members since 2005. PetroCaribe members have saved an estimated US$921million spread between PetroCaribe's 1 per cent financing rate and the cost of raising money on the credit markets, according to official figures (Mander, 2008). Combined with the PetroCaribe loan facilities and funds for social development projects, the agreement is proving vital to the survival of some CARICOM economies.

Within the context of energy resource diplomacy, it remains to be seen whether Venezuela will be able to deliver on the promises of President Chávez. A great deal depends on the capacity of Venezuela to deliver product effectively. Investment in and maintenance of Venezuela's oil fields have diminished as PdVSA has been forced to give more money to the government to finance social spending. None of this implies that Caribbean countries should reject a generous offer. They should, however, accept the largesse with the understanding that they will increase their energy independence by strengthening regional energy cooperation and developing alternative sources of energy.

PetroCaribe's regional impact and the Dominica response to ALBA may have damaged the coherence and integrity of CARICOM. Consequently, there are some lessons and recommendations for the region.

First, oil and energy supplies have become proxies for geopolitics. The regional leadership should strengthen mechanisms for monitoring the ongoing changes in the international geopolitical environment brought about by the dynamics of energy supply and consumption, and the potential impact on Caribbean countries.

Second, the management of CARICOM relations with Venezuela should be approached regionally. The impact of PetroCaribe/ALBA on the economy, politics, and diplomacy of CARICOM states has shown the inability of the region to respond effectively to what some critics have called Venezuela's 'bribery diplomacy'. Member states have adopted different postures toward Caracas or specific Venezuelan policy initiatives. Dominica's decision to support the ALBA initiative emphasised the ease with which Venezuela could capture geopolitical space within CARICOM.

Third, the PetroCaribe model of regional energy cooperation is based on the primacy of Venezuelan oil, current largesse, and the use of ideology as a strategy for regional cooperation. It is not a model for the future. Venezuelan largesse beyond Chávez is not guaranteed. The Caribbean needs a clear vision of regional energy cooperation or integration. At its best, such a policy would integrate the region's energy policy with trade, economic, environmental, security and foreign policies, while broadening dialogue with producing and consuming nations alike. The alternative scenario is that regional consuming countries will continue to feel heightened insecurity over access to supplies.

Fourth, Venezuela's resource diplomacy, and the PetroCaribe and ALBA experiences in the Caribbean, also highlight a more profound process. While the CARICOM region has yet to construct a single regional economy, and endow its institutions with executive authority for the urgent implementation of decisions, individual countries are now more willing to explore the options of multiple integration schemes simultaneously. Perhaps as regions become more diluted there is a case to be made for more flexible and dynamic models of regional integration that could include various levels of cooperation. In the end, countries do not have friends, they have interests.

References

Altmann, Josette (2008) 'ALBA: ¿un proyecto alternative para América Latina?', Madrid, Real Instituto Elcano, 17 April.

Arreaza, Teresa (2004) 'ALBA: Bolivarian Alternative for Latin America and the Caribbean', *Venezuelaanalysis.com*, 30 January, http://www.venezuelanalysis.com/analysis/339, accessed on 21 May 2008.

Arriagada, Genaro (2006) 'Petropolitics in Latin America: A Review of Energy Policy and Regional Relations', Inter-American Dialogue, *Andean Group Working Paper*, December, http://www.thedialogue.org/publications/2006/winter/arriagada.pdf, accessed on 21 May 2008.

BBC Caribbean (2006) 'Trinidad Warns against Chávez Deal', 6 January.

Bryan, Anthony T. (2007) 'Trinidad and Tobago' in Sidney Weintraub (ed.) *Energy Cooperation in the Western Hemisphere: Benefits and Impediments* (Washington, DC: CSIS Press): 366–404.

Bryan, Anthony T. and Roget V. Bryan (1999) *The New Face of Regionalism in the Caribbean: The Western Hemisphere Dynamic*, North South Agenda Papers 35 (Coral Gables, FL: The University of Miami).

Carrington, Edwin (2008) 'Remarks by His Excellency Edwin W. Carrington, Secretary-General, Caribbean Community, on the Occasion of the Opening of the Eleventh Meeting of the Council for Foreign and Community Relations (COFCOR), 7 May 2008, St John's, Antigua and Barbuda', *Caricom Press Release* 121/2008, 08 May.

CNN (2007) 'Venezuelan Leader Chávez presides over oil summit in Cuba', 22 December, http://edition.cnn.com/2007/WORLD/americas/12/21/cuba.petroleum.summit.ap/index.html

EIU (2008) 'Venezuelan Politics: Power pursues power', Economist Intelligence Unit Country Briefing, 14 August.

ENERGY Caribbean (2007a) 'Petrotrin Fighting Venezuelan Onslaught', *ENERGY Caribbean Yearbook, 2007–08* (Port of Spain, Trinidad: MEP Publishers):12–13.

ENERGY Caribbean (2007b) 'Is an energy plan for the Caribbean still relevant?', *ENERGY Caribbean Yearbook, 2007–08* (Port of Spain, Trinidad: MEP Publishers): 6.

Energy Information Agency (2008) *Venezuela Energy Profile*, 16 May, http://tonto.eia. doe.gov/country/country_energy_data.cfm?fips=VE, accessed on 20 May 2008.

Girvan, Norman (2008) 'Alba, PetroCaribe and Caricom: Issues in a New Dynamic', 29 May, http://www.normangirvan.info/alba-petrocaribe-and-caricom-issues-in-a-new-dynamic-by-norman-girvan/ accessed on 26 August 2008.

Grenade, Wendy (2005) 'An overview of regional governance arrangements within the Caribbean Community (Caricom)', in Joaquín Roy and Roberto Domínguez (eds), *The European Union and Regional Integration: A Comparative Perspective and Lessons for the Americas* (Miami: University of Miami/Jean Monnet Chair): 167–83.

Hutchinson-Jafar, Linda, (2008) 'Venezuela pushes Trinidad out of Caribbean oil market', *Reuters*, 4 August, http://www.reuters.com/article/GCA-Oil/idUSN 0134094520080804, accessed on 26 August 2008.

Jamaica Gleaner (2008) 'Petrocaribe debt reaches $33b: State to lend out $12b more from fund this year', 16 April.

Jamaica Observer (2008) 'Jamaica port authority turns to PetroCaribe for financial assistance', 13 August.

Kozloff, Nikolas (2005) 'Venezuela's Chávez: Oil is a Geopolitical Weapon', *Council on Hemispheric Affairs*, 28 March.

Lewis, Vaughn A. (2008a) 'What purposes for Caribbean integration today?', Paper presented at the Third Sir Arthur Lewis Lecture, University of the West Indies, St Augustine's 2008 Nobel Laureate Celebrations, 15 April.

Lewis, Vaughn A. (2008b) 'Political leadership and Caribbean integration', 4 June, Mss.

Mander, Benedict (2008) 'Chávez widens cheap oil finance network', *Financial Times*, 21 July, http://www.ft.com/cms/s/0/e3f5e5d0-5766-11dd-916c-000077b07658.html, accessed on 26 August 2008.

Newsday (2008) 'TT backs Caricom neighbors', 16 March.

Payne, Anthony (2007) *The Political History of CARICOM* (Kingston, Jamaica: Ian Randle Publishers).

PetroleumWorld.com (2005) Full text of 'PetroCaribe Agreement, 2005', 10 July, http://www.petroleumworldtt.com/storytt05071002.htm, accessed on 26 August 2008.

Richards, Peter (2008) 'Is ALBA more than a storm in a teacup?', *Caribbean 360.com*, 4 March.

West Indian Commission (1992) *Time for Action*, Black Rock, Barbados.

WOLA (2007) 'Venezuela after the Re-election of Hugo Chávez: Political Dynamics and Policy Challenges', Washington Office on Latin America (WOLA) Conference Report, July.

Wood, Anthony (2005) 'The Case against PetroCaribe', Statement by the Minister of Energy, *Barbados Nation*, 18 September.

9

The CARIFORUM–EU Economic Partnership Agreement: Impediment or Development Opportunity for CARICOM SIDS?

Debbie A. Mohammed

The economic partnership agreement (EPA) initiated in December 2007 between CARIFORUM countries (CARICOM states[1] plus the Dominican Republic) and the European Union (EU) is an historic agreement providing the framework for a new economic relationship between the two regions. This 'trade for development' partnership replaces decades of asymmetrical preferential trade and aid[2] for CARICOM states with progressive market liberalisation and ultimately, reciprocal trade between its partners.

Already, the EPA has become a contentious issue. Some CARICOM leaders and negotiators hail the EPA a success, insisting it is a vehicle for reducing poverty and achieving sustainable development. The EPA, they assert, will provide the investment and technology impetus required to diversify and grow the region's economies, improve competitiveness, and generate employment.

While supporters underscore the Agreement's development dimension, sceptics maintain that it only vaguely addresses the issue of development. They see it as nothing more than a free-trade agreement being forced upon the region by the EU and point to the latter's decision to negotiate separate regional EPAs with the African, Caribbean and Pacific (ACP)[3] countries as part of its strategy to weaken the bloc's negotiating power and push its free-trade agenda. They warn that CARIFORUM's commitment to open nearly 90 per cent of its goods and services sectors over the next 25 years (DR1, 2007) will be detrimental to the growth and poverty-reducing objectives of CARICOM microstates that face increasing economic vulnerability precisely because of free trade. They are therefore calling for a renegotiation of the EPA (Girvan et al., 2008).

Some member governments are unsure if and how new institutions mandated by the EPA will work with CARICOM's decision making organs, particularly the Heads of Government Conference (HOGC) and the Council for Trade and Economic Development (COTED). The failure of the Caribbean Regional Negotiating Machinery (CRNM)[4] to formally report on the outcome of the EPA negotiations has prompted COTED, the organ responsible for trade and economic matters within CARICOM, to mandate an independent review of the EPA through a 'Reflections Group'[5] before the agreement is signed and becomes legally binding.

Debate is raging as to whether the EPA will facilitate or impede the development of CARICOM microstates. Concerns centre on vulnerability as a function of the region's smallness and island characteristics, which supposedly limit its range of productive activities and capacity to shift quickly into more competitive areas. Ranked among the smallest states in terms of population size (Mohamed, 2002), CARICOM countries are also heavily dependent on foreign trade (Payne and Sutton, 1993), making growth susceptible to externally driven events.

CARICOM microstates also face resource and capital constraints, weak industrial sectors and export concentration in a few commodities, all of which impede their ability to respond effectively to trade liberalisation and intense competition. As such, the pace and scope of market liberalisation impacts the region's development prospects, becoming a major issue for CARICOM in international trade negotiations fora.

Undoubtedly, the EPA will have profound implications for CARICOM states in terms of their economic growth and development potential; but it portends much more. It underscores economic globalisation as the defining logic of a new relationship between states, premised solely on equality of access to markets and investments. As free-trade arrangements (FTAs) become the strategy of choice for countries to increase market share, economic vulnerability associated with small size, resource limitations, and openness is being sidelined in favour of resilience via innovative coping strategies that facilitate integration into the global economy.

Both the vulnerability and resilience arguments have been advanced to explain CARICOM's competitiveness challenges in the face of free trade. Regardless of the approach adopted, certain facts are unchanged. First, the region's inherent vulnerabilities make growth and economic transformation quite difficult. Secondly, despite three decades of preferences and aid under the EU–ACP Lomé/Cotonou Conventions, the region has been unable to realise significant economic transformation, growth stimulation and new exports development (Patterson, 2004). Thirdly, in today's global economy, competitiveness and growth are more dependent on created advantages than endowed resources. Given these facts, the CARIFORUM–EU EPA becomes an important 'test case' for the region since it will determine whether inherent vulnerabilities are deterrents to growth and competitiveness under such a trade regime, or whether CARICOM microstates can create advantages to overcome economic vulnerability and grasp opportunities afforded by the EPA.

The EPA is a comprehensive trade pact covering liberalisation of goods, services and investment markets. Ideally, it should be assessed in its entirety; however, the scope and size of the Agreement make analysis of a specific area more manageable.

This chapter will focus its analysis on the Services Chapter of the EPA for a number of reasons. Services are now the fastest growing component of world trade and are deemed critical to the diversification strategies of most CARICOM economies. Although tourism has been the major source of revenue and employment generation for CARICOM states,[6] countries are transitioning into other service activities in the face of dwindling EU preferences for commodity exports. Furthermore, services are linked to the role of governments as providers of public/social services[7] at nominal prices. CARICOM states have thus far been unwilling to negotiate liberalisation of their services sectors.

Given the stated objectives of the EPA and the importance of services to the region, this chapter seeks to assess whether the CARIFORUM–EU EPA can facilitate the development of dynamic, competitive *service* exports in CARICOM countries. The first section provides the contextual basis for analysing the EPA and its development implications for CARICOM states. It places export-led development within the framework of economic globalisation and trade liberalisation and links sustained country exports to new drivers of competitiveness. Some link CARICOM's lack of competitiveness and its reliance on EU preferences to the region's economic vulnerability, while others maintain competitiveness and resilience are developed through appropriate strategies and accompanying policies, citing other small states that have been able to build globally competitive niche exports.

The second section elaborates Title II of the EPA – investment, trade in services and E-commerce – while section three critically analyses the development implications of Title II for CARICOM states. The EPA's supporters are optimistic that it can provide important growth opportunities for the region's services exports. The author argues that while the EPA may offer some long-term benefits to the region's services sector, the EU's strategy of aggressive market penetration coupled with CARICOM's un-preparedness and incapacity to turn perceived opportunities into tangible export growth may prove to be the greatest obstacles. Finally, the last section provides some prescriptions for building service sector competitiveness under the EPA, which can assist CARICOM countries in diversifying their economies and promote greater integration into the global economy.

The trade for development paradigm and CARICOM reality

Free-trade advocates contend that export-led growth is the only way for poor countries to achieve growth rates necessary to catch up with developed economies. They point to the phenomenal growth of the Asian economies in the 1970s and 1980s and the recent surge of the BRICs,[8] as evidence that liberalisation of trade and investment can accelerate country growth and development. The free trade lobby has been so persuasive that export-led growth, as espoused by the Washington Consensus,[9] has become the *de facto* global development model and the legitimising philosophy for trade liberalisation today. Free trade is an inescapable reality that countries, irrespective of size or 'readiness', must now accept.

Under this 'trade for development approach', private enterprise and mobile production factors have become the major drivers of economic growth. Keesing (1967) and Bhagwati and Krueger (1973) note that free trade and ensuing global competition force domestic firms to improve efficiency and innovativeness to remain competitive. Since firms continually invest in upgrading learning processes and production techniques, free trade promotes increased productivity and specialisation based on cost efficiencies, which increases employment and welfare in nations. Free trade and investment opportunities are especially important for developing countries because of their capacity to stimulate growth, alleviate poverty, and increase living standards.

Yet the reality for CARICOM microstates has been loss of competitiveness, declining market access and adverse movements in commodity terms of trade, resulting in 'weakened export capacity, rising trade deficits and increased economic vulnerability' (Carrington, 2005). According to Carrington the region's trade deficit jumped from US$1.2 billion in 1994 to US$3.4 billion in 2001 because the unit value of seven of CARICOM's 11 most important exports fell between 1995 and 2000.[10] Nine of 14 independent CARICOM countries now rank among the 25 most vulnerable countries in the world and 13 are among the 50 most vulnerable (Carrington, 2005).

Although market liberalisation can facilitate increased trade, it is also creating a grab for markets that is fuelling intense competition. Firms must now defend market share both at home and abroad. Information and communication technologies (ICT) are increasing mobility productive factors enabling them to move quickly to the most attractive locations. Technology and knowledge inputs are the main sources of value added and the principal determinants of competitiveness. The interval between new technology developments and their application to products and services is now measured in mere months, making the advantage of 'first on the market' fleeting. As such, the ability to constantly produce new, knowledge-intensive goods or services or to differentiate existing products is the crux of today's successful competitiveness strategies.

Countries such as Australia and Ireland recognise that this new competitive landscape requires strategies involving government, research centres and private enterprise to ensure that innovation aids existing advantages to create continuous competitive advantages. This provides the basis for sustained national and global market dominance. The success of states such as Iceland, Malta, and Ireland suggests that small, resource-deficient states can become globally competitive if creative strategies and policies are adopted. Dynamic country growth and competitiveness may be more a function of identifying and developing niche markets, building globally recognised domestic brands, tapping into diasporic networks and targeted planning rather than size or free trade.

While some small states are carving globally competitive niches, CARICOM countries have struggled to cope with eroding trade preferences, declining commodity export prices and loss of competitiveness. Caldentey (2006: 7) observed that the region experienced declining export competitiveness from 1990–2005, with the gap increasing to over 20 per cent of GDP in 2005. This continuing deterioration extends to service exports, which have been declining since 1985. In essence, the rate of growth of imports into CARICOM states has been outpacing that of exports, currently resulting in mounting account deficits and indebtedness. Over the period 1990–2005, outstanding debt for the larger[11] economies grew from 60 to 79 per cent of GDP, while debt for the smaller economies[12] increased from 35 to 95 per cent for the same period (Caldentey, 2006: 9).

CARICOM's economic vulnerability is often attributed to small size. Its miniscule markets, capital bases and limited resource endowments have shaped economic systems that rely heavily on revenue generated from a narrow range of exports, as well as from foreign direct investment and customs duties to finance government expenditure. Prices for CARICOM's major exports (sugar, rice, rum, bauxite, coffee and bananas) have experienced steady decline in international commodity markets, while demand for imports remains high. As a result, terms of trade position have worsened, weakening the region's export capacity and increasing its economic vulnerability.

CARICOM countries have been at the forefront of calls for Special and Differential Treatment (SD&T), particularly by pushing for longer timeframes for accessing EU preferences and opening domestic markets to external competition. Patterson (2005) noted:

> There is a lack of empathy for the challenges facing small, vulnerable developing economies, with relatively high per capita incomes. Only the destitute gain attention. Apprehension is increasing, particularly as governments contemplate their ability to finance export diversification, concurrent with fiscal fallout from reduced tariffs.

These sentiments were endorsed by Richard Bernal (2005), head of the CRNM and lead CARIFORUM negotiator for the EPA, who noted that:

> Rather than pressing for the abandonment of preferences, rich nations should be examining ways of maintaining them as long as possible, and identifying tangible compensatory measures to ameliorate the effects of preference erosion.

Interestingly, defenders of the EPA including the CRNM and current Jamaican prime minister, Bruce Golding, accuse sceptics of clinging to preferences, labelling them 'a kind of mendicancy that we need to purge ourselves of' (*Jamaica Gleaner*, 2008). Some business organisations and commentators (*Trinidad Guardian*, 2008) suggest that the EPA presents significant opportunities for the region, which domestic firms can tap into and exploit and insist that preferences, not free trade, have been responsible for the region's uncompetitive position and its underdevelopment. They urge CARICOM to 'accept and engage' the new age of trade liberalisation as this creates efficiencies and hones competitiveness. As host of the 2009 Summit of the Americas and Commonwealth Heads of Government Conference, Trinidad and Tobago is seeking to brand itself as a global player, while carving a niche as the region's financial capital in the hope of exploiting opportunities in the EPA.

The EPA-Title II – investment, services and e-commerce

The CARIFORUM–EU EPA has been described as WTO-plus, covering not just liberalisation of trade in goods but also liberalisation of services and investments, competition, intellectual property rights, e-commerce and trade-related measures. Another feature of the EPA is its emphasis on regional integration since an expanded CARICOM offers greater scope for product diversity and investment opportunities to drive trade. The EU has positioned itself as the 'natural leader of the drive to open trade in services' calling for 'deeper and broader commitments to market access and national treatment' (Europa, undated). Since CARICOM's export of manufactured goods to the EU has been relatively insignificant, liberalising the services sector was the obvious 'next step' for both parties.

Services exports are the fastest growing component of world trade (Stephenson, 1999: 72). Prabir (2006) notes that global trade in services increased from US$825 billion in 1980 to US$4.4 trillion in 2004 and accounts for one-third of global employment. ICTs are revolutionising the global services trade, introducing a new mode of doing business, 'E-commerce', and with it the potential for capturing markets globally.

Although the EU is the world's leading exporter of services with 28 per cent (ESF, 2007), the disparity between services' contribution to GDP and employment (77 per cent) and its share of external trade prompted calls for trade policy to harness the growth potential of the services sector. The European Services Forum (ESF) has advised the EU that new trade agreements must include a comprehensive package of services liberalisation covering market access, national treatment, most favoured nation treatment (MFN) and substantial sector coverage since 'European service companies can no longer afford to watch their competitors gaining new market access in countries with which an FTA has been signed' (ESF, 2007).

A key EU strategy for consolidating its leadership of global services trade appears to be through cross-border supply of services. On CARICOM's side, services exports account for over 50 per cent of GDP; however, this is still heavily concentrated in tourism (Jeffrey, 2007). Greenaway and Milner's policy study of EU expansion concluded that potential opportunities exist for increased CARICOM tourism exports as well as increased EU investment inflows into the region (Greenaway and Milner, 2001: 80, 82). Since tourism accounts for 60 per cent of CARICOM's exports to the EU (CRNM, 2008d) the region's negotiating strategy was to tap into the lucrative EU market of 457 million population with per capita GDP US$32 501 (2004).

Key sectors to be liberalised under the EPA include tourism, E-commerce, telecommunications, as well as financial, cultural, and entertainment services subject to the GATS Modes of service supply. Although the EU will reportedly liberalise 90 per cent of its service sectors, most of the liberalisation relates to Modes 1 and 2 of the GATS. Interestingly, this EPA combines Mode 1 (cross border supply) and Mode 2 (consumption abroad) as cross border services. Under Chapter 3 (16), the principles of national treatment and (3:18) MFN are afforded to all cross-border suppliers of services.

On the more ticklish issue of Mode 3 – commercial presence – the EU has listed some exclusions and limitations in certain sectors. Under Title II Chapter 2 (6), national treatment and MFN (9) are afforded to commercial presences and investments in all economic activities except for certain sectors.[13] Also, while the EPA excludes national and international air transport services, it allows for investment in areas where EU providers have a competitive advantage, including aircraft repair and maintenance, ancillary services including ground handling services, rental services of aircraft with crew, and airport management services.

Like investment, the expectation is that CARICOM service exports will increase through Mode 4 (presence of natural persons). The EU has allowed market access in 29 sectors provided a contract is secured,[14] but has restricted CARIFORUM providers to no more than 90 days in a calendar year. Further, Chapter 4 (2: ii) specifies the persons that can enter either party's jurisdiction; these include managers, specialists, graduate trainees and business service sellers. Self-employed professionals can access the EU in 11 sectors upon evaluation of their economic need.

For CARIFORUM countries the level of liberalisation reflects a 'clear asymmetry' (CRNM, 2008b) because sectoral coverage is between 65 and 75 per cent. However, the Dominican Republic will liberalise more than 90 per cent of its services. The services liberalised by CARIFORUM reflect their positive economic contributions, which can be enhanced through injections of investment and new technologies (CRNM, 2008b). Also included are sectors deemed important for generating economic activity and returns through outsourcing contacts from EU firms (CRNM, 2008d).

The importance of tourism to CARICOM's economies is addressed in section 7 (50), which seeks to prevent suppliers from engaging in anti-competitive behaviour. Articles 51 provides for transfer of technology to CARIFORUM states while Article 52 encourages participation of small- and medium-size enterprises. Article 54 addresses the sustainability of tourism by exposing CARIFORUM services suppliers to various financing programmes, while Article 55 outlines commitments to encourage compliance with environmental and quality standards.

The entertainment sector is another area in which CARICOM states already exhibit some competitive advantage and can enjoy sustained advantage over time. Inclusion of entertainment and commitments on market access, particularly via Mode 4, was deemed critical to CARICOM's services-led development strategy. The fact that 27 EU countries will liberalise entertainment services covering *inter alia* music, dance, theatre, visual arts, and sculptors attests to CARIFORUM's achievements. The EU's proposals in entertainment services impose 'certain controls and conditions'; however, these do not apply to the number of persons entering under this commitment.

The EPA has become a 'high stakes' game in which CARICOM states will relinquish their preferences safety net in favour of market liberalisation as the engine of growth and development. The gamble is whether opening the region's potentially lucrative but vulnerable services sectors to EU investors and service providers will yield the medium-to-long-term investment and competitiveness payouts required to stimulate growth and reduce poverty.

Assessment of Title II: Impediment or opportunity for CARICOM?

The link between services liberalisation and investment is a crucial one for trade-dependent CARICOM states. Since services account for over 62 per cent of total exports, many see services liberalisation under the EPA as an opportunity to facilitate growth and revive flagging economies. Further, as a net capital-importing region CARICOM requires investment facilitation to expand service export capacity and to develop other sectors.

Careful analysis of the commitments and sectors liberalised by the EU suggests that these arrangements present serious short- and long-term challenges for CARICOM states. Furthermore, the benefits of service liberalisation, while heavily skewed in the EU's favour, are at best minimal for most CARICOM countries.

EU services trade with CARIFORUM countries for the period 1999–2003 reveals that the EU recorded a net services deficit of Euro 976 million (Manduna and Thompson, 2007: 41). Total service imports from CARIFORUM averaged Euro 1672 million with travel (Euro 1000 million) accounting for the largest share. By contrast, EU travel exports to CARIFOURM averaged only Euro 105 million over this period. CARIFORUM also registered surpluses in transport linked to tourism (Euro 114 million), communications services (Euro 42 million) and government services (Euro 17 million).

The EU exhibited trade surpluses in computer and information services, other business services, financial services, construction services, and insurance services (Manduna and Thompson, 2007). It should be noted that personal, cultural and recreational services exports were negligible for both CARIFORUM (Euro 1 million) and the EU (Euro 2 million). The fact that the EU has opened up more than 90 per cent of its services under the EPA must be viewed as part of a broader strategy of harnessing existing and potential ACP markets for its service firms and, in the process, consolidating its position as the world's leading exporter of services. While negotiators on both sides are quick to point out the extensive list of services liberalised by the EU, CARIFORUM countries, and in particular, CARICOM, has thus far exhibited relative trade advantage only in tourism.

Concerns that the EU would give few concessions on Mode 4 issues despite these being critical for most CARICOM service providers are now realised since the vast majority of services have been liberalised only via Mode 1. Since many CARICOM providers will be unable to utilise this mode, it effectively paves the way for expansion of EU E-commerce and Internet services firms, which the ESF identified as priority sectors. Recognising that E-commerce offers a new mode of doing business and that IT and computer services enable E-commerce, the EU has successfully incorporated liberalisation of telecommunications services, computer related services, advertising services and some financial services into the EPA.

There is also unease that the EU will use GATS non-discrimination provisions (national treatment and MFN) and substantial sector coverage to rapidly extend regionally agreed services liberalisation at the country level since Chapter 1 (3) requires parties to enter into further negotiations on investment and services liberalisation no later than five years after the EPA enters into force. This is likely to place undue pressure on many of these states to increase their service commitments.

Market liberalisation and non-discriminatory obligations covering such a wide range of services will be challenging for CARICOM states. Potential outflows of CARICOM services are likely to be minimal relative to the trade and investment inflows from EU providers in the short to medium term. There are concerns that market liberalisation will encourage 'crowding out' in successful service sectors (e.g. financial, insurance, distribution) possibly resulting in mergers/acquisitions of domestic firms by larger EU firms, creation of regional firms and/or the exit of weaker firms from the industry.

The issue of market dominance must also be addressed. Larger, more established EU firms are likely to dominate various sectors. While the EPA makes provisions for a competition authority to guard against anti-competitive practices and abuse of dominant positions, detection and prosecution can be complicated and lengthy. Obligations that afford national treatment and MFN to EU firms can further complicate the situation. The relative newness of incorporating competition law and policy into the region's legislative frameworks will also present some challenges.[15]

These concerns are particularly significant for the tourism sector, the principal generator of revenue and employment for most CARICOM states. Full liberalisation of this sector can have negative consequences for small entrepreneurs. Investment trends in tourism favour 'in-house, all inclusive' operations where the entire chain of activities – from ticket purchase to hotel and transportation bookings to ground activities – is performed by one company. Although Section 7 (52) encourages partic-ipation of small and medium enterprises, there is no indication as to how this will be achieved. Again, national treatment and MFN become significant since attempts to promote small firms within certain sectors can be construed as discriminatory and in breach of the EPA.

CARIFORUM negotiators maintain that substantial investment inflows are required to finance diversification and develop potentially lucrative service exports. However, FDI becomes meaningful only if it facilitates development of sectors deemed a priority by the receiving country. There are concerns that EU investments will move into the more developed countries and sectors[16] intensifying disparities in regional development and sectoral imbalances. Singh (2003) contends that there is little evi-dence linking investment liberalisation to growth since this is a complex process impacted by a range of factors. Although growth and productiv-ity rates are impacted by the quality of investment, portfolio investment is now the major source of cross border financing. This is worrisome since such investments are speculative in nature and often have tenuous link-ages with the wider economy resulting in macro-economic instability in the event of sudden capital withdrawals.

Singh (2003) suggests that FDI is no panacea for development since investment without accompanying factors like competition policy; skilled labour and comprehensive regulatory frameworks will have little developmental impact. Furthermore, FDI must complement rather than replace domestic capital to produce sustained national economic growth.

The question of how much of the gains from development of these sectors actually remain in the region is important since sector growth and economic diversification are premised on liberalisation.

An analysis of foreign investment patterns in certain CARICOM countries[17] from 1990 to 2004 reveals that FDI flows amounted to 8.6 per cent of GDP while profit repatriation flows amounted to 4.7 per cent. Profit repatriation represented over 50 per cent of FDI during this period (Caldenty, 2006: 10). Cost of fiscal incentives introduced to attract FDI were found to be 'exceptionally high with import-related tax concessions in the selected countries averaging more than 10 per cent of GDP' (Caldenty, 2006: 11).

Despite generous incentives, Caldenty notes FDI flows have been uneven and increased only slightly over the last decade. Further, government made foreign exchange-intensive concessions tend to limit the effectiveness of taxation as an instrument for equitable distribution of income and balancing national accounts. If net transfers into these economies are compared with revenues foregone as a result of incentives to FDI, these countries actually transfer resources to the rest of the world instead of being resource beneficiaries (Caldenty, 2006: 11). This view is supported by Singh (2007) who notes that 'it is increasingly becoming clear that the benefits of foreign investment have been fewer than expected while costs have been much bigger ... disappointment with certain kinds of foreign investment has put a big question mark on the benefits of investment liberalization.'

Apart from tourism, the majority of CARICOM's service exports will be restricted to Mode 4. Procedures for mutual recognition of professional qualifications and certification must first be developed and accepted by the CARIFORUM–EC Trade and Development Committee (CETDC) before service providers move to a client's jurisdiction.[18] Criteria and attributes defining specific types of artisans and entertainers must also be decided and agreed to by the CETDC before CARICOM's professionals and artists can benefit from Title II.

Given asymmetries in infrastructure, technical expertise and financial capital, it is doubtful if most CARICOM countries have the capacity to take advantage of these 'opportunities'. Similarly, establishment of a Joint Council and CETDC to implement the EPA leaves little room for CARICOM's major decision-making organs – the HOG and the COTED – in respect to trade. There are questions as to how the EPA will be operationalised within the framework of the CARICOM Single Market and Economy (CSME) – a regional development strategy that promotes competitiveness and integration into the global economy through efficiencies gained from resource pooling, market enlargement and technology and knowledge sharing. These issues can affect the progress of the CSME and impact development of internationally competitive service exports.

From 'vulnerability' to 'resilience'

Although the EPA presents some development challenges for the region, renegotiating will do little to improve competitiveness and development outcomes since the fundamental problem of a clear development strategy and related policies required to inform trade negotiations remains. The region lacks an entrepreneurial spirit since many firms are risk-averse, leaving governments to underwrite new ventures. There is little emphasis on research and innovation as creators of new advantage and no real commitment to building a single regional economy to compete globally. This EPA may be the trigger needed to force CARICOM countries to seriously address regional integration, economic diversification and competitiveness. The development component of the EPA, though vague, can be used to transform CARICOM economies and build competitive service exports if appropriate competitiveness models and complementary policies are employed.

Although various sectors will be liberalised there is little correlation between these sectors and the readiness or capacity of domestic providers to grasp potential opportunities. Market access becomes meaningless if CARICOM providers are unable to compete, or if their numbers are too insignificant to make market entry worthwhile.

CARICOM countries must first identify service niches and begin building internationally recognised product and country brands. This requires a clear development vision to guide policy direction. Policy-makers must also recognise the link between innovative macro-economic policies, industrial policy and trade policy in producing dynamic, globally competitive products. Mapping out the role of services exports in a restructured economy and identifying precisely how these feed into industry and vice versa provides the framework for service sector identification and development.

Service sector competitiveness is a critical issue now that most services will be liberalised. Building competitiveness within these sectors will be key to sustained export performance under the EPA. Development assistance under the EPA can be utilised *inter alia* to increase technical capacity, promote innovation, improve marketing and distribution channels and encourage entrants into these targeted sectors.

A precondition for international competitiveness must be a firm's ability to capture domestic and regional markets.[19]

The competitiveness model calls for collaboration by major stakeholders within the economy (government, service providers, research, development, marketing, and financial organisations). This provides a platform for knowledge and technology dissemination and sharing information on global service trends that enable local firms to differentiate service products in terms of superior quality, competitive price, and reliable and superior service. The government's role is critical, providing the policy and marketing frameworks necessary for firms to build globally recognised brands.

Nationally competitive firms expanding into the regional market can capture scale economies associated with larger market size. The CSME is therefore key to the formation of regional firms that through alliances, acquisitions or mergers can hone strategies, pool investments and expertise, access technologies and distribution networks that can translate into distinct competitive advantages and provide the launch pad into the global market.

It is imperative that the development and assistance facilities in the EPA be used to improve telecommunications and computer and related capacity and infrastructure within the region since these are the input services that lead to the development of other services and goods within economies. Furthermore, their strategic importance to the region is evident in light of offshore financial activities, which many CARICOM states are moving into, as well as E-commerce activities that will become the major mode for economic transactions in the near future. Developing regional capacity and infrastructure in transport, professional, and financial services will also be critical to the region's growth and development. The development provisions in the EPA must focus on these as priority areas. The challenge for CARICOM is to move beyond preferences and vulnerabilities and identify new development strategies that harness regional integration to build globally competitive firms.

Notes

1. The Caribbean Community (CARICOM) consists of 15 member states – Antigua and Barbuda, the Bahamas, Barbados, Belize, Dominica, Grenada, Guyana, Haiti, Jamaica, Montserrat, St Kitts and Nevis, St Lucia, St Vincent and the Grenadines, Suriname, and Trinidad and Tobago.
2. The Lomé Conventions I–IV (1975–99) provided a framework for trade and development cooperation between the EU and ACP group of countries. Under

Lomé, the EU allowed duty-free entry for most ACP agricultural exports and established a preferential pricing and quota system for a few dominant ACP agricultural exports. ACP countries were allowed to impose tariffs on imports from the EU. Under the Cotonou Agreement, which replaced the Lomé Convention in 2000, both sides agreed to negotiate a trade regime that is more WTO compatible. The creation of regional EPAs involving the EU and individual regions of the ACP are meant to reflect this new regime.

3. Under the EPA negotiations ACP countries are split into six regional groups, each of which is negotiating a separate EPA with the EU. These groups are: West Africa; East and Southern Africa (ESA); Southern Africa Development Community (SADC); Central Africa; the Caribbean (CARIFORUM); and the Pacific. CARIFORUM is the only region to sign a full EPA with the EU to date.

4. The CRNM was created by CARICOM to harness the region's trade and negotiating expertise to develop, coordinate and execute an overall negotiating strategy with respect to various external trade negotiations. The CRNM negotiated the EPA on behalf of CARIFORUM countries.

5. In February 2008 the COTED agreed to a 'review process' of the EPA by 'Reflections Group' involving various stakeholders. Recommendations of this group were to be conveyed to heads of government prior to their 7–8 March Inter-sessional conference in the Bahamas.

6. Except Suriname, Guyana and Trinidad and Tobago.

7. These include health services, public transportation, education, amenities (water, electricity) and security.

8. Emerging economic giants Brazil, Russia, India and China.

9. This refers to ten major areas of reform that have been identified by the IMF and World Bank as ways to improve macro-economic and financial problems in poor economies. They include: fiscal discipline, tax reform, trade liberalisation and investment and market liberalisation.

10. Sugar, rice, bananas, rum, bauxite, coffee and cocoa.

11. Barbados, the Bahamas, Belize, Guyana, Jamaica, Trinidad and Tobago and Suriname. The highest indebtedness ratios were exhibited by Jamaica (143 per cent) and Guyana (140 per cent) in 2005.

12. Antigua and Barbuda, Anguilla, Dominica, Grenada, St Kitts and Nevis, St Lucia and St Vincent. St Kitts and Nevis (153 per cent), Dominica (119 per cent) and Grenada (91 per cent) recorded highest debt to GDP ratios for 2005.

13. Including mining, audio-visual services and national and international air transport services, *other than* aircraft repair and maintenance services, selling and marketing of air transport services, computer reservation system (CRS) services, ancillary services facilitating operations of air carriers, e.g. ground handling services, rental services of aircraft with crew, and airport management services.

14. For a full list *see* CRNM – Getting to know the EPA-Services and Investment. http://www.crnm.org/documents/ACP_EU_EPA/epa_agreement/Getting_to_ Know_ the_EPA_Services_and_Investment_revised_final.pdf.

15. To date only two countries, Barbados and Jamaica, have operational competition authorities. Trinidad and Tobago will soon have a fair trade commission operational and CARICOM has indicated that the regional Competition Commission will be launched soon.

16. Trinidad, Jamaica and Barbados, in tourism, financial services, energy-related services.
17. Grenada, St Kitts and Nevis, St Lucia, St Vincent and the Grenadines, Belize, Barbados, and Jamaica.
18. The Joint CARIFOURUM–EC Council will manage overall implementation of the EPA and will be assisted by the CETCD whose mandate covers all aspects of trade and development cooperation as stipulated in the EPA. See Part 5 Article 4 of the EPA Final Agreement.
19. The Platform Approach to International Competitiveness was developed by this author, see Mohammed (2005).

References

Bernal, Richard (2005) 'Trade Preferences Important For Small, Vulnerable Economies', *RNM Update*, http://www.crnm.org/documents/updates_2005/rnmupdate0510.htm, accessed on 10 February 2008.

Bhagwati, J.N. and A.O. Krueger (1973) 'Exchange Control, Liberalization, and Economic Development', *American Economic Review* 63 (2): 419–27.

Caldentey, E.P. (2006) 'Financing for development and the institutionalization of finance', XXXVIII Annual *Caribbean Monetary Studies* Conference, Barbados, http://www.ccmsuwi.org/Files/amsc/ecaldentey_pap06.pdf, accessed on 3 March 2008.

Caribbean Regional Negotiating Machinery (CRNM) (2008a) *The CARIFORUM–EU Economic Partnership Agreement*, http://www.crnm.org/documents/ACP_EU_EPA/epa_agreement/EPA_Text_060308.pdf, accessed on 20 January 2008.

Caribbean Regional Negotiating Machinery (CRNM) (2008b) *Highlights Re Services and Investment in the CARIFORUM–EU Economic Partnership Agreement (EPA)*, http://www.crnm.org/documents/ACP_EU_EPA/epa_agreement/Dec%2018-Web-Services&%20Investment%20in%20EPA.pdf, accessed on 3 March 2008.

Caribbean Regional Negotiating Machinery (CRNM) (2008c) *Getting to know the EPA*, http://www.crnm.org/documents/updates_2007/special_rnmupdate_on_epa.htm, accessed on 28 February 2008.

Caribbean Regional Negotiating Machinery (CRNM) (2008d) *Getting to know the EPA: Provisions on Services and Investment*, http://www.crnm.org/documents/ACP_EU_EPA/epa_agreement/Getting_to_Know_the_EPA_Services_and_Investment_Final.pdf, accessed on 29 January 2008.

Carrington, E. (2005) 'Caribbean Urges More Support For Small States', *Jamaica Information Service*, http://www.jis.gov.jm/special_sections/CARICOMNew/caribbeanUrges.html, accessed on 5 January 2008.

DR1 (2007) 'EPA is Good News for DR', *Dominican Republic Trade, CAFTA and Business Information*, http://dr1.com/trade/articles/433/1/EPA-is-good-news-for-DR/Page1.html, accessed on 12 January 2008.

Europa Secretariat General of the European Commission (undated), 'External Trade', http://ec.europa.eu/trade/gentools/faqs_en.htm#ser, accessed on 7 March 2008.

European Services Forum (ESF) (2007) *ESF Position Paper on EU Free Trade Agreements*, http://www.esf.be/pdfs/documents/position_papers/ESF%20Position%

20Paper%20on%20EU%20Free%20Trade%20Agreements%20-%20final.pdf, accessed on 10 February 2008.

Girvan, N., H. Brewster and V. Lewis (2008) *Renegotiate the EPA*, http://www. normangirvan.info/wp-content/uploads/2008/03/renegotiate-the-epa-rev1.pdf, accessed on 27 March 2008.

Greenaway, D. and C. Milner (2001) *Implications of European Union Enlargement For CARICOM Countries*, CRNM and InterAmerican Development Bank Regional Technical Cooperation Project, ATN/JF/SF-6158-RG, http://www.crnm. org/documents/studies/Implications%20of%20EU%20Enlargement%20-% 20Greenaway%20&%20Milner.pdf, accessed on 12 March 2008.

Jamaica Gleaner (2008) 'Golding slams EPA critics – Says they suffer from mendicancy', 1 February, http://www.jamaica-gleaner.com/gleaner/20080201/ business/business6.html accessed on 27 March 2008.

Jeffrey, H.B. (2007) 'Strategy for the Development and Export Promotion of Professional Services in Guyana', *Trade in Services Workshop*, Ministry of Foreign Trade and International Cooperation/Commonwealth Secretariat, February, http://www.moftic.gov.gy/Speeches/SPe.MOFTIC-COMSEC.htm, accessed on 1 April 2008.

Keesing, Donald B. (1967) 'Outward-looking Policies and Economic Development', *Economic Journal* 77 (306): 303–20.

Manduna, C. and K.A. Thompson (2007) *The Emergence of an EPA – A CARICOM Perspective*, http://www.tralac.org/pdf/20071002_THOMPSON_MANDUNA_ The_Emergence_of_an_EPA_CARICOM21Sept.pdf, accessed on 4 March 2008.

Mohamed, A.N. (2002) 'The Diplomacy of Micro-States', *Discussion Papers in Diplomacy*, The Netherlands Institute of International Relations, http:// www.clingendael.nl/publications/2002/20020100_cli_paper_dip_issue78.pdf, accessed on 5 January 2008.

Mohammed, D.A. (2005) *Global Competitiveness of Trinidad and Tobago in the Services Export Sector: A Case Study of the Information Technology Industry*, Unpublished PhD dissertation, University of the West Indies, Trinidad.

Patterson, P.J. (2004) Address by Prime Minister of Jamaica at the Launch of Negotiations for Caribbean/EU Economic Partnership Agreement, http:// www.crnm.org/documents/press_releases_2004/Hon.%20P.J.%20Patterson%20 Speech%20EPA%20Launch.pdf, accessed on 29 March 2008.

Patterson, P.J. (2005) *New Global Realities Demand New CARICOM Trade Policy*, http://www.   jis.gov.jm/special_sections/CARICOMNew/newGlobalRealities. html, accessed on 12 January 2008.

Payne, Anthony J. and Paul K. Sutton (1993) 'The Commonwealth Caribbean in the New World Order: Between Europe and North America?' *Journal of Interamerican Studies and World Affairs* Vol. 34 (4): 39–75.

Prabir, D. (2006). International Trade in Services: Evolving Issues for Developing Countries, WTO/ESCAP/ARTNeTAdvanced Regional Seminar on Multilateral Negotiations in Services for Asian and Pacific Economies, Kolkata, 19– 21 September, http://www.unescap.org/tid/projects/negoservice_prabir.pdf, accessed on 2 April 2008.

Singh, K. (2003) *Multilateral Investment Agreement in the WTO – Issues and Illusions*, http://www.wto.org/english/forums_e/ngo_e/multi_invest_agree_ july03_e.pdf, accessed on 3 March 2008.

Singh, K. (2007) 'International Investments: Is Policy Pendulum Swinging Back?', *Countercurrents.org*, http://www.countercurrents.org/singh250707.htm, accessed on 10 February 2008.

Stephenson, S.M. (1999) 'Approaches to Liberalizing Services', Policy Research Working Paper 2107, May (Washington, DC: World Bank Development Research Group).

Trinidad Guardian (2008) 'EPA Madness', 21 February, http://www.guardian.co.tt/archives/2008–02–26/bussguardian3.html, accessed on 30 March 2008.

10
From Afterthought to Centre Stage: The Caribbean and the Summit of the Americas Process

Daniel P. Erikson

In April 2009 the 34 elected leaders of the nations of the Western hemisphere will gather in the twin island nation of Trinidad and Tobago for the fifth Summit of the Americas. This event will offer an opportunity to renew the sense of purpose in inter-American relations following a period of deepening strain. Fifteen years will have passed since the first Summit of the Americas was held in Miami, Florida in 1994, and the initial sense of enthusiasm and convergence that accompanied the early years of the summit process have since given way to increasing tension and rancour. Indeed, the sharp divisions that emerged during the fourth Summit – the ill-fated meeting in Mar del Plata, Argentina that collapsed in disarray in November 2005 – left a bitter taste in the mouths of many presidents and prime ministers, calling into question whether hemispheric summitry had become an exhausted project. The stakes are high, therefore, for the 2009 summit to set hemispheric affairs on a sounder foundation and create a framework to bring new ideas and energy into the summit process.

The fifth Summit of the Americas will be significant for many reasons, most notably because it will offer the first opportunity for the new US president, Barack Obama, to set forth a clear agenda for hemispheric affairs and meet many counterparts for the first time. Indeed, this will be the first Summit of the Americas for more than half of the attendees, including leaders from countries such as Mexico, Canada, Argentina, Bolivia, Chile, Ecuador, Guatemala, Nicaragua, and Peru, as well as several Caribbean countries including Barbados, Jamaica and St Lucia. Cuba is likely to be excluded once more on the grounds that it is not a democracy. The 2009 meeting comes at a moment when discussions on free trade and democratic consolidation, long considered the two core goals of the summit process, are more likely to produce ill will than bonhomie. Efforts to negotiate the Free Trade Area of the Americas (FTAA), initially conceived at the Miami summit in 1994, collapsed entirely at the Mar del Plata summit in 2005. The convergence around democratic norms has made significant progress, including the ratification of the Inter-American Democratic Charter by all 34 participant countries in the fall of 2001. However, in practice, the level of agreement on how to define democracy is little more than skin deep, with particularly sharp splits between Venezuela and the United States on a number of issues. Thus, the participants in the 2009 summit are wary of lingering too long on the topics of trade or democracy, and the risks of reigniting old disagreements and unravelling the summit agenda that such topics pose.

The special role of the Caribbean is another unique feature of the Fifth Summit of the Americas. The summit host, Trinidad and Tobago, is the first Caribbean country to host this meeting since the process began in 1994. With a population of 1.3 million and a land mass that is only a fraction of the size of most Latin American countries (although the second largest island territory in the English-speaking Caribbean) Trinidad and Tobago is by far the smallest nation ever to host such a logistically complicated and politically sensitive gathering. Hosting a Summit of the Americas is far more than merely a ceremonial role. Since these meetings are principally organised by a national secretariat financed and staffed by the host country, this means that diplomats and officials from Trinidad and Tobago will be the chief organisers of the summit and take the lead in drafting summit documents. Moreover, the Fifth Summit of the Americas will place Trinidad and Tobago – and more broadly, the Caribbean as a whole – at centre stage when hemispheric leaders gather in the capital city of Port-of-Spain in 2009. This level of attention is a far cry from the peripheral role played by Caribbean leaders at the first summit of the Americas, and it elevates the region from a historically marginal position to centre stage.

The role of the Caribbean nations in the Summit of the Americas process presents one of the most intriguing examples of small-state diplomacy in a multilateral forum that the Western hemisphere has to offer. The Caribbean remains the most linguistically and politically diverse region in the Western hemisphere. In the Spanish-speaking Caribbean, there is Cuba, one of the few remaining communist states in the world and a perpetual target of isolation by the United States; the Dominican Republic, which is treated as a member of good standing with the Latin American bloc of countries; and Puerto Rico, which remains a US commonwealth and thus excluded from any gathering where state sovereignty is required. Haiti, the French and Creole-speaking Republic that has long remained stalled on the path of democratic transition, has nonetheless been a full participant in the Summit of the Americas process since its inception, which coincided with Haiti's final decisive shift away from military rule. The 12 countries of the English-speaking Caribbean, ranging in size from Jamaica and Trinidad and Tobago to the micro-states of the Organization of Eastern Caribbean States (OECS), were charter members of the Caribbean Community (CARICOM), now a 15-member grouping that includes Suriname and Haiti, who joined in 1995 and 2002 respectively. (The British territory of Montserrat has been a member since 1974, but, like Puerto Rico, lacks the sovereign status required to participate in international summitry.) Thus, there are 14 CARICOM members that participate in inter-American summitry, representing more than 40 per cent of the 34 participating nations, and only a narrow sliver of the hemisphere's territory and economic output. Caribbean participation is thus central to the universality of the Summit of the Americas project, even as the region itself has been hard-pressed to pursue its interests among the jostling of larger powers such as the United States, Brazil, Mexico, Canada and Venezuela.

This chapter examines the evolution of the Summit of the Americas process since 1994 and how the members of the Caribbean Community sought to pursue their interests on a stage shared with much larger regional powers. Through their single-minded pursuit of winning recognition for special treatment for small economies, Caribbean countries did win some victories during the summits, even though the main treaty under negotiation, the FTAA, was ultimately placed on hold on account of resistance from several South American countries. Now that the Summit of the Americas is being planned for Trinidad and Tobago in 2009, it is a particularly opportune moment to examine how the small-state diplomacy practised by the Caribbean has been played out in this vital yet increasingly contentious forum.

From Miami to Mar del Plata: A hemispheric vision unravels

When US President Bill Clinton convened the Summit of the Americas in Miami in 1994, it represented an effort by the US to assert new leadership in the hemisphere while building on the convergence of several favourable trends in the region. More than a quarter-century had passed since the last hemispheric summit was held in 1967, but the nations of the Americas had now entered a dramatically different era.

The fall of the Berlin Wall in Eastern Europe in 1989 and the subsequent collapse of the Soviet Union in 1991 definitively marked the end of the Cold War, which had created deep political divisions between the US and several Latin American countries. Moreover, a wave of democratisation in the late 1980s and early 1990s meant that most countries in the hemisphere had moved away from authoritarian regimes and were now firmly placed in the democratic column. Indeed, by the time the summit was held in December 1994, 34 of the 35 countries in the hemisphere had elected leaders, with Fidel Castro's Cuba remaining the outlier. Of course, the democratic record of many other countries remained far from perfect. Mexico remained under the control of the long-lived authoritarian PRI regime, although this did not stop the US and Canada from including it in the North American Free Trade Agreement (NAFTA), which was passed by the US Congress and signed by President Clinton in 1993. Haiti's first democratic elections in 1990 were soon followed by a military coup that ousted President Jean-Bertrand Aristide in 1991, and he spent three years in exile in the United States before being restored to Haiti by a US-led military intervention in October 1994. Still, the US deemed it a favourable moment to reinvigorate hemispheric collaboration, and the Clinton administration was anxious to demonstrate that its interests in the hemisphere went beyond single issues such as Cuba, Haiti and NAFTA.

In December 1994 the 34 democratically-elected leaders of the Western hemisphere met in Miami to launch a process that the Clinton administration advertised as an effort to 'open new markets and create a free trade area throughout our hemisphere and bring together our nations to improve the quality of life for all of our people' (Clinton, 1994). In fact, Clinton's fulsome engagement with Latin America, highlighted by his repeated mentions of Simon Bolívar, peaked in Miami, a city whose skyscrapers were bathed in the colours of the flags of the hemisphere for the occasion. After three days of deliberations, the summiteers did produce a 23-point plan of action that addressed everything from hemispheric free trade to strengthening the role of women in society, leading the president to proclaim, 'Mission Accomplished' (Adams, 1994). At the very least, the summit had laid the framework for a process that could eventually unify the hemisphere behind the ideals of democracy, free trade, and sustainable development.

The cornerstone of the Miami summit, and its successive iterations, was the launch of negotiations for the FTAA. By 2005 the US government had expressed hope that the Americas would be united, creating the biggest market in the world by linking 850 million consumers with

$13 trillion worth of goods and services from Alaska to Tierra del Fuego (Clinton, 1994). The proposed FTAA represented a significant expansion of the recently signed NAFTA treaty, significantly decreasing tariff and non-tariff barriers to trade in a region that already traded heavily with the United States. Between 1985 and 1993 US exports to Latin America more than doubled from $30 billion to $80 billion. US investment in Latin America grew similarly, from $28.7 billion in 1985 to over $100 billion in 1994 (Walte, 1994). As a region Latin America imported almost half its goods from the United States in 1994. Additionally, Latin America was one of few areas with which the US maintained a trade surplus (to the tune of $13 billion in 1993). From the US perspective the FTAA would cheapen existing trade, promote further trade, and stimulate investment and capital flows. Using the same type of rhetoric that encouraged the passage of NAFTA, Clinton explained the need for the FTAA, saying, 'We simply must be able to export more of our goods and services if we are going to create more high-wage jobs' (Goshko and Behr, 1994). While the Caribbean leaders present voiced support for the FTAA, they were in fact slow to recognise a way to take advantage of the proposed strategic shift towards regional integration. Instead, they mainly focused on pressing their concerns regarding the phasing out of quotas for Caribbean bananas, threatening to devastate the industry. These pleas, however, fell on deaf ears as far as the US and Central American leaders present were concerned.

While often overshadowed by the FTAA, the Miami declaration committed to action in the following areas: preserving and strengthening the community of democracies of the Americas; promoting prosperity through economic integration and free trade; eradicating poverty and discrimination in the hemisphere; and guaranteeing sustainable development and conserving the natural environment for future generations. In fact, only one of the 23 points in the action plan was devoted to free trade. Hemispheric organisations like the Pan-American Health Organization and the Organization of American States (OAS) were called to join governments in working to advance the non-trade agenda. The OAS received mandates to follow up on provisions to promote democracy, protect human rights, promote cultural values, combat corruption, reduce the threat of terrorism, build mutual confidence, and encourage the development of an information infrastructure.

The Miami Plan of Action addressed the contentious trade issue forcefully, but diplomatically. It coupled reductions in tariffs with social issues to make it more palatable to Latin American governments. Workers' rights, intellectual property rights, and subsidies – three significant hang-ups during the NATFA debates – were mentioned as areas in which 'balanced and comprehensive' agreements could be reached. Nonetheless, the product of the Miami summit was a skeleton of a map, a plan to plan. At best it laid out detailed directions for arriving at the goals of the summit, using smaller ministerial or vice ministerial meetings between larger summits to iron out the complex details. Between the 1994 Miami summit and the second iteration in Santiago in 1998, there were 15 lower-level meetings on trade alone. These proceeded on schedule and were relatively successful at achieving consensus. Six months after the Miami summit, the ministers of the 34 countries responsible for trade met at the Denver Trade Ministerial where they agreed to form 7 of 12 working groups called for by the Miami Plan of Action for harmonisation on specific areas. The Caribbean Community scored its first major victory at this time by pushing for a working group on smaller economies to be chaired by Jamaica. The remaining five working groups were created at the 1996 Cartagena Trade Ministerial and by the fourth FTAA trade ministerial at San José, Costa Rica; the ministers were able to lay out a concrete structure for FTAA negotiations to take place following Santiago. The Caribbean countries remained active participants throughout the ministerial meetings, but they were unable to defuse several minor points of contention that emerged between MERCOSUR countries and the US. When confronted with accusations that his government had been deliberately dragging out the ministerial proceedings, Brazilian Foreign Minister Luiz Felipe Lampreia retorted, 'I think we have been given 10 years by the presidents (to integrate) and we should use all of those 10 years' (Hall, 1995).

The second Summit of the Americas took place in Santiago, Chile in April 1998. The Santiago plan of action stipulated that official trade negotiations begin in accordance with the schedule set out in the 1998 San José ministerial. Specifically, nine negotiating groups were set up on market access, investment (Dominican Republic vice-chair), services (Bahamas vice-chair), government procurement, dispute settlement, agriculture, intellectual property rights, subsidies, and competition policy. Results from the negotiating groups were to be reported to the Trade Negotiations Committee no later than December 2000. The Dominican Republic served as vice-chair of the investment group and the Bahamas was the vice-chair of the services group, allowing the two Caribbean countries to help steer subsequent negotiations. In addition, Santiago designated Canada as the first chair of the FTAA process and set up an order for rotating chairmanship. Beyond the trade agenda the primary focus of the Santiago summit was education. Leaders reiterated their commitment to ensure universal completion of primary education, and at least 75 per cent completion of secondary education by 2010 as agreed to at the Miami summit. The plan of action charged the governments, the OAS, the IDB, the World Bank, and several other institutions to cooperate in order to reach this goal.

Although all of the summit participants pledged to continue the trade negotiations in good faith, beneath the surface signs of tension were already beginning to emerge, as was evident in the next round of ministerial trade talks that took place following the Santiago summit. The fifth trade ministerial in Toronto broke down after trade ministers failed to negotiate a framework agreement that would begin to finalise the FTAA process. During this session the Caribbean nations put forward a united front to insist that adjustment assistance be afforded to small economies for the transition to free trade, but the proposal received a cool reception from the developed economies. The Caribbean position, together with Argentina's preference to work within the MERCOSUR framework, ultimately prevented any agreement from being reached (Weinberg, 1999). The negotiations were further complicated by the fact that US Trade Representative Charlene Barshefsky did not attend the Toronto meetings, choosing instead to send her deputy so that she could remain in Washington to lobby (unsuccessfully) for 'fast-track' trade promotion authority. The lack of trade promotion authority from the US certainly did little to spur trade ministers into action. In the same way that the San José ministerial laid out the Santiago talks and the work plan following the president's summit, Toronto was designed to lay the groundwork for the Quebec City summit which was originally scheduled to take place in November 1999 immediately following the ministerial.

While disappointing in many respects, the Toronto ministerial did succeed in extending the FTAA process. Ministers scheduled an additional meeting 18 months later in Buenos Aires to precede the Quebec City summit. Amid protestors in Buenos Aires, trade ministers agreed to a framework for negotiations that would see the FTAA implemented by the beginning of 2006. To get around sticky issues such as labour provisions, environmental concerns, and adjustment periods for small economies, the ministerial declaration from Buenos Aires allowed consideration for each of these issues at a later date, but ensured that only provisions with unanimous consent would be undertaken.

In April 2001 the hemisphere's leaders gathered at the third Summit of the Americas in Quebec City ratified the agreement put forth by the Buenos Aires ministerial on trade – but, in effect, only put off serious discussion over the most contentious issues. There were several more pressing concerns. A crowd of 30 000 protestors delayed the opening ceremony of the summit and commanded more headlines than the 34 heads of state gathered there. 'We expected this,' a senior Bush administration official said upon the president's arrival at his first Summit of the Americas. 'You can't have a trade summit these days without tear gas; it would be like having a cheeseburger without cheese' (Sanger, 2001). President Bush also used the summit to announce the Third Border Initiative, which provides a framework for US–Caribbean security cooperation that complemented the summit process. Bush and his Venezuelan counterpart Hugo Chávez were two notable first-time participants in the Summit of the Americas process in Quebec City. Chávez was the only head of state not to vote in favour of completing FTAA negotiations by January 2005. At the closure of the Quebec City summit, Argentine President Fernando de la Rua predicted a more productive summit under his country's leadership at Mar de Plata, saying, 'The next summit we will hold in Argentina will not require walls for those coming to oppose, but it will have space for those coming to applaud' (Mutume, 2001).

The four years between the 2001 summit in Quebec City and the 2005 gathering in Mar del Plata were characterised by turmoil in world and hemispheric affairs that presaged deepening divisions in the Americas. On 11 September 2001, the day that al Qaeda terrorists hijacked four planes and unleashed their attack on New York and Washington, Secretary of State Colin Powell was with hemispheric leaders gathered in Lima, Peru to sign the Inter-American Democratic Charter that had been agreed to several months earlier in Quebec. He quickly left for Washington after the document was ratified, and the US soon became embroiled in its operations in Afghanistan. Eighteen months later, the US invasion of Iraq in 2003 provoked a global upsurge in anti-Americanism that turned President Bush into an increasingly unpopular figure abroad. Meanwhile, in Latin America, a series of events including the Argentine financial default in December 2001, the attempted coup to oust Chávez in April 2002, and the collapse of governments in Bolivia, Ecuador and Haiti deepened a sense of disappointment with the US. The small countries of the Caribbean were consumed with their own set of tensions, including a stark drop in the tourist trade following 9/11, frustration with the flow of criminal deportees from the US and Canada leading to rising crime and violence, and increasing scepticism about how the Caribbean could benefit in the context of a free-trade pact. The February 2004 ousting of Haitian President Jean-Bertrand Aristide by armed thugs sparked particularly strong protest within CARICOM, who objected to seeing one of their own spirited away in a US-chartered plane and deposited in Africa. Several CARICOM countries pressed for an inquiry into Aristide's ousting to be conducted by the OAS or the UN, but the US, which strongly opposed such a move, squelched the efforts.

Against this backdrop of deepening unease, Venezuelan President Hugo Chávez planned to use the fourth Summit of the Americas in Mar del Plata, Argentina, as a forum for rallying his left-wing base on the continent and airing grievances with the United States. Formally, the main issue on the agenda was whether or not to continue negotiations for an FTAA, but off the agenda, the summit quickly became a populist sideshow. The trade agenda began to break down on several fronts. Latin American countries complained that US farm subsidies were insurmountable non-tariff trade barriers unfairly allowing America to corner the agricultural market. An equally strong contingent complained that labour standards and environmental provisions must accompany any free-trade document. The small economies of the Caribbean expressed concerns that, at the current pace, their economies would be overwhelmed by exposure to a more open market. They demanded more time to adjust to the proposed FTAA provisions. The members of the South American Common Market, or MERCOSUR, also commanded a strong contingent that sought to slow down integration. In a desperate attempt to forge an agreement, Argentine Chancellor Rafael Bielsa offered to draw up a document that included two postures, pro and anti-FTAA, essentially suggesting that the hemisphere agrees to disagree. Mexican President Vicente Fox countered that the rest of the nations should continue without Venezuela and MERCOSUR states. In the end, the heads of state issued a paltry final statement with no mention of FTAA, terrorism, or regional security – only 30 items related to the purported theme of the summit: 'creating jobs to fight poverty and strengthen democratic governance.' In the end, the Caribbean nations joined 29 other countries in favour of continuing FTAA negotiations, despite all the difficulties. However, the disagreement of five key countries, Venezuela plus the MERCOSUR group of Brazil, Argentina, Uruguay, and Paraguay, meant that the FTAA would be placed on the back-burner, perhaps forever.

Moreover, as in Quebec City, the Mar del Plata summit was dominated by protestors. Chávez and his allies organised a 'People's Summit' attended by 300 Cubans dressed in red and white jumpsuits, Argentine soccer legend Diego Maradona, and over 50 000 protestors. As the summit collapsed, many hailed the rise of the new left in Latin America. Chávez took advantage of an unpopular US president and a region somewhat fed up with America's free-trade gospel and created a perception that a US-led process of hemispheric integration would be all but impossible. Speaking before a crowd of thousands, Chávez declared, 'Each one of us brought a shovel, a gravedigger's shovel, because here in Mar del Plata is the tomb of the Free Trade Area of the Americas' (quoted in Reel and Fletcher, 2005). The reality was that the existing tensions in Mar del Plata merely revealed how far the Summit of the Americas process had fallen short of the vision of convergence and community that had characterised the discussions in Miami 11 years earlier. Now, as the hemisphere prepares for the next summit to take place in Trinidad and Tobago in 2009, the question remains whether Caribbean diplomacy can help to heal a hemisphere torn asunder.

Caribbean summit diplomacy: Fits and starts

During the 15 years since the first Summit of the Americas, many Caribbean countries have been torn between judging the summit process as a glass half full or a glass half empty. In particular, the small, English-speaking countries of the CARICOM felt largely marginalised during the 1994 Miami summit, having been excluded from the agenda-setting process and invited only at the last minute. From its earliest days, the summit process placed the US–Latin America relationship at its core, with Washington principally soliciting input from the major Latin American economies and, to a lesser degree, Canada.

Speaking before a meeting of the Association of Caribbean States in 1995, Prime Minister Patrick Manning of Trinidad and Tobago proposed establishing a Caribbean free trade area by 2000 in order to make the region a relevant negotiating force at hemispheric trade meetings, arguing that 'the international community is addressing trade matters with an urgency which demands that the Caribbean galvanise itself through similar actions, if we are not to be left behind' (Gibbings, 1995). Beginning with the Miami summit, Caribbean countries argued forcefully that the special needs of small states be accounted for in the broader integration process. Indeed, the concept of 'special attention for small states' has been at the crux of the Caribbean position on the FTAA and central to the region's negotiating strategy at the summits. Still, the larger countries generally viewed the Caribbean to be peripheral to the negotiating process and doubted that Caribbean states would be able to adhere to the timetables. Against this backdrop it is ironic to note that the FTAA process eventually broke down on account of severe disagreements between the two largest states – the United States and Brazil – resulting from disputes over how to handle the sensitive agricultural sectors.

The nations of the Caribbean are involved in political and economic integration at two levels, regional and hemispheric – and so far they have had much more tangible gains from the former. The nations that make up CARICOM have, in theory, much to gain from hemispheric integration. But the Summit of the Americas process, having failed to deliver a FTAA, leaves the Caribbean little with which to work. For the time being, economic and social issues have taken a back seat to security and it does not appear likely that the Caribbean will receive the attention it desires on these issues at the upcoming summit in Trinidad and Tobago.

That is not to say that Caribbean diplomacy has made little to no contribution to the summit negotiations, including the assuming of substantial coordination responsibilities. The Dominican Republic and Jamaica were the responsible coordinators of the mandates on civil society following the second summit. As a result, a regional technical seminar on participatory methods for managing biodiversity and coastal resources in the Caribbean was held in Barbados in September 1998. The Sub-regional Seminar on Internal Migration in the Caribbean was held in Kingston, Jamaica in October 1998 as a follow-up to the mandate on migrant workers from the second summit. Jamaica helped co-coordinate the mandate on prevention and control of the 'illicit consumption of and trafficking in narcotics and psychotropic substances and related crimes' following the Santiago summit. The 28th regular session of the Inter-American Drug Abuse Control Commission (CICAD) met in Trinidad and Tobago in October 2000 for follow up. The accomplishments of the CICAD meeting included gaining support for a multilateral evaluation mechanism process and, for the first time, the participation of various sectors of civil society within the sessions. Pursuant to the mandate on 'Building Confidence and Security among States,' the special security concerns of small island states in the Caribbean were discussed in the high-level meeting held in San Salvador in February 2008 and in the OAS Committee on Hemispheric Security.

Trinidad and Tobago, the Bahamas, and the Dominican Republic held vice-chair positions for FTAA negotiating groups between the Miami and Santiago Summits. At the Fifth Trade Ministerial of the FTAA process in Toronto, 1999, Trinidad and Tobago was given the chair of the investment negotiating group for an 18-month period. Under the 'Science and Technology' mandate from the Santiago Summit, a course entitled 'Labelling and Net contents of Pre-packaged goods' was held in Jamaica in the winter of 1999. This course was an attempt to familiarise Central American and Caribbean countries with the basic principles of labelling and re-distribution of pre-packaged goods, as well as harmonising standards in those areas. In addition, CARIMET (Caribbean Metrology) participated in Inter-American Metrology System (SIM) meetings with a goal of harmonisation of measurement and standards in the region, followed by the hemisphere.

While the disastrous outcome in Mar del Plata may have seemed to negate much of the energy that the Caribbean countries have poured into the Summits of the Americas, the reality is more complicated. The most contentious issue for the Caribbean in the summit process thus far has been the objective of securing special treatment for small economies under the proposed FTAA, which the larger countries acknowledged a need for in principle but proved unwilling to address with significant concessions. As a result, if the Mar del Plata meeting had produced the framework for the FTAA as originally planned, the Caribbean would have been in a tight spot: being presented with an agreement that was economically untenable to support but politically damaging to oppose. Given that the Caribbean Community enjoys the perception that its members support free trade and can be counted on as steady US allies, the failure of Mar del Plata actually saved them from having to admit that the Caribbean did not support an FTAA on the terms the US was dictating. Indeed, the Caribbean raised concerns on a number of issues leading up to Mar del Plata; government procurement in particular, such as the state purchasing of goods and services, is a significant boon to many Caribbean economies that are struggling to achieve the economies of scale necessary to compete in the global economy. If procurement had been limited by the mandates the US had put forward in the FTAA negotiations, the outcome would have considerably undercut native firms. Protecting national companies is a key concern for many Caribbean governments, but their pleas often fell on deaf ears during the FTAA process.

Indeed, while many Caribbean leaders enjoy attending the summits and meeting with their counterparts from the United States, Canada and Latin America, there is deep discontent among many diplomats over whether the summits can achieve real gains for the region. Moreover, the Caribbean Regional Negotiating Machinery (the trade arm of CARICOM) has been actively negotiating trade agreements with a range of partners including Canada and the European Union, meaning the region is less dependent on the fortunes of the FTAA. The Mar del Plata summit, in particular, left a bad taste in the mouths of many participants from the Caribbean. One Caribbean diplomat, in reference to the breakdown in diplomacy in Mar del Plata, recalled, 'We were totally isolated when it came to the conflicts that would arise. Some of the other countries would treat our issues with a yawn, while others thought we were nitpick-ing.' Furthermore, while the United States has been a key player in the summit process and will remain so in 2009, the new president will have a long way to go to repair the strained relationship between the United States, Latin America and the Caribbean. Few Caribbean diplomats are optimistic that a new administration will be able to gather hemi-spheric support prior to 2009. According to one high-level Caribbean diplomat stationed in Washington, 'New administration or not, the con-tentious issues that caused the fallout at Mar del Plata have not been solved.'

Can the summit be saved? The Trinidad gamble

Now Trinidad and Tobago will inherit the divisive set of issues and personalities that led to the 2005 breakdown when it hosts the fifth Summit of the Americas in 2009. It will be the largest single test faced by a Caribbean country during the summit process, posing logistic, diplomatic, and security challenges. Trinidadian Prime Minister Patrick Manning views the summit as an opportunity to consolidate his legacy as a regional leader, and he has appointed distinguished Trinidadian diplomat Luis Alberto Rodriguez as the summit coordinator. Already Caribbean countries are benefiting from the choice of Trinidad as the summit location, as the region will have a host country that is knowl-edgeable about regional groupings and instinctively knows how to include its Caribbean neighbours for the first time. Several of the key meetings of the Summit Implementation Resource Group (known as SIRG meetings) are scheduled to take place in the Caribbean in the fall of 2008 and joined by top diplomats from across Latin America, as well as from Canada and the US. Still, signs of tension are already emerging around such issues as whether the new Cuban leadership should attend the summit now that Fidel Castro has retired, a suggestion that riles the Bush administration but may in fact be greeted with more interest by the next US president. By focusing on common issues such as energy and the environment, and downplaying the thorny topics of democracy and trade, Trinidad hopes to restore the spirit of collegiality that domi-nated during the first two summits in 1994 and 1998, before the tensions of 2001 and the protests of 2005 cast doubt upon the viability of a hemi-spheric summit process. If the 2009 Summit of the Americas proves to be successful, then it will be Caribbean stewardship that helped regional integration get back on track.

References

Adams, David (1994) 'Skeleton in place for huge trade bloc', *St Petersburg Times*, 12 December.

Clinton, Bill (1994) 'Remarks on Goals of the Summit of the Americas', Miami, FL, 9 December.

Gibbings, Wesley (1995) 'Caribbean Trade: Road to ACS Integration Filled with Potholes', *Inter Press Service*, 19 August.

Goshko, John M. and Peter Behr (1994) 'The Americas Open 3-Day Trade Summit', *Washington Post*, 10 December.

Hall, Kevin G. (1995) 'Brazil's call to 'go slow' holds sway at summit', *Journal of Commerce*, 3 July: 1A.

Mutume, Gumisai (2001) 'Trade Police Repression Marked Summit of the Americas', *Inter Press Service*, 22 April.

Reel, Monte and Michael A. Fletcher (2005) 'Anti-US Protests Flare at Summit', *Washington Post*, 5 November.

Sanger, David E. (2001) 'Bush will press free-trade issue at Quebec talks', *New York Times*, 21 April: A1.

Walte, Juan J. (1994) 'Hemispheric huddle is all about growth', *USA Today*, 8 December: 4A.

Weinberg, Paul (1999) 'Trade: Heavy going at FTAA Negotiations', *Inter Press Service*, 7 November.

Part 3
Case Studies: Small States' Diplomacy vis-à-vis International Organisations

11
Bringing an Elephant into the Room: Small African State Diplomacy in the WTO

Donna Lee

Small state diplomacy is increasingly relevant to multilateral trade negotiations in the World Trade Organization (WTO). This is because small developing states have come to play an increasingly active and vociferous part in WTO negotiations, especially during the current Doha Round of talks. Indeed, developing country activism has been a major factor in the ongoing delay in concluding the Doha Round.[1] Several of the very active developing countries are small states. This suggests that small states are now beginning to play a key role in WTO negotiations and contrasts with the conclusions of a recent study of small states in the WTO which claims they remain marginal, vulnerable and weak (Grynberg, 2006).

The conclusions in the Grynberg (2006) edited volume are reached through an outcome-based analysis. While this is useful in highlighting the continuing structural difficulties small states face in the WTO system, it provides only partial insight into the impact of small states in the WTO. By contrast, my analysis stresses the impact of small state diplomacy on WTO processes in the cotton talks, rather than merely outcomes, and proceeds to argue that small states have succeeded in changing these processes by positioning themselves at the very centre of these talks. I find evidence that small developing states are able to punch above their weight as Edis has previously claimed (Edis, 1991). In sum, small state diplomacy has provided traditionally perceived weak small states with the capacity to collectively say 'no' and, therefore, to block multilateral trade agreements. They have this capacity not only because they have developed collective diplomatic strategies in the context of a changing negotiation process (discussed below) but also because negotiations are very different in the WTO to what they were in the GATT. The GATT process was dominated by the US and the EU countries and, largely as a result of the Principle Supplier Rule,[2] the negotiating process was in effect a bilateral one. In the 1980s the emergence of the Cairns Group kick-started a process of procedural change as other GATT members sought greater involvement in the negotiations, using negotiating alliances around particular issues (in the Cairns Group agricultural subsidies case) as a platform to achieve this. A key characteristic of the WTO has been the growth, indeed proliferation, of negotiating groups all seeking to influence outcomes in the negotiations. As Narlikar (2003) has commented, with the growth of strategic alliances, the WTO process begins to look as tangled as a bowl of spaghetti. With this increasingly complex multilateral process has come the rising tendency towards collapse and stalemate in WTO Trade Rounds (Wilkinson, 2006).

The most visible location of multilateral trade negotiating is the episodic and often highly stylised WTO Ministerial Meetings – the latest of which took place in Hong Kong in December 2005. Significant negotiating also takes place at the regular sector negotiating groups, such as the WTO Agriculture Negotiating Committee.[3] Wolfe (2006) has also highlighted the enormous amount of informal as well as formal diplomatic activity that takes place in and around the WTO headquarters in Geneva where African countries have a growing, though still tiny, presence. In addition, small African state diplomatic activity on trade issues has developed in other international organisational forums, such as the United Nations Economic Commission for Africa (UNECA), regional forums like the African Union, and sub-regional forums, such as the Southern African Development Community, the Economic Community of West African States, the Common Market for Eastern and Southern Africa, and the like.

In this chapter I focus on small African state diplomacy in the formal WTO Ministerial meetings of the Doha Round. By examining the diplomatic strategies of Benin, Burkina Faso, Chad and Mali, also known as the Cotton 4, or C4, in the current cotton talks during this round of negotiation, this chapter develops a process-based analysis of small state diplomacy in the WTO. The C4 is a small but very active group in the WTO. It has succeeded in playing a significant role in challenging the process of the agricultural negotiations in general, and the cotton talks in particular. It has done so by using its limited diplomatic assets very effectively, developing a diplomatic strategy of building social networks and bargaining alliances among other African countries, other developing countries, and NGOs, around the issue of cotton. Indeed, they have accented the issue of cotton so effectively that it has become the elephant in the room of the Doha Round negotiations; an issue that looms large and will not go away. And by building alliances with other states, as well as networks with non-state actors, these four small African developing states have become important players in the process and form of the Doha Round as it has evolved. By raising their own collective game in the WTO and encouraging other groups to support their demands, they have shifted from being mere objects of trade talks to being subjects in the trade negotiations. And while some argue that small states remain weak in their bargaining with the strong despite alliance formation (Drahos, 2003), the development of collective negotiating strategies and the building of social and policy networks with other states, as well as NGOs, offers small African states a means of compensating for their relatively small size. Does the increasing activism of small developing states through collective diplomacy and social network formation in the WTO highlight that small size need not mean small impact and that size does not matter in the WTO?

This chapter begins to address these issues of size in the WTO context by mapping the 'smallness' of the four small cotton-producing countries (C4). The issue of smallness is then discussed in the context of the international political economy of world cotton production and trade in order to show the importance of the commodity to small state development and, in turn, the fundamental importance of developing a successful diplomatic strategy within the WTO to secure a satisfactory agreement on cotton. The final section discusses the cotton negotiations and the diplomatic strategies of the C4 as they negotiate to achieve concessions on cotton from the US and EU in the Doha Round.

Mapping smallness in Africa: The Cotton Four

As we may expect, each of the C4 countries share a number of small state characteristics.[4] Each, for example, has a small population of fewer than 14 million, with most people living in rural communities. Each has a relatively small economy when measured in terms of Gross Domestic Product (GDP).[5] Each is also heavily dependent on a single commodity, cotton, which provides 40 per cent of their annual export earnings (Fleshman, 2006). In Mali, for example, a third of the population works in the cotton sector (Oxfam International, 2007: 14). In all four countries cotton is grown on small family plots and accounts for over 50 per cent of rural household income. Cotton production is undergoing privatisation or has already been privatised as a result of World Bank and International Monetary Fund policy conditions for receiving Structural Adjustment Credit loans (Oxfam International, 2007). All four states – particularly

Chad and Mali – have relatively high levels of trade to GDP.[6] The C4 can all be said, therefore, to be competitive small economies but with high levels of exposure to international trade.

Small and successful: Africa's comparative advantage in cotton production

In terms of production, cotton is a remarkable success story for the C4. The cotton sector in West and Central Africa has enjoyed growth rates of more than ten per cent almost each year for the last decade. Cotton is, therefore, seen as a potential driver of development in the C4 states. Oxfam, for example, finds that 'Cotton producers are considered better off and more capable of emerging from poverty than other farmers', and in Burkina Faso 'literacy and school attendance rates in cotton producing regions are higher than the national average' (Oxfam International, 2007: 7–8). Until the depression of world cotton prices – caused mainly by increases in developed country subsidies, particularly in the US – began in the late 1990s, poverty levels in cotton-producing countries were falling.[7] According to the US Department of Agriculture, in 1994–95 the world price for cotton was 76.12 American cents per pound. In 2001–02 that had fallen to 28.49 cents per pound and small increases since leave current 2006–07 prices at 44.62 cents per pound. In Mali, for example, research by Oxfam found that until this fall in the price of cotton, nine out of ten farmers were able to repay their loans. Levels of indebtedness are now increasing, however, such that only four out of ten African cotton farmers are able to service their loans. Worse still is that 'some farmers are forced to sell assets such as livestock or farming equipment, reducing their productivity for the next farming season' (Oxfam International, 2007: 19). Evidence from US Department of Agriculture data comparing 2006 and 2007 production clearly displays this effect. Across the C4 countries production levels have been falling. Burkina Faso produced some 33 per cent less this year compared with last and Mali produced some 28 per cent less in the same period. Before this recent drop cotton production in the region had increased by 14 per cent between 1999 and 2002, but export earnings fell by 31 per cent at the same time owing to depressed market prices (WTO, 2003a).

US cotton subsidies are a significant factor in falling market prices for cotton.[8] It is little wonder, then, that the C4 would seek to use the Doha Round negotiations to dismantle these cotton subsidies. Throughout the Doha talks cotton prices have fallen, C4 cotton farmers have been producing at a loss while experiencing rising levels of indebtedness, and as a result they have been forced to sell their assets.

The cotton issue in the Doha Round

Cotton came to prominence in the Doha Round in April 2003 when the C4 sent a 'Cotton Initiative', to the WTO Director-General. The Cotton Initiative made wide-sweeping proposals including the elimination of domestic payments and export subsidies on cotton in the period 2004–06. The C4 hoped the Initiative would prompt purposeful discussions in the Doha Round on cotton at the forthcoming Cancún Ministerial Meeting in September 2003 and thereafter (WTO, 2003b).

The position of the C4 was quite straightforward but none the less challenging, particularly for the US which makes huge domestic payments to its cotton producers. To date there has been little progress on the cotton negotiations despite high levels of activism by the C4 and their supporters in the Africa Group,[9] the Group of 20 (G20),[10] and the Group of 90 (G90)[11] (Lee, 2007). At the current time of writing (March 2008) the Chair of the Agricultural Negotiations Committee has published a revised draft of 'modalities' (formulas for cutting tariffs and trade-distorting subsidies), which will kick off another set of meetings. The hope is that agreement on these modalities can be reached in the next few months in time to complete the Doha Round in 2008. The draft contains a formula for reducing domestic support for cotton and commitments on market access, and repeats the 2005 Hong Kong Ministerial Declaration's commitment to prohibit export subsidies for cotton (WTO, 2008b). The Doha Round is, however, still a long way from being concluded – if indeed it can be concluded at all. Realistic hopes for the elimination of US domestic cotton payments have been set back by the passage of the new US Farm Bill in the House and Senate. The new Bill maintains the high levels of domestic subsidies in cotton. Perhaps only further recall to the Dispute Settlement Mechanism (DSM) can lead to meaningful reductions in US subsidies since it is possible to argue that much of the progress on cotton subsidies has been forced through by the 2005 WTO Appellate Body ruling against the US on Uplands Cotton,[12] which bolstered the direct influence of the C4 in the Doha talks (Zunckel, 2005). The cotton case suggests that small developing states can best influence the rules governing trade where the rule of law prevails. The DSM, as the Uplands Cotton Ruling shows, offers an important supportive judicial framework to small African state diplomacy.[13]

The draft modalities now on the table, however, do incorporate many of the concessions the C4 have spent five years bargaining for, though they are yet to be agreed upon by the Agriculture Negotiating Committee. Moreover, given that WTO agreements are made on an all or nothing basis (the 'Single Undertaking'[14]), there remains the risk that negotiations in the other sectors such as non-agricultural market access will stall and prevent implementation of the concessions on cotton. That said, the fact that the concessions are in draft represents some achievement for C4 diplomacy and serves to challenge traditional views that small developing states are vulnerable and weak in multilateral trade negotiations. In terms of process, small African state diplomacy has also had a marked impact in the Doha Round. How have they done this? What are the diplomatic assets of the C4 in the Doha talks?

Diplomatic assets of the Cotton Four

The C4 have sought to build their diplomatic capacity at the WTO making use of limited bargaining resources. WTO membership helps in diplomatic capacity building since small developing states receive significant technical assistance to help them understand the WTO agreements and process. Programmes such as the WTO's Joint Integrated Technical Assistance Programme to Selected Least Developed and other African Countries, as well as the International Trade Commission (ITC) and the United Nations Conference on Trade and Development (UNCTAD), provide legal and economic training for diplomats to prepare for trade negotiations. Both Benin and Burkina Faso have benefited from these schemes since 2000 (Bernal, 2001).

First has been the cohesiveness of the C4 and the Africa group on the cotton issue that has enabled the C4 and other African states to synchronise their diplomatic capacities and diplomatic strategies during the Doha Round. This has been done through weekly meetings of the Africa WTO Group (Geneva-based African trade representatives), UNECA – which hosts workshops for African trade negotiators to prepare for Ministerial meetings – and the African Union Conference of Ministers of Trade. These are examples of how small developing countries have raised their deliberative capacity by enhancing the skills of their delegations through increased manpower, training and better preparation.[15] More noticeable, however, has been the establishment of developing country coalitions such as the G20, the Africa Group, and, to a lesser extent, the G90,[16] which have all at one stage actively opposed the major powers in the Doha Round on key issues, such as agriculture, cotton, implementation, and the Singapore Issues. These coalitions serve, among other things, to increase the diplomatic capacity of small developing countries by pooling their delegations, and by providing a focus to draw in NGO expertise to assist in the negotiations. Alone, many small countries have at best one or two delegates involved in the Ministerial meetings. Such meagre presence is hardly sufficient given the huge numbers of formal and informal meetings across an extensive range of trade issues, often very technical in nature. By pooling resources at the Ministerial meetings as well as in the Agriculture Negotiating Committee, small African countries can overcome some of their capacity deficit.[17] The involvement of state and non-state representatives, as well as NGOs such as Oxfam, in these negotiations enhances the possibility for small states to be heard and have an impact on the outcomes of these negotiations. In particular, NGO groups add to the deliberative capacity of small states in the WTO through direct formal lobbying activities at the WTO. They also provide much needed policy, trade and economic expert analysis. In the case of Oxfam, for example, this can take the form of very detailed reports on the cotton sector in small Africa states (Oxfam International, 2007). In addition, civil groups have been active in US capitols, lobbying media groups in particular, to highlight the impact of US domestic cotton subsidies on cotton farmers in Central and West Africa. This has led to editorials supporting the C4 in the *Washington Post* and the *New York Times*. With the support of these state alliances and non-state actor networks the C4 have successfully obstructed moves by the major powers to complete the Doha Round.

Added to these the C4 have a 'vision' for cotton and for development. This is a key diplomatic asset. It is, interestingly, a simple vision that links the issue of cotton to the broader development agenda in the context of the ideology of trade liberalisation. Since this is the ideological basis of the WTO system, the C4 argue simply for free markets rather than a radical new economic order. The C4 are demanding only that the US and the EU implement WTO rules on cotton subsidies and, more generally, to implement the Uruguay Agreement on agricultural subsidies. As such, the greatest diplomatic asset of the C4 is that they have been able to capture the moral and ideological high ground which, in turn, has facilitated the formation of alliances and networks as mentioned above. In the cotton negotiations (but also the wider agricultural talks) 'might is not right' and the US have been on the back foot in the agriculture talks for much of the Doha Round. Furthermore, since the discourse is one of trade liberalisation, the C4 and other developing countries have been able to shift the talks away from the vulnerability and entitlement framework of 'special and differential treatment' towards a more progressive development framework, emphasising development rights and liberal trade.

Is size relevant in the WTO?

The C4 have played a role in delaying completion of the Doha Round. Supported by the Africa Group, the G20, the G90, and NGOs – such as Oxfam – Benin, Burkina Faso, Chad and Mali have utilised their limited diplomatic assets to compensate for the structural bargaining constraints caused by their small size. The fact that two of the four small African cotton producing countries now sit on the Agriculture Negotiating Committee is one example of the rebalancing of forces within the WTO in favour of small developing countries.

In all aspects the Africa Group (incorporating the C4) have created the conditions that Drahos (2003) suggests are necessary in order to overcome unequal bargaining between small and major states (he uses the terms weak and strong) in trade negotiations. Yet some dynamics of the agricultural trade negotiations continue to work against small developing country influence. These dynamics include: the continued tendency for the negotiations to be dominated by the US and EU (who recently formed the so-called Group of 8, which then grew to the Group of 12); the American use of bilaterals with developing countries to undermine solidarity in developing country coalitions; the existence of a range of preferential trade agreements (PTA) between African countries and the US and the EU, which provide potential retaliation measures should African countries not cooperate with their patrons; the presence and continued emergence of new competing strategic alliances (such as the Group of 33 and the Like-Minded Group) that all strive for influence; as well as the dynamics within the Africa Group – having members who are net importers of agricultural products and thus benefit from subsidised food, as well as members who seek market access and thus lose out because of developed country subsidies – which undermines African solidarity in the wider agriculture negotiations. The Africa Group is far from homogeneous and has found it difficult to sustain collective action in the Doha Round on issues other than cotton. Yet how many of these dynamics relate to size? The dominance of the majors certainly reflects their superior negotiating capacities that are a result of the size and expertise of their delegation teams compared with small states. Also, strategies that have been used by small states to adjust for size – forming alliances to pool resources and increase negotiating capacity and expertise – have not been as successful as delegates and scholars hoped they would be because of structural weaknesses within some alliances. Other factors not related to negotiating capacities but more to weakness (as Drahos (2003) conceptualises developing countries), seem to be equally significant. Small African states are often weak in WTO negotiations because of their overall economic dependence on the US and EU. A range of PTAs and aid programmes create economic dependency. Therefore, the impact of smallness seems to be relevant where it can also be linked with economic weakness. But even then it is not the sole determining factor. In what follows I explore some of these issues of size.

The cotton negotiations are a useful case study for exploring the relevance of size for a number of reasons. First, because the major protagonists in the cotton negotiations, the C4, are set against one of the major powers in the WTO, the US, this case provides a useful exploration of the issue of unequal size in multilateral trade negotiations and how small states might compensate for unequal size. The cotton issue in the WTO is an example of how small African states have employed their diplomatic assets to develop effective diplomatic strategies to enhance their diplomatic capacity in order to influence the negotiations, and thus compensate for smallness. It is also a case in which we can explore the issue of weakness or vulnerability. The C4 are not inherently weak, vulnerable states in the cotton sector in the traditional sense. They are in fact the most competitive cotton producers in world trade and enjoy substantial comparative advantages in the sector. As such this is an atypical and unusual story of small state competitiveness in international production. The usual narrative of small 'weak' states – especially small African states – is one of low competitiveness, low comparative advantage and dependency on preferential access to developed country markets through PTAs (see Heron, 2008). The C4 are only weak in the sense that they are more vulnerable than, say, the US to fluctuations in market prices and because they cannot block US market price distorting policies.

Conclusion

As the various chapters in this book have shown, there is huge interest in the distinctive responses and strategies of small states to developments in international economic governance in global institutions such as the WTO. Small states have come to play an increasingly proactive and assertive role, particularly in WTO trade talks. Changes in the decision-making processes of the WTO, driven by calls within and outside the WTO for more openness and transparency, and by the impact of the 'Single Undertaking', as well as the growth in WTO membership and the increased formal involvement of civil society groups have reduced the exclusivity of WTO decision-making. Especially marked is the reduced (though not eliminated) dominance of the US and EU. The challenge for small developing states is to use this changed environment to exert more influence over outcomes. So far the story is very much one of increasing activism in WTO processes (including the DSM). Ensuring that concessions for small African states are included in any Doha agreement will require translating activism into substantive influence.

Small African states such as Benin, Burkina Faso, Chad and Mali have limited but significant diplomatic assets and have employed these to develop a resilient diplomacy in the WTO. Alliance formation and issue linkage have been used effectively to delay and stall a Doha agreement. By forging alliances and networks between themselves and with other small- and medium-sized powers, as well as non-state actors, the C4 have ensured that the issue of US (and to a lesser extent EU) domestic subsidies in cotton is the elephant in the room; an issue that constantly looms large in the Doha negotiations.

What this case study of the C4 has demonstrated is that the changing nature of WTO decision making has created opportunities for small developing countries to actively oppose and challenge the major powers in the WTO, such as the US and EU. By focusing on size in relation to social relations and social processes within the WTO (the formation of alliances and networks) rather than adopting a more conventional approach to size focusing on structural issues, I have highlighted the diplomatic assets and opportunities for small African states in the Doha talks. These assets have enabled the C4 countries to significantly influence the process of the Doha talks. This suggests that smallness is less relevant in the WTO than perhaps it was in the GATT. That said, the WTO remains a challenging environment, the negotiating capacities and resources of small states – even when they are pooled following alliance formation – are still insufficient to force trade liberalisation on the majors. Any significant progress on trade liberalisation, as the case of cotton (and the recent case between Antigua and the US over Internet gambling) illustrates is more often the product of the coming together of the judicial process of the DSM with the negotiating process.

Notes

1. The original timetable for the Doha Round set the end of 2004 as the deadline for completion.

2. This rule formalised the domination of the major players in GATT by stating that countries need only negotiate with trade partners who could offer the largest concessions in return for their own concessions. This ruled out any participation by small countries although the outcomes would extend to all other member states through the most favoured nation (MFN) principle of the GATT (Bernal, 2001: 5).
3. The Agriculture Committee is comprised of some 36 or 37 members and currently chaired by Crawford Falconer of New Zealand. Benin and Chad are members of this committee along with Egypt and Cote d'Ivoire (WTO, 2008a).
4. There is of course considerable debate about how to define a 'small state' but although fixed definitions relating to factors such as GDP and population size are clearly arbitrary (Baehr 1975; Mosser 2001) they can nevertheless provide a useful starting point for cross-country analysis.
5. The World Bank ranked Chad 120th, Burkina Faso 126th, Mali 127th and Benin 134th out of 183 countries in terms of GDP (millions of US dollars) (World Bank, 2007).
6. The trade to GDP ratios for the C4 for the period 2003–05 was 97.6 (Chad), 60.0 (Mali), 48.1 (Benin) and 34.5 (Burkina Faso) (WTO 2007).
7. For details and data on the fall in world cotton prices see Oxfam, 2007.
8. For a detailed discussion of US cotton subsidies see Lee and Smith (2008).
9. The Africa Group consists of 44 members from the African Union.
10. The G20 group includes Argentina, Bolivia, Brazil, Chile, China, Colombia, Costa Rica, Cuba, Ecuador, Egypt, Guatemala, India, Indonesia, Mexico, Pakistan, Paraguay, Peru, the Philippines, Nicaragua, South Africa, Thailand and Venezuela. El Salvador was originally a member but it withdrew at the Cancún Conference.
11. This Group comprises members of the Africa Group, the Least Developed Country Group, and the African, Caribbean and Pacific states group.
12. For details of the ruling on US Uplands Cotton see WTO documents on Dispute Case DS267 at http://www.wto.org (Home page)
13. The DSM ruling on the Antigua–US gambling dispute is another example of this.
14. The Single Undertaking of the WTO, agreed to in the Uruguay negotiations, requires members to accept the entire Trade Round package or reject it entirely. Developing countries had opposed the introduction of the Single Undertaking in the Uruguay negotiations arguing that it was a mechanism that forces developing countries to accept the whole package or opt out (Wilkinson, 2006: 90).
15. The WTO has provided funds and technical assistance to help developing countries improve their negotiating skills. The United Nations ECA has also provided much needed expert advice and analysis of WTO negotiations, policies and procedures to the Africa Group.
16. The G90 comprises all the developing and less developed country members of the WTO.
17. For details of African delegations in multilateral conferences see Walker (2004).

References

Baehr, P. (1975) 'Small states: a tool for analysis', *World Politics* 27 (3): 456–66.

Bernal, R.L. (2001) 'Small Developing Economies in the World Trade Organisation', Paper presented at the World Bank conference 'Leveraging Trade, Global Market Integration and the New WTO Negotiations for Development', Washington DC, 23–24 July.

Drahos P. (2003) 'When the Weak Bargain with the Strong: Negotiations in the World Trade Organization', *International Negotiation* 8 (1): 79–109.

Edis, R. (1991) 'Punching above their weight: How small states operate in the contemporary diplomatic world', *Cambridge Review of International Affairs* 5 (2): 45–53.

Fleshman, M. (2006) 'Trade Talks: Where is the Development?' *Africa Renewal* 20 (1), http://www.citizenstrade.org, accessed on 19 March 2008.

Grynberg, R. (ed.) (2006) *WTO at the Margins: Small States and the Multilateral Trading System* (Cambridge: Cambridge University Press).

Heron, T. (2008) 'Small States and the Politics of Multilateral Trade Liberalisation', *Roundtable: The Commonwealth Journal of International Affair* 97(395): 243–57.

Lee, D. (2007) 'The Cotton Club: The Africa Group in the Doha Development Agenda', in D. Lee and R. Wilkinson (eds) *The WTO After Hong Kong: Progress in, and Prospects for, the Doha Development Agenda* (London: Routledge).

Lee, D. and N. J. Smith (2008) 'The Political Economy of Small African States in the WTO', *Roundtable* 97 (395): 259–71.

Mosser, M.W. (2001) 'Engineering Influence: The Subtle Power of Small States in the CSCE/OSCE' in E. Reiter and H. Gartner (eds) *Small States and Alliances* (New York: Physica-Verlag).

Narlikar, A. (2003) *International Trade and Developing Countries: Bargaining Coalitions in the GATT & WTO* (London: Routledge).

Oxfam International (2007) 'Pricing Farmers out of Cotton: The Costs of World Bank reforms in Mali', Oxfam Briefing Paper No. 99.

Walker, R.A. (2004) *Multilateral Conferences: Purposeful International Negotiation* (Basingstoke: Palgrave Macmillan).

Wilkinson, R. (2006) *The WTO; Crisis and Governance in Global Trade* (London: Routledge).

Wolfe, R. (2006) 'New Groups in the WTO Agricultural Trade Negotiations: Power, Learning and Institutional Design', Canadian Agricultural Trade Policy Research Network, Commissioned Paper CP 2006-2.

World Bank (2007) 'World Development Indicators Database, 1 July 2007', http://web.worldbank.org, accessed on 30 October 2007.

WTO (2003a) 'Poverty Reduction: Sectoral Initiative in Favour of Cotton', Joint proposal by Benin, Burkina Faso, Chad, and Mali, WTO TN/AG/GEN/4, 16 May.

WTO (2003b) WT/MIN(03)/W/2/Add.1, 15 August.

WTO (2007) 'Trade Profiles: Statistics Database', http://www.wto.org, accessed on 30 October 2007.

WTO (2008a) Agriculture Negotiations Chairperson's Texts, 8 February. http://www.wto.org, accessed on 19 March 2008.

WTO (2008b) 'Revised Draft Modalities for Agriculture', TN/AG/W/4/Rev.1

Zunckel, H. (2005) 'The African Awakening in United States – Upland Cotton', *Journal of World Trade* 39 (6): 1071–94.

12
Confronting Vulnerability through Resilient Diplomacy: Antigua and the WTO Internet Gambling Dispute with the United States

Andrew F. Cooper

Antigua has many of the structural characteristics of a vulnerable country. As a small island state in the Eastern Caribbean, with a population of approximately 68 000 people, Antigua remains overshadowed by its larger regional neighbours – Jamaica and Trinidad and Tobago – never mind the major global powers. In economic character Antigua lost its traditional export industry (sugar) decades ago. Although boasting 365 beaches, Antigua has not built up a mass tourism industry. Moreover, its susceptibility to severe hurricanes serves as an obstacle to doing so. In political/diplomatic terms, Antigua has been held back by the image of corruption, which has been the result of the rule of a family dynasty (the Birds) for most of its post-independence existence.

Yet, if structurally vulnerable, Antigua demonstrates some noticeable ingredients associated with resilience (Baldacchino and Milne, 2000; Prasad, 2004). Small vulnerable countries exhibit an ability to find and develop niches in the global economy in a variety of ways. Some countries do it via the tourism industry. Others find it in the hosting of offshore financial centres (OFCs). Still others have moved into far more explicitly unorthodox areas, such as shipping registries, passport sales, and the issuing of stamps. These activities involve a degree of 'selling sovereignty' in return for rent/licensing collection (Palan, 2002).

Since the late 1990s Antigua's economic niche has been the Internet gambling (or gaming) industry. This industry shares many of the features of the other activities listed above. In large part Antigua's gambling industry is 'offshore' in the sense that most of its entrepreneurs and consumers are non-Antiguans. As with other similar industries the economic stakes are high; the global industry was estimated to be worth about $12 billion in 2006 (Christiansen Capital Advisors, 2007), and a full range of competitors exist, extending across Antigua, Costa Rica, Curacao, Gibraltar, Isle of Man, and Alderney. As with other 'offshore' industries, the Internet gambling industry suffers from negative stigmatisation. The stigmatisation of these intersecting industries – with Antigua as a prime site for irregularities – was at the forefront of two legal cases directed against specific individuals considered to have contravened American money-laundering laws. In the first, indictments were made against two individuals from the US (William Scott and Jessica Davis Dyett) who were accused of channelling some 250 million dollars of wagers from World Wide Tele Sports. A second, with far greater ramifications, involved charges under the 1961 Wire Act against Jay Cohen who, with another US partner, had established a major Internet gambling company in Antigua (World Sports Exchange), to the amount of between US$100 and US$200 million a year.

Unlike other 'offshore' industries, however, the Internet gambling dispute (sparked by the imprisonment of Cohen after he returned to the US to fight the charges) led to a formal and protracted case at the World Trade Organization (WTO), beginning in 2003 and continuing up to the present time. Given the asymmetrical power difference between the two countries, this time-line is itself highly significant. With its massive power resources, contesting this issue in bureaucratic/legal terms did not raise issues of over-stretch for the US; Antigua, at least in terms of state capacity, was at the other end of the spectrum. With an economy approximately 0.007 per cent the size of the US, the case has all the flavour of what Robert Keohane (1969) termed a struggle between Gulliver and a Lilliputian. To give just one illustration of the extent to which its resources are outmatched, Antigua's ambassador at the WTO at the start of this case (Sir Ronald Sanders) also served as the High Commissioner to the United Kingdom (Beattie and Williams, 2005).[1] In contrast, the US could bring to the negotiations a strong team from the United States Trade Representative, the Justice Department as well as the Department of State.

Reinforcing this image of resilience is the fact that Antigua was not only trying to defend its interests in a services area, it was doing so in a new sophisticated sub-set of the gambling industry that had some considerable potential to 'leapfrog' over its established bricks and mortar component. Antigua had not built up a physical replica of the Las Vegas or Atlantic City casino model – or even an equivalent of a Mississippi steamboat floating gambling site. The Antigua gambling industry was a virtual one, located in cyberspace. The case is a rare example of a challenge under the General Agreement on Trade in Services (GATS), yet it is more remarkable in its position as the first WTO dispute revolving around Internet sites.

If Antigua can be credited for taking the enormous risk of taking on the US, it could not do so on its own. Antigua had the sovereign status to take the dispute to the WTO on the basis that the US was denying access to its market to services provided by the Antiguan Internet gambling industry. Nonetheless, the government of Antigua lacked both the material and human resources to do so by itself. A puzzle arises about how Antigua was able to negotiate so effectively when its resources were so strained. The answer lies in the fiction that it was the Antiguan state that did all the running in this case. At the formal level Antiguan officials presented themselves in a skilful manner. This was not only true of Sir Ronald Sanders but also Ambassador Dr John Ashe, Sanders' successor, and Dr Errol Cort, Antigua's Minister of Finance and the Economy, who were active on the case. Underpinning and underwriting the case for Antigua, though, was the highly globalised Internet and remote gambling industry. Formal *de jure* authority through the state structure was wedded to the *de facto* strength of a new form of private authority.

Still, this outsourcing approach highlights the degree of resilience brought to the case by Antigua. In normative terms, the off-loading by Antigua of some negotiating responsibilities to private actors constituted another form of commercialising sovereignty. In practical terms, however, the case serves as an excellent example of what a small state can do to respond to the dynamic changes imposed by globalisation. Amid sharply weakened capabilities in other areas the Internet remote gambling business has been seized upon as a panacea in a high stakes game of international political economy, in which a country in the position of Antigua must constantly seek new ways to reposition themselves within the new division of labour (Commonwealth Secretariat/World Bank, 2000; Payne and Sutton, 2007).

Antigua: Orthodox follower or regional eccentric?

Consistent with most of the general images of resilience laid out in this book, Antigua's approach on the Internet gambling case did not emerge out of a set development strategy. What facilitated it was not a commitment to a proactive state or the overall building of state capacity. Rather, the approach was *ad hoc* and opportunistic. Much of the novelty of the case came from the unconventional nature of the Antigua political/diplomatic culture as a source of strength as much as weakness.

Traditionally, Antigua can be categorised as an orthodox follower of the big players in world affairs. In particular, Antigua has demonstrated almost uniform support for US interests. In the 1980s the US was allowed to install military and communication facilities near the international airport to keep the region under surveillance (Coram, 1993). When other members of the Organization of Eastern Caribbean States (OECS) visited Libya (amid promises from Colonel Moammar Gaddafi that he would provide a substitute market for bananas) Antigua refused to do so.

Domestically Antigua provided a putative bulwark against radicalism. Tim Hector, a former black power leader, provided a robust challenge to the political status quo. But the cutting edge of his alternative approach was provided through his journalism via *Outlet*. And even Hector appeared to mellow over time. Offside with the political establishment for most of his life (and jailed at one point under the Public Order Act) Hector moved to a more accommodating stance shortly before he died, taking on the position of an unpaid adviser on regional affairs.

The political culture in Antigua took on an exaggerated form of stability. The hero of the trade union movement in the sugar industry, Vere Bird, parlayed his charismatic personality into a long period of domination extending before and after independence in 1981 (with only a short spell out of power from 1971 to 1976) up until he eventually retired from politics in 1994. The ten-year struggle to succeed him as both leader of the Antigua Labour Party and as prime minister was a fierce contest between two of his sons, Vere Jr. and Lester, with Lester Bird eventually triumphing.

Economically Antigua took on many of the standard characteristics of what Payne and Sutton term 'open dependent' development (Payne and Sutton, 2001). The Birds were willing to entertain various options in order to try to pursue growth, including tax havens, export processing zones, a site for cruise ships, and Internet remote gambling. Albeit full of problems, this approach provided considerable flexibility in development.

Underneath this orthodox surface, however, the political regime made Antigua the regional eccentric. On repeated occasions the Bird family was implicated in notorious scandals, including shipments of Israeli arms to Colombian drug traffickers in 1990 leading to a public inquiry by the prominent British QC Louis Blom-Cooper.

At odds with the image of Antigua as a well-managed country in terms of its economic structure, 'Birdism' (or 'the Aviary' as the locals termed it) was criticised both externally and internally for its regulatory flaws. This problematic image has already been framed with respect to the perception of a lack of proper public accounts. Internally the criticism was directed at the opportunism and inefficiency of Birdism. Instead of a well thought out, sustained strategy after the demise of the sugar industry, the government went from economic option to option on an opportunistic basis.

This opportunism was wedded to a sense of arbitrary decision-making. Even in the online gambling industry the treatment provided to different businesses was striking. The failure of Aladdin's Gold led to intense speculation that the disgraced proprietor (Edie Hadeed) had found protection from the government because of his well-placed uncle (Aziz Hadeed), a senator and minister of state in the Bird government. Another gambling proprietor (the operator of Sportsoffshore) who complained about the government's mode of regulation in 2001 found himself bundled onto a plane in his underwear in the middle of the night, served with an extradition order to the US on tax evasion charges.

The overall flavour attached to Birdism was that of a regime comfortable with corrupt practices, willing to do things such as facilitate the location of a toxic waste dump or selling off the sand of its twin island (Barbuda) without notice. As one analyst observed by the early 1990s: 'Antigua has over two decades acquired the regrettable image of being the most corrupt society in the Commonwealth Caribbean' (Thorndike, 1993).[2] Having become a private fiefdom for the ruling family dynasty, and its courtiers, state power became the route to accumulate resources and dispense either largesse or punishment.

The weakness of this reputation meant that it was much harder for Antigua to mobilise a networked or alliance approach that Donna Lee traces in the cotton case (see Chapter 11). As the case progressed Antigua picked up some support from other members of the WTO, including a number of larger actors that adopted the status of 'third parties' in the case. Nonetheless, on a formal state-to-state basis Antigua, from the outset, took on the US by itself. Unlike other protracted and high profile Caribbean-related WTO cases, above all the long and bitter 'bananas war', neither CARICOM (the Caribbean Community and Common Market), the OECS, nor the Eastern Caribbean Central Bank have played major mobilising roles in drumming up support for Antigua's position, although the OECS' technical mission to the WTO offered some limited help.

Antigua's strength came from its willingness to embrace an unorthodox approach, especially under the Bird government. Once Antigua decided it would take the US on it was an enthusiastic proponent of unconventional methods. Out-muscled by the US, Antigua substituted skill not only through its own small cast of diplomats but through the use of 'outsourced' expertise.

Mobilising in an unconventional fashion

In terms of its own negotiating capabilities via the WTO Antigua was at an absolute disadvantage to the US. Unlike the US, Antigua had very little in-house expertise on the international trading system. Any initiative to take on the US through (and, as it turned out, beyond) the dispute settlement mechanism process would be a costly and time-consuming undertaking. As Dr Errol Cort, Antigua's Minister of Finance and the Economy noted:

> there are direct costs to the government in terms of our participation. Ambassador Dr. John Ashe has been a key person in this whole equation ... Dr. Ashe has been at most, if not all of the sessions in Geneva and part of the team meeting with the various other country delegations to lobby support ... I've been to the WTO myself a couple of times, so its not an inexpensive venture. (Campbell, 2007)

Moreover, many of the successful tactics used by small states in other struggles with dominant actors were less effective in the WTO case. The existence of solidarity in the domestic society of Antigua is striking, as it cut across the deep divide between Birdism and the divergent opposition forces that eventually triumphed under the leadership of Baldwin Spencer in March 2004. But this availability of solidarity continued to be of less salience in this case than in others, such as that of the Panama Canal case or military bases. The WTO case was engaged at the technical and legal level with little public outlet. Unlike these other cases of asymmetrical struggle there was no space for marches, demonstrations, or protest rallies.

Antigua did engage in public diplomacy by targeting the wider international public opinion. A sense of being a victim in the international arena was deeply ingrained. This attitude was in good part carried over from older struggles, especially the fight with the Organisation for Economic Co-operation and Development (OECD) and the Financial Action Task Force over the regulation of tax havens. What Antigua claimed as justice in that case was the establishment of a level playing field, in which both

OECD and non-OECD countries played by the same rules with respect to such matters as the exchange of information on tax matters. Under acute pressure to comply with the OECD campaign on transparency, Antigua voiced its concern with equality. In the words of Sir Ronald Sanders: 'It is patently and blatantly obvious that no level playing field exists and jurisdictions, such as Antigua and Barbuda ... are being placed at a serious disadvantage' (BBC Monitoring International Reports, 2003).

The strength of this public diplomacy was embellished in the online gambling case by two factors. First, state officials argued that the creation of an online gambling industry was a successful extension of 'open' market strategies promoted for small countries, such as Antigua, by international institutions like the World Bank. The barrier to consolidation of this still fragile market was promotion of a prohibition regime by the US that caused a chill in the industry. Since the initiation of legal proceedings against certain promoters of the business in Antigua, especially the case against Jay Cohen under the Wire Act, the Antigua component of the industry had scaled back from 119 casino operations employing 3000 people in 1999 to 28 operations and 500 workers in 2003 (albeit still retaining a high number of Internet sites) (Government of Antigua and Barbuda, 2004).

Second, Antigua appealed to its record of heightened regulation since the start of the offensive against OFCs. In terms of process, Antigua emphasised its willingness to make concessions so long as these were made as part of a bona fide mode of consultation. As an advocate for Antigua phrased it: 'We are trying to influence public opinion as much as we can as a small country. We're hoping our willingness to compromise will get us the right ear and a negotiated solution will come about' (Sparshott, 2006).

In terms of substance, considerable emphasis was laid on the great strides Antigua had made on establishing an orderly regulatory framework for the Internet gambling industry. At odds with its problematic reputation in other areas of governance, Antigua branded itself a confident leader of the online gambling business. The message from state officials throughout the case was that Antigua, notwithstanding the punishment meted out to Jay Cohen and other forms of legal action, had nothing to be embarrassed by: 'It is more than just a little ironic that the United States Department of Justice has chosen to single out for prosecution a well-known gaming service provider from Antigua, a jurisdiction that has been leading global efforts to license, regulate, supervise and oversee a robust yet clean and safe gaming industry over the internet' (Ashe, 2005).

It was clear to Antigua that by itself public diplomacy was not going to be enough to pursue a winning case. In principle, Antigua could differentiate the status of the Internet gambling industry, not only with clearly illegal activities such as drug running (Griffith, 1997) but other forms of poorly regulated economic activity. In practice, though, what was needed for success was good technical preparation and support. Given the enormous cost and sophistication of such an approach, some considerable offloading of responsibility for the case had to be given over to the online gambling industry itself.

There is some anecdotal evidence that the online gambling industry bankrolled the WTO case. In explaining how Antigua was able to take on the burden of such an onerous case, Finance Minister Cort revealed to a local reporter that: '[We have been] able to muster the resources ... with the help of the industry' (Campbell, 2007).

An interview by Paul Bluestein with Jay Cohen, in prison outside of Las Vegas, confirms both the motivation and the extent of the involvement of the gambling industry as backers of the WTO case. In Bluestein's words: 'The Antigua government hesitated to file a case, citing one of the biggest inequalities of the WTO system; a dearth of funds and legal expenditure that often shuts out small countries. Antigua's budget is US$145 million a year, and a trade case promised to cost at least US$1 million. The gambling industry finally agreed to pay the bill' (Bluestein, 2006).

All of the major players in the industry, whether or not they operated sites out of Antigua, had a direct stake in the outcome given the importance of the US market. All supported what Andrew McIver, finance director of Sportingbet.com (which had its servers in Antigua, and had built up close ties with the government of Antigua) called a campaign designed to impart 'continual bits of pressure on the US' (*New Media Age*, 2005). These included well-known traditional brands such as Ladbrokes and William Hill in the UK and other firms, all of which would move to capitalise if Antigua won the case and the US shifted its position away from a prohibition regime. As a representative of Boyles Sports in Ireland stated at the time of the appellate ruling: 'we would naturally target [the US] if the opportunities arose' (Dalby, 2004).

The extent of the 'deep pockets' with respect to this financial support can be gauged by the fact that Antigua was able to employ two very different types of lawyers. One component of its legal apparatus was handled by Mark Mendel, a self-styled maverick who was the public face of the case. Mendel (a partner of the firm Mendel Blumenfeld of El Paso, Texas) was a friend of Jay Cohen's and although he had no deep expertise in international trade law, he added a robust sense of emotional commitment to taking on the US, generally, and the US Justice Department, in particular. In contradistinction to Mendel's public enthusiasm, a top-flight legal team (with Craig Pouncey and Lode Van Den Hende as the principals) from Herbert Smith's trade and WTO practice in Brussels provided the deep expertise needed to battle the US. 'Herbies' was one of the world's leading firms for international litigation, with over 1000 lawyers. With its headquarters in London and other offices in Europe and Asia, it also had extensive experience working for the US on other controversial cases such as bananas and hormone treated beef (*The Lawyer*, 2004).

The unanticipated resilience of small state diplomatic agency

The WTO case on Internet remote gambling confirms the impression that in particular situations small states can punch above their weight in international relations; Antigua neutralised the massive asymmetrical divergence between itself and the US in a number of ways. It gained relative, albeit not absolute, control of the negotiations by taking the case to the WTO, where legal and technical arguments had predominance over the power distribution of the two protagonists.

Antigua could also take advantage of the uneven approach adopted by the US to the case. The argument by the US that Internet gambling should be prohibited was undercut by its allowance of Internet gambling in its own domestic horse racing industry, a gap that caused the most complication for the US position within the WTO case. To help a domestic industry that was under stress, Congress passed the Interstate Horseracing Act in the 1970s. Under the provision related to horse racing betting operations, no prohibition was placed on any activities including Internet gambling. Once accorded this legal exceptionalism, the industry hung on to it with firm tenacity.

Instead of the mobilisation of good arguments in the context of the WTO, the US resorted to escalated modes of enforcement. This approach was signalled by the late night passage in the Senate (followed in short order by passage in the House of Representatives and Presidential approval) of a ban on credit card and electronic payments for gambling wagers just before the congressional recess in September 2006. The legislation was passed largely by stealth, as the then Senate Majority Leader Bill Frist attached the measure to the 2006 SAFE Port Act, the objective of which was to increase protection of American ports. Furthermore, the legislation maintained the exception for off-track betting parlours for racetracks

Although this approach allowed the US to exert some control (by its coercive unilateral power directed at leaders of the offshore gambling industry), it also underscored the ambivalence of the US to the WTO process. By comparison Antigua demonstrated the importance, not of intrinsic, but of contingent resources (Habeeb, 1988), where a small state directs a disproportionate amount of its capabilities on a specific issue-area.

Moreover, as time passed, the US backed itself into a corner on the offshore Internet gambling case with far more complications, rather than potential exit strategies, being revealed. The unilateral crack-down on offshore gambling opens up the possibility for Antigua and its supporters to exploit the tensions in the US political system on gambling, especially with the ascendance of the Democrats in Congress. It also opens up the possibility of a wider strategic alliance between the forces behind a global regulatory regime of Internet gambling against the champions of prohibition (Garrahan and Yee, 2005).

The choice of unilateralism by the US also exposed it to charges that it is a backslider on its WTO commitments. The US has kept delaying its final response on the case, neither moving to adapt its own domestic laws (on horse racing) in line with the WTO ruling or offering compensation to Antigua for its ban on offshore internet gambling sites. Such stonewalling shows the problems small states have in extracting benefits from the WTO process, as any direct retaliatory measures against US goods or services would have detrimental cost effects for their own domestic populations.

To keep up the negotiating pressure on the US, Antigua filed for US$3.44 billion in annual compensation from the compliance panel established by the WTO (a vast amount given the size of Antigua's economy). But when the US eventually announced in May 2007 that it would be non-compliant, by the virtue of withdrawing its commitment on betting services under Article 21 of the GATS, it offered only compensation to the amount of $500 000 for lost annual revenue.

In terms of tangible outcomes the case shows the limits of resilience. The concessions Antigua did receive through the WTO's binding verdict as announced by the final Arbitrator panel report on 21 December 2007 proved a disappointment. Gaining the right to suspend copyright protections on US intellectual property to the sum of US$21 million a year – without any form of financial compensation – was not the outcome Antigua had wanted. Instead of bringing Internet gambling into the mainstream as a respectable and responsible industry, Antigua was being nudged towards other areas of trade that create new problematic reputational issues in terms of perceived piracy and counterfeiting.

What makes this case innovative, however, was Antigua's willingness to go on the offensive in taking on the US. Unlike the cotton club – and indeed much of the work of other groups from the global South – the focus was not placed on blocking the initiatives coming from the North. On the Internet dispute, Antigua took its good arguments to the WTO and stuck with it. This was true of the Bird government. But it was also true of the government of Baldwin Spencer, a more conventional administration. Instead of being resilient by 'rule bending' – a more common feature of small state diplomacy (Baldacchino and Milne, 2000; Prasad, 2004) – Antigua pushed ahead on the WTO dispute through operational bending, outsourcing much of its diplomacy with financial support from the international gambling industry. By doing so Antigua demonstrated an unanticipated power of agency. The normative consequences of this approach can be debated. But in terms of a model for future activity this approach serves as a compelling model for other small and supposedly vulnerable countries.

Notes

1. Subsequently Dr John Ashe became Antigua's ambassador to the WTO. See Sanders (1989) for conceptions of diplomacy for small island states.
2. See also Larry Rohter (1997).

References

Ashe, John W. (2005) 'Antigua reacts to indictments of gaming operators', Press Release, 22 May.

Baldacchino, G. and D. Milne (eds) (2000) *Lessons from the Political Economy of Small Islands: The Resourcefulness of Jurisdiction* (London: Palgrave Macmillan).

BBC Monitoring International Reports (2003) 'Caribbean States appeal to the OECD for a level playing field on tax', 4 March.

Beattie, Alan, and Frances Williams (2005) 'Antigua and US both claim win in WTO gambling row', *Financial Times*, 7 April.

Bluestein, Paul (2006) 'Against All Odds', *Washington Post*, 4 August.

Campbell, Patricia (2007) 'Gaming fight with US costs Antigua millions', *Antigua Sun*, 1 March.

Christiansen Capital Advisors (2007) Home page, www.cca-i.com, accessed on 28 May 2008.

Commonwealth Secretariat/World Bank (2000) *Small States: Meeting Challenges in the Global Economy*, final report of the Commonwealth Secretariat/World

Bank Joint Task Force on Small States, March (London and Washington DC: Commonwealth Secretariat/World Bank), http://siteresources.worldbank.org/PROJECTS/Resources/meetingchallengeinglobaleconomyl.pdf, accessed on 28 May 2008.

Coram, Robert (1993) *Caribbean Time Bomb: the United States: Complicity in the Corruption of Antigua* (New York: William Morrow).

Dalby, Douglas (2004) 'WTO opens up US door for Irish bookies', *Sunday Times*, 14 November.

Garrahan, Matthew and Amy Yee (2005) 'Antigua bets on UK in online gambling battle', *Financial Times*, 22 June.

Government of Antigua and Barbuda (2004) '2005 Budget Statement: Foundation for a Fresh Start' 30 November, http://www.ab.gov.ag/gov_v2/government/statsandreports/statsandreports2005/2005budget.pdf, accessed on 26 August 2008.

Griffith, Ivelaw L. (1997) *Drugs and Security in the Caribbean: Sovereignty Under Siege* (University Park, Penn.: Pennsylvania State University Press).

Habeeb, William Mark (1988) *Power and Tactics in International Negotiations: How Weak Nations Bargain with Strong Nations* (Baltimore: Johns Hopkins University Press).

Keohane, Robert O. (1969) 'Lilliputians' Dilemmas; Small States in International Politics', *International Organization* 23 (2): 291–310.

The Lawyer (2004) 'Herbies help Antigua in WTO outsourcing victory', 5 April.

New Media Age (2005) 'WTO ruling on Antigua could open US market to UK bookies', 7 April.

Palan, Ronen (2002) 'Tax Havens and the Commercialization of State Sovereignty', *International Organization* 56(1): 151–76.

Payne, Anthony and Paul Sutton (2001) *Charting Caribbean Development* (Gainesville: University of Florida/Macmillan).

Payne, Anthony and Paul Sutton (2007) 'Repositioning the Caribbean within Globalisation', *Caribbean Paper* 1 (Waterloo: CIGI).

Prasad, Naren (2004) 'Escaping Regulation, Escaping Convention: Development Strategies in Small Economies', *World Economics* 5 (1): 41–65.

Sanders, Ron (1989) 'The Relevance and Function of Diplomacy in International Politics for Small Caribbean States', *Round Table* (312): 413–44.

Sparshott, Jeffrey (2006) 'Antigua gambles on trade case with US', *Washington Times*, 5 July.

Rohter, Larry (1997) 'The Real Caribbean: Paradise Stops at the Beach's Edge', *New York Times*, 16 February.

Thorndike, Tony (1993) 'Revolution, Democracy, and Regional Integration in the Eastern Caribbean', in Anthony Payne and Paul Sutton (eds), *Modern Caribbean Politics* (Baltimore: Johns Hopkins University Press).

13

The Path to 'International Finance': Bringing (Caribbean) Offshore Financial Centres In; Attenuating the Western Grand Narrative

Don D. Marshall

The aim of this chapter is three-fold: it challenges over-determined, hegemonic accounts on the rise of offshore financial centres (OFCs); it seeks to establish the co-constitutive role of OFCs in shaping the cultural *habitus* of 'financialisation'; and it begins to account for the growth and resilience of Caribbean OFCs, tracing their roots/routes back to the development of institutionalised finance and public credit in England (circa 1670). This discussion calls into question the uncontested assumption that many of the problems of regulating the international financial system stem from the growth of OFCs. This assumption is at the heart of measures aimed at combating tax avoidance and evasion, tracking terrorist finance, and revising banking confidentiality principles. It animates the constructed category of the Caribbean or Pacific 'tax or asset haven', and can be located within the literature on the OFC phenomenon as either complex or fascinating when not posing problems of legitimacy. I treat the thrust for global financial re-regulation as part of the dilemma of neoliberalism: the pressures to further consecrate capital mobility world-wide continually run up against the limitations of the primary political unit (the nation-state) and arrangements for global governance structures that lack political legitimacy and accountability. But I attend to the broader knowledge produced on global financial flows as largely mired in silences and premature closures over the question of OFCs and their general resilience.

The dramatic evolution of global finance in the last three decades has seen intensified competition among the world's major cities to become prominent control centres of global financial flows. However, Western knowledge producers are displacing the 'hegemony' effect with a positive diversity of spaces, seeking to order every space on a singular grid/axis of 'modern' or 'primitive' (undeveloped), 'global' or 'non-global' (forgotten), or 'core' versus 'peripheral'. These binaries shape the ways in which, for example, banking cities are known and financial services centres are understood and legitimised. Such binaries are transfigured in the hegemony argument that financially powerful states are responsible for designing the (deregulated) financial order that was to replace the Bretton Woods agreements.[1] Here the banking and credit management practices of countries like Bermuda, the Commonwealth of the Bahamas (hereafter, the Bahamas), Barbados, the Cayman Islands, Hong Kong and the then-condominium of the New Hebrides (today's Vanuatu) are evaded where their activities were for a long time interwoven in the fabric of British commercial, industrial and financial markets, extending back at least to the eighteenth century. What is insufficiently acknowledged is how these and other colonial spaces were an integral part of historical global finance, as is how the postcolonial states, as sites of agency, would subsume the offshore financial services strategy under their nation-building strategies. Today the flexibility and adaptability of these very offshore financial centres assist in the operations of modern capital, its designs penetrating into the 'everyday life of global finance' (Langley, 2002). Debates within Western and non-Western studies on tax and investment planning, as well as recent discussions on the international financial architecture and regulatory scrutiny of financial systems around the world, have broadened awareness of the grey, interconnected world of fiscal and finance systems. But neoliberal precepts, market morality, and imperial and metropolitan biases influence the trajectories of the intellectual culture of financial studies. It is in this context that OFCs from former colonial geographies occupy the status of the 'curious', much unlike financial centres of the imperial core.

This chapter discusses how OFCs have become socially discredited. It seeks to accomplish this by unveiling some of the relevant narratives of eviction and rhetorical strategies at play, counter-balancing these with greater attention to the specificity of English-speaking Caribbean OFCs – the emergence of which is discursively 'read off' as epi-phenomena to Western market developments. This rejoinder amounts to an appeal to historicise the region's international political economy, noting the varying degrees some Caribbean colonial societies and economies were/are configured by the predilections of merchant capital.

The focus on the English-speaking Caribbean is intended to update the Western (meaning Anglo-American) encounter with the Caribbean. Although the Caribbean lies at the heart of the Western hemisphere and was historically pivotal to the 'rise of the West', it has nevertheless been spatially and temporally erased from the imaginary geographies of Western modernity. This is despite the consumption of its 'natures', flows,[2] and 'scapes'. Caribbean OFCs have become a special point of entanglement in the alignment of core Western interests in establishing the mobility rights of capital, tracking terrorist finance, and penalising tax evasion. I argue that from the vantage point of the Caribbean region, globalisation is experienced as late-imperial travel culture. This occurs through a process of flows of re-regulations, money, tourists and international business activities that include ship-chartering, shipping registers, aircraft-basing, reinsurance, film-making, mining and oil production and development, property development, cross-border equipment leasing and writers' royalties (circa 2008). This point is brought to bear in the review of narratives/debates on the origins and nature of financial globalisation. This brings the discussion back on track towards understanding the integral role of OFC jurisdictions, their mutually reinforcing cultural effect on high finance, and socio-economic development implications of the host countries themselves.

Master narrative of financial globalisation qua financialisation

The geographies of global finance encompass cities – some dubbed financial districts, others tax shelters, tax havens or offshore financial centres – that together constitute spaces of money flows. The varying terminologies signify a wider contest over legitimacy, one that involves a complex interplay between language and power. Currently, there is an international policy constellation around capital mobility, tracing criminal money and tracking terrorist finance, and this has been made possible by a), the 'extraordinary power' of Washington, Wall Street, Main Street and London before and increasingly since the events of 11 September 2001 (or 9/11); and b), the discursive hegemony of scientific finance. An epistemic community of largely Western experts 'fluent in finance', together with other policy specialists, are busily constructing norms in international tax policy and financial transactions through newly constituted international authority structures; transactions and tax policy initiatives that deviate from the standards so determined are being classified as suspicious. Indeed, financial stability discourses argue that Pacific and Caribbean OFCs are despised collectives. The narratives rely on Western literary protocols reminiscent of the colonial/imperial condescension found in the tropological narratives of Anglo-American travellers. The authoritative constructions convey the impression of

Pacific and Caribbean OFCs as temptress or tax havens of considerable intrigue. To feminise OFCs is to devalue their history and contribution to financial market civilisation.[3] At minimum, in my view, these representations and discourses confine the OFCs to the status of being 'connected through subordination' to more global financial operations and processes. The knowledge produced about the rise of finance and the financial sector in late modern capitalism use a similar characterisation.

The conflation of the literature seeking to address financial globalisation and financialisation arises as part of a broader body of work seeking to establish globalisation as both epoch and epistemological. For some authors, the compelling globalisation metaphor is meant to illuminate interconnections tying together the fates of men, women and households in different states/regions in the world system. Here, the world is marked by a unique holism – a technological and telecommunications novelty in capitalism's recent turn. Others acknowledge technological change, emphasise world system continuity but speak in terms of historical episodes of globalisation.[4] Generally, mainstream globalisation discourses fixate on the flows of capital and finance as well as the flows of people across borders. Indeed, the rise of innovative developments in global financial markets, along with their grip on individuals, households, firms and governments, remain an ongoing concern in the work on financialisation. The research converges around debates on regulation and the legitimacy of the global financial architecture.[5] Notwithstanding the 'efflorescence of approaches' to the question of financial globalisation and innovation, the literature invariably appears as a project of creating ever more exacting measures to gauge the competition between places in their 'globalness', 'globality' or 'centrality'. Offshore financial centres, in this grand narrative, generally remain unspecified.

This continues to be quite odd as the United Nations estimates that about $8 trillion are held in offshore companies and accounts (Mitchell, 2000). Figures produced by Oxfam point to $6–7 trillion, but this is nevertheless equivalent to a third of global GDP (Oxfam, 2000). For specificity, some estimate that a total of US$9 trillion resides in, or passes through, Caribbean OFCs alone (Thorndike, 1989; Kochen, 1991; Palan, 2002).

OFCs focus on providing a wide array of financial and business services for modern businesses and individuals. While there are distinct legal and policy considerations present in many offshore jurisdictions, the legislative, regulatory and tax framework is less restrictive compared with an investor's (onshore) home-base. Financial confidentiality – inherent in liberal precepts on individual rights and recognised as the Tournier principle[6] – girds the activities of OFCs, but discretionary service among the most competitive OFCs extends to effective counsel on money and portfolio management, tax planning, and leveraging the melding of national capital markets. Currently, the confidentiality protections of the offshore jurisdiction conflict with onshore extra-jurisdictional tax and money laundering investigations. The sneak terrorist attacks on New York and Washington of 9/11 provided the basis for enhancing the search for anomalies in the international financial system to prevent terrorist financing. Previously, the anti-money laundering regulation of the 1980s and 1990s was aimed at tracing the illicit gains of the criminal underworld (particularly in the narcotics and arms trade) and of corrupt public officials. Since 9/11 the emphasis is on security through prior identification and exposure of suspicious transactions. Know-Your-Customer guidelines have been amplified by the new imperative to shut down terrorist-funded networks. Next are the claims that the OFCs are engaging in unfair tax competition, as they provide favourable or non-existent taxes to individuals and companies (see the OECD Harmful Tax Report of 2000). This leads to the argument that tax evasion is being encouraged. A range of specific measures and initiatives have been undertaken by the (US-based) Internal Revenue Service to monitor onshore businesses and individuals that do business offshore, such as increasing reporting requirements on those who utilise OFCs. Altogether these challenges have been met in the Caribbean with some relaxation of strict standards of confidentiality and allowance of disclosure when a sufficient reason is provided (Belle-Antoine, 2002). As the Caribbean engages the re-regulation resolve of international agencies, state-managers are careful to defend the right of any sovereign nation to determine its tax policy. Tax planning is an important cog to the region's determined 'export services' strategy that complements high-end tourism promotion. But cumulatively the negative spiel produced after 9/11 about sham havens, terrorist cells and the like, could lead to a disassembling of the confidentiality framework that allows for attractive investment in the OFCs on the part of legitimate businesses and individuals.

Financial globalisation loosely refers to the process through which money, value and credit constitute a capital sphere sufficient to spawn networks and centres offering financial services. Two overlapping developments remain crucial to this account. One refers to the US-led campaign for capital mobility from the 1980s; the other refers to the subsequent coercive pressure applied to governments in the global South by international financial institutions (IFIs) to deregulate their capital markets. This merged well with parallel advances in communications technology marked by the proliferation of Internet and high-tech stock.

In sum, financial globalisation is held to be the outcome of a wave of innovations and deregulation that have led to the broad integration of national markets (circa 1980).

Scholars such as Benjamin Cohen (1996) presented finance-capital, conceptualised as largely autonomous and self-activating, as a 'mastering force' undermining national sovereignty and scope for domestic policy intervention. This was in contrast to the postwar Bretton Woods order when finance was seen as the 'servant' of economic production, and financial flows were subjected to capital controls (see Helleiner, 1993). The greater the flows of capital in and out of domestic banking systems around the globe, the more it was claimed that 'finance' had become as important an element in the world system as commodity trade and productive capital. The literature coming out of the 1990s debated the extent and scope of increased capital mobility and the implications for state-management. One camp lamented(s) that financial globalisation was (is) eroding much of the authority of the contemporary sovereign state.[7] Scholars of another persuasion took issue with the very portrayal of the world financial market as singular and akin to a seamless web (Eichengreen et al., 1995; Fiege, 1995; Cohen, 1996). Others addressed the neoliberal critique of the welfare and interventionist state reminding neoclassicists and financial globalisation proponents that inexorable tides of global economic flows did not mean the elimination of political structures of national states. Indeed financial instability and economic uncertainty throughout the 1990s led to pragmatic responses in the direction of re-regulating international finance and resolving the institutional fragmentation among states that frustrated the effective functioning of markets.

The literature's predominant explanation of the internationalisation of capital references developments emanating from the emergence of the Eurodollar market (1957). The narrative then chronologically turns to President Nixon's decision to devalue the US dollar (1971); the subsequent spawning of bank deregulation policies across core countries; how this was also driven by increasing trade in Eurodollar futures; and how these developments altogether facilitated the quest to 'go global' in search of efficiency, markets, and increased returns on the part of core firms and corporations. Stock exchanges expanded to form intricate networks offering ever more financially innovative products and opportunities for speculation. By the start of the 1990s Susan Strange would express misgivings about the 'the casino character' of international finance. Research produced along similar cautionary lines follows two broad trends. One interrogates the limits and strains of liberal internationalism, querying the legitimacy deficits that abound in the complex maze of international financial regulatory or administrative networks.[8] The second features discussion about the merits and demerits of finance-led growth regimes. This is where neoclassical studies on finance, girded by liberal economics, physics and mathematics, would come under unwitting interrogation by social enquiries into the effect of high finance on currency stability, development policy and debt management.[9] But altogether the 'internationalisation of capital' narrative turns out to be about the transatlantic integration of Euopean and North American capital, rendering the promotion of 'boundless financial services' by OFCs parenthetical (Johns and Le Marchant, 1993).

The seminal issue of capitalism's predisposition to crisis does not surface in the analytical schema of neoclassical work on high finance.[10] This is in contrast to research produced within the Marxist tradition, the world systems schools, political geography, institutional economics of the Karl Polanyi and John Maynard Keynes variety, as well as in International Political Economy (IPE). The crisis of Keynesianism, however, intensifies in this 'age of shareholder value' (*The Economist*, 2006). It is reflected in the rise to respectability of scientific finance and how this interacts with an ongoing restructuring of the global political economy that requires rolling back the economic and social borders of the state and satisfying neoliberal criteria of fiscal and monetary responsibility. Or, as one scholar neatly surmised: 'Nowadays, neoclassical economics' domination of development theory is on par with that of high finance's neoliberal power over development policies' (Herrera, 2006). This kind of specificity is apparent in the literature emphasising financialisation.

'Financialisation' signifies the growing and systemic power of finance and financial engineering under contemporary capitalism.[11] This field of inquiry extends to debates on whether the stock market is a legitimate and autonomous site for the valorisation of the market; how to curtail short-term speculative capital flows; and the reliability of professional accounting criteria for assessments of asset values. Pragmatic reassessments abound also on the question of deregulating capital controls, a discussion that usually re-enlivens debate on whether 'the market' really does know best (Thrift, 2005). As most accounts go, the power of finance and financial engineering would come to beckon the need for international policy coordination unlike any other period in the previous century. From around the 1990s, elite global actors began consistently encouraging governments to subject their macro-economic management to the needs of a 'finance-led growth regime'. This was the route to securing a maximally open world market for attracting and facilitating investment flows. This advice is part of a univocal discourse shared by neoliberal policy specialists and experts drawn from scientific finance, which encourages faith in the calculation of risk and trading in uncertain futures.

Under macro-economic conditions of a finance-led growth regime, firms increasingly pursue strategies designed to enhance shareholder value. Asset price bubbles have to be monitored by fund-managers to ensure that the companies' investment spread is not exposed to depreciating risk. Consultancy firms who develop, market and sell shareholder value strategies could advise(d) companies to live up to stock market expectations as a condition for success (Thrift, 2001). This produces tension in the spheres of the financial and productive economies, for the financial economy transposes its internally generated shocks into the productive economy.[12] The state is expected to secure a market order backed by sound economic fundamentals in order to attract facilitating foreign investment to its shore.

It is the growing exposure of all institutions and arrangements to the opportunities of financialisation, as well as to the more familiar pressures of globalisation, that have made the distribution of power within corporations and financial networks so fluctuating and unpredictable in the last few years (Blackburn, 2006). The volatility in the stock and credit markets from the summer of 2007, triggered by a sub-prime mortgage crisis in the US, has led to an off-loading of risky stocks by companies and investors world-wide.[13] Immediately the blame was placed on the decision to grant mortgages to persons of 'low credit value', and others with 'no income, no job and no assets' – the so-called 'ninja loans'. This distracts attention, however, from the intrinsic practice of recycling private capital through the stock market. This practice allows for some stock price manipulation, enhancing the value of shares in the highest performing capital – which, for some considerable time, has been the property development market. It is because firms routinely employ value-based management techniques to enhance shareholder value at the expense of product market expansion, and R&D that it is possible to speak of the rule of the capital market. This delineates the contours of what Stephen Gill (1995) would refer to as an emerging 'market civilisation'.

In other words, credit extension and market valuation combine to produce new social values. This is encoded in late-modern forms of financial self-discipline where civility is associated with the mastering of outstanding obligations that arise from extended borrowing. New financial identities are being constructed, Langley (2004) writes, through discourses of credit-worthiness that hail the 'responsible' individual as one who copes with credit card management, shares trading, mortgage repayments and pension fund commitments – sufficient to sustain his/her consumer freedom. Here one can add that while credit worth functions represent a bestowal of social honour, the rich preserve their high net-worth status and social superiority through the pursuit of wealth management options and lucrative investment vehicles in OFCs. Indeed the full contours of financialisation extend beyond the rule of capital markets. It relates to deeper commodification processes occasioned by innovations in commercial-dealing capital and information technology as well.

Classical debates on the role and force of capital live vicariously through their refraction in the current body of work on high finance. The liberal preoccupation with banking regulations, market relations, accumulation strategies and global institutional coordination of the same conditions demonstrates the 'dialogue of the deaf' that exists between its advocates and others whose concern is from the vantage point of the materially displaced and the socially excluded. What is conspicuously understated across the various disciplines, however, is the complex interplay of OFCs in the present world financial order. The 'tool kit' of innovative instruments such as trusts and bank accounts, as well as the wide array of financial services for modern businesses and individuals, make the OFC a complex creature.[14] Take the idea of offshore banking, for example. Any entity wishing to carry on 'banking business' as defined by the 1969 Banks Act in Bermuda is required to obtain a licence. There are only three licensed banks in Bermuda and so it is possible to conclude that within its profile, there is little offshore banking in Bermuda.[15] Yet some 90 international banks use the island, primarily through equity interests in Bermuda exempted companies, to carry on a wide range of financial activities, such as leasing, real estate ventures, group financing, collective investment schemes and the like. This is the result of intelligent regulation and entrepreneurial business acumen on the part of foreign and local principals involved.

Johns and Le Marchant (1993) initially, and Palan (1998; 2002; 2006) particularly, sought to capture OFC linkages within the circuitry of global finance and business (see also Johns, 1983). In the case of Johns and Le Marchant, they establish the contiguity of offshore and onshore financial centres, their respective specialisms and relationship to international banking practices. It is when discussion turns away from the OFCs in the British Isles and towards explanations about the rise of the so-called tax havens across the different zones (Caribbean-Central American, European, Middle East and Asia-Pacific) that we are asked to consider such factors as, in the case of the Caribbean, its shared time zone with New York, and the seizure of opportunities created in the wake of the Eurodollar market. The impression conveyed is that opportunist pragmatism was the decisive factor that led to the growth of Caribbean OFCs. This is too narrow an explanation as it does not explain why some countries were successful at this strategy and others were not.

Palan's work generally seeks to determine the nature of sovereignty under restructuring global capitalism. We are offered the following insights: one, sovereignty and self-determination played an enabling and constraining role in the development of the realm we know today as the offshore economy;[16] two, that these juridical enclaves, while marked by less stringent government interference, were created to better facilitate the more mobile economic sectors within the country's sovereign space and; three, that this cohabitation (between offshore and onshore, domestic and international) will continue to feature a constant cat-and-mouse game of state and business innovation, followed by multilateral and bilateral responses to close the loopholes. These insights serve as a counterfoil to early arguments extolling the decline of the state in the wake of globalisation. His work also sheds light on the blurring lines between international offshore practices and onshore practices. Noteworthy is how deregulation and re-regulation imperatives since 1970 were the outcome of contingent consequences arising from activities across the world of financial 'shores'. But these observations notwithstanding, Palan also focuses too strictly on processes occurring at a global level to explain the OFC phenomenon. Further, he treats the offshore world as one 'where millionaires and corporations roam in search of financial advantage' (Palan, 2006). This depiction revives romantic imperialist discourses justifying the re-regulation of OFCs as key to international financial stability. From the point of view of Caribbean OFCs, their histories have remained largely evacuated, their IPE is exoticised as 'secrecy' shelters, and their existence legally affirmed, but socially unmoored.

Early modern finance and the colonial encounter: Bringing Caribbean OFCs in

The orthodox portrait of contemporary global finance requires a concession to the sphere of historical commercial capitalism. It is here that the genealogy of financial services emerges. The creation, buying and selling of credit; the historical role of merchant capital; the overlapping histories of gambling and financial trading in seventeenth-century Europe; and the emergence of professional speculators and their struggle for political legitimacy and respectability by the end of the nineteenth century – all form part of the hard-wired logics that propelled the evolution of international finance. These processes were enacted on the stormy ground of European imperialist expansion and colonial formations. Geoffrey Kay's (1975) study of historical merchant capital informs us about the role of merchants as creditors in European colonialist expansion and the rise of commerce during the years of the triangular trade.[17] The spaces produced by merchant capital and the cultural coding left behind in its wake is given little consideration. The Anglophone Caribbean commercial heritage, for example, was shaped by developments in early modern finance (circa 1700). The prevalence of merchant and trading activity would later produce a domestic preference among Caribbean colonial elites for commercial dealing risks over industrial deepening ones. These characteristics travelled well into the shaping of the postcolonial states and political economies of most of these islands.

Reading Neal (1990), Germain (1997) and de Goede (2005), the emergence of paper money and public credit in England marked the birth of modern science. Gambling on a wide variety of uncertainties was part and parcel of early modern finance. While no conceptual distinction existed between gambling and financial practices, as they were both strategies for profiting from an uncertain future, the concept of risk allied to the idea that it was humanly calculable provided the possibility for financial trading to be accorded some scientific respectability. But the struggle for political and moral legitimacy would persist through to the twentieth century.

The emergence of public credit in England merged well with the development of a range of financial instruments, including futures and other speculative contracts. The second half of the seventeenth century saw the development of institutionalised finance and public credit in England as English society was transforming from a feudal aristocracy to one oriented towards commerce and trade (Dickson, 1967). This period saw the emergence of London as one of the principal financial centres in the world. Indeed London, Antwerp and Amsterdam were centres of commercial capitalism, more anonymous and more coherently regulated than the frontier or the countryside. While there were earlier sophisticated financial networks in Florence, Italy (fifteenth century) and other European cities in the sixteenth century, the sheer volume of borrowing and investment by the English government fostered financial innovations such as new partnership banks, new insurance offices and sophisticated trade in stocks and debt certificates (Germain, 1997). While the invention of state credit and national debt can be regarded as monetary transformations inaugurating modern finance, this does not mean that the conceptual apparatus of modern finance sprang up naturally and consistently in the wake of the Financial Revolution (spurred by the English need to finance the war against France). Even more than the invention of financial instruments, the Financial Revolution must be thought of as the articulation of moral and political spaces in which these instruments became possible and were condoned (de Goede, 2005).

Trade in derivatives has been controversial since its first appearance in early modern Europe. Financial instruments such as options and forward contracts emerged in conjunction with the longer time horizons brought about by voyages of discovery and colonial conquest. For instance, the *Amsterdame Beurs* (Amsterdam stock market) emerged early in the seventeenth century as a secondary market for shares of the imperial shipping company, the Dutch East India Company (Germain, 2000; Neal, 1990). In this historical context, the Amsterdam money market developed sophisticated techniques of trading, including options to sell or buy stocks for a stipulated price, forwards and short sales.[18] These trading techniques served gambling as well as investment purposes as a distinction between the two was not consistently made.

Credit relied heavily on the social construction of trust, honour and obligation. More specifically, credit pertains to respect and trustworthiness in business matters and indicates a source of honour and authority. Aristocratic society recognised the seventeenth-century gentleman as truth-teller *par excellence*, in contrast to women, enslaved peoples and servants. The plantation economies constructed in the Anglophone Caribbean were financed by British and western European merchants who extended lines of credit to the 'gentleman planters' of the period. These merchants benefited from investments in the slave trade and other commercial trade.

The emergence of commercial-dealing capitalism made a more thorough individualism possible. As the accumulation of wealth from trade, slaving and colonies deepened, a calculative rationality began to permeate urban culture across Europe and the newly independent USA. Competing conceptions of manhood in late eighteenth-century USA were based on dominant ideals fashioned out of the aristocratic pieties of the Old World and a romantic rugged individualism associated with exploration of travel in the New World. Kimmel (2002) points to three masculine archetypes as an unfolding outcome as elite American and English culture pitted ill-gained wealth and dubious morality against hard work and civic virtue. There was the Genteel Patriarch, an ideal inherited from Europe. Here manhood meant property ownership at home, and this was enhanced by overseas possessions. The Genteel Patriarch of early nineteenth-century vintage represented a dignified aristocratic manhood, 'committed to the British upper-class code of honour and to well-rounded character, with exquisite tastes and manners and refined sensibilities' (Kimmel, 2002: 137). The second type of manhood was the Heroic Artisan, again inherited from Europe, and an honest toiler either of his family farm or his urban craft shop. His public manner was formal and his virtue was tied to his honesty, independence and dedication to skilled craftsmanship. The third archetype was the wealthy trader or merchant, referred to by Kimmel as the 'Self-made Man'. This was the *nouveau riche* of capitalist economic life in Europe and, like his American counterpart, he was temperamentally restless, mobile, shrewd, chronically insecure and 'desperate to achieve a solid grounding for a masculine identity' (ibid.). Here a man's wealth was uncomfortably linked to the volatile marketplace and imperial exchange relations, where fortune is as easily unmade as it is made. In the place of visibility and sturdiness of wealth embodied in land, the possibilities for wealth based on circulation and credit rested in the commercial activities of the transatlantic slave trade and the imperial plantation political economy.[19] Money-as-pledge provided a basis for sturdy financial networks on the precondition of a gentlemanly ethic. These financial networks fashioned by the social connection and cross-over between metropolitan merchants, local ones and planters in places like the Bahamas, Barbados and Bermuda provide clues to the ease with which these countries could later, and successfully, proffer offshore financial services.

Plantations were central units in the colonial Caribbean. The mode of production relied on the deployment of forced labour and the application of appropriate technologies sufficient for the steady supply of cotton in the case of the Bahamas, and cane sugar and other by-products from other islands to imperial Britain. The social relations of production were shaped by psycho-cultural anxieties that targeted black bodies. White male planters and merchants owned the means of production and were the dominant figures in the colonial legislatures through to the twentieth century. The most important economic function of the merchants was to provide both absentee and resident planters with operating capital as there were no formal financial institutions in the colonies. The network of credit often extended from metropolitan merchants to the planters in the colonies, with the local merchants as intermediaries (Johnson, 1996). These were also middlemen in the colonies' import–export trade and progenitors of leisure travel.

Barrow (2004) informs us that by 1750 the 'bachelor plantations' had given way to a visual aesthetic of grandeur in order to produce the effect of 'welcoming societies'. Early travellers to the Caribbean would refer to the spatial ordering of nature – tropical fruit, flora, fauna, forms of cultivation and buildings – as a sign of civilised control and progress (Pratt, 1992). Nineteenth-century depictions of the Caribbean as romantic escape and piratical adventure represented another way of envisioning the region as a natural Eden. The representation of the tropical island both as cultivated Paradise and desert isle would play a crucial part in the history of European literature, philosophy and arts.[20] These ways of representing and viewing the Caribbean were exploited by the post-Emancipation planter-merchant elite in order to encourage an increase in travel by male, white elites of postcolonial America and Britain. An increase in white tourist traffic would net increase business in their import-trade endeavours, shipping interests, guest-houses and inns and stimulate economic activity in the heavily indebted plantations (see Beckles, 1990). This was the tropical island commoditised as a scenic and therapeutic economy for convalescence and indulgence. William Paton writing in 1887 referred to the Barbadian planters and merchants as 'graduates in the sciences of hospitality, masters of the art of entertaining, genial and sociable by instinct, self-possessed, courteous, and polite' (see Paton, 1888).

The period between 1838 through to the dawn of the twentieth century marked the further economic and political dominance of merchant capitalists. This was brought about by the widespread need for credit among the colonies' labouring classes. The economies bore a corporate-commercial imprint with merchant capital integrating commercial agriculture, salt production, the sponge fishery trade (in the Bahamas), shipping and distribution, and the retail cluster of shops, finance houses, bars and inns (circa 1920). This historical legacy in part would later account for the ease of intra-elite consensus on the provision of financial and holiday resort services as a coping strategy against deteriorating rates of return in traditional exports.

The point was made earlier that dominant accounts on the origins of OFCs rely on outside-in explanations. We are informed about the implications of the example set by Switzerland in its (1934) passage of the Swiss Banking Law that made the violation of bank secrecy a crime (Palan, 1998). Many other European jurisdictions (for example, Luxembourg and Austria) were to follow suit extending protection to the accounts of foreigners. Further impetus was provided by developments following the creation of the Eurodollar market: the growth of incomes subject to substantial personal taxation in OECD countries; the growth of multinational corporate activity; and improvements in transportation and especially communications that would make the use of offshore financial services easily accessible. All of this pre-supposes permissive regimes on the part of governments. Host governments in the Caribbean chose to pursue the OFC option as an important aspect of economic diversification, but it required legislative, financial and business infra-structure that was/is more flexible than orthodox infrastructures – one that catered exclusively to the needs of non-resident investors. The question is why some countries could easily pursue the provision of offshore financial services and others could not. Or, to repeat Frankel's (1975) initial query: Why did the 'most spectacular growth' of US overseas bank branches in the period (1965–75) '[take] place in the Caribbean'? (Frankel, 1975: 5). Palan (1998: 639), after observing that 'the Caribbean havens developed phenomenally fast during the 1970s', attributed this to activities of American and Canadian banks that would 'develop neighbouring tax havens in the Caribbean'. He would also add that '[f]ugitive criminals introduced many of these havens to the business, while others emulated their successful brethren'. This is an inadequate explanation with orientalist underpinnings, presenting the Caribbean as tame, indulgent space.[21] What is required is a closer look at the political economies dominated as they are/were by the proclivities of merchant capital.

Barbados, Bermuda, the Bahamas and Antigua: Domestic class formation and resilience of the financial services sector

The first entrenched merchant-finance institution in the region was established in Barbados in 1840. The Barbados Mutual Life Assurance Society (BMLAS) was established at a time when British capital and hegemonic interests were primarily occupied with the 'East' and opening China for trade. The BMLAS was created by local merchants to raise capital to support the plantation and commercial interests in the colony. It managed to save planters from the wave of bankruptcies that affected their Jamaican and Guyanese counterparts following full Emancipation (1838), and the passage of the Sugar Duties Act (1846).[22] Today the BMLAS is de-mutualised and has been renamed SAGICOR Company. It is an entrenched institution and typifies those that have shaped the corporate-commercial character and portfolio of Commonwealth Caribbean economies. Its Board of Directors retains descendants of the planter-merchant elite as well as black professional managers, accountants and attorneys-at-law; it has dominant or significant interests in most of the leading economic and commercial establishments and public utilities in the country; it has incorporated the family businesses (that is, the merchandising stores) into the SAGICOR family; and interlocking directorships and insider trading so long normalised remains unaffected by the passage of the Fair Competition Act of 2002.[23] The provision of free primary, secondary and tertiary education by the Barbadian state from the 1960s has resulted in a steady growth of professionals in the fields of accounting and management which, in turn, services the circulation of commerce. Auditors and fiduciaries would encourage vigilance, innovation and consolidation among credit unions, insurance companies and leading conglomerates. Indeed it could purchase the portfolio of the fraudulent Bank of Credit & Commerce International (BCCI) and establish the Mutual bank back in the early 1990s.

Similarly, the merchant capital class in the Bahamas would consolidate its dominance from the middle to late nineteenth century. Rather than a monopoly of land, the important elements in this elite's economic and social control were a monopoly of the credit available to the majority of the population and the operation of a system of payment in truck. According to Johnson (1986), the credit and truck systems frequently left the lower classes in debt. Merchants also expanded their wealth through the sponge trade. The Nassau Sponge Exchange in the Bahamas was established in 1884 for the auction of sponges and division of the proceeds. By 1935 limits were placed on the value of advances that could be made to the captains and seamen, but merchants as financiers profited from all stages of the sponging operations in their capacities as outfitters, owners of schooners and brokers (Craton and Saunders, 1998). One historian pointing to the significant impact of this economic activity in the first two decades of the twenthieth century noted that the Bahamas realised US$200 000 annually from the sponge trade (Corfield, 1938).

Given the region's historical experience in financial management, the emergence of the transnational corporation in the prevailing IPE, and the increasing number of high net worth Westerners (circa 1960), various Caribbean governments moved to create an offshore financial extension to their host economies. This was possible in some cases through the public provision of: one, formal education and national scholarships, a measure that would create a high quality of professional support services (for example, lawyers, accountants, chartered financial analysts); two, the signing of double taxation treaty arrangements;

and/or three, the passage of enabling legislation and policy measures.[24] Sovereignty actualised through the exercise of fiscal autonomy gave expression to broader understandings of self-determination. Certainly, self-determination was/is not necessarily tethered to the goal of political independence. The Cayman Islands, Bermuda and Montserrat defended financial confidentiality regulations and tax policies in the manner of a trespass into public policy. The existing Exchange of Information Treaty between the US and Cayman Islands, for example, requires the United States to state the reason for the request of confidential information, and the Cayman Islands reserves the right to refuse the request if it violates public policy or any privilege.[25] The Bahamas Independence Constitution of 1973 preserved and subsequently expanded the English common law duty of confidentiality. Unlike other Caribbean OFCs, it has not signed any tax treaties with other states or agreements for exchange of information except agreements covering mutual assistance in cases of drug trafficking.

The interplay of comity and sovereignty is especially apparent in the Bahamas. The application of comity dictates that the jurisdiction with the more important justification should prevail. Belle-Antoine (2002) observes that Caribbean courts do scrutinise disclosure requests to determine if they are legitimate and not just 'fishing expeditions'. The Bahamas government particularly seeks to ensure that onshore justifications for disclosure are related to crime prevention rather than mere tax purposes.

The commercial circuit continues to give Caribbean countries like Barbados its character and its low-risk profile. Real estate and property development, insurance, finance and banking, transport, communications, import-trading, and construction predominate in the Barbadian economy with tourism serving as the main foreign exchange earner and, the state, the biggest employer. Agriculture and manufacturing lag behind not only in terms of their respective contribution to the national GDP but at the intersection of global and hemispheric imperatives as well. Merchant capitalists are not so much part of the ruling class as they are society's leading class. This is also the case with other Caribbean countries that function as conduits for international finance – Antigua, Bermuda, the Cayman Islands and the Bahamas, where commercial-dealing capitalists predominate. They operate in a network of interlocking spheres of capital, encompassing the production, commodity circulation, and credit spheres. Their social position, values and expectations register deeply into material society. The state-managers, on the other hand, largely consist of Creole professionals, a petit-bourgeois group not sited in the business community, but drawn to public service and career enhancement.

Many of the powerful names in early Bermudian colonial history reappeared among the list of the economic elite in 1968. This was confirmed by the Wooding Commission Report which stated that in Bermuda 'economic power, banking power and political power have historically been and still are concentrated in the same hands' (The Wooding Commission, 1968). Well-known colonial/merchant names such as Tucker, Cox, Smith, Cooper, Gibbons, Vesey, Trott, and Paton appeared among the list of directors of the island's leading financial and commercial institutions. The Commission Report also alluded to the strong merchant capital foundations of the country when it added:

> Effective power in Bermuda lay with the white oligarchy and it is not surprising that members of the small oligarchy became in time bankers and commercial entrepreneurs. They had the opportunity, the means and the training, and they were thus enabled to lead and to entrench themselves. (Wooding Commission, 1968: 9)

The Bermudian financial community has expanded to include local black and expatriate professionals. Altogether this class fraction remains the principal defender of the country's dependency status to the British government. The country had had a long experience (extending back to 1938) at using its status as a British dependent territory to encourage rich individuals, particularly from the US, to establish private trusts in its offshore sector in order to avoid US taxes.[26] The postwar years saw this activity expand to include exempted companies established to handle the affairs of local (that is, Bermudian) and Bahamian planter families along with their agricultural plantations. In addition, private banks went on to manage the wealth and investments of some rich US families and their estates. The considerable degree of autonomy afforded to Bermudians in the management of its legislative and financial affairs has produced a pragmatic accommodation to UK dependency status. Today there are over 8000 registered international exempted companies in Bermuda's register and it is the largest captive insurance market in the world. Tax issues nevertheless remain a contentious one for US regulators but this has not threatened the country's reputation. A UK commissioned (2000) 'Review of Financial Regulation in the Caribbean Overseas Territories and Bermuda' noted that its authorities well exceeded minimum requirements in many areas such as captive insurance, company formation and private trusts.[27] Elite confidence in pursuing the 'offshore' option has been buoyed by the April 2006 decision of the New York Stock Exchange's Transaction Network Services, Inc. (TNS) to operate from premises at 7 Reid Street, Hamilton, Bermuda. TNS is a leading network and data communications provider. The company's new point-of-presence in Bermuda enables local traders to 'connect to more than 1000 financial community end-points around the world, representing over 450 buy and sell side institutions, market data providers, software vendors, exchanges and trading venues' (Business Wire, 2006).

Antigua and Barbuda's dispute with the US government over Internet gambling, for example, presents a case study of frontier expansion by an OFC as it seeks to ensure new rules of commerce in an online age.[28] The dispute at once challenges Washington's effort to prohibit online gambling while simultaneously testing the ability of the WTO to enforce its own standards. St Kitts and Antigua operate Internet casinos exploiting the potential for online gambling. This adds to the offshore sports betting niche that the Antiguan authorities are seeking to develop. There are 32 licensed online casinos in Antigua, employing 1000 persons and generating annual revenues of US$130 million dollars (Klapper, 2007). In 2003 the Antiguan government instigated a trade complaint against the US claiming that the ban violated Antigua's rights as a fellow member of the WTO. A WTO panel ruled against the US in 2004; its appellate body upheld the decision one year later; and in March 2007 the WTO upheld that ruling for a second time and declared Washington out of compliance with its rules. The US government will either reverse course and allow Americans to place bets online legally with offshore casinos or impose a ban on its citizens against all forms of Internet gambling, including the online purchase of lottery tickets. The latter action will likely produce a credibility and political backlash in the campaign for free-flowing global trade. Antigua's exercise of state-sovereignty in fashioning a strategy to attract global sources of income and investment, as well as defending it in its international bargains, should be understood as part of the country's adjustment to the challenges of neoliberal globalisation.

The propagation of the welcoming society construct of the plantation era, the durability and adaptability of merchant capitalists, merchant-finance institutions like SAGICOR/BMLAS, the Nassau Sponge Exchange and Antigua's e-commerce strategies bear witness to the existence of a predilection for the 'service' sector in the Caribbean. The hitherto well developed, corporate-commercial and legal environment of the region prior to governments' usage of offshore services as part of their tourism package, bespeaks of more than merely a current fashion for 'selling sovereignty'.

Summary

This chapter has emphasised the need for a truly global reading of the rise and nature of high finance. OFCs often appear in the literature only in relation to the globalisation of crime and detecting trans-boundary financial offences. These are not anachronistic spaces.

Antigua, Barbados, the Bahamas and St Lucia continue to pursue a services-led development strategy, tying high-end tourism promotion with the provision of offshore financial services. I refer to the purchase of timeshares in luxury villas, the purchase of condominiums and villas, and high-brow indulgence in recreational golf and polo in the 'escapist' offshore isles. This builds on an historical predilection towards services among the traditional elite and, later, an ease of consensus among the professional middle strata of attorneys, career politicians, accountants and bankers. But varying tensions arise among Caribbean OFCs from the tourism side of the strategy. The host societies are increasingly marked by disarticulations. Land and property purchases are increasingly out of the reach of resident populations and socio-ecological challenges pose limits to the sustainability of golf and polo-based tourism. It is in these circumstances that Caribbean governments may yet encourage further innovation in the provision of wealth management and business services to non-residents as part of an overall economic renewal strategy. There is every possibility that the very high net-worth clientele the region woos may become participants in venture philanthropy initiatives of a social and productive nature, consistent with the states' developmental goals.

Notes

1. This is with reference to the core of the Bretton Woods monetary system, fixed rates, and the dollar–gold standard.
2. I refer to flows of people, commodities, texts, images, capital and knowledge – mobilities of many different kinds.
3. Here when we use the term 'feminise', we are referring to the representation of femininity within masculinist discourses of gender. The effect of these discourses is a binary representation of gender in which femininity is tied to female bodies and masculinity to male bodies. The language that seeks to capture this binary construction of reality 'otherises' femininity.
4. For a closer reading of the intellectual trajectories within globalisation literature, see Amoore et al. (1997: 179–96). For an affirmative reading of globalisation, see Chow (2003).
5. For discussion on regulation and questions over the legitimacy of global financial regimes, see the following anthologies on the subject: Cutler et al. (1999); Soederberg (2001); and Germain (2001).

6. I refer to an early English case, *Tournier* vs. *National Provincial Bank*, where the court held that bankers had a contractual duty not to disclose a client's financial information. Subsequent adoption of this principle was undertaken by many countries. The United Kingdom itself expanded Tournier to cover areas other than banking. Certainly common law confidentiality is not absolute as under Tournier and disclosure is permitted in instances where it is in the public interest; by compulsion of law; when it is in the best interests of the banker; and with the implied consent of the customer. For more on this see Belle-Antoine (2002).

7. See for example, Wachtel (1990); Robertson (1992); Strange (1995).

8. This shadows protests of 'global civil society' against unaccountable supranational regulatory authority structures.

9. Indeed the sharp disagreements across fields of knowledge over liberalisation of exchange controls, capital markets, investment and trade may be an allegory of the classic debate in political economy posed by Adam Smith's *Wealth of Nations* and Karl Marx's *Das Kapital*.

10. For examples of work in the IPE and critical geography tradition that address capitalism as crisis-prone, see Arrighi (1997); Harvey (2001; 2007).

11. For a representative sample of the work on financialisation, see the special issue (2000) of *Economy and Society*, particularly, Aglietta (2000); Froud et al. (2000); Lazonick and O'Sullivan (2000); Seabrooke (2006). Also see Langley (2004); Blackburn (2006); Beck (2002); Gill (1995); Thrift (2005).

12. In this environment it is the financial world of hedge funds, investment banks, ratings agencies and private equity concerns that predominates with 'risk-management' the new mantra (see Blackburn, 2006; Beck, 2002).

13. As occurred in the Dubai index, Paris Bourse, London's FTSE, Tokyo's Nikkei Index, the Sydney Futures Exchange and New York's Dow Jones Index. For more on this see the story produced by the Associated Free Press and published in the *Sydney Morning Herald*, 20 August 2007 'Markets Brace for a Volatile Week'. Also see Martin (2007).

14. HedgeWorld.com, which is based in Bermuda and was launched in September 1999, claims to have been the first e-commerce-enabled Web site serving the needs of the hedge fund and global alternative investment industry.

15. The three licensed banks that appear on the Bermuda stock exchange are: the Bank of Bermuda Ltd, the Bank of N.T. Butterfield & Son Ltd, and the Bermuda Commercial Bank Ltd. The former two, and larger, banks have each been in existence for over 100 years. As at 31 December 1994 the consolidated assets of the three banks were some $12.4 billion, while the assets under their administration were valued at several times that amount. See http://www.offshore-manual.com/taxhavens/Bermuda.html, accessed on 29 September 2007.

16. In offshore economy, Palan includes finance, manufacturing, online casino gambling, call centres, and outsourcing to niche industries and activities. See Palan (1998; 2002; 2006).

17. For more on merchant capital's tendency, see Kay (1975). The triangular trade refers to the trade in bodies, goods and credit across the Atlantic and the Americas, featuring mainly England, West Africa, the Caribbean and the colonial America.

18. Short-selling is the practice of 'selling a borrowed security'. Short-sellers sell a security or commodity that they do not own for delivery at a later date, thus profiting from price declines. See Karpoff (1994).
19. For more on who made fortunes from the slave trade, see Knight (1978).
20. I refer to the European tradition of landscape painting and classical allegory also. The Caribbean has been portrayed in various texts as Edens and Utopias. By the late nineteenth century its hinterland was represented as either the site of Paradise lost or the location of piratical adventure as in Daniel Defoe's *Robinson Crusoe*. It is also the site imagined for the enactment of the master–slave dialectic as in William Shakespeare's *The Tempest*.
21. Here we get the sense of a social space marked by despotism, law enforcement laxities, and the failure of self-regulation.
22. Briefly, the Sugar Duties Act (1846) imposed higher import duties on sugar exported from the West Indies into Britain. Already beleaguered by the loss of their traditional (slave) labour supply and the price-fall of sugar, many Jamaican and Guyanese plantations soon went into bankruptcy. For more on this, see Williams (1970).
23. See the Fair Competition Act CAP326C, Laws of Barbados, http://www.commerce.gov.bb/Legislation, accessed 27 September 2007.
24. For legislation created to stimulate offshore and non-resident business see those of Barbados: the International Business Company (IBC) Act of 1965, forerunner to the 1991 International Business Act, the Exempt Insurance Act of 1983, the Offshore Banking Act of 1984, which has been replaced by the 2002 International Financial Services Act, and the 2001 Electronic Transactions Act. For Acts passed see: http://www.lawandtaxnews.com/html/bermuda/jbrlatolaw.html, accessed 27 September 2007.
25. Agreement Between the Government of the United States of America and the Government of the United Kingdom of Great Britain and Northern Ireland, including the Government of Cayman Islands, for the Exchange of Information Related to Taxes, 27 November 2001, US–Cayman Islands (2001).
26. Indeed Bermuda's ship registry extended further back to the early 1700s. As part of the British registry, Bermuda-registered ships flew the red ensign and were therefore entitled to the protection of the British Royal Navy.
27. This was carried out by KPMG to assess the extent to which Overseas Territories comply with international standards and good practice. See http://www.cimoney.com.ky, accessed 28 September 2007.
28. This case is analysed in greater depth in Cooper's chapter.

References

Aglietta, M. (2000) 'Shareholder Value and Corporate Governance: Some Tricky Questions', *Economy and Society* 29 (1): 146–59.
Amoore, L. et al. (1997) 'Overturning Globalisation: Resisting the Teleological, Reclaiming the Political', *New Political Economy* 2 (1): 179–96.
Arrighi, Giovanni (1997) *The Long Twentieth Century* (London: Verso Books).
Barrow, V.M. (2004) 'A Genealogy of Barbadian Tourism: The Welcoming Society and Contemporary Narratives of Resistance', *Journal of Eastern Caribbean Studies* 29 (2): 50–75.

Beckles, H. (1990) *A History of Barbados: From Amerindian Settlement to Nation-State* (London: Cambridge University Press).

Belle-Antoine, R. (2002) *Confidentiality in Offshore Financial Law* (Oxford: Oxford University Press).

Blackburn, R. (2006) 'Finance and the Fourth Dimension', *New Left Review* (39): 39–70.

Business Wire (2006) 'Communications Service Provider Establishes Presence in Bermuda; TNS Establishes Office and Gateway to Worldwide Extranet on Island', 5 May, http://findarticles. com/p/articles/mi_m0EIN/is_2006_May_5/ai_n1634 7183, accessed on 28 September 2007.

Chow, E. (2003) 'Gender Matters: Studying Globalisation and Social Change in the 21st Century', *International Sociology* 18 (3): 443–60.

Cohen, B. (1996) 'Phoenix Risen: The Resurrection of Global Finance', *World Politics* 48 (2): 268–87.

Corfield, G.S. (1938) 'Sponge Industry of the Caribbean Area', *Economic Geography* 14(2): 201–6.

Craton, M. and G. Saunders (1998) *Islanders in the Stream: A History of the Bahamian People, Volume 2: From the Ending of Slavery to the Twenty-First Century* (Athens and London: University of Georgia Press).

Cutler, C., V. Haufler and T. Porter (eds) (1999) *Private Authority in International Affairs* (New York: State University of New York Press).

de Goede, M. (2005) *Virtue, Fortune and Faith: A Genealogy of Finance* (Minneapolis: University of Minneapolis Press).

Dickson, P.G.M. (1967) *The Financial Revolution in England: A Study in the Development of Public Credit 1688–1756* (London: Macmillan).

Economist (2006) 'Goldman Sachs and the Culture of Risk', 29 April.

Eichengreen, B., A.K. Rose and C. Wyplosz (1995) 'Exchange Market Mayhem: The Antecedents and Aftermath of Speculative Attacks', *Economic Policy* (21): 294–307.

Fiege, E.L. (1995) 'The Underground Economy and the Currency Enigma', *Public Finance*, Supplement, 49: 119–36.

Frankel, A.B. (1975) 'International Banking: Part 1, Business Conditions', in *Economic Review of Federal Reserve Bank of Chicago*, September: 5–14.

Froud, J., C. Haslam, S. Johal and K. Williams (2000) 'Shareholder Value and Financialisation: Consultancy Promises, Management Moves', *Economy and Society* 29 (1): 80–110.

Germain, R. (1997) *The International Organisation of Credit* (Cambridge: Cambridge University Press).

Germain, R. (2000) 'Globalisation in Historical Perspective' in R.D. Germain (ed.) *Globalisation and its Critics: Perspectives from Political Economy* (London: Macmillan).

Germain, R. (2001) 'Global Financial Governance and the Problem of Inclusion', *Global Governance*, Special Issue: The New International Financial Architecture 7(4).

Gill, S. (1995) 'Globalisation, Market Civilisation and Disciplinary Neoliberalism', *Millennium: Journal of International Studies* 24 (3): 399–423.

Helleiner, E. (1993) 'When Finance was the Servant: International Capital Movements in the Bretton Woods Era', in P.G. Cerny (ed.) *Finance and World*

Politics: Markets, Regimes and States in the Post-Hegemonic Era (Cheltenham: Edward Elgar).

Herrera, R. (2006) 'The Neoliberal "Rebirth" of Development Economics', *Monthly Review* 58 (1): 38–50.

Johns, R.A. (1983) *Tax Havens and Offshore Finance: A Study of Transnational Economic Development* (New York: St Martin's Press).

Johns, R.A. and C.M. Le Marchant (1993) *Finance Centres: British Isle Offshore Development Since 1979* (London and New York: Pinter).

Johnson, H. (1986) ' "A Modified Form of Slavery": The Credit and Truck Systems in the Bahamas in the Nineteenth and Early Twentieth Centuries', *Comparative Studies in Society and History* (London: Cambridge University Press): 729–53.

Johnson, H. (1996) *The Bahamas from Slavery to Servitude, 1783–1933* (Gainsville: University Press of Florida).

Karpoff, J.M. (1994) 'Short selling' in P. Newman, M. Milgate and J. Eatwell (eds) *New Palgrave Dictionary of Money and Finance*, Vol. 3 (New York: Macmillan).

Kay, G. (1975) *Development and Underdevelopment* (New York: St Martin's Press).

Kimmel, M. (2002) 'The Birth of the Self-made Man' in R. Adams and D. Savran (eds) *The Masculinity Studies Reader* (London and Oxford: Blackwell Publishers): 135–52.

Klapper, B.S. (2007) 'US May be Target in Gambling Dispute', *Washington Post*, 23 May, http://www.washingtonpost.com, accessed on 4 September 2007.

Knight, D. (1978) *Gentlemen of Fortune: The Men who Made their Fortunes in Britain's Slave Trade* (London: Frederick Muller Ltd).

Kochen, A. (1991) 'Cleaning Up by Cleaning Up', *Euromoney*, April: 73–7.

Langley, P. (2002) 'The Everyday Life of Global Finance', Paper presented at the British International Studies Association Convention, London School of Economics and Political Science, December.

Langley, P. (2004) 'In the Eye of the "Perfect Storm": The Final Salary Pensions Crisis and Financialisation of Anglo-American Capitalism', *New Political Economy* 9(4): 539–58.

Lazonick, W. and M. O'Sullivan (2000) 'Maximising Shareholder Value: A New Ideology for Corporate Governance', *Economy and Society* 29(1): 13–35.

Martin, J. (2007) 'American Home Mortgage Implodes', Jason Martin Financial Rebel, 31 July, http://www.financial rebel.com/news, accessed on 20 August 2007.

Mitchell, D. (2000) 'An OECD Proposal to Eliminate Tax Competition would Mean Higher Taxes and Less Privacy', Heritage Foundation Backgrounder #1395, 18 September.

Neal, L. (1990) *The Rise of Financial Capitalism: International Capital Markets in the Age of Reason* (Cambridge: Cambridge University Press).

Offshore Manual (2007) 'Bermuda', http://www.offshore-manual.com/taxhavens/ Bermuda.html, accessed on 29 September 2007.

Oxfam (2000) 'Tax Havens: Releasing the Hidden Billions for Poverty Eradication', *Oxfam Policy Papers*, 6, http://www.oxfam.org.uk/policy/papers/taxhvn/ tax1.htm.

Palan, R. (1998) 'Trying to Have Your Cake and Eating It: How and Why the State System has Created Offshore', *International Studies Quarterly* (42): 625–44.

Palan, R. (2002) 'Tax Havens and the Commercialisation of State Sovereignty', *International Organisation* 56 (1): 151–76.

Palan, R. (2006) *The Offshore World: Sovereign Markets, Virtual Places and Nomad Millionaires* (Ithaca, NY: Cornell University Press).

Paton, W.A. (1888) *Down the Islands: A Voyage to the Caribbees* (London: Kegan Paul, Trench & Co).

Pratt, M. L. (1992) *Imperial Eyes: Travel Writing and Transculturation* (London: Routledge).

Soederberg, S. (ed.) (2001) 'The New International Financial Architecture', *Global Governance* Special Issue: The New International Financial Architecture 7(4).

Strange, S. (1995) 'The Defective State', *Daedalus: Journal of the American Academy of Arts and Sciences* 124 (2): 55–74.

Thrift, N. (2001) 'It's the romance not the finance, that makes the business worth pursuing', *Economy and Society* (30): 412–32.

Thrift, N. (2005) *Knowing Capitalism* (London: Sage).

Thorndike, T. (1989) 'Offshore Finance: A Major Industry for the Caribbean', in *Latin America & Caribbean Review, World of Information*: 24–6.

US–Cayman Islands (2001) *Worldwide Tax Treaties*, Doc. 2001–29858, art. 2, http://www.taxanalysts.com, accessed on 27 September 2007.

Wachtel, M. (1990) *The Money Mandarins: The Making of a New Supranational Economic Order* (Armonk, NY: M.E. Sharpe).

Williams, E. (1970) *From Columbus to Castro: The History of the Caribbean, 1492-1969* (London: Deutsch).

Wooding Commission, The (1968) *Bermuda Civil Disorders 1968, Report of Commission and Statement by the Government of Bermuda*, Hamilton.

14
Cultural Industries and Cultural Policy in the Context of Globalisation: An Agenda for SIDS

Keith Nurse

Small Island Developing States (SIDS) share many similarities beyond the issue of size. Many are former colonies and their economies are structured as plantation economies where production is dominated by one or two agricultural and mineral commodity exports and by export-oriented manufacturing in clothing and electronics. Consumption, on the other hand, is largely import-oriented accounting for the high share of trade in the national economy. SIDS are also characterised by the dominance of tourism in their economies, as well as their heavy reliance on foreign aid, which has been in decline in the post-Cold War environment. Remittances from diasporic communities have been a key new source of foreign exchange, in many instances outpacing Foreign Direct Investment (FDI), aid and other external sources of capital (Nurse, 2004a).

These economies are increasingly vulnerable in the current context of WTO trade liberalisation owing to the erosion of preferences in exports such as bananas, sugar and clothing (Alexandraki, 2005). Tourism, though significant to national development in terms of employment and export earnings, has historically generated low levels of local added value and is subject to strong external control by transnational tour operators, hoteliers and airlines. These trends signal that these economies are required to find new and more sustainable sources of employment, exports and growth.

This chapter argues that the cultural industries sector is an area of the global economy where SIDS enjoy some comparative advantage in production but not in the distribution and marketing elements of the value chain. For SIDS there is a window of opportunity given the rise of the digital economy and the increasing commercialisation of the arts. The view is that cultural industries may offer more sustainable development options since they draw on the creativity and enterprise of local artists and communities.

The chapter identifies ways in which SIDS can benefit from the increased commercialisation of the arts and cultural industries. It will also outline the main challenges and opportunities for SIDS in the global cultural economy as well as give broad recommendations by drawing on the experience of the Caribbean.

Globalisation, technological change and the cultural industries

The area of culture has grown in salience in global development issues on account of the rising share of cultural goods, services and intellectual property in world trade, as well as the threats and opportunities to cultural diversities and identities associated with contemporary globalisation. Also, there is increasing awareness that the protection and promotion of cultural diversities is vital to achieving universal human rights, democratic freedoms and sustainable development.

The arts and the cultural sectors are well recognised as means of artistic expression and symbols of national and regional identity. The cultural sector can be defined as an aesthetic and social space where spiritual values, psychic meaning and bodily pleasures are displayed, enacted and represented. From this perspective cultural production, promotion and preservation are important areas for investment as they bolster cultural identities and ultimately the cultural confidence of a society. This is considered to be particularly important in plural or multicultural societies in addressing the challenges of social stratification and social injustice.

In economic terms the cultural/creative industries sectors can be categorised based on the extent of copyright embodied in the product or service.[1] As Figure 14.1 illustrates, a large part of the cultural sector is embodied in what is defined as the creative core, industries for which copyright is the central feature of manufacture, performance, broadcasting, distribution, retail, and so on. The other category is interdependent copyright industries, activities that generate equipment that service the creative core (e.g. musical instruments). The last category is the partial copyright industries, those activities that only have a portion of their production attributable to copyright; for example, fashion design, costuming, advertising, architecture. The cultural/creative industries sector is also distinctive in that it has several transaction networks

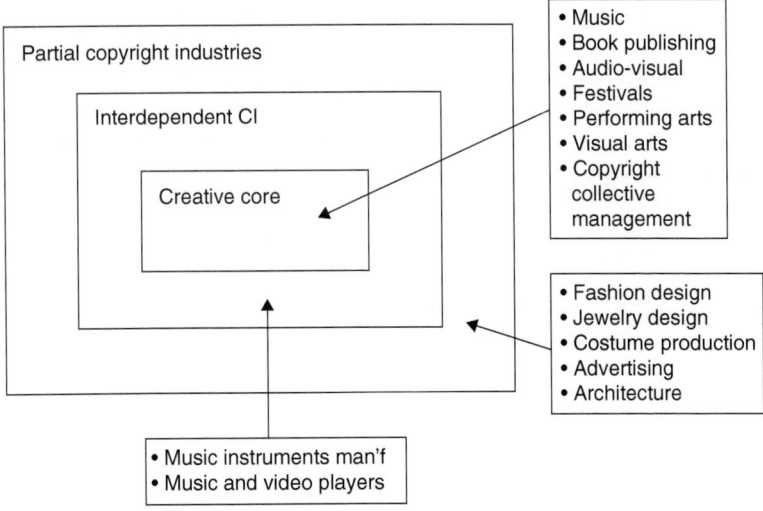

Figure 14.1   Typology of cultural/creative industries
Source: Nurse, 2006.

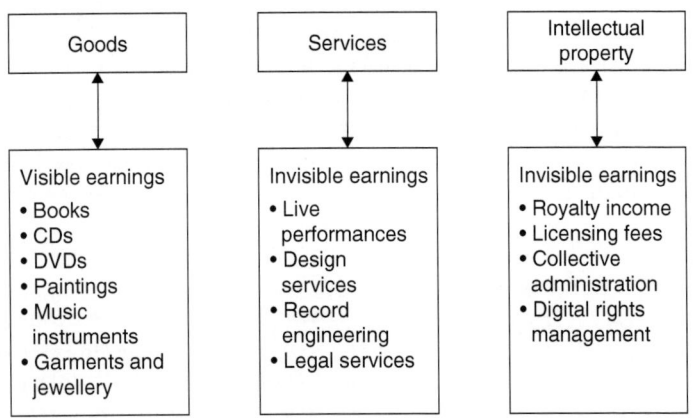

Figure 14.2   Income streams in the cultural/creative industries
Source: Nurse, 2006.

and income streams (see Figure 14.2). The sector generates income from the sale of goods (e.g. merchandise sales), the provision of services (e.g. professional fees), and the licensing of intellectual property (e.g. royalties).

The cultural sector plays a dual role in that it is an arena for identity formation and also an economic sector with growth potential, including its role as a key driver of consumer demand for tourism services, information and communication technologies, e-commerce and Internet services. The cultural industries describe the role of cultural entrepreneurs and arts enterprises, for-profit as well as not-for-profit, in the production, distribution, and consumption of film, television, books, music, theatre, dance, visual arts, multimedia, animation, and so on.

The cultural industries sector is one of the fastest growing sectors of the world economy. Best estimates value the sector at 7 per cent of the world's gross domestic product (UNCTAD, 2004). Recent estimates show that trade in the cultural economy has increased at an unprecedented average annual rate of 8.7 per cent over the last decade. Services also enjoyed a rate of growth of 8.8 per cent. Exports of creative products were valued at US$ 424.4 billion in 2005, up from $227.5 billion in 1996 (UNCTAD/UNDP, 2008).

Factors attributing to this growth are: rapid techno-economic change in products, distribution, and marketing (e.g. e-books, iTunes, Amazon.com); the increasing commercialisation of intellectual property, particularly copyright; the shift towards a post-industrial economy where personal, recreational and audio-visual services have expanded as a share of the economy; the strong cross-promotional linkages with sectors like tourism (e.g. festival tourism); and the convergence of media, the increasing concentration of large firms and the expansive growth of the digital economy (e.g. the Internet and e-commerce) that allows for easier production, distribution and consumption as well as infringement (e.g. piracy, file swapping) of cultural products, services and intellectual property.

New digital, information, and communication technologies have revolutionised the industry in terms of production processes, distribution channels, and consumption modes. Low-cost digital recording technologies have facilitated the diffusion of sound, text and image production by small entrepreneurs without any appreciable compromise in quality. For example, feature films can be shot digitally at a fraction of the cost of older analogue technologies. Mass production technologies have been challenged by niche production and mass customisation (e.g. ring-tones, print-on-demand services, movies-on-demand, interactive media and social networking sites like MySpace and YouTube). The proliferation and diffusion of production makes this stage of the value chain the most competitive, and consequently, prices and margins have been driven down in recent years.

The convergence of the telecoms, telephony, the Internet and cultural content has revolutionised product sales and marketing, changed the nature of piracy and royalties collections, as well as upset the balance between the major content distribution/marketing companies and the independents, thus giving the consumer greater choice. However, these gains are dependent on wider access to Internet services internationally, the growth of broadband and wireless access, and the expansion of interoperability between content providers/creators, digital distribution channels (e.g. online subscription services like iTunes) and consumption devices (e.g. mobile phones, iPods). All of this would not be possible without digital rights management facilitating consumer usage rights while protecting the works of creators from unauthorised distribution and unfair use.

Transformations in the cultural industries sector have been complemented by the emergence of a trade policy framework and regime facilitating the harmonisation and internationalisation of copyright regulations (WTO–TRIPs; World Intellectual Property Organization [WIPO] copyright and digital treaties); the liberalisation of cultural industries under WTO–GATS; and the protection of cultural diversity (e.g. UNESCO Convention on the Protection and Promotion of the Diversity of Cultural Expressions[2]) (Van den Bossche, 2007). Each country and region needs to evaluate the implications of the trade policy context and make proposals in regards to multilateral negotiations. At the intra-regional level SIDS also need to reduce barriers to trade and greater facilitation of the movement of artists and cultural workers.

For SIDS the introduction of culture into global trade rules and governance is an issue of immense concern. In many respects it is a contest between the liberalisation of trade in cultural goods and services under the WTO and the promotion of cultural diversity through the UNESCO Convention. The Convention calls for the parties to incorporate culture into sustainable development and for international cooperation to support the development of the cultural industries and policies in developing countries through technology transfer, financial support and preferential treatment.

Many SIDS supported the adoption of the Convention based upon its potential to contribute to cultural diversity and to facilitate more balanced trade in cultural goods, services and intellectual property. The key challenge for many developing countries is that while the convention is a legal instrument that is binding it does not generate commitments to signatories as obtains under the WTO. In this sense the convention may encourage more artistic production but it does not guarantee space in the

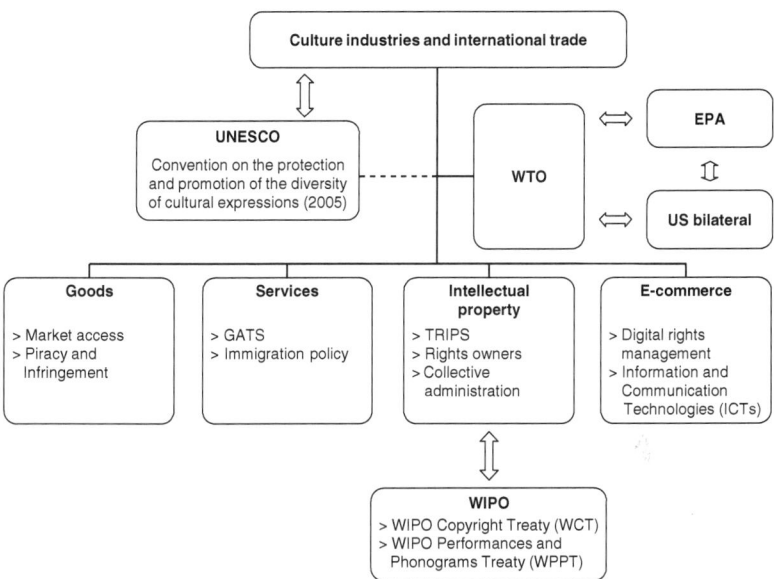

Figure 14.3 Diagram linking culture industries and international trade to trade, industrial, and intellectual property policy
Source: Nurse, 2006.

market. This brings the issue of cultural entrepreneurship to the forefront of the discussion because no legal framework can legislate for who will get into the market or will proliferate in the global, regional or national cultural economy. Therefore, the principal issue is to ensure flexibility within the evolving rules-based trading system such that developing countries can promote cultural entrepreneurship. Here the key concern is whether developing countries will be able to meaningfully participate in the expansion of this sector of the world economy through the application of a range of industrial and innovative policy initiatives (see Figure 14.3).

The cultural industries sector in SIDS

While the developing countries are rich in terms of creativity and cultural expressions, there is a genuine disparity between capacities of the developed and developing countries when it comes to producing and disseminating their own cultural expressions, thereby

Table 14.1   Cultural industries exports and imports, merchandise trade, selected Small Island Developing States, 2002

	Barbados	Fiji	Jamaica	Mauritius	Singapore
Population	257 000*	773 000**	2 528 000**	1 127 000*	2 987 000*
Total exports in core cultural goods	901.3	410.4	482.5	6 171.4	2 000 989.4
Total imports of core cultural goods	16 793.2	6 470.4	52 713.2	15 803.70	639 514.6
Balance	−15 891.90	−6 060.00	−52 230.70	−9 632.30	131 474.80

Notes: Population data is for the following years, 1995* and 1996**.
Source: UNESCO, 2005.

reducing the opportunities of developing countries to contribute actively to diversity at the international level. (Ministry of Education, Government of Finland, 2007)

The cultural industries sector plays a vital role in forging identity. Cultural industries are not just informed by societal mores and habits, they also shape society through the ways in which it represents these mores and habits in text, sound, and images. The cultural industries are also synergistic in that they provide a competitive platform for innovation in other sectors like tourism, clothing and textiles, ICTs, as well as traditional commodity exports. In this sense the cultural sector is critical to an alternative development strategy that draws on the creativity and enterprise of local artists and communities.

In several SIDS the cultural industry sector is making an increased contribution to GDP, exports and employment. A comparison of the performance of Mauritius with that of other SIDS in the global cultural economy shows that most operate with a large trade imbalance, the exception being Singapore. Table 14.1 provides export and import data on cultural merchandise trade for a selected group of SIDS, specifically those that are known to have some export capabilities (Jamaica and Barbados from the Caribbean and Fiji in the Pacific). What the table shows is that although these SIDS are known for their arts and cultural industries they still have a significant deficit in the trade of cultural goods. Part of the explanation is that the table has data only for merchandise trade and does not include trade in services, royalties earnings, and earnings from cultural, heritage and festival tourism where these economies are able to generate some earnings. It is also that in most SIDS the capacity to document and measure the economic flows and exports is largely underdeveloped.

The data on selected SIDS fits with the general pattern in that the world trade in cultural goods is highly concentrated in a few developed and emerging market economies (UNESCO, 2005). The structure of world trade in the cultural/creative industries in 2002 was such that Europe (EU 15) was the major exporter, accounting for approximately 52 per cent of the market. Asia is the next biggest exporter and fastest rising region (largely because of the rapid expansion coming from East Asia and China, particularly) with 20.8 per cent of the world market. North America's relative share declined from 25 per cent in 1994 to 17 per cent in 2002, which makes it the third largest export region. The 'Other Europe' region is next with 6 per cent. Latin America and the Caribbean (LAC) have expanded their share from 1.9 per cent to 3.0 per cent over the period. Oceania and Africa together share 1 per cent of the market.

Europe is the main importer, accounting for 40 per cent of world demand, compared with the North American share of approximately 30 per cent. Both regions had 4 per cent changes in share with the United States rising and the EU dropping. Asia is third with approximately 15 per cent of global imports, a slight improvement over 1994. The LAC and Oceania regions' shares have declined marginally from 4.4 per cent to 3.6 per cent and from 3.9 per cent to 2.5 per cent, respectively. Africa has stayed steady at about 1 per cent. The United States has an impressive trade balance with the rest of the world. The top ten sales territories, primarily North America, Europe and Japan, account for 80.7 per cent of the world market.

In most developed market economies, the cultural industries account for 2–5 per cent of GDP and have generated consistent and stable growth in the last decade as exemplified in a rising share of employment and exports. Similar trends are observed in some large developing countries, such as India, Mexico, and Brazil, which have strong capabilities in the audio-visual sector and large home and diasporic markets. Table 14.2 provides data on the impact of GDP and employment on the cultural industries in Latin America and shows that the sector is making a sizeable contribution to these economies. As is to be expected, Brazil ranks the highest with a GDP contribution of 6.7 per cent and an employment share of 5.0 per cent. However, even a smaller economy like Uruguay has impressive figures to report with 6.0 per cent and 4.9 per cent shares in GDP and employment, respectively.

Table 14.2 Cultural industries' contribution to select Latin America economies

Country	Base year	Cultural industries impact	
		GDP	Employment
Argentina	1993	4.1%	–
	1994	–	3.5%
Brazil	1998	6.7%	5.0%
Columbia	2001	2.01%	–
	1999–2002	–	27 724*
Chile	1990–1998	2.0%	2.7%
Uruguay	1997	6.0%	4.9%
Venezuela	1997–2000	3.0%	35 329**
	2001	2.3%	–

Source: OAS, 2004.
Notes: *Jobs in three sectors: publishing, phonography, and film-making. **Jobs in four sectors: graphic arts, radio, advertising, and film-making.

The case of the Caribbean

The Caribbean's contribution to the global cultural economy has been significant. It is often noted that the region's impact has been large relative to its size. It can also be argued that the Caribbean enjoys strong artistic capabilities in fields such as music, literature, the visual arts, the performing arts and the audio-visual sector. For example, in the literary arts the region has produced intellectual giants like Derek Walcott, V.S. Naipaul, George Lamming, Edward Braithwaite, Patrick Chamosieau, Jamaica Kincaid and Earl Lovelace.

The Caribbean enjoys a competitive capability in cultural production; however, the problem is that the creativity of its artists has not been backed up by an entrepreneurial, managerial and marketing capability from within the Caribbean's business sector, nor has there been strong state support, facilitation or leadership. This is the essence of the problem that plagues several sectors of the cultural industries in the region.

This section provides a brief analysis of the Caribbean experience. The focus is principally on the music industry and festivals since these are the sectors with the best data and because they are the sectors that have made the greatest economic impact.

The music industry

Caribbean music and artists have had a significant impact in recent years. Shaggy's album *Hotshot* was the best selling album world-wide for 2001.

Artists like Sean Paul, Elephant Man, Beenie Man and Bounty Killa have enjoyed high international sales. Bob Marley's catalogue continues to be among the top ten in terms of world sales. Other parts of the region have seen their nationals enjoy international success: Arrow, from Montserrat, has sold in excess of 4 million copies of 'Hot, Hot, Hot' and enjoys an active performance schedule; Guyana's Eddy Grant and his recent remake of 'Electric Avenue' had chart success in the UK in 2001; the Baha Men, from the Bahamas, in a remake of Trinidadian Anselm Douglas's 'Who Let the Dogs Out' topped the world music charts in 2001 and has generated significant publishing income from commercials, movies and sporting events.

Jamaica continues to be the primary source for musical innovation in reggae and dancehall music in spite of the fact that the genres have spread to many parts of the globe. Reggae is now recognised as one of the major genres of music and has gained recognition from international music awards such as the American Grammys. It is conservatively estimated that the music industry employs 15 000 people and controls 15–20 per cent of the US$300 million in reggae music sales (see Table 14.3). In addition, reggae is one of the main elements in Jamaica's destination branding and has created a strong demand-pull

Table 14.3 Economic contribution of Caribbean music industry

Territories	Foreign exchange earnings (US$m)	Employment	Key drivers
Jamaica	80–100	15 000	• Recording industry • Live performance • Music publishing • Festival tourism
Barbados	20–25	n.a.	• Live performance • Recording industry • Festival tourism
Eastern Caribbean	20–25	n.a.	• Festival tourism • Live performance • Recording industry
Trinidad & Tobago	50–60	n.a.	• Festival tourism • Live performance • Recording industry • Music publishing • Music instruments

Source: Nurse, 2003a.

for tourists through music festivals like Reggae Sunsplash and Reggae Sumfest (Nurse, 2002a).

The music industry in Barbados, which is estimated to earn US$20–25 million, is driven largely by overseas performances by soca artists and music bands, performance fees in the hotel and hospitality sector, and earnings from festival tourism, namely the Barbados Cropover and the Barbados Jazz festival. The recording industry has grown with the overseas success of soca artists and has attracted many artists from the southern Caribbean to record there.

The music industry in the Eastern Caribbean is largely driven by festival tourism, which accounts for over US$20 million. The St Lucia Jazz festival alone contributes US$14 million in visitor expenditures. Other major festivals are the Dominica World Creole Music festival and the St Kitts music festival which are estimated to earn US$800 000 (Nurse and Tull, 2003) and US$1.2 million (Sahely and Skeritt, 2003), respectively. Each festival generates strong visitor demand from regional and diasporic tourists and creates high media value that adds to destination appeal (Nurse, 2004b). The recording industry, though embryonic, has begun to contribute to the regional and international calypso and soca circuit.

Trinidad and Tobago produces a wide range of musical genres including calypso, soca, pan, chutney, rapso, and parang. Like many of its counterparts the music industry is driven largely by live performances at home, regionally, in the diaspora and in international mainstream markets. Other drivers of the sector are the recording industry although it suffers from high levels of piracy and low levels of radio airplay. Music publishing is an emerging source of earnings with the shift towards a digital entertainment economy (e.g. digital broadcasting, iTunes, ringtones). Another element of the sector is the production and export of steelpan instruments (the major merchandise export in the cultural sector), most of which are sold in the educational music market in North America and Europe. In Trinidad and Tobago the music and related cultural industries are estimated to earn over US$50 million in foreign exchange and rank among the top ten export sectors (Nurse, 2003b).

Festivals, tourism and diaspora

Caribbean festivals have also made a significant impact on the regional tourism sector in terms of creating a new tourism season and/or filling the void in the tourism calendar by boosting flight arrivals and improving hotel occupancy levels. Caribbean festivals have done much to generate new tourism demand from the short-break travel market as well as from

Table 14.4 Festival tourism economic impact

Festivals	Year	Arrivals	Visitor expenditures US$m
Trinidad and Tobago Carnival	2004	40 455	28.0
St Lucia Jazz festival	2000	11 041	14.8
Barbados Cropover	2000	3 485	3.2

Source: Nurse, 2005.

diasporic and intra-regional tourist groupings that are largely omitted in the tourist marketing plans of most Caribbean tourism organisations. The spending of festival tourists, considered 'new' or incremental and is counted as an export industry, has been very significant as a share of total visitor expenditure, where the data on visitor arrivals have been documented by exit surveys.

The main finding is that festivals create a strong demand-pull for visitors. The best case is Trinidad Carnival – the largest festival in the region in terms of visitor arrivals and expenditures. Arrivals have grown by 60 per cent since the late 1990s such that by 2004 there were over 40 000 visitors who spent approximately US$28 million, over 10 per cent of annual visitor expenditures (see Table 14.4). The festival with the next best performance was that of St Lucia Jazz, which had 11 041 visitors and expenditures of $14.8 million in 2000. The Barbados Cropover festival, after a significant drop in arrivals in the late 1990s, attracted 3485 visitors in 2000 that spent $3.2 million in visitor expenditures.

Caribbean festivals have been pivotal, especially carnivals and indigenous music festivals, to the development of the cultural industries and arts sector. Festivals give a fillip to the entertainment sector through creating new clients, markets and media exposure, thereby facilitating export expansion. It also stimulates infrastructure development, heritage conservation and investment into the arts. Festival tourism also makes an important contribution to the wider economy in that it (1) increases government tax receipts, generates employment and sectoral linkages between the tourism, travel and cultural industries: (2) is a cost effective means of building destination image and attracts new business sponsorship and cross promotion opportunities; (3) has a multiplier effect on the wider economy and a spill-over effect on ancillary sectors like the media and advertising industries, auto rentals and restaurants.

Caribbean music, arts and festivals have been exported with the proliferation of Trinidad-styled carnivals, which can be found throughout

Table 14.5   The economic impact of diasporic Caribbean carnivals

Diasporic carnivals	Attendance	Festival expenditures
Caribana, Toronto	1 million	Cnd$200 million
Labour Day, New York	3.5 million	US$300 million
Notting Hill, London	2 million	Stg£93 million

Source: Nurse, 2004c.

the Anglophone Caribbean and in over 60 cities in the North Atlantic where there are large diasporic populations (Nurse, 1999). The diasporic Caribbean carnivals are an important feature of the cultural industries in Trinidad and Tobago, Barbados and the Eastern Caribbean because they account for a large percentage of the year-round work for musical artists and other carnivalists, such as costume designers. These carnivals have grown rapidly since the early 1990s and are now the largest street festivals and generators of economic activity in their respective locations (see Table 14.5). The 'Notting Hill' carnival attracts over 2 million people over two days and generates over £93 million in audience and visitor expenditures. Similarly, the 'Labour Day' carnival in New York earns US$300 million while the 'Caribana' festival in Toronto generates CND$200 million.

Challenges and opportunities

The challenges for the cultural industries in SIDS go beyond lack of talent, product or market. The main challenge is that of establishing new and alternative art forms and genres in global, regional, and national markets that are increasingly saturated with content from the main cultural exporters (e.g. the US, UK and India). Participating in these markets is not just a matter of building competitiveness, but also calling for changing tastes and lifestyles that are not easily achieved without heavy marketing and alliances with global firms.

SIDS are also faced with a number of challenges that are associated with small and peripheral economies such as weak management and information systems, shortage of skilled personnel, low levels of training, poor manufacturing and service facilities, uncompetitive packaging and branding, weak marketing and distribution channels, high levels of copyright infringement and piracy, and weak rights management and royalties collections. There also tends to be an historical, institutional and commercial bias against indigenous content in the home markets that marginalises and chokes off local entrepreneurship, investment and market development.

The key opportunities relate to changes such as rising domestic cultural content in developing countries, the growth of diasporic markets and networks, the increasing interest in 'authenticity' and indigenous culture in the tourism industry, cost reductions in new digital technologies, the growth of global media (e.g. cable TV, satellite radio, Internet), and the emergence of Internet marketing and broadcasting. However, access to foreign markets and media are constrained by the high cost of marketing, the oligopolistic structure of markets and the restrictive business practices of the transnational companies.

In this context existing strategies for ensuring competitiveness and sustainable development are inadequate. It is against this backdrop that recommendations for developing the potential of the cultural industries through the application of industrial, trade and innovation policies must be made.

The foregoing analysis illustrates the specificity of the industrial challenge facing the cultural industries. It suggests that there are three specific areas for industrial intervention, which differentiates from the traditional goods sector. The first intervention required is that of intellectual property protection. The cultural industries cannot survive in the marketplace without adequate protection from copyright infringement. Without such protection cultural entrepreneurs would be at the mercy of piracy, bootlegging, counterfeiting and other forms of infringement such as unlicensed broadcasting. For example, music is one of the easiest forms of art to pirate as a result of the wide diffusion of reproduction technologies such as recordable compact discs and Internet based filesharing and peer-to-peer formats like My.MP3.com, Gnutella, Napster and Grokster. The latter technologies have helped to expand the demand for music but have also had a negative impact on the music industry with declining sales to the tune of 5 per cent year on year since the late-1990s (IFPI, 2006).

The second key intervention that is required is investment in research and development, which in the cultural industries means investment in human and creative capital. For example, in the music industry this is referred to as artists and repertoire (A&R). This is a critical area because the cultural industries start with creativity and it accounts for a large share of investment. The cultural industries sector is estimated to spend at least 15 per cent more of its turnover on research and development, on average, than other industries.[3] Investing in creative capabilities calls for the establishment of training institutions as well as support mechanisms for young artists and cultural entrepreneurs.

The third key intervention for the cultural industries relates to marketing. Audience loyalty is difficult to build and predict, hence the need for significant resources in terms of marketing and building a brand. What is also evident is that there is product differentiation based on genre. This calls for life-style marketing or niche marketing. Based on this industrial context, analysts argue that:

> Building up a diversified industrial structure and reaching a critical mass are essential in order to sustain increasing competition. Maintaining competitiveness requires financial and marketing muscle in order to assemble financing for intellectual and artistic production; to pay the high fees demanded by talented or world famous authors, movie stars, film directors, or singers; to bear the relevant risks; to obtain consumer loyalty by promoting massively the product or the brand (the author) over a variety of media; to bundle the rights and protect them; and to be able to gain from ancillary markets such as merchandising. Vast global distribution networks are critical in maximizing returns and spreading the risk and cost over larger markets. (UNCTAD/ILO, 1995)

The cultural industries are also faced with the problem of externalities because of the difficulty of excluding free riders, for example, in activities like festivals which generate significant value in terms of media exposure, destination imaging and visitor expenditures in travel, accommodation, and shopping (Casey et al., 1996). In addition, public investment and corporate sponsorship in the cultural industries are often blocked for socio-political reasons because popular culture genres often embody anti-establishment themes. This is particularly evident in the region's music industry, which is produced by marginalised groups for whom music is an act of resistance to cultural and political domination (Nurse, 2002b; Ho and Nurse, 2005).

Cultural industries and cultural policy

Cultural policy is by definition nation-state specific and so is being squeezed by globally-dispersed creative industries and by international trade rules that seek to limit national exceptionalism. Content convergence means that cultural policy has a shrinking sector-specific envelope to work as a bigger mix of new content policies come to the fore, and a set of formidable challenges in collaboration, and the design and delivery of policy and programmes.

> The arts, cultural and creative industry sectors will need to get used to thinking of themselves and acting as part of a broader coalescence of interests encompassing the content-rich service industries such as education and learning, publishing, design, communications devices, and e-commerce. (Cunningham, 2002)

Governments and corporate sectors in most SIDS have not fully appreciated the new directions in the global economy and the ways in which their economies can diversify to meet new challenges and take advantage of emerging opportunities. In addition, the cultural industries are not seriously regarded as an economic sector; the key stakeholders in the industry are poorly organised and the sector's economic value remains largely undocumented. In this context, policy measures have typically been absent and when there have been investments and initiatives they have tended to be short-lived and misdirected. Changing the mindset of governments and the corporate sector is key for transforming the sector's viability, but it is equally important for the industry stakeholders to become better organised and provide a more sustained and cohesive advocacy capability.

In broad outline, the key policy interventions would entail a number of initiatives from a wide array of stakeholders: the state including various ministries and agencies (e.g. tourism organisations, intellectual property offices, trade facilitation agencies) along with industry associations, non-governmental development organisations and international development agencies. A short list of the main recommendations for fostering a regional environment conducive to the development of the cultural industries includes the following:

- Improved government-industry relations through the harmonisation of government policy on trade, industrial and intellectual property policies. Proactive policies aimed at promoting cultural diversity and investment in the cultural sector should be preserved in bilateral and multilateral negotiations (e.g. WTO) and in inter-regional arrangements (e.g. the CARIFORUM–EU Economic Partnership Agreement).
- Harmonisation, simplification, and implementation of intra-regional trade measures to facilitate the deepening of the regional market; for example, common customs regimes and procedures. Key issues are the freedom of movement of cultural workers and equipment. Also

important is a reduction of tariffs and taxes on inputs for creative products.

- Documented economic impact of the cultural industries through the establishment of cultural observatories. Establishment of benchmarks, targets and policy measures to promote employment generation, enterprise development, industrial upgrading and export expansion.
- Increased local and regional content on the airwaves (e.g. radio and TV) through local content legislation/regulation where needed. Encouragement and facilitation of the 'uploading' of local and regional content onto the World Wide Web, for example, through the webcasting of festival and events.
- Development of cultural industry associations to represent the interest of the sector and also to develop a code of ethics and standards for remuneration rates and work practice, particularly for cultural workers who provide services to the hotel, hospitality and advertising sectors. An overarching regional council of industry associations would help to achieve some critical mass in terms of networking and advocacy.
- Improved access to finance, credit and business support services for emerging and export-ready firms and artists. Establishment of booking agencies and trade/export facilitation centres. Much of this can be done through aggregator websites. These measures should be matched by market development grants and financing for participation in trade fairs.
- Entrance into double-taxation treaties with trading partners to address the issue of withholding taxes. The inclusion of specific provisions on cultural goods and services in investment promotion contracts for investors.
- Copyright exploitation, protection and collective administration are vital components of the industrial and export upgrading agenda. Parallel initiatives are required in anti-piracy and public awareness campaigns in the regional and diasporic markets. National and regional rights management centres need to be established for multiple areas of the cultural industries (e.g. music, book publishing, visual arts).
- Expansion of the linkages between the cultural industries, the tourism sector and the wider economy, for example, through festivals like the Pacific Festival of Arts and the Caribbean Festival of Arts. Facilitation and encouragement of new marketing strategies targeted at the diasporic and intra-regional markets as well as cultural tourists.
- Development of Internet-readiness for alternative broadcasting, marketing and distribution of cultural goods, services and events.

Establishment of a stronger e-commerce platform and a regional warehousing and fulfilment system for sales and distribution of cultural goods and services.

- Upgrading of the human resource capabilities of the cultural sector through technical training in the arts at the secondary and tertiary levels, as well as training in arts administration, management, and cultural entrepreneurship. Increased funding and human resources for regional art institutes, forge alliances with similar institutions overseas, and establish scholarships for training.
- The marketing and branding of the region's cultural industries requires significant investment. The region already enjoys much market appeal. This needs to be translated into stronger commercial opportunities for distribution over the Internet as well as expanded destination branding for cultural tourism.

Conclusion

This chapter argues that cultural industries are a critical catalyst for identity formation and nation building, and reinforce and expand the cultural confidence of the SIDS and the diasporic communities. It also argues that investing in the cultural industries provides worthwhile returns because the sector generates new, high value-added and indigenous forms of employment, production and exports, aids in the diversification of mono-production economies and facilitates a more competitive development platform. The conclusion is that the cultural industries should be viewed as a critical strategic resource in the move towards creating sustainable development options.

Achieving the above goals does require some resource mobilisation that can only be determined on a case-by-case basis. Some SIDS have more commercialised arts and cultural industries while some have stronger export capabilities and the required institutional and organisational resources. Also some sub-sectors are more commercialised than others in terms of the domestic, regional and diasporic markets providing a platform for internationalisation.

SIDS have small markets that have operated as a disincentive to investment in some sub-sectors of the cultural industries. Exports to regional, diasporic and extra-regional markets are critical to overcoming the diseconomies of scale. The cultural industries are also often viewed as risky investments because of the volatility of consumer tastes and the difficulties in predicting market demands. Consequently, the main source of capital has tended to come from private individual and family savings rather than from banks and credit facilities. Development grants and small business financing are appropriate for emerging sectors of this sort.

Historically the cultural arena has not been seen as a priority area in national budgets or in overseas development assistance when compared with the resource demands of traditional economic activities (e.g. sugar, bananas, rice and rum). Also when there are resources for the cultural sector it tends to be allocated for tangible and built heritage. Intangible heritage has traditionally attracted fewer resources.

Notes

1. For further details see WIPO (2003).
2. The Convention (http://www.unesco.org/culture/en/diversity/convention/), which was adopted in October 2005,
   a) recognises that 'cultural diversity forms a common heritage of humanity';
   b) notes that 'cultural activities, goods and services have both an economic and cultural nature because they convey identities, values and meanings, and must therefore not be treated as solely having commercial value';
   c) and reaffirms the rights of sovereign states to 'maintain, adopt and implement policies and measures that they deem appropriate for the protection and promotion of the diversity of cultural expressions on their territory'.
3. The Recording Industry Association of America estimates that the investment in talent by the music industry averages 15 per cent of turnover, which is higher than most key industries.

References

Alexandraki, Katerina (2005) 'Preference Erosion: Cause for Alarm', *Finance & Development*, March: 26–9.

Casey, B., R. Dunlop and S. Selwood (1996) *Culture as Commodity? The Economics of the Arts and Built Heritage in the UK* (London: Policy Studies Institute).

Cunningham, Stuart D. (2002) 'From Cultural to Creative Industries: Theory, Industry, and Policy Implications' *Media International Australia, Incorporating Culture & Policy* (102): 54–65.

Ho, Christine and Keith Nurse (eds) (2005) *Globalization, Diaspora and Caribbean Popular Culture* (Kingston, Jamaica: Ian Randle Press).

IFPI (2006) *The Recording Industry in Numbers, 2005* (London: IFPI).

Ministry of Education, Government of Finland (2007) *Fair Culture – Culture for Sustainable Development*, Background Paper for conference: Fair culture? Culture for Sustainable Development, 29–30 May, http://www.minedu.fi/OPM/Tapahtu-makalenteri/2007/05/reilu_kulttuuri. html, accessed 30 May 2008.

Nurse, K. (1999) 'Globalization and Trinidad Carnival: Diaspora, Hybridity and Identity in Global Culture', *Cultural Studies* 13(4): 661–90.

Nurse, K. (2001) *The Caribbean Music Industry* (Bridgetown: Caribbean Export Development Agency, Tradewins), 1(7).

Nurse, K. (2002a) 'Bringing Culture into Tourism: Festival Tourism and Reggae Sunsplash in Jamaica', *Social and Economic Studies* 51 (1): 127–43.

Nurse, K. (2002b) 'The Caribbean Music Industry: Enhancing Export Capabilities' in Keith Nurse and Marie-Claude Derne (eds), *Caribbean Economies and Global Restructuring* (Kingston, Jamaica: Ian Randle Press).

Nurse, K. (2003a) *The Caribbean Music Industry: Building Competitiveness and Enhancing Export Capabilities in an Emerging Sector* (Bridgetown: Caribbean Export Development Agency).

Nurse, K. (2003b) 'Trinidad Carnival: Festival Tourism and Cultural Industry', *Event Management* 8 (3): 223–30.

Nurse, K. (2004a) 'Migration, Diaspora and Development in Latin America and the Caribbean', *International Politics and Society* (2): 107–26.

Nurse, K. (2004b) 'Festival Tourism in the Caribbean: An Economic Impact Assessment' in Philip Long and Mike Robinson (eds) *Festivals and Tourism: Marketing, Management and Evaluation* (Sunderland, UK: Business Education Publishers).

Nurse, K. (2004c) 'Globalization in Reverse: The Export of Trinidad Carnival' in Milla Riggio (ed.) *Culture in Action: Trinidad Carnival* (London: Routledge): 245–54.

Nurse, K. (2005) *Festival Tourism in the Caribbean* (Washington DC: Inter-American Development Bank).

Nurse, K. (2006) *The Cultural Industries in CARICOM: Trade and Development Challenges*, report prepared for EU PROINVEST and Caribbean Regional Negotiating Machinery, http://www.crnm.org/documents/cultural_industries/Final_Cultural_Industries_ Study_21Dec07.pdf, accessed 30 May 2008.

Nurse, Keith and Joanne Tull (2003) *The World Creole Music Festival: An Economic Impact Assessment* (Roseau, Dominica: National Development Commission).

OAS (2004) 'Study for Theme 1: "Culture as an Engine for Economic Growth, Employment and Development"' (Organization of American States/Inter-American Council for Integral Development).

Sahely, Leah and Shirley Skeritt, 'St. Kitts Music Festival 2003: Economic Impact Assessment and Visitor Profile', July.

UNCTAD (2004) *Creative Industries and Development*, Paper presented at UNCTAD Eleventh Session, Sao Paulo, June, TD(XI)BP/13.

UNCTAD/ILO (1995) *Media Services: A Survey of the Industry and Its Largest Firms* (Geneva: UNCTAD).

UNCTAD/UNDP (2008) *Economy Report 2008: The Challenges of Assessing the Creative Economy: Towards Informed Policy-making* (Geneva and New York: UNCTAD/UNDP), http://www.unctad.org/creative-economy, accessed May 2008.

UNESCO (2005) *International Flow of Selected Cultural Goods and Services, 1994–2003* (Montreal: UNESCO Institute for Statistics), http://www.uis.unesco.org, accessed 2 March 2006.

Van den Bossche, Peter (2007) *Free Trade and Culture: A Study of Relevant WTO Rules and Constraints on National Cultural Policy Measures* (Amsterdam: Boekmanstudies).

WIPO (2003) *Guide on Surveying the Economic Contribution of the Copyright-based Industries* (Geneva: WIPO).

15
The Caribbean Confronts the OECD: Tax Competition and Diplomacy

William Vlcek

This chapter presents a case study of small state diplomacy with an exploration of the confrontation between small states hosting offshore financial centres (OFCs), and the Organisation of Economic Co-operation and Development (OECD) over its 'harmful tax competition' project.[1] In this analysis, diplomacy is understood as a relationship between states involving dialogue and negotiation (Evans and Newnham, 1998: 129). Diplomacy is, in the words of Martin Wight (1986: 113), 'the system and the art of communication between powers'. With this quotation it is worth noting for the context of the following analysis that his posthumous text was titled *Power Politics*. While the analytical approach within this chapter does not follow the realist perspective of Wight, state power and the relationships of power between states nonetheless are central to this analysis.

In a situation between an international organisation with restricted membership and a group of non-member states, the power relations are more complex than simple raw calculations of military and economic resources (Cline, 1980). In these circumstances we are dealing with what has been identified as the second dimension of power, the ability to set the international agenda and, most importantly, influence what topics are never considered for inclusion on that agenda. Possession of the ability to shape and formulate the agenda is possession of the power to limit and control the alternatives or options available as possible courses of action (Berenskoetter, 2007: 7–9). Where the first dimension of power is the realist conception of power, the ability for actor 'A' to convince actor 'B' to take an action that 'B' would not otherwise take, this second dimension leaves 'B' with no choice but to act as desired by 'A' because alternatives are not on the agenda (Berenskoetter, 2007: 4–7). Beyond these two dimensions there operates the situational awareness of the weaker participant. Such awareness means that 'B' is quite likely to act in order to satisfy 'A' because 'B' recognises the weakness of their position regardless of the legitimacy of 'A's case.[2] Quentin Skinner identified the situation as representing a Third Concept of Liberty (following Isaiah Berlin's work on the two concepts of liberty), namely that individual liberty, or freedom of action, is limited by the recognition that we live in an awareness of our dependence upon others, which in turn forces us to constrain our choices and actions (Skinner, 2002).[3] Thus, it may be the case that 'B' acted not because it was the correct choice or because there were no alternatives, but simply because of a dependence on 'A', limiting choices either to resist (and be subjected to punishment) or comply. The case study presented in this chapter is one of resistance in the face of implied sanctions by the OECD and its member states.

The chapter is structured in four sections; the first provides a discussion of the nature of power for the situation of relations between the OECD and small Caribbean states. The second section explains the creation of 'harmful tax competition' as an international problem that requires collective action guided by the OECD. The third section is a summary of specific points in the chronology of the relations between the OECD and those jurisdictions that it labelled as tax havens. The final section explains the discursive power embedded in this case (and similar ones) for diplomatic relations between a dominant international organisation and non-member (often developing) states. It must be acknowledged that a similar size-related dynamic operates within the OECD itself, which was represented by internal dissent with the tax competition project. Reservations towards both the scope and approach of the project were expressed by several smaller members of the OECD, and were explained in some detail in an annex to the OECD's first report, but were subsequently relegated to minor references buried in footnotes. Switzerland was firm in its disagreement and of particular note is the position taken by Luxembourg, the smallest member of the OECD and host for an international financial centre accused of sponsoring a 'preferential' tax regime (by the European Union as well as by the OECD).

Power relations between small states and multilateral institutions

In an article published by *International Organization* in 2005, Michael Barnett and Raymond Duvall made a convincing case for the need to look at power in international politics beyond the realist construction of brute force, whether in its economic or military forms (Barnett and

Duvall, 2005). It has certainly been the case that small states find themselves confronted with materialist forms of economic power, such as the Financial Action Task Force's (FATF) use of a 'blacklist' to discipline non-cooperative non-member jurisdictions in the international campaign against money laundering (see Marshall, Chapter 13 this volume). In order to understand why international 'naming and shaming' through the use of a blacklist was not successfully implemented in this case, the analysis must consider more nuanced permutations of international power, how it is deployed, and in particular, how it is subsequently resisted. For Barnett and Duvall (2005: 42) 'power is the production, in and through social relations, of effects that shape the capacities of actors to determine their circumstances and fate'.

Absent from Barnett and Duvall's analysis of power is the creation of the purpose behind the use of power in the international arena. The application of their model to the case of global governance adequately addressed the power features embedded in the institutions and structures behind global governance, for example the World Bank and World Trade Organization (WTO). It included the use of power by large states to define the international institution and delimit its operational boundaries, yet the analysis failed to address the power relations embedded in the determination of the agenda for each of these sites of global governance. It is this aspect of power that is pivotal for the case of the OECD and OFCs. How did it come about that, first, a problem such as 'harmful tax competition' was determined to exist and, second, that the OECD was the appropriate forum in which to engage the problem?

This form of power, the capability and capacity to determine what a valid subject for discussion is, and what remains silent, invisible and unknown, forms a third dimension to power in the international arena. In essence the third dimension is the power to shape or determine what is 'normal', a move beyond the first dimension of forced compliance and the second dimension of structural limitation. The power to establish what is normal is more than simply controlling the agenda, for it succeeds in shaping the surrounding discourse for an emerging agenda such that competing perspectives are never revealed. As Steven Lukes phrased it, 'is it not the supreme and most insidious exercise of power to prevent people, to whatever degree, from having grievances by shaping their perceptions, cognitions and preferences in such a way that they accept their role in the existing order of things . . .?' (Lukes, 2005: 28). Refining Lukes's analysis of power, John Gaventa placed the three dimensions of power described by Lukes into a larger construct. His power cube situates, on one face, the levels of power (supranational, national and subnational), which then intersects with the forms of power (invisible, hidden and visible), and another face comprising the spaces of power (closed, invited and claimed/created) (Gaventa, 2007: 206). His analysis sought to incorporate the changes to inter-state (and power) relations brought about by globalisation. Thus, we find features that are represented in this chapter's case study throughout this multi-level, multi-dimensional model for power in international politics today. The diplomatic efforts taken by small states came from both national and supranational levels in a space that was first closed to them and then subsequently opened, while the forms of power were most often visible despite cases of invisible and hidden power. However, the space they found was not welcoming on account of OFCs remaining outside the OECD, forcing them to engage with the OECD Secretariat and member states in specially created groups that imply equal representation, such as the Global Forum on Taxation.

The relevance for this discussion of power to the case of the OECD Harmful Tax Competition Initiative may be further understood with reference to the analysis of Rainer Hülsse on the creation of new objects of global governance. Hülsse used the FATF and its anti-money-laundering campaign as a case study to describe what he named the 'problematisation' of a global issue. He observed that the first step taken by promoters for a new international regulation or standard is frequently a campaign to persuade others that a global problem, such as money laundering or harmful tax competition, actually exists. His central question is particularly relevant for if the problem is obvious, then why the need to convince others that it exists before persuading them of the need for global governance? Clearly, from the perspective of small states in this case study, it was not a global problem but simply a problem for OECD member states who, through the G7, commissioned the OECD to label OFCs as a global problem. The academic discussion of tax competition before 1998 centred on abstract analysis involving the relationship between the tax regimes of two notional states (Bacchetta and Espinosa, 1995; Razin and Sadka, 1991; Wilson, 1991; Janeba and Peters, 1999). The problematisation of tax competition as 'harmful' was therefore an exercise in defining the 'normal' for tax competition in the international arena, a form of discursive power. The next section outlines the discourse used by the OECD to establish harmful tax competition as a global problem.

Tax competition as an international problem

The OECD has constructed a perception that the low-tax regimes offered by OFCs to non-resident persons (natural and legal) pose a threat to the tax base of OECD members. In 1998 the OECD released the first public report from their project, *Harmful Tax Competition: An Emerging Global Issue*, in which it described tax competition 'as "poaching" as the tax base "rightly" belongs to the other country' (OECD, 1998). This viewpoint is fundamental to the case, arguing some forms of tax competition are harmful and that globalisation is partly responsible for this threat to OECD states. It fits with the economistic argument against an inefficient global allocation of finance capital brought about by tax competition (Wilson, 1999). Yet at the same time it fails to acknowledge any rationale or desire on the part of the persons that are using an OFC to reduce their tax obligations.[4] By focusing on the perception that member state revenue was lost owing to tax competition, the OECD left a gap into which small states would insert a wedge that would delay, if not defeat, the project. The wedge placed focus on political questions aroused by the OECD, rather than staying in the domain of its established competence for the technical aspects of taxation (Sharman, 2006: 129–34). The prime minister of Barbados declared, for example, 'The power to tax is a sovereign right that cannot be compromised and certainly cannot be yielded to institutions which have no standing in law to determine the tax policies of other countries.' (Commonwealth Secretariat, 2000a: 2) The failure to include affected jurisdictions in the formative stages of the project led to accusations of neo-colonial action against small states (Sanders, 2002). More explicitly from a Caribbean perspective, the OECD project was viewed as a campaign by large white states against small black states.

One example of the above-mentioned technical competence of the OECD Secretariat has been its Model Tax Convention. Additionally, it has had a working group studying tax competition since at least 1977, when the OECD Council adopted a recommendation encouraging member states to 'strengthen their powers to detect and prevent international tax avoidance and evasion, and to develop exchanges of information between tax administrators' (Gordon, 1981: 31). The latest campaign against tax competition emerged from the 1996 G7 Summit in Lyon (OECD, 1998). Space does not permit a full exploration of the tax competition literature, which at a minimum goes back to Charles Tiebout's 1956 article 'A Pure Theory of Local Expenditures' (Tiebout, 1956). Let it simply be noted here that while there is general agreement on the existence of tax competition, there is no agreement on whether it is in fact harmful, rather than beneficial.[5] The advancement of communication technologies and transportation over the past two decades now permit easy access to foreign (offshore) financial institutions by more individuals and smaller firms. Consequently, the perception is that the member states of the OECD initiated the project in order to retain their present tax revenue base (Vlcek, 2004).

In presenting this project to the wider non-OECD community, tax competition was 'problematised' as a global issue. Tax competition permits individual free-riders (persons and firms) to benefit from the public goods provided by their state of residence without contributing tax towards state maintenance. The OECD described a situation where states foster competition with their tax regimes and thereby reduce tax receipts in the free riders' home locations. 'In a still broader sense, governments and residents of tax havens can be "free riders" of general public goods created by the non-haven country' (OECD, 1998: 15). In other words, small states are benefiting from the public goods financed by large states. Alternatively, in the language used by some economists, tax competition distorts investment and produces inefficient outcomes (Wilson, 1999). Essentially, it was necessary for the OECD to build a convincing case that tax competition was a source of harm with global proportions that required a collective global solution, rather than it simply being an effort by a collection of large states intent on retaining the financial assets that they were presently losing to the OFCs. Clearly it failed in that regard as critics immediately made the case that the project was all about lost tax revenues and not about global equity. '[M]etropolitan countries have long been happy to accept "capital flight" financial flows from developing countries, and there has been no talk of harmful competition with regard to such flows.' In his presentation before the Caribbean Group for Cooperation in Economic Development's session on the 'Offshore Financial Sector', Compton Bourne (Pro Vice-Chancellor, University of the West Indies) concluded that the OECD project was really 'a struggle over the location of the international financial services industry' (Caribbean Group for Cooperation in Economic Development, 2000). Nonetheless, the OECD has established the terms of the debate and a conceptual framework for the creation of an international regime involving national-level taxation.[6] Finally, the hidden power of the OECD to create this discourse is reflected by its presence in academic publications, NGO initiatives, and the impact analyses found in financial and banking industry publications.[7]

The power and resistance of small states

Resistance to the OECD developed slowly and was often framed with language similar to the above quotation from Bourne. For example, the Commonwealth Heads of Government (1999) argued for 'the right of member countries to compete in the international financial markets, through the provision of both onshore and offshore financial services'. Perceptions had shifted by 2000 and the OECD released its second report containing its list of tax haven jurisdictions, preparatory for the later creation of a final list of 'uncooperative tax havens' (OECD, 2000: 16–18). Many of these same jurisdictions were also under pressure from the FATF, which had released its own list identifying Non-Cooperative Countries and Territories (NCCT) (see Marshall's chapter). The material impact on the small jurisdictions, both perceived and experienced, generated in turn the substance of the threat implicit within the OECD's planned list.[8] The OECD report listed 35 jurisdictions that met its technical criteria to be determined a tax haven (OECD, 2000: 17). Prior to the report's publication, however, the OECD announced that it had advance commitments from six jurisdictions to co-operate with the project, though they were not named in the report itself. The jurisdictions identified as tax havens were permitted 12 months in which to make a commitment to cooperate with the OECD project. Failing to provide an indication of their commitment meant that they would be identified as an uncooperative tax haven on a list initially scheduled for publication in July 2001.

Consequently, the OECD initiative was a major topic at the September 2000 Commonwealth Finance Ministers Meeting in Malta with its headline status and six numbered paragraphs in the meeting's Communiqué. The Communiqué conveyed the ministers' concern that the scheduled publication date for the list represented an 'impediment to constructive dialogue'. At the same time, ministers 'strongly reaffirmed the right of sovereign nations to determine their own tax policies'. The Commonwealth finance ministers requested that the Commonwealth Secretariat facilitate multilateral dialogue 'in appropriate ways' (Commonwealth Secretariat, 2000b). As a fellow international organisation whose membership included many of the listed jurisdictions, the Commonwealth offered a site of international power capable of offsetting the OECD. It functioned as a means to aggregate individual small state voices as a single, more substantial, collective voice. The Commonwealth Secretariat arranged a high-level consultation meeting in January 2001, and at this juncture, a form of 'diplomacy via press release' developed.[9] The meeting was announced via press release on 23 November 2000, stating that the Secretariat was using 'its good offices to facilitate these consultations' (Commonwealth News and Information Service, 2000). Initially, the press releases, both individual and those issued jointly by the Commonwealth Secretariat and the OECD Secretariat, relayed the confidence with which the parties held, entering into discussions and any indication of the chasm existing between respective positions was completely absent. The statement released prior to the meeting in Barbados, for example, noted that it would 'provide the first real opportunity for multilateral dialogue between the OECD and other jurisdictions on "harmful tax competition"' (Commonwealth Secretariat, 2001a). The meeting was described afterwards in a press release as 'a frank, open and ultimately fruitful exchange of views' (Commonwealth Secretariat, 2001b).

The momentum of the OECD project began to fade following statements by the US Secretary of the Treasury in May 2001 concerning the OECD 'working group that targets "harmful tax practices"', and echoing statements from Caribbean leaders.

> I am troubled by the underlying premise that low tax rates are somehow suspect and by the notion that any country, or group of countries, should interfere in any other country's decision about how to structure its own tax system. (O'Neill, 2001)

Subsequent media reports suggested 'The threat of sanctions for small island states accused of supporting tax evasion is receding' (BBC News, 2001). An OECD spokesperson insisted, however, that the OECD Secretariat did not feel that statements from the US would have a significant impact on the progress of the project (Carroll, 2001). That assessment was in part correct, as the small jurisdictions continued to provide commitment statements to the OECD Secretariat, even though they did not follow the format of the OECD's Memorandum of Understanding.[10] Starting with the Isle of Man, these statements would be conditional, qualified by a requirement for impartial and equivalent treatment for all jurisdictions, regardless of whether it was a member of the OECD or not (Peter-Szerenyi, 2003).

The next meeting of the Global Forum on Taxation was in October 2003, when a select group of 20 OECD members and 20 OFCs gathered in Ottawa, Canada for two days. The vague concept of a 'level playing field' had emerged as a central issue for small states, consistent with the conditional statement contained in their commitment letters requesting equivalent treatment to that given OECD states. As seen in the closing statement from the meeting in Ottawa, 'virtually all participants' were committed to principles of transparency and effective exchanges of information. Transparency and information exchanges had replaced tax competition as a discourse amenable to the US administration. Another working group was formed with a mission to develop a proposal for creating a 'global level playing field', an initial step for the re-focused OECD project (OECD Global Forum on Taxation, 2003).[11]

The resilience of small states to maintain their position on equal treatment remained a feature in subsequent meetings of the Global Forum, seeking agreement on standards for transparency and information exchanges (Spencer and Sharman, 2006). The OECD, however, has returned to a hidden application of its power, and incorporated aspects of its desired information exchange provisions in a more recent revision to the Model Tax Treaty. The revised Article 26 (2004) focused on bank secrecy laws, but crucially failed to guarantee information exchanges. Consequently, when a jurisdiction does not collect an income tax, it is not likely to have the necessary institutional structure to collect such information (Spencer, 2005a; Spencer, 2005b). Moreover, a tax treaty is a bilateral agreement and, as documented by the Commonwealth Secretariat, very few small jurisdictions are party to these tax treaties (Stoll-Davey, 2007). The target for this hidden deployment of power appeared to be among those states with the densest collection of bilateral tax treaties, the member states of the OECD with bank secrecy laws, and not the OFCs. Because of the nature of the OECD's operating principles this tactic achieved limited success, as Austria, Belgium, Luxembourg and Switzerland all registered reservations with the revised Model Treaty article (Spencer, 2005a: 11). In sum, the overall purpose behind the treaty's revision is not entirely clear, at least in terms of increased transparency and the exchange of information by national tax administrations, and it will remain unclear until there is a significant increase in tax treaties negotiated with OFC jurisdictions.

Discursive power in diplomacy

Several points concerning small states and their diplomatic relations with international organisations arise from the preceding discussion. The first involves the global governance aspects of offshore finance. As demonstrated by this case, Hülsse's argument, the problematisation of global issues leading in turn to global governance, failed to interrogate the *national* origins for any initial problem statement. An analysis of the creation of the FATF and the establishment of money laundering as a problem of both global stature as well as global concern must look past the origins of the organisation to the establishment of money laundering as a distinct criminal activity in the US prior to 1989. Any international problem ultimately has a domestic point of origin. The discourse regarding the dangerous nature of money laundering is that it tears the very moral fabric of society. Permitting criminals to benefit from their ill-gotten gains could lead the law-abiding to question the usefulness of their lawful conduct (Pieth, 2002; Alldridge, 2003). A similar domestic discourse exists in the case of tax avoidance, elevating it from national levels of concern to harmful tax competition concerns believed to exist in the international political economy.[12]

In the case of the OECD and the Caribbean, it was a matter of international politics and negotiation among sovereign entities. These negotiations reproduce the sovereign status of the participants as independent territorial jurisdictions representing a distinct population with their unique interests and desires. As an international organisation, neither the OECD nor its Secretariat represented a specific national constituency, instead proclaiming that it acted on behalf of all citizens in tackling the issue of harmful tax competition as a threat to global welfare (OECD, 1998: 8). At the same time, the 1998 report emphasised that it was not an attempt to impose some optimal rate of tax upon individual domestic constituencies. 'Countries should remain free to design their own tax systems as long as they abide by internationally accepted standards in doing so' (Organisation for Economic Co-operation and Development, 1998: 15). Confronted by the assertions of sovereignty that accompanied the observation that small states were absent from the initial report's development, the OECD found itself in a position where it had to follow through and act on its claim to multilateral participation and inclusiveness (Sharman, 2006). The diplomatic posture of small states was to remain firm and insist on equal treatment.

It is a rather facile conclusion to declare that the change of policy in Washington, DC undermined the collective effort of the OECD. Certainly the continued use of bilateral tax agreements between the US and select small jurisdictions demonstrated that the US remained vigilant against the use of OFCs for tax avoidance. However, resistance from small jurisdictions involved issues of equal treatment and a level playing field, tactics that present just as much a discursive dilemma for the OECD with US support as it does for the OECD without US support. The preference of the US to establish tax information exchange agreements (TIEAs) with small Caribbean jurisdictions reflects its dominant market presence in the local financial sector, as well as its demonstrated unilateral use of financial sanctions.[13] For the case of the OECD and harmful tax competition, the discursive influence of the OECD Secretariat was weakened from the start by the immanent critique of Switzerland and Luxembourg. Subsequent policy changes by a new US Administration directly challenged the discursive position of the Secretariat and opened a space for small states to resist the problematisation of tax competition. Strategies of qualified acquiescence developed, in which commitments were offered with the explicit expectation of equal treatment independent of economic and material power. Diplomatic representatives for the small states demonstrated their resilience through claims for equal recognition with OECD states, overturning the aggressive timetable and original objectives established by the OECD. At the same time, participants from Caribbean states will readily argue that the entire process left a bitter aftertaste.

Notes

1. As stated repeatedly throughout my work, I use the term offshore financial centre (OFC) to re-emphasise and underscore the distinct territorial separation between jurisdictions and their sovereign right to establish independent legal structures governing finance, trade and taxation. The presence of the term 'tax haven' in this chapter is used 'under erasure' (following Jacques Derrida) owing to its prevalence in OECD documentation and related literature.

2. For reasons of space the question of the legitimacy of the OECD project will not be addressed, though one argument made by critics was that the OECD did not possess legitimacy as it was not an appropriate forum to produce international standards affecting non-member jurisdictions (see Vlcek, 2008a: 72–3).

3. This point is made with respect to trade negotiations by Lee, Chapter 11 this volume.

4. This aspect of the issue has been studied as a question of 'tax morale', see Feld and Frey, 2002; Feld and Frey, 2005; Frey and Torgler, 2007).

5. Several starting points to the literature include Edwards and Keen, 1996; Schulze and Ursprung, 1999; Wilson, 1999.

6. Avi-Yonah (2007), for example, argued that an international tax regime has emerged as a consequence of OECD action over the past decade, a claim that will not be debated in this chapter. See also Thomas (2002).

7. Examples include Johnston, 1999; Avi-Yonah, 2000; Langer, 2000; Oxfam, 2000; Samuels and Kolb, 2001; Edwards and de Rugy, 2002; Lopatin, 2002; Hishikawa, 2002; Shapiro and Schröder, 2003; Hampton and Sikka, 2005).

8. For an analysis of blacklisting as a tool used by international organisations to discipline compliance with their standards of conduct, see Sharman (2007).

9. In an analysis of the re-regulation of offshore finance Bill Maurer described a 'politics by press release', following Greg Rawlings' analysis of the 'regulatory dialogue' between the OFCs and international organisations like the OECD as a case of 'compliance by press release' (Maurer, 2008: 13; Rawlings, 2007: 59).

10. To review copies of the commitment letters, see http://www.oecd.org/document/19/0,3343, en_2649_33745_1903251_1_1_1_1,00.html.

11. My critique of the 'level playing field' approach to equitable treatment in world politics is contained in Vlcek, 2008b.
12. At the time of writing Liechtenstein is at the centre of a German tax evasion scandal, see e.g. (Crawford and Esterl, 2008).
13. As seen, for example, with the case of the Commercial Bank of Syria (BBC News, 2006; US Treasury, 2004; US Treasury, 2006).

References

Alldridge, P. (2003) *Money Laundering Law: Forfeiture, Confiscation, Civil Recovery, Criminal Laundering and Taxation of the Proceeds of Crime* (Oxford: Hart Publishing).

Avi-Yonah, R.S. (2000) 'Globalization, Tax Competition, and the Fiscal Crisis of the Welfare State', Harvard Law Review 113 (7): 1575–676.

Avi-Yonah, R.S. (2007) 'Tax Competition, Tax Arbitrage and the International Tax Regime', Bulletin for International Taxation 61 (4): 130–9.

Bacchetta, P. and M.P. Espinosa (1995) 'Information Sharing and Tax Competition Among Governments', *Journal of International Economics* 39 (1–2): 103–21.

Barnett, M. and R. Duvall (2005) 'Power in International Politics', *International Organization* (59): 39–75.

BBC News (2001) 'US Eases Stance on "Tax Havens"', BBC News Business ed., last revised 20 July, http://news.bbc.co.uk/1/hi/business/1446603.stm, accessed on 26 August 2008.

BBC News (2006) Syrian bank 'blacklisted' by US. BBC News, 2006, last revised 10 March, available at http://news.bbc.co.uk/1/hi/business/4795536.stm, accessed on 26 August 2008.

Berenskoetter, F. (2007) 'Thinking about power' in F. Berenskoetter and M.J. Williams (eds) *Power in World Politics* (London and New York: Routledge).

Caribbean Group for Cooperation in Economic Development (2000) CGCED Meeting Proceedings – Session for the Offshore Financial Sector, World Bank.

Carroll, A. (2001) 'Tax havens no more?', *Private Banker International* (7).

Cline, R.S. (1980) *World Power Trends and U.S. Foreign Policy for the 1980's* (Boulder, Colorado: Westview Press).

Commonwealth Heads of Government (1999) The Durban Communiqué: Durban, South Africa 12–15 November 1999 (London: Commonwealth Secretariat).

Commonwealth News and Information Service (2000) 'Announcement for "High-level Consultations on Harmful Tax Practices" to be held in Barbados 8–9 January 2001', London, Commonwealth Secretariat.

Commonwealth Secretariat (2000a) 'The Implications of the OECD Harmful Tax Competition Initiative for Offshore Financial Centres', FMM(00)(O)4 (London: Commonwealth Secretariat). Available at http://www.thecommonwealth.org/papers/oecd/FMM(00)(0)4.doc, accessed on 7 October 2002.

Commonwealth Secretariat (2000b) Commonwealth Finance Ministers Meeting, St Julians, Malta, 19–21 September 2000 – Communiqué (London: Commonwealth Secretariat) http://www.thecommonwealth.org/Templates/Internal.asp?NodeID=141664, accessed on 24 March 2008.

Commonwealth Secretariat (2001a) 'Commonwealth and OECD Countries to hold high-level consultations on "harmful tax competition"', Information &

Public Affairs Division, http://www.thecommonwealth.org/Templates/Internal. asp?NodeID=34634, accessed on 24 March 2008.

Commonwealth Secretariat (2001b) 'OECD, Commonwealth Agree to Work Towards Global Cooperation on Harmful Tax Practices', Information & Public Affairs Division, http://www.thecommonwealth.org/Templates/Internal.asp? NodeID=34633, accessed on 24 March 2008.

Crawford, D. and M. Esterl (2008) 'Theft of tax data hits bank clients around the globe', *Wall Street Journal* Europe (Brussels), 25 February: 1, 6.

Edwards, C. and V. de Rugy (2002) 'International Tax Competition: A 21st-Century Restraint on Government', Policy Analysis (431).

Edwards, J. and M. Keen (1996) 'Tax competition and Leviathan', *European Economic Review* (40): 113–34.

Evans, G. and J. Newnham (1998) *The Penguin Dictionary of International Relations* (London: Penguin Books).

Feld, L.P. and B.S. Frey (2002) 'Trust Breeds Trust: How Taxpayers Are Treated', *Economics of Governance* 3 (2): 87–99.

Feld, L.P. and B.S. Frey (2005) 'Illegal, Immoral, Fattening or What?: How Deterrence and Responsive Regulation Shape Tax Morale' in C. Badja and F. Schneider (eds) *Size, Causes and Consequences of the Underground Economy: An International Perspective* (Aldershot: Ashgate).

Frey, B.S. and B. Torgler (2007) 'Tax morale and conditional cooperation', *Journal of Comparative Economics* 35 (1): 136–59.

Gaventa, J. (2007) 'Levels, spaces and forms of power: Analysing opportunities for change', in F. Berenskoetter and M.J. Williams (eds) *Power in World Politics* (London and New York: Routledge).

Gordon, R.A. (1981) *Tax Havens and Their Use by United States Taxpayers – An Overview* (Washington, DC: United States Government Printing Office).

Hampton, M.P. and P. Sikka (2005) 'Tax avoidance and global development', *Accounting Forum* 29 (3): 245–8.

Hishikawa, A. (2002) 'The Death of Tax Havens?', *Boston College International & Comparative Law Review* 25 (2): 389–418.

Janeba, E. and W. Peters (1999) 'Tax Evasion, Tax Competition and the Gains from Nondiscrimination: The Case of Interest Taxation in Europe', *Economic Journal* (109): 93–101.

Johnston, D.J. (1999) 'Taxation and social progress', OECD Observer, January, http://www1.oecd.org/publications/observer/215/e-editorial.htm, accessed on 20 March 2002.

Langer, M.J. (2000) 'Harmful Tax Competition: Who Are the Real Tax Havens?', *Tax Notes International*, 18 December: 1–9, http://www.freedomandprosperity. org/Articles/tni12-18-00.pdf, accessed on 20 April 2002.

Lopatin, M. (2002) 'Tax avoiders rob wealth of nations', *Observer* (London), 17 November.

Lukes, S. (2005) *Power: A Radical View,* 2nd edn (Basingstoke: Palgrave Macmillan).

Maurer, B. (2008) 'Re-Regulating Offshore Finance?', *Geography Compass* 2 (1): 155–75.

OECD Global Forum on Taxation (2003) OECD Global Forum on Taxation, Ottawa, 14–15 October. Closing Statement by the Co-Chairs, OECD, http://www.oecd.org/document/0/0,2340,en_2649_34897_16643264_1_1_1_1, 00.html, accessed on 24 March 2008.

William Vlcek 277

O'Neill, P. (2001) Treasury Secretary O'Neill Statement on OECD Tax Havens, PO-366 ed., Office of Public Affairs, 2003, http://www.treas.gov/press/releases/po366.htm, accessed on 24 March 2008.

Organisation for Economic Co-operation and Development (1998) *Harmful Tax Competition: An Emerging Global Issue* (Paris: OECD Publications).

Organisation for Economic Co-operation and Development (2000) *Towards Global Tax Co-operation: Progress in Identifying and Eliminating Harmful Tax Practices* (Paris: OECD Publications).

Oxfam (2000) *Tax Havens: Releasing the Hidden Billions for Poverty Eradication* (London: Oxfam GB), http://publications.oxfam.org.uk/oxfam/display.asp?K= 20040623_2316_000034, accessed on 24 March 2008.

Peter-Szerenyi, L. (2003) 'The OECD's artificial approach to tax havens: Part 2', *Journal of International Taxation* 14 (3): 10–26.

Pieth, M. (2002) 'Financing of Terrorism: Following the Money', *European Journal of Law Reform* 4 (2): 365–76.

Rawlings, G. (2007) 'Taxes and Transnational Treaties: Responsive Regulation and the Reassertion of Offshore Sovereignty', *Law & Policy* 29 (1): 51–66.

Razin, A. and E. Sadka (1991) 'International tax competition and gains from tax harmonization', *Economics Letters* 37 (1): 69–76.

Samuels, L.B. and D.C. Kolb (2001) 'The OECD initiative: Harmful tax practices and tax havens', *Taxes* 79 (3): 231–60.

Sanders, R.M. (2002) 'The Fight Against Fiscal Colonialism: The OECD and Small Jurisdictions', *Round Table: The Commonwealth Journal of International Affairs* (365): 325–48.

Schulze, G.G. and H.W. Ursprung (1999) 'Globalisation of the Economy and the Nation State', *World Economy* 22 (3): 295–352.

Shapiro, M. and F. Schröder (2003) 'Money Laundering and Tax Havens: The Hidden Billions for Development', Conference Report, No. 3, (New York: Friedrich-Ebert-Stiftung) http://www.fesny.org/docus/ffd/money_laundering. pdf accessed on 12 March 2005.

Sharman, J.C. (2006) *Havens in a Storm: The Struggle for Global Tax Regulation* (Ithaca and London: Cornell University Press).

Sharman, J.C. (2007) 'The Bark is the Bite: International Organisations and Blacklisting', unpublished manuscript.

Skinner, Q. (2002) 'A Third Concept of Liberty', *Proceedings of the British Academy* (117): 237–68.

Spencer, D. (2005a) 'Tax Information Exchange and Bank Secrecy (Part 1)', *Journal of International Taxation* 16 (2).

Spencer, D. (2005b) 'Tax Information Exchange and Bank Secrecy (Part 2)', *Journal of International Taxation* 16 (3).

Spencer, D. and J.C. Sharman (2006) 'OECD Proposals on Harmful Tax Practices: A Status Report', *Journal of International Taxation*, 17 (10): 24–42.

Stoll-Davey, C. (2007) *Assessing the Playing Field: International Cooperation in Tax Information Exchange* (London: Commonwealth Secretariat).

Thomas, K.P. (2002) 'The Politics of an Emergent Global Regime for Controlling Tax Competition', *Policy Studies Journal* 30 (2): 270–84.

Tiebout, C.M. (1956) 'A Pure Theory of Local Expenditures', *Journal of Political Economy* 64 (5): 416–24.

US Treasury (2004) 'Treasury Designates Commercial Bank of Syria as Financial Institution of Primary Money Laundering Concern', JS-1538 ed., Office of Public Affairs, http://www.treasury.gov/press/releases/js1538.htm, accessed on 24 March 2008.

US Treasury (2006) 'Treasury Issues Final Rule Against Commercial Bank of Syria. US Financial Institutions Must Terminate Correspondent Accounts', JS-4105 ed., Office of Public Affairs, http://www.treas.gov/press/releases/js4105.htm, accessed on 24 March 2008.

Vlcek, W. (2004) 'The OECD and Offshore Financial Centres: Rearguard Action Against Globalisation?', *Global Change, Peace and Security* 16 (3): 227–42.

Vlcek, W. (2008a) *Offshore Finance and Small States: Sovereignty, Size and Money* (Basingstoke: Palgrave Macmillan).

Vlcek, W. (2008b) 'A Level Playing Field and the Space for Small States', Manuscript under review.

Wight, M. (1986) *Power Politics*, Second edn (Harmondsworth, Middlesex: Penguin Books).

Wilson, J.D. (1991) 'Tax competition with interregional differences in factor endowments', *Regional Science and Urban Economics* 21 (3): 423–51.

Wilson, J.D. (1999) 'Theories of Tax Competition', *National Tax Journal* (52): 269–304.

Afterword: Vulnerability as a Condition, Resilience as a Strategy

Anthony Payne

As this book amply shows, small states continue to interest us, but they also continue to puzzle us. We know that more small states exist than ever before and that most seem to survive while some indeed do prosper. But we also know that there is still no agreed definition of what constitutes a small state and certainly no sharp dichotomy between a small and a large state. It may actually be the case that no firm category of analysis will ever be carved out in this field of study. Even if this is so, it does not mean of course that we should abandon the study of how seemingly small states behave in different spheres of action and at different times. In fact, we need to recognise the multiple natures of the small state phenomenon and focus on their variations in practice. This book, thus, does well to address the 'diplomacies' of small states, for there is no typical or characteristic diplomacy of a small state to identify and explain.

The editors, Andrew F. Cooper and Timothy M. Shaw, have sought to position the book at the cutting edge of the study of small states by positioning these states somewhere between vulnerability and resilience in the early twenty-first century. This reflects a recent change of mood in thinking about how such states should be considered. As they explain in their introduction, doubts were expressed in the 1950s and 1960s about the core viability and capacity to exercise sovereignty of small independent states. Thereafter, once it became apparent that many such territories, having been granted sovereignty, had not simply folded up and disappeared, the conventional wisdom came to note their inherent vulnerability, understood above all in economic and social, but also lately too in ecological, terms. The editors do me the honour of quoting at the outset of their opening chapter something that I wrote in 2004 in a review of the role played by small states in the global politics of development, suggesting that 'small states are mostly acted upon by much more powerful states and institutions' and that 'vulnerabilities rather than opportunities', thus, 'come through as the most striking manifestations of the consequences of smallness'. Of late, however, the debate has been moved somewhat to the point where Cooper and Shaw argue that small states can no longer 'be seen simply as structurally weak Lilliputs in a system controlled by the big and strong'. In putting it this way, they may exaggerate slightly the emphasis of the old literature (for in the most nuanced interpretations small states were never 'simply' seen as structurally weak), but they unquestionably capture the spirit of the new and currently fashionable approach, which is to stress not what small states cannot do, but rather what they can do, and have done, to survive and chart a course in global affairs.

The person who has done the most to open up this line of argument is Lino Briguglio of the University of Malta. He has in effect urged that resilience should replace vulnerability as the focus of analytical attention. He has not contributed himself to this collection of essays, but it is his definition of resilience as 'the coping ability of an economically vulnerable country' – that 'ability to recover from or adjust to change' – that is counterposed by Cooper and Shaw to my observation about vulnerability at the very start of the book. What is more, several other authors cite Briguglio's work, thereby placing themselves within this mode of thinking. Indeed, as already indicated, the book as a whole is introduced by the editors as representing a 'privileging of resilience and resourcefulness', with a view explicitly to bringing about a reconfiguration of the image of small states within the conventional narrative. I believe, however, that the book actually reaches a subtly different conclusion from this prognosis. To me, the argument that seems to emerge from the many interesting case studies presented suggests that we should not in fact seek to move on too quickly to substitute a focus on vulnerability for one on resilience, but rather that we should see if we can manage to link up these two apparently competing conceptual frameworks in a fruitful and symbiotic way. I suggest in what follows of this short conclusion the steps by which I think we might do that.

Step 1: Do not throw away the concept of vulnerability

We should establish first of all whether we think that all the features of the global economic and political order, previously thought to establish the preponderance of vulnerability as a defining feature of small states, were misconceived, or alternatively have gone away. The concept of vulnerability arose out of the study published by the Commonwealth Secretariat in 1985, prompted in good part by the political reaction to the United States' invasion of the small Commonwealth Caribbean state of Grenada a year or so earlier. It has thereafter been amplified and illustrated in the many annual volumes produced by the Secretariat delineating the particular economic problems facing small states, as well as being refined conceptually to a high degree in all of the work done in various fora on the notion of a vulnerability index. Briguglio and his colleagues contributed extensively to this approach, taking the lead in adding the notion of ecological vulnerability into the mix. Any attempt to assemble complex and interrelated data into a composite index cannot but over-simplify to an extent. Put differently, the vulnerability index always needed to be deployed sensitively. But that was generally how it was incorporated into other analyses and my view is that the whole vulnerability discourse impressively went towards establishing that small states were genuinely characterised by a common set of core economic and social characteristics that, collectively and cumulatively, defined their particular predicament.

The political dimension was always more awkward to integrate into the vulnerability perspective, in large part because politics depends substantially on subjective perception. Nonetheless, it was a part of the original debate about vulnerability, derivative in the first instance of the fact that Grenada, as it were, stayed invaded by the United States despite an overwhelming vote condemning that action within the United Nations General Assembly. That invasion was a dramatic illustration of the pitfalls of small size, to be sure, and has not become a norm in international affairs. Nevertheless, one has only to note in the pages of this book how small Caribbean states have danced to the tune of PetroCaribe whistled by the current Venezuelan regime, how they were pushed to sign up to a controversial Economic Partnership Agreement with the European Union when backed up against an externally imposed deadline, or how they were completely marginalised within the unfolding Summit of the Americas process by the assertion of the concerns of both the United States and the larger South American (also notionally developing) states. Clearly, smallness still generates a basic vulnerability in the political, as well as the economic, social and ecological, equation. In short, I suggest that the concept of vulnerability still captures effectively the underlying structural condition of small states seeking to make their way in the current global order. We should not therefore dispense with such a perceptive way of framing the issue in an excessively zealous pursuit of novelty for its own sake.

Step 2: Move on from the plaintive diplomacy of vulnerability

We should scrutinise closely all the evidence that bears upon the important practical and political question of whether or not the manner and mode of diplomacy that has mostly flowed out of the vulnerability discourse has worked to any significant degree. In their introduction Cooper and Shaw dub this a 'strategy of crying "vulnerability"'. It is an apt turn of phrase. From the mid-1980s onwards small states commonly protested their plight in global affairs. They were ignored, marginalised, beleaguered. They deserved to be treated differently/more fairly. Theirs was, in effect, a moral claim for attention that purported to override the conventional power-political dynamics at work in a situation. In part, this may have just been an attempted tactic, a way of making a case. But in all probability, it was a consequence of small state leaders and elites internalising to a considerable extent the sense that their countries were vulnerable and lacking in policy options. This is almost impossible to prove, but is in my view a plausible way of reading some of the diplomacies of this period. It also fits in with some of the analyses that have been offered over the years regarding the cultural condition of dependency in some parts of the world, such as the Caribbean and the Pacific, populated by a large number of small states.

The evidence suggests, however, that the diplomacy of wallowing in vulnerability has signally failed to work for small states. Maybe this is a commentary on the moral tone of the last 20 or so years of global politics; maybe it reveals the essential *realpolitik* of international relations. Either way, it seems to be true. A good deal of the evidence has in fact been assembled in this book. We heard that the impassioned and indeed poignant address to the United Nations 'Earth Summit' of 1992 delivered by President Gayoom of the Maldives, in which he spoke as 'a representative of an endangered people' threatened by sea-level rise, actually achieved very little. We were advised that the standard claim of small states that they be given 'special and differentiated (S&D) treatment' within global trade negotiations conducted under the auspices of the World Trade Organization has fallen on deaf ears in an era attuned to reciprocity in trade matters. We saw that the World Bank, heavily lobbied by many small states with the backing of the Commonwealth Secretariat, formally accepted that small states did have special characteristics that should be noted by global institutions, but nevertheless backed away from instituting a new country category to give force to this perception. We also know now, with the collapse of the Doha round of trade talks at the end of July 2008, that the energetic cotton diplomacy of the small states of West Africa failed to move the big protectionist interests of the Western developed countries, even though the moral case that they made for fairness of treatment was viewed by many observers as compelling. In short, again, I suggest that the lesson is clear, and has been well learned by those analysts interested in moving the debate forward towards the concept of resilience: plaintive diplomacy does not do the job. An excessive preoccupation with vulnerability easily leads to defeatist, misinformed and inappropriate diplomacies.

Step 3: Rethink resilience not as a quality but as a strategy

We should in the light of this second argument begin to take on board the notion of resilience, but we should rethink the way that the concept has thus far been deployed in the small states debate. As indicated earlier, it has been conceived by Briguglio and his followers as essentially an ability, an ability 'that may be inherent or nurtured'. This is where I have a problem with the formulation. I have not been convinced by anything that I have yet read in this genre that definable, inherent, core qualities of resilience can be found in the make-up of particular economies, polities or societies, still less that such qualities can be specified in relation to small states as a category. I can see, however, that greater resilience, viewed relatively, can be built and/or nurtured, that it can be seen as a goal of policy to be pursued and, if they are to be effective, the nature of the building and nurturing must relate to the inherited and path-dependent conditions that prevail at the point of embarking on the policy. I am not therefore persuaded of the merits of attempts to construct a resilience index to replace, or even sit alongside, a vulnerability index. This book does not, as it happens, contain a chapter that brings forward this endeavour, which is a pity because several of the case studies refer implicitly to such an enterprise (or else, put more critically, do not fully define what they mean by resilience). I would suggest, therefore, that we proceed by conceiving of the pursuit of resilience as an appropriate strategy of development for small states and thus use the concept as a benchmark against which we can begin to explore again, and more fully than before, some of the older arguments about the merits of diversification, the need to open up new and alternative markets, the case for developing new products and services, and so on and so forth, that were always part of the debate about coping with vulnerability (just as they were also part of an even earlier debate about 'living with dependency' conducted by myself and others in relation to the political economy of the Caribbean in the 1970s!).

We again find examples in the pages of this book of the kinds of diplomacies that have flowed, and should in the future flow even more assertively, from this vision of pursuing a broad strategy of development geared to building greater resilience. For example, the argument has been made that the newly independent government of Singapore deliberately chose from the mid-1960s onwards to seek to generate a measure of what later came to be called 'soft power' by reference to the global promotion of a distinctive 'Singapore Model of Development' grounded in the notion of state and society acting in unison. It was also shown how a shift of perception on the part of the political elite in Iceland from the late 1990s onwards has given rise to a much more activist and self-confident pursuit of its interests in international relations over the last decade. Iceland is said, in effect, to have re-evaluated its size, to have chosen a new and larger size for future purposes. Within the Caribbean and Pacific regions, the familiar home areas of small states, no such equivalent examples of bold, innovative, successful new diplomacies were identified. Although, some recall might perhaps have been usefully undertaken of aspects of the foreign policy record of the People's Revolutionary Government of Grenada between 1979 and 1983 when, for a brief period at least, the concept of 'a big revolution in a small country' generated a dynamism on the world stage that was quite striking when considered against the resources at the disposal of the leadership. Generally, though, Commonwealth Caribbean countries have been slow to adapt to the fast changing global order of the last 20 years, focusing in the main on mounting a rearguard action against the encroachment of neoliberalism. But this only means that the challenge has still to be met: the need to rethink diplomacy in the region and to link it directly to resilience-building remains an imperative.

Step 4: Integrate the analysis of resilience and vulnerability

We can then take the final step in the direction of a better analysis of small states, explicitly recognising that an excessive emphasis on vulnerability without a sense of the need to build resilience becomes self-defeating, and also that resilience cannot really be understood meaningfully outside of an understanding of the structural context of vulnerability. The first point is exactly that made by Briguglio and other critics of the early work on vulnerability; the second is the main point

I have been trying to make in these concluding remarks. It is all very well, for example, highlighting the way that some small states have become experts in 'slipping subtly through the nets of conformity' or exercising the 'power of the powerless'. Manifestly, we need to analyse and dissect the various options that small states are increasingly adopting in order to seek a viable and satisfactory location in the global political economy, whether it be via the establishment of offshore financial centres, the pursuit of remittances, aid and other forms of rent-seeking, or even the more unorthodox dimensions of 'selling sovereignty' in relation to military bases, fishing rights, shipping registries, passports, stamps, country codes or internet domain names. The cunning, ingenuity and political skill involved can certainly be admired and the increased resilience thereby generated assessed and noted. But it does not make sense to go to the next stage and assert or imply that these various diplomatic and financial techniques constitute constructive elements of a coherent and sound strategy of development on the part of small states. They are actually the desperate measures taken by states that do not really have other effective developmental choices. In other words, they grow out of a fundamental vulnerability, even if they contribute for the moment to a greater resilience.

E.M. Forster wrote in *Howard's End* that 'it is the vice of a vulgar mind to be thrilled by bigness, to think that a thousand square miles are a thousand more wonderful than one square mile, and that a million square miles are almost the same as heaven'. Students of small states are thus, by definition, not given to vulgar thinking! In fact, we occupy an interesting and important field of study within contemporary global affairs. But we must now surely position ourselves not so much 'between' vulnerability and resilience, as in the title of this book, but rather at a point on the analytical spectrum where we see these two concepts as mutually constituting the politics of small states.

Index

ACP states   xi, 49, 160, 161
  see also EPAs, EU, South
Africa   viii, ix, x, 9, 11, 14, 48, 82, 97,
    124, 186, 195–204, 251, 283
  see also South, South Africa
agriculture   196, 200
aid   51, 52, 53, 74–5, 76, 77
Antigua   11, 14, 35, 59–60, 83, 91,
    148, 151, 152, 204, 207–17, 233,
    235, 237, 238
  see also Caribbean, Internet
    gambling, OECD, US
AOSIS   25, 29, 30, 35
Argentina   178, 184, 185, 186, 252
Asia   viii, 251
Asian values   66, 70, 71–9
  see also development, Singapore
Association of Caribbean States (ACS)
    187
  see also Caribbean, CARICOM

Baldacchino, Godfrey   xvii, 13,
    21–40, 42
  see also Malta
Barbados   vii, 2, 12, 15, 25, 26, 41,
    49, 82, 97, 105, 109, 110, 148,
    150, 178, 188, 220, 233, 235, 238,
    250, 254, 255, 268, 271
  SIDS conference   25, 26
  see also Caribbean, CARICOM
big states   2, 14, 23, 26
  see also BRICs, EU, US
Brazil   98, 143, 146, 154, 186, 187,
    251, 252
BRICs   2, 5, 11, 14, 163
Briguglio, Lino   xv, 1, 3–4, 6, 12, 15,
    24, 43, 280, 283, 234
  see also Commonwealth, resilience,
    vulnerability

Canada   2, 75, 100, 106–7, 121, 178,
    180, 181, 183, 184, 185, 187, 190,
    256, 271
  see also NAFTA, OAS, US

Caribbean   viii, ix, xii, 1, 3, 7, 8, 9,
    12, 14, 15, 48, 81–93, 96–113,
    135, 144, 147, 152, 160–73,
    178–90, 211, 219–38, 245, 251,
    252–62, 264–74, 281, 284
  non-independent   81–93
  see also ACP, Antigua, Barbados,
    CARICOM, Jamaica, T&T
CARICOM   8, 9, 91, 93, 96–113, 143,
    148, 149–52, 153, 154–8, 160–73,
    180, 187, 188, 189, 211
CARIFORUM   160–70, 259
CRNM   189
CSME   93, 100, 151, 156, 171, 173
  see also Caribbean, regionalism
carnivals   255–6
  see also cultural industries
China   23, 53, 54, 56, 66, 68, 69, 72,
    75, 76, 121, 123, 126, 127, 143,
    251
  see also BRICs, Taiwan
CIGI   xvi, xvii, 14
civil society   65, 70, 102, 204
  see also NGOs, non-state actors, soft
    power
climate change   29, 30, 32, 33
  see also sea-level rise, vulnerability
Clinton, William   73–7, 180–2
Cold War   vii, xi, 3, 27, 53, 66,
    132, 181
  see also post-Cold War
Commonwealth   xii, xiv, xvii, 6, 9,
    10, 13, 21, 24, 26, 41, 42, 44, 65,
    68, 135, 165, 211, 269, 270, 272,
    281, 282
  CHOGM   10, 165
competitiveness   163–73, 257
copyright   245–9
cotton   11, 196–204, 211, 217, 283
  C4 196–204
country-codes   6, 57–8
cruise ships   6, 10, 210
  see also tourism